A QUIET CASE OF ETHNIC CLEANSING : THE MURDER OF BANGLADESH'S HINDUS

A Quiet Case of Ethnic Cleansing

The Murder of Bangladesh's Hindus

(Second Enlarged Edition)

DR. RICHARD L. BENKIN

Foreword by

Samir Kalra, Esq.
Director and Senior Fellow for
Human Rights,
Hindu American Foundation

AKSHAYA PRAKASHAN
NEW DELHI

First Published: 2012
Second Enlarged Edition: 2014
Reprint: 2019
Second Reprint: 2024

ISBN-13: 978-81-88643-52-3

Price: Rs. 600

Published by Harish Chandra for
AKSHAYA PRAKASHAN
208, M.G. House, 2 Community Centre
Wazirpur Industrial Area
New Delhi - 110 052
Tel.: 011-4161 0957, Mob.: 98184 52269
e-mail: harish@akshayaprakashan.com
Website: www.akshayaprakashan.com

Printed at D.K. Fine Art Press (P) Ltd., Delhi–110 052.

This book is dedicated to the Bangladeshi Hindus and to all victims of the terrorist plague that is called international jihad. This book also is dedicated to those men and women who are engaged in civilization's epic battle against international jihad—sometimes quietly, sometimes loudly, sometimes because of and sometimes in spite of their national governments, and always without regard to the deadly social and political philosophies of our day, multiculturalism and political correctness.

Most of all, this book is dedicated to my wife and daughter.

"Man goes into the noisy crowd to drown his own clamour of silence."

—Rabindranath Tagore, Bengali Poet, 1861-1941
from "Stray Birds," 1916

"It is not enough to be compassionate; you must ACT."

—Tenzin Gyatso, Fourteenth Dalai Lama, 1992

"The only thing necessary for the triumph of evil is for good men to do nothing."

—Edmund Burke (attributed)

Contents

New Author's Preface for Second Printing

I was in Bangladesh in February 2013, and of the many things that happened while I was there, two in particular indicate the extent of the problem we face. They also indicate how Hindu inferiority is institutionalized and is an accepted element of Bangladesh's social fabric. It is not the work of "a few radicals," which is the standard apologetic by the Awami League and its enablers; and the rationale that several senior Bangladeshi officials tried to use (unsuccessfully) to dismiss the evidence in this book.

On February 20, I had a rather heated exchange with Bangladesh's Home Minister, Muhiuddin Khan Alamgir. Advocate Rabindra Ghosh, the tireless Bangladeshi human rights activist, helped arrange the meeting at Mr. Alamgir's Dhaka office and was present. I am sure the Home Minister expected a pleasant courtesy call full of smiles and photo ops; what he got was something quite different. I told him that I came to deliver a message. "Atrocities against Hindus in Bangladesh have been able to go unnoticed heretofore," I said "At the very least, I told him, they have been ignored enough so that those who can do something to stop them are able to pretend they do not exist. But that time is drawing to a close—and I have had discussions in at least two foreign capitals which confirm that. The opportunity for Bangladesh is this. It either can get on top of the process by taking certain concrete actions, or it can be the passive recipient of what might come."

The Home Minister went immediately into denial mode, but in a very interesting way. At first he insisted that things were fine for Hindus in Bangladesh, which took all of a few moments to refute with verified evidence. I told him that respectfully, I begged to differ and that Bangladesh's human rights record at this point was "atrocious." He then repeated that he "did not know of any such things," which not incidentally was the exact wording used by Bangladesh's US Ambassador Akramul Qader when he was faced with the same evidence.[1]

I wondered out loud how I could spend most of my time in Chicago and uncover things that he says he cannot. It did not make any sense. Plus I pointed to Rabindra Ghosh and noted that he has piles of evidence that he has vetted personally and which confirm my allegations and talked about our recent trip to the tiny village of Balai Bazar in far northern Dinajpur's Chirir-Bondar Upazila. Advocate Ghosh and I arrived there about six months after this tiny village of 75 Hindu families was attacked by over 100 marauding Muslims. The attackers went from home to home, stealing whatever they found valuable, destroying everything else, and torching the homes, razing several to the ground. They went from farm to farm, destroying crops and stealing the livestock. They beat the mean and abused the women, unfortunately a regular feature of such attacks. Even though the villagers identified many of the perpetrators, the government has not responded. The attackers are threatening to come back and "finish the job" if the Hindus do not leave Bangladesh; and the only thing stopping them is four Muslim policemen who come to the village of their own accord but who also told us they are fearful because they know they cannot be there all the time.[2]

And what was the Bangladeshi Home Minister's response to this tragic situation faced by the villagers? He neither denied their suffering nor addressed the allegations of Awami League inaction. He instead told me that he had been to the United States and had "seen the enclaves of the Red Indians."

---

[1] Private meeting between the Ambassador and me at the Bangladeshi embassy in Washington, May 25, 2012.

[2] Visit by Dr. Richard Benkin and Advocate Rabindra Ghosh, February 15, 2013.

He also kept repeating that "33 people were killed in Connecticut," referring to the Sandy Hook Elementary School shooting where 27 people were murdered. My response was "yes, and?" waiting for him to say *something, anything* about how he would help his fellow Bangladeshis; but that was never forthcoming. He also tried to counter my argument by saying that "union membership is declining in the US."

"What in the world kind of response is that to the ethnic cleansing of Hindus in your country," I said as even he realized that his defenses fell flat. So, he said that I should send him evidence of any crimes and he personally would see that they are prosecuted.

"You mean to tell me that here you are the Home Minister of the country and you're dependent on some guy from Chicago to bring you evidence? I think you have much bigger problems then we thought." I also reminded him that the very fact that the Home Minister needs to take a personal role in this indicates the depth of their problems. These things should be prosecuted as a matter of course on the local level by local officials.

The Home Minister was explicit in saying that Bangladesh did not have to do anything further; that there was no problem for Hindus or any other minorities in Bangladesh. I told him that I did not come here to have a debate but to give him a message—which he did not pick up before since he already had his canned response ready. So I repeated it clearly and slowly. He tried to go back to Connecticut and laugh until I mentioned that he should consider what would it be like if, in reaction to his government's complicity in this ethnic cleansing, increased tariffs or other things made it impossible for Bangladesh to sell its garments competitively; or if the UN decided that a nation involved in these things should not provide peacekeeping troops.

That got his attention. So he complained that fixing the problem would be costly, especially if I carried out my "threat" and reduced the little income they have. In other words, he admitted that something in fact can be done; it is just too costly to do it. Given the way I have seen Bangladesh waste money on building false images of itself, massive corruption, and more; his response was not just callous but criminal as he would let the atrocities continue because he found it too expensive to fix them!

As we parted, he asked if I was from the CIA.

Update: Two days later, I sent Alamgir the evidence he requested, along with new cases I had just uncovered.[3] I also sent the material to several influential lawmakers in Washington who have been working with me, one of whom referred it to the Senate Foreign Relations Committee. As of this writing, the Bangladeshi Home Minister has neither responded nor taken any perceptible action.

The night before that encounter, two Hindu Members of Parliament (MPs) came to my hotel for what they believed was to be a pleasant and insubstantial meeting of smiles, mutual compliments, and hand wringing about what "they" are doing to Bangladesh's Hindus. They represent Dinajpur and Khulna, two areas in Bangladesh where anti-Hindu abuse is a way of life, and where the Awami League government continues its predecessors' practice of purposely turning a blind eye to this quiet case of ethnic cleansing. It is from where these two MPs, who claim to represent the Bangladeshi Hindu community, sit silently while their coreligionists are slaughtered. Having recently returned from one of their districts where I met their victims, I was in no mood for their sort of false solidarity. So, after a brief introduction, I asked, "Okay, tell me what you—as Hindu MPs—are doing about the ethnic cleansing of your people here."

"We have done many things, "answered the man from Khulna.

"Many things? You know that's [a lie]," I replied sharply. "Hindus in your district are being raped and killed, their land

---

[3] Evidence letters included as Appendix III.

snatched, *Mandirs* destroyed; and no prosecutions. So, don't tell me that you're doing 'many things.'"[4]

I asked them how many Hindu MPs there are in the *Jatiya Sangsad.* When they told me 17, I was outraged that with that large a bloc they have done nothing for their people. Their excuse was that the Awami League, not they, were at fault; and I reminded them how I have been urging minorities to form their own political party.

"Right now, the Awami League doesn't have to do anything. They know you'll vote for them anyway. And the BNP doesn't have to do anything because they know you won't vote for them."

Rabindra Ghosh, I said "has extensive evidence that there are Members of Parliament heavily involved in stealing land from Hindus, and even in rapes and other atrocities. You know what your enemies think of you as you sit next to them smiling? 'We can steal their land, rape their daughters and sisters, and just give them a few Taka.'"

Someone then tried to complain about their "problems," which really angered me. "[Do] you think I don't have problems? Or that he [Rabindra Ghosh] has none? [Your] 'problems' are just an excuse for not doing what's right."

I reminded them that an American Christian, former US Congressman Bob Dold raised the issue of the Bangladeshi Hindus on the floor of the US House, while they remain silent. I noted that Rabindra Ghosh has enough direct and verified evidence of atrocities so that Hindu MPs can begin each session of the *Jatiya Sangsad* by reading a new one in the record and perhaps become agents of change.[5]

Unfortunately, though a month has passed between our encounter and this writing, none of the Bangladeshi Hindu

---

[4] Two days later, a delegation of Hindus from Khulna met me in Dhaka carrying more evidence of unprosecuted atrocities against Hindus there, including the case of a young Hindu woman who was abducted last year and still is missing. Police refuse to help.

[5] Two more Members of Congress, Ed Royce and Tulsi Gabbard, have since raised the issue in the US Congress.

MPs have taken the suggested action or any other. To be sure, the country has been lurching from one crisis to the next, and their silence could be understood, even if not justified. Perhaps they will take action—or if they do not, perhaps the voters might find other representatives who will.[6]

For years, people like Rabindra Ghosh and I have been struggling against a system and a government that wants to keep the issue buried while keeping the destruction of Bangladesh's Hindus going strong. More and more young Bangladeshis are also working toward the same end and have been beaten both by Islamists and the police. Not all of them are Hindu. Saleh Akram Marin is a young Muslim who founded the Bangladesh Crime Prevention Society, which emphasizes that the actions against Hindus are contrary to existing Bangladeshi law, and the government's failure to treat them as such is part of Bangladesh's law and order problem, as well as a human rights travesty. We can understand if the victimized villagers we met do not feel empowered to act and are fearful of the consequences if they do. But Bangladesh's Hindu MPs are in a position of leadership. They have power and prestige and can do something to help save their people; but they do not. They remain silent.

While the actual atrocities against Hindus and against Hinduism in Bangladesh are themselves horrific to anyone with even a gram of decency; these two incidents show us how our struggle goes beyond just displaying them. One shows a government that is no less complicit in this quiet case of ethnic cleansing than any of its forebears; yet asserts it is not, while those powers that can force it to take responsibility for these sins refuse to do so. The other shows how those

[6] Richard L. Benkin, "Look at ourselves to find Culprits for the Ethnic Cleansing of Hindus in Bangladesh," Struggle for Hindu Existence; March 28, 2013. http://hinduexistence.org/2013/03/28/gutless-hindu-mps-in-bangladesh-plight-of-bangladeshi-hindus-as-we-are-guilty/

Bangladeshi Hindu community leaders who have the power to act—such as the Hindu MPs—do not. They remain silent, and they let their silence act as tacit confirmation of the Awami League government's duplicity.

The struggle continues.

Dr. Richard L. Benkin
Chicago, USA

April 2013

Foreword

For years, Bangladesh has successfully portrayed itself as a moderate Muslim democracy and escaped serious censure for its deplorable human rights record. In those rare instances when it has been criticized by the international community or human rights organizations, the plight of the persecuted Hindu minority has largely been ignored. *A Quiet Case of Ethnic Cleansing: The Murder of Bangladesh's Hindus* shatters the myth of Bangladesh as a moderate Muslim nation and delves deeply into the origins and causes of the violence and oppression that has plagued its Hindu community. The culmination of tireless activism and rigorous independent research, Dr. BenkinÌs fascinating account brings a much needed voice to the millions of Bangladeshi Hindu victims who have suffered violence, discrimination, and indignity in silence.

Since its birth as an independent nation in 1971, Bangladesh has implemented a number of measures to expand the constitutional and legal role of Islam, while institutionalizing prejudice and bigotry against its minority Hindu population. Hindus have also faced routine acts of violence, including murders, rapes, forced conversions, temple attacks, abductions, and land encroachments. Religiously motivated violence in Bangladesh has particularly impacted Hindu women and young girls, and has been utilized as a weapon of subjugation.

Moreover, the dramatic decline in the Hindu population is indicative of a deliberate attempt to forcibly remove Hindus from Bangladesh. As Benkin points out, Hindus comprised approximately 33% of the population in 1947 (in the territory now encompassing Bangladesh), but were less than 20% by 1971. And in 2001, Hindus represented less than 10% of the population, while today many sources estimate that Hindus are only 8%. This massive population loss cannot be explained through normal birth rates or as a natural phenomenon, but instead signify an intentional effort to irreversibly change the demographics of this South Asian nation.

Drawing nuanced comparisons with the Holocaust and other historical cases of genocide and ethnic cleansing, Benkin forcefully argues to label what is happening to Bangladeshi Hindus is nothing short of ethnic cleansing. These comparisons are not intended to demonstrate equivalency in the nature and scope of the crimes, but rather to ensure that we no longer continue to ignore the clear warning signs that exist, as we have done so often in the past.

In the case of Bangladesh, the ethnic cleansing of Hindus can best be described as "quiet and steady," as it has gone essentially unnoticed by the world. The international community's failure to notice or stop the cleansing, however, in no way diminishes the sheer magnitude of the calamity.

Tracing developments from pre-independence Bangladesh, Benkin systematically outlines the multitude of factors responsible for the ongoing ethnic cleansing of Hindus, including the increased radicalization of the Bangladesh polity, the complicity of corrupt government officials at all levels of governance, discriminatory laws, and the widespread failure to act in defense of the victims. In particular, he spends considerable time describing the vast appropriation of Hindu-owned land under the Vested Property Act (VPA) and demonstrates its impact on the forced migration of Hindus from Bangladesh. He further notes the significant personal benefits accrued by local politicians and the consequent unwillingness of successive governments to end the blatantly racist law.

Benkin also shows, contrary to commonly held perceptions, that the plight of Hindus under the purportedly "secular" Awami League government has not significantly improved compared to previous regimes. Despite several opportunities to institute reforms and prosecute attacks on Hindus, the recently elected Awami League has chosen instead to maintain the status quo. From failing to rescind the remaining vestiges of the VPA, to not returning confiscated properties under the Act, the Awami League has continued the discriminatory policies of its predecessors. Additionally, it has declined to repeal the eighth amendment of the constitution, which recognizes Islam as the official state religion, while allowing radical Islamist parties, such as Jamaat-e-Islami, to expand their influence.

A Quiet Case of Ethnic Cleansing closely examines the situation in Bangladesh within the broader context of the global expansion of pan-Islamism, but carefully distinguishes between Islam the religion, and radical Islam and international jihad as a destructive political ideology. Similarly, it identifies the dangerous convergence of Islamists and communist political parties in perpetuating the victimization of Bangladeshi Hindu refugees living in India's West Bengal state. Benkin provides an insightful account into the lives of these refugees, who lack formal legal status in India and struggle to survive. Based on his investigations and first-hand accounts, he demonstrates the ongoing danger the refugees face from Islamist attacks and the failure of corrupt West Bengal officials and police to protect them.

Far from being politically correct, Benkin is equally critical of the ineffective leadership of those who claim to represent the interests of Hindu refugees in West Bengal, and their incessant concern for personal comfort over improving the conditions of their constituents. He is similarly contemptuous of Hindus in India and the diaspora for their widespread apathy towards the plight of their co-religionists from Bangladesh.

The uniqueness of *A Quiet Case of Ethnic Cleansing,* however, lies not only in its description of the origins and causes of the ethnic cleansing of Bangladeshi Hindus or the culpable parties, but in its ability to suggest comprehensive strategies to address the situation. As Benkin appropriately notes, the Bangladeshi government has no incentive to modify its behavior absent pressure from the U.S. or international community. Although the U.S. currently lacks a coherent foreign policy towards Bangladesh, he argues that it can use its significant economic leverage to bring about meaningful change.

A Quiet Case of Ethnic Cleansing, therefore, makes a compelling and impassioned plea to urgently end the persecution of Bangladeshi Hindus, while providing practical recommendations that merit our immediate attention. It is a seminal and comprehensive work that contributes immensely to our understanding of the factors that have led to the ethnic cleansing, and serves as a powerful call to action.

Samir Kalra, Esq.
Director and Senior Fellow for Human Rights
Hindu American Foundation
www.HAFsite.org

Author's Preface

From time to time, I get the opportunity to speak about the destruction of Bangladesh's Hindus to audiences that do not already share my understanding of the situation and its root causes. These are often (but not always) western groups that know little about the dynamics playing themselves out in South Asia; nor do they know that Hindus and other minorities are being persecuted in Bangladesh or that the country is year by year coming under the thumb of radical Islam. It might be a college campus, a synagogue, or even Washington, DC; or in a more general gathering. I relish these opportunities because these people—the Bangladeshi Hindus—are going through their trauma knowing that few people outside of their community care enough to do anything about it. At a 2008 press conference in Lucknow, India, I said that "everyone in India knows that the Bangladeshi Hindus are [at risk] but no one seems to be stopping it."[1] In the West, most people do not know about it and the few who do are not getting the message across to others; and none of them are stopping it either. To the victims, the reason hardly matters. The horror I have confronted inside and outside of Bengal is not just what is happening there, but perhaps even more so *everyone's* silence in the face of it. And that is what has to change if we are going to stop this "quiet case of ethnic cleansing."

When I speak at these venues in the west or in South Asia, I am confronted by the same tactic, even if the motives of

[1] "American Jew fights for Bangladeshi Hindus," *The Times of India; Lucknow*. February 21, 2008.

those who use it differ; even if their sincerity does, too. That is an attempt to hijack our agenda of educating people about this monumental crime, the millions still at risk, and our moral duty to act on their behalf until we have stopped it. The first attempt at hijacking comes whenever people in the audience have read up on me and find that I am Jewish and a Zionist—and very proud of both, by the way. Sometimes with a raised hand, sometimes only with a raised voice, someone will ask how I can talk about oppression of a minority and ignore 'what Israel is doing to the Palestinians.' At different times, there might be someone who asks me how as an American I can justify 'US actions' or something like that. Again for the record, I am very proud of being an American and a patriotic one at that. So, I sometimes have felt the need to stand up for the US and Israel.

Interestingly, the anti-American rants happen far more frequently within the United States than elsewhere. There have been times, I must admit, when I answered them because I jump at any chance to argue against slogans and slander with facts and figures—especially if the venue is a college campus. Most of the time, however, I have offered to do so *after* this important talk.

But when that fails, I can always count on some of my adversaries trying to pry people's attention away from the human rights tragedy by calling me 'anti-Muslim' or 'Islamaphobic.' I generally offer a quick disclaimer—as I do with a small chapter in this book—that rebuts the charge and then pushes ahead.

And that is the purpose of this Preface. Whether I am giving a speech or talking to officials in Washington or elsewhere, it is imperative that I never let the topic stray from the essential reality of what we are fighting. For if we are complicit in entangling our message with one or another of those charges it loses its pristine quality and moral imperative. As much as it might pain me to admit it, people can take positions different from mine without being dishonest or uninformed. We should welcome principled debate. *But when it comes to the brutalization of the Bangladeshi Hindus, there is only one morally defensible side: stopping it and saving the victims.* To the extent that we allow anyone to prevent that focus by hijacking our agenda because we feel obliged to defend a point or because we are afraid what others might say; we are complicit in the human rights travesty being committed against the Bangladeshi Hindus.

Although I have recently co-founded a human rights NGO, Forcefield, I am really just a guy with a day job who through a number of circumstances became aware of this and other injustices. In 2003, I was working with a Bangladeshi Muslim journalist named Salah Uddin Shoaib Choudhury. He had contacted me because, he said, his people received nothing but biased and hate-filled information about Israel and the Jewish people. As a journalist, he said, he wanted to change that and asked me to help. And so we worked together for several months, and actually began finding some success. But in November of that year, Bangladeshi police arrested him as he was about to board a plane for a speech in Israel. (We found out later they had been tracking his activities for some time, and that his own brother-in-law was a major informant for the government.) Bangladeshi security forces held him incommunicado for hours before moving him to the Central Dhaka Jail. But as they were dragging him away, he saw his brother in the crowd and cried out to him: "Call Dr. Benkin. Ask him to please help me."

And so what do you do in such a situation? What can you do other than everything in your power? At first, there was no one who cared; no one who even wanted to hear about it. Eventually, however, one of the giants on Capitol Hill in Washington—then Congressman, now Senator Mark Kirk of Illinois, a veteran of human rights struggles going back to the Soviet *Refuseniks*—heard me and responded in a relentless and committed way. Together, we secured Shoaib's freedom after 17 months of imprisonment and torture.[2] And we did so by doing nothing more than speaking the truth and refusing to shut up, refusing to be polite.

Early on, I realized something: the Bangladeshi government and the Islamists who ran that show arrested and tortured this journalist because they believed they could; because they believed no one would raise a fuss about it; because they believed that no one would care. Making them see that they were wrong in that was the key to freeing Shoaib. Letting them know in a thousand different ways was critical to our success. We also had to do it constantly and relentlessly because these people believe we have the attention span of a mosquito and no moral backbone. The very same thing is true of what—in many cases the same—Islamists are doing to the Hindus of Bangladesh.

The book's final chapter covers this most important issue of how we can take effective action. For when addressing those numerous groups, meetings, and seminars, I grow weary of going to one after another and watching the same individuals shake the same ineffective fists at the same enemy. We cannot afford to do that anymore; more importantly, the Bangladeshi Hindus cannot afford that. Talking is easy; acting even in the face of danger takes courage. Every day that we do nothing, we are confirming our enemy's belief that no one cares; that the world would rather wring its hands after it is all over and wonder 'how could it have happened' than to take the action necessary to prevent it.

I owe a sincere debt of gratitude to so many people without whom this book would not have been possible. There are my friends and allies in India, first and foremost: Amitabh Tripathi and Madhuri Singh, who always took care of me and opened

---

[2] In January 2007, I was in the Bangladeshi capital of Dhaka and found a man who was a principal guard at the prison at the time Shoaib was there. While he did not see the torture himself, he did see its effects as Shoaib was brought back to his cell after each interrogation.

my mind and many doors; and Bikash Halder who first contacted me and asked me to help save his people, and who has been my companion, guide, and translator as we traveled West Bengal together. There is Dr. Daniel Pipes who has provided financial support for my trips and their educative functions, as well as the guidance only a most incisive and educated mind can provide. And there is the Not-for-Profit human rights organization, Forcefield (http://www.forcefieldnow.org) which also has provided some funding for my human rights endeavors and has been a vehicle to help fight this quiet case of ethnic cleansing; to my co-founder and friend, Miriam Guttman-Jones of Australia. My gratitude goes also to the US Hindu community, especially the Chicago area community. There are so many people to thank, far more than I can name here; but I want to extend a special thank you to Prasad Yalmanchi, Kamlesh Chauhan, and Bhavna Shinde. Thanks to Harish Chandra and Akshaya Prakashan for supporting this book and my efforts. And special thanks to the many elected officials in Washington, Jerusalem, and New Delhi, who have helped me learn how to get things done in their capitals. Special thanks go to Congressman Robert Dold of Illinois, who has carried the torch of this struggle with me; and extra special thanks go to US Senator Mark Kirk also of Illinois, who was the first person in Washington to believe in me and offer his help without seeking anything in return except the knowledge that he, too, was helping to save lives.

Most of all, I am eternally grateful to my family, both immediate and extended. Without their support for my sometimes monomaniacal, always intense and committed activity, none of this would be possible.

In preparing to write this book, I took some time to review the private notes I made while I was in India over the last few years. I found the following especially significant to help frame the issue we are facing. I wrote it while on a flight from Kolkata to New Delhi on March 26, 2009.

> It took a while before we were in the air and so I can see us being late by a half hour or so. Still, it has given me time to think. The worst mass murderers count on the fact that the sheer unbelievability of their actions will make it difficult or impossible for people to convince others of them until they are finished. Stalin and Mao—the two greatest mass murderers of our time in terms of numbers—also counted on "true believers" who could never admit to themselves that their understanding of communism as a people-first, grand ideology was horribly wrong. They took millions of fellow travelers with them down this primrose path while millions of innocents died. The same protection allowed the Kmere Rouge to push ahead with their killing fields and millions more dead. . .
>
> When I was a youngster and began understanding what was done to my people by the Nazis, I once asked my mother, "Mom, why didn't American Jews do something about this?' She responded that "we really had no idea what was happening. We heard stories, but nothing about mass murder." Later when I started making these trips to South Asia to stop the murder of Pakistani and Bangladeshi Hindus, she and other loved ones often were concerned for my safety. She asked me if the things happening were really that bad why we never read about it in our papers or hear about it in the media.
>
> "Good question," I responded. "You remember what you said when I asked you why American Jews never did anything to help stop the Holocaust? You said that you just had no idea that it was happening."
>
> "That's right," she said. "We didn't."
>
> "But that didn't mean the murders weren't happening. Just because the papers never reported it didn't mean that our families weren't being killed, did it? Same thing now."

And that's what we have to remember. If we today repeat the deadly and shameful actions of the past, knowing what we now know, how can we possibly still consider ourselves decent people?

Dr. Richard L. Benkin
Chicago
October 25, 2011

CHAPTER ONE

MILLIONS KILLED; MILLIONS AT RISK; BILLIONS SILENT

The Hindus of East Bengal[3] *are dying; they are being eliminated slowly and steadily. Of that there is no doubt; it is an objective fact supported by extensive amounts of data. As readers will see, the Hindus of West Bengal are up next for destruction; and the deliberate and ongoing attempt to destroy both communities is part of the international jihad that threatens all people, Muslims and non-Muslims alike. With its decades-long silence, the world is complicit in the ethnic cleansing of millions of Bangladeshi Hindus.*

Shmuel Zygielbojm was a young Jewish leader smuggled out of the Warsaw Ghetto in 1941. Before he was, however, he watched his family and community systematically looted of their possessions, robbed of their dignity, their status as citizens, the humanity that their neighbors and others once saw in them, and in many cases their lives. Like the rest of the city's Jews, he was forced from his home in 1940 and herded into the cramped and unsanitary Warsaw Ghetto. Things were so bad in the ghetto that besides the random shootings, arbitrary hangings, and deportations, typhus ran rampant and 1941 "records indicate" that one quarter of all the deaths were "attributed to starvation."[4] Zygielbojm had seen the harsh

[3] Please note that throughout this book, the terms, "East Bengal," "East Pakistan," and "Bangladesh" are often used interchangeably as they refer to roughly the same piece of real estate. Used in different contexts, they might refer to specific political designations or time periods; but they always refer to an area where Hindus have lived for millennia, long pre-dating Islam, and in that context, the three terms are singular.

[4] Alan L. Buchman, MD, MSPH, editor. *Clinical Nutrition in Gastrointestinal Disease.* (Slack, Incorporated: Thorofare, NJ, 2006), p. 38. Also see Emmannuel

reality of an enemy with genocide in its eyes. Unlike many of his fellow Jews, he could not pretend that it was just another difficult period that would pass on its own; or that the oppressors would somehow decide to stop their horrible activities. Having confronted the cold truth of reality, he saw the end to which they inevitably would lead without the lenses of false hope and rationalization. Thus, when he escaped he had one goal in mind—and only one: get to England. Get to England and tell the world what was happening to the Jews of Europe. Because he was convinced that once the world knew—the *good* people of the world, those who were the guardians of civilization and of that which is right and just—they would stop the inhuman slaughter in the ghettos, in the open fields, and in the death camps, that we later came to call the Holocaust.

And so he told the Americans. He told the British. He told the French and Polish governments in exile. He told the press and even representatives of the Jewish agencies. "Zygielbojm pounded on the doors of embassies, sent cables to heads of state (including Roosevelt) and addressed public meetings. No audience was too small, for he was aflame with indignation."[5] He did this relentlessly for two years, but none of those "good people" did anything about it. And that is what's important: they *did* nothing. Did they believe him? Did they *not* believe him? Or were they unsure? To the victims, it did not matter. The only thing that did matter is that no one who could have helped them *did* anything.

... Ringelblum, *Notes from the Warsaw Ghetto,* edited and translated by Jacob Sloan. (Schocken Books: New York, 1974). The book contains the insightful journal of renowned historian and ghetto resident, Emmannuel Ringelblum. On page 97, Sloan notes that the average daily food ration in the ghetto (during the best of times) was 800 calories.

[5] *The Last Letter From Szmul Zygielbojm,* The Bund Representative With The Polish National Council In Exile, May 11, 1943. Yad Vashem Archives, O-55 (Jerusalem: Yad Vashem The Holocaust Martyrs' and Heroes' Remembrance Authority, 2004). Also quoted in Arthur D. Morse. *While 6 Million Died.* (Ace Publishing Corporation: New York, 1967), p. 57.

By May 12, 1943, Zygielbojm must have come face to face with the horrible realization that no one was going to save the Jews of Europe. Because on that date, Shmuel Zygielbojm committed suicide, partly because of what *was* happening in Nazi-occupied Europe and partly because of what *was not* happening in what is only sometimes accurately termed "the free world." In his suicide note he wrote, "By my death I wish to make my final protest against the passivity with which the world is looking on and permitting the extermination of the Jewish people."[6]

Imagine the horror of watching your loved ones—parents, siblings, family, friends, and neighbors brutalized and murdered in often horrible fashion; exterminated as if they were nothing more than vermin! Imagine Zygielbojm's horror as he, like my own uncle, Mendel Gold (*z'l*), watched Nazis murder his wife and children. But as horrible as that must be, it is impossible to think of anything more horrible than going through all of it with the knowledge that the world—those "good" people—do not even care; and that they are essentially telling the murderers, 'go ahead, we won't try to stop you! They're only *Jews,* anyway.'

Despite the commonly accepted narrative, the allies knew exactly what was happening to the Jews in Nazi Europe; and Zygielbojm was not their only source of information about anti-Jewish atrocities that year.[7] Several Jewish escapees made their way to the West and reported on the carnage to Jewish agencies in countries like Switzerland. Well before Pearl Harbor, newspaper reports of Nazis murdering Jews began showing up in America's heartland. On January 25, 1941 for instance, the *Nevada State Journal* reported "wholesale killings in the streets of Bucharest," Romania.[8]

---

[6] Quoted in *ibid*, p. 58.

[7] See among other works, Walter Lacquer, *The Terrible Secret: Suppression of the Truth about Hitler's "Final Solution."* (Henry Holt and Company: New York, 1980).

[8] "Toll of Dead in 'Civil War' Termed Great." *Nevada State Journal,* Reno, Nevada; January 25, 1941, p. 1

On October 30, Reuters "quoted French reports saying more than 1,000 Jews had been shot dead by Germans who forced them to kneel in wholesale grave trenches in Northern Poland."[9] From 1941 onward in England, highly respected newspapers including the *Times of London, Manchester Guardian,* and others reported "the Nazis' systematic massacres of the European Jews."[10] Yet, their governments did not act. Many officials dismissed the reports as hyperbole or propaganda. Perhaps they simply could not deal with yet another moral imperative; perhaps they found them too horrific to believe. Recognize, however, that some of these leaders made a conscious decision to keep the information secret.[11] Thus, the British Ministry of Information noted in July 1941 that "a certain amount of terror was needed in British home propaganda," but reports of Nazi atrocities were to be used sparingly and "not with the Jews."[12] There also were many for whom, even if the reports were true, the deaths were seen as nothing more than collateral damage in the war. This perspective was not new. A mere two years before open hostilities, the allies sacrificed the Jews and others in Czechoslovakia as the price (that is, collateral damage) of appeasing their god of even a false peace at any price. Most people remember then Prime Minister Neville Chamberlain's famous statement that this agreement with "Herr Hitler" brought "peace for our time."[13] But few of them know what Chamberlain said only three days earlier, which provides us

---

[9] "Frenchmen Urged." *Morning News,* Florence, SC; October 30, 1941, p.6.

[10] *Op. Cit., The Terrible Secret,* p. 92.

[11] *Ibid.*

[12] Quoted in *Ibid,* p. 91.

[13] The full text of the statement is: "My good friends, this is the second time in our history that there has come back from Germany to Downing Street peace with honour. I believe it is peace for our time. We thank you from the bottom of our hearts. And now I recommend you to go home and sleep quietly in your beds." Speech from window of 10 Downing Street, September 30, 1938, quoted in *The Times of London*, October 1, 1938; and in Elizabeth Knowles, editor, *Oxford Dictionary of Modern Quotations,* (Oxford University Press: Oxford, 1991), page 62.

with insight into how world leaders rationalize inaction against people other than their own.

"How horrible, fantastic, incredible it is that we should be digging trenches and trying on gas-masks here because of a quarrel in a far away country between people of whom we know nothing."[14] In 1938, the people of Czechoslovakia were expendable; in 1941, it was the Jews. And as we will see below, there is a new crop of expendable people today. If a British Prime Minister could say this about a "far away country" in Europe, how much easier can contemporary western leaders say this about a group of Asians half way around the world from United Nations (UN) headquarters in New York?

Chamberlain and his allies decided in 1938 that it was best not to think about the victims because, well, there were more "important" issues that they wanted to resolve—or more accurately, delay resolving—than the fate of Czechoslovakia's people. By 1941, their *official* position changed in principle but not effect; that is, they acknowledged (to themselves but not to the public) the human rights issue in Nazi Europe but said that the best way allied governments could help the victims was to win the war. They even held a conference in Bermuda to formalize it—but the truth was something quite different. One conference delegate protested the decision and called it "a façade for inaction."[15] A façade it was, which the allies demonstrated prior to the war with incidents like that of the *S. S. St. Louis.* The S. S. St. Louis (or more technically, the M.S. St. Louis) was a German cruise ship that left Hamburg in May 1939, with almost 1,000 Jews fleeing murderous persecution in Germany. But under direct orders from President Franklin Roosevelt, the United States (US) would not even let it dock, let alone unload any refugees. Canada also refused, and the United Kingdom (UK) accepted

[14] Broadcast speech, September 27, 1938, quoted in *The Times of London,* September 28, 1938 and in *Ibid.*

[15] Op. Cit., *Morse,* p. 57.

about a fourth of them. They sent the others to suffer their fate at the hands of the Nazis. Even if we ignore all of that and accept the allies' protestations of their good intentions, their strategy was a deadly failure. Because even though they did win the war, the sad fact is that the majority of Holocaust victims died *after* the allies told Zygielbojm that the best way to help the victims was to ignore them.[16]

Even before Zygielbojm's valiant but vain efforts, the signs were there. They were there ever since the 1930s when the Nazis started talking about their desire to see all Jews out of Germany; when they began taking away their rights and justifying it by saying that Jews were less "German" than others in the country, that they were not Germans at all; when their fellow citizens were encouraged to treat them as such knowing they could do so with impunity; and when the laws of the land supported their brutalization and impoverishment.[17] Quite a few people criticize the use of comparisons with Nazi Germany because they have been so overused and are thereby trite or even strained. The criticism is apt, and of course it is no great accomplishment to talk about how bad the Nazis were. It's not really going out on a limb. But what *does* take guts is to recognize when the same signs that existed for Europe's Jews in the 1930s are there today for others and to do something about it; because it *is* happening today. It is *all* happening today; not to the Jews, but to the Hindus of Bangladesh; and if the words "*Never again!*" mean anything, we need to prevent another holocaust.[18]

---

[16] *The Destruction of the European Jews - Revised and Definite Edition 1985*, (Holmes and Meier Publishers, Inc.: Teaneck, NJ, 1985), Table B-3, p. 1220

[17] The most notorious codification of these acts is known as the Nuremburg Laws (1935). There are numerous works about their role as a stepping stone to genocide. See, for instance, Raul Hilberg, *The Destruction of European Jews* (Chicago: Quadrangle Books, 1961) and Ian Kershaw, *Hitler 1889-1936: Hubris* (New York: W.W. Norton, 1999). A copy of the original document is on display in the Skirball Cultural Center, Los Angeles.

[18] This book contains quite a few references to Nazi Germany, and there is a tendency for many people to discount such comparisons because they are so . . .

There are an estimated 13 to 15 million Hindus in Bangladesh, and every one of them is facing a protracted effort at ethnic cleansing.[19] Although their situation has not reached the level of horror experience by the Jews under Hitler, the parallels are striking. Individually, they have experienced murder, ritualized gang rape, child abduction, beatings, land seizures, property theft, deliberate impoverishment, and forced conversion (to Islam) at the hands of their fellow citizens.[20] Bangladeshi police often participate in these activities, as do party and government officials, but most of the perpetrators are average Bangladeshi citizens. The criminals are prosecuted on rare occasions, and those who have been faced light sentences if any at all. More often, the police have refused to pursue the matter and often allege that no crime ever occurred. Occasionally, they might make a visible show of picking up accused parties only to release them quietly shortly thereafter with no charges.

Under something called the Vested Property Act (VPA), which will be explained below, the Bangladesh government is empowered to and often does seize Hindus' land at any moment on the flimsiest of pretexts. The resulting

overused and often in simplistic and inappropriate ways. I am no less tolerant of such facile uses of a horrific set of events; and I find their overuse an insult to the memories of the victims. But I am using it rather extensively in this book **precisely because the parallel is appropriate,** certainly in the similar end foreseen by Islamists for Bengali Hindus and Nazis for Jews. If that recognition awakens the world to action, then this will be one the most important uses of the comparison since World War II.

[19] One might take technical exception with the use of "ethnic cleansing"; specifically, that about 99 percent of all Bangladeshis belong to the same ethnic group (Bengali). While that is technically correct, we use the term ethnic cleansing because of the reality it represents; because people can understand what is happening to this identified minority population in Bangladesh.

[20] Crimes such as forced conversion, however, did not exist for the Jews in Nazi Germany, as there was no ideology that allowed Jews to become Germans as the Nazis defined them. They and their progeny were forever outside the pale of legitimacy. Unlike Europe's Jews, Bangladesh's Hindus might avoid a violent end by abandoning their faith and heritage and converting to Islam.

impoverishment or an official's "suggestion," then forces the victims to emigrate, if they have not been driven out already, which provides the basis in Bangladeshi law for the land transfer under the VPA. Every Bangladeshi government has been complicit in this most egregious case of ethnic cleansing. It did not matter if it was a military dictatorship, the more openly Islamist Bangladesh Nationalist Party (BNP), or the more liberal Awami League, which holds power as this book is being written and as anti-Hindu activities are increasing. In Bangladesh, the lives of most Hindus are in constant jeopardy.

Of the millions who have been forced out, the lion's share now live in West Bengal, India, and they are at risk as well. So, too, are their children. In my travels through West Bengal, I have taken enough testimony to be convinced that these refugees are subject to regular attack by Islamists from both sides of the border. Let me share just one incident with you from February 2008. West Bengal—the Indian state that borders Bangladesh on the West—was only recently freed of communist rule that lasted for over three decades; and there is evidence that communists and Islamists are cooperating in South Asia. As my colleagues and I traveled from one refugee colony to another, the ruling Communist Party of India/ Marxist (CPIM)[21] became aware of our efforts and tried to thwart them. And so we played something of a game where they would try to beat us to these camps and intimidate the refugees into remaining silent. They were especially keen about stopping any testimony about ongoing attacks the refugees were facing in the CPIM's fiefdom and therefore attacks that the CPIM could stop if it wanted to do so. We had to overcome these efforts because they would block the flow of information to the US. So we would alter our itinerary to keep them guessing about what our next stop would be.

[21] The CPIM ruled West Bengal, often with an iron fist, from 1977 until 2011 when it was voted out of office. References to my own and others' interaction with the CPIM refer to the period when that communist party still ruled West Bengal.

It meant that they could not intimidate the people into silence, which was their aim and *modus operandi;* and we tended to be successful in thwarting their efforts, but not all the time.

Our adversaries succeeded in beating us to one camp, pretty far to the north, located in the Darjeeling District, near the borders of Nepal, Bangladesh, and Bhutan. On that day, by the time we arrived in the camp, the local commissar was already there, and he had cautioned the people not to speak of any recent events that might cast a bad light on the CPIM or West Bengal government. We were able to gather a large crowd in the ersatz village square nonetheless. The communist official approached me and with no prompting or introduction on my part said, "Only the CPIM should solve problems in West Bengal." That was all I needed. Sometimes speaking to him directly in English, but always having my colleagues translate our exchange into Bangla for the benefit of the refugees, we started an often heated debate.[22]

"I should think that any *decent* government would care more about solving people's problems than who solves them," I replied.

But in automaton like fashion, he merely repeated; "Only the CPIM has a right to solve our problems."

"Really," I said. "Have you looked around here? Does it look like you are doing anything for these people? Huh? Answer me!"

---

[22] During my missions to West Bengal, I was always accompanied by Bengali associates, and in particular, my associate, ally, and representative in West Bengal, Bikash Halder. Bikash is himself a Bangladeshi Hindu whose family fled to India when he was a child. Some of my conversations on these missions were held in English, but in many cases, Bikash and others would act as my translator. In the case here, for instance, the CPIM official accosted me with his initial statement in English, and part of our public debate was held in English. At times, however, he lapsed into Bangla (the *lingua franca* of Bangladesh and West Bengal) and my English was difficult for him to understand. In those instances, Bikash translated, which also let the people in the village (non-English speakers) hear my arguments and see that they could stand up to officials who were enabling their victimization. Note, then, that incidents described in this book might have transpired in English or in Bangla with Bikash or others translating the conversations.

He did not.

"I thought that's what you communists say you're all about, helping the people. It doesn't look like you're doing them any good around here."

He in fact starting saying how Communism was oriented toward the people, "unlike Americans," and what followed was a rather lively—and public—debate between the two of us about the pros and cons of communism; with me most avidly taking the "con" side. For the most part, however, he seemed nonplussed over my aggressiveness toward him. It seems that CPIM officials in West Bengal are not used to people "talking back" to them. So, I kept pushing him about what they were doing to help the people here and protect them from attack, something he was never able to answer. It became rather intense at a few points, especially when my adversary said that the CPIM was dedicated to the people, and I repeated what I said earlier and for which he had no response: "It doesn't seem to be working out that well *for the people* if you have to intimidate them to shut up—and there are a lot of places in West Bengal where the people are suffering even more." After a pause, I added, "And you and your cronies know it!" That was when Bikash Halder, my Bengali ally and representative who lives in West Bengal, had to step in and separate us. Things calmed down after that, and the two of us smiled and shook hands—although I can only imagine what he was thinking about me given what I was thinking about him and his red masters.

Nonetheless, our public argument made it clear that he was under orders not to leave as long as we remained in the village attempting to get unfettered testimony from the refugees. Unfortunately, his presence seemed to be working. Despite the potential anonymity that a relatively large crowd affords, people were reticent to speak about anything that might anger the ever-present commissar. I would ask them to talk about their experiences either in Bangladesh or since they crossed into India and was met with a brief but awkward silence.

Finally, someone would stand up and start talking about how Muslims attacked him or his family and seized their land; and even how the *Bangladeshi* police advised them to leave the country rather than pursue a case against the perpetrators. That would have been fine, but they always made sure to add that the events occurred at some point in the safe and distant past, certainly at some time prior to the CPIM's ascension to power in 1976.[23] Any time I asked the assembled if they ever face attacks by Bangladeshi Islamists teaming up with local Muslims, they were eerily silent, and I always detected a few furtive glances from them in the commissar's direction.

My asking the refugees about the West Bengal government's collusion in attacks there was rather unexpected because the West Bengal government was not really my focus at that point. I had heard rumors of such attacks but had not yet confirmed their frequency. The West Bengal government's obsession with me and my activities, however, led me to wonder what prompted its concern. *What was it trying to hide?* In fact, I came to West Bengal, naively perhaps, expecting to find support and solidarity from a government glad to see a human rights activist trying to help its people and stem the flow of refugees across its long and porous border. It was only when I encountered the opposite—obstruction and opposition—that I was led to ask the people if they were subject to attacks on this side of the India-Bangladesh border, as well. But people were not going to talk about it given the commissar's presence; and I suppose I could not blame them.

---

[23] A general caveat seems obligatory. Throughout this book, I will refer to incidents and direct quotations about atrocities committed by Muslims. This is not an indictment of all Muslims, but the violence described here is motivated by communal hatred. The victims do not just happen to be Hindus. They are attacked *because* they are Hindus, and this must be understood as part of international *jihad*. Moreover, it is the language of the victims, and I must remain true to them. Finally, this caveat would not be necessary and the world would not conflate Islam, Muslim, and Islamist if *Muslim* leaders denounced *radical Islam* consistently and unequivocally.

Still, I pressed on and continued to ask the same question in different ways—which also proved a sterile exercise. Finally, however, and not too long before I was ready to give up, one elderly woman rose and turned to the commissar. Looking right at him with undisguised contempt she said, "I'm not afraid of anyone" and proceeded to defy his order. She told me that, absolutely, the little village has to face frequent attacks from Islamists. Many of them cross over from Bangladesh, and many are from surrounding villages that used to have mixed Hindu and Muslim populations but are now exclusively Muslim.[24] She also said, again staring at the CPIM official, that West Bengal militia on the border are notoriously corrupt and accept bribes to turn the other way during the illegal border crossings by radical Muslims and their sympathizers.[25] I half expected her to spit on the ground with disgust at the Bengali communist and accuse him of betraying his own people. She never did, but she did say that the government never prosecutes the local attackers, either. Although she was telling us that her *people* are powerless in West Bengal, this lone, courageous woman was anything but that. No government threat was going to stop her from speaking her mind. She had an internal strength that all of us would covet, and both she and her fellow refugees deserve our support and committed defense.

The war against Bangladesh's Hindus has been proceeding

---

[24] One concrete way you could tell that the Hindu population had left was by noting the lack of those small but ever-present Hindu temples that stand wherever there are Hindus in India. My colleagues and I would drive through these villages on our way to the refugee colonies and note their absence. Worse still, we would see an occasional *Mandir*, but it was clear from the disarray that no one had cared for it in some time. There were no recent gifts of food or fresh flowers, and the gates remained barred.

[25] The same level of corruption and bribery has been documented with regard to illegal cattle smuggling, which is rampant between West and East Bengal. See Richard Benkin, "Smuggling of cattle must stop," *The Daily Pioneer*, October 5, 2009, and Anuradha Dutt, "Criminal Slaughter," *The Daily Pioneer*, September 23, 2009.

for decades, but this book is more about our failure to do anything about it than it is about the actual perpetrators and their passive supporters. Think about it a minute. When Bangladeshi Islamists and politicians began the process of cleansing the country of its Hindu population:

- Barack Obama was an elementary school kid in Hawaii;
- Richard Nixon was President of the United States;
- Indira Gandhi was Prime Minister of India;
- Leonid Brezhnev was running a vibrant and menacing USSR;
- The Shah was the undisputed ruler of Iran;
- The United States was fighting in Vietnam;
- Zimbabwe was still known as Southern Rhodesia;
- The fall of *apartheid* was another 20 years away;
- No one had ever heard of AIDS;
- There would be no internet or Windows for eleven years;
- And all phones had cords, many still had dials.[26]

That is how long we have allowed Bangladesh to get away with a steady attack on its minority populations in general and Hindus in particular. That is how long the world has blithely patronized a country that has an openly racist law, the Vested Property Act which gives the government legal title to impoverish its Hindu population to force it from the country.

And that is how long the international community has provided the various governments of Bangladesh the financial wherewithal to carry out this program of ethnic cleansing. In the three-year period, 1988-1991 alone, they received almost $5 billion in unrestricted aid from a dozen countries

---

[26] This considers only the process that has occurred since the founding of Bangladesh as an independent nation. It does not include what went on when the area was part of Pakistan and when Hindus fell from just under one third to less than one fifth of the population.

and the United Nations.[27] Donor nations might periodically recognize Bangladesh's oppression of its minority population, but they never have gotten tough with the Islamic State[28] and conditioned aid on ending that oppression. In 2004, a group of donor nations meeting under the auspices of the World Bank did declare a halt to Bangladeshi aid; but their reason was its government's unfulfilled promises to "control crime and corruption and promote good governance." Its oppression of minorities was only noted as a "concern" in separate statements not tied to the cessation of aid. Moreover, the stoppage was temporary, and when the aid was reinstituted it was not done so because the Bangladeshis made any discernable progress on its treatment of Hindus or other minorities. Neither have any of the world's supposed guardians of human rights ever seriously taken up the issue of anti-Hindu actions supported or allowed by the government of Bangladesh or addressed the blatantly racist Vested Property Act. The UN has no problem looking aside while Bangladeshi Hindus are eliminated. It consistently looks the other way at minority oppression and is even complicit by propping up Bangladesh's economy with receipts from troops serving as peacekeepers. In fact, since February 2010, either Bangladesh or Pakistan has provided more UN peacekeeping troops than any other nation in the world; and the world body never seems to get the irony of the fact that neither country can keep the peace inside its own borders.[29]

If the rest of the world is content to sit on the sidelines while millions of Bangladeshi Hindus are killed, brutalized, or

---

[27] Compiled by the Committee for International Campaign (on behalf of Chittagong Hill Tracts people), 2008. The information can be found at: http://www.angelfire.com/ab/jumma/faid.html. Unless otherwise noted, money is expressed in US dollars.

[28] In 1977, the Bangladeshi constitution was amended, formally defining Bangladesh as an Islamic state. In 2011, the Bangladeshi Supreme Court gave the ruling Awami League the ability to change that, but it declined to do so.

[29] For years, Pakistan contributed the greatest number of peacekeeping troops with Bangladesh a close second. In May 2009, for example, Bangladesh . . .

stripped of their rights, should we really be surprised? Truth be told, we stink at this stuff! It is truly a mystery how we can continue calling ourselves the "civilized world" at all. For if we were judged on the basis of the moral action we have taken in recent history to prevent oppression and genocide, any objective court would declare us to be guilty: guilty of supreme cowardice. Try to think about any time when we have taken strong and effective action to prevent massive slaughter, brutality, or expulsion. It does not matter if we call it genocide, ethnic cleansing, or simply mass murder; our record of moral action with regard to them is a sad one for the victims and a disgraceful one for what it says about us. The international community responds to oppression and mass murder only after the lifeless bodies are piled too high to ignore. To be sure, pious statements of condemnation, memorials for the victims, and studied outrage are indeed the order of the day—but only *after* our inaction allows far too many deaths; almost all of them brutal and most accompanied by torture and untold indignities. Wherever we look, we find that history's monsters have been able to motivate most of their followers—average citizens all—to wipe out another people by demonizing and de-humanizing the latter. This gives those average citizens leave to commit these crimes in the name of self-defense or some other fabricated explanation of a supposed higher good.

None of these demons have been shy about their intentions either. None of them acted without telling the rest of us what they intended to do; yet, the world allowed them to implement their murderous intentions. In 1922, Hitler told an associate,

---

provided 9,849 troops; Pakistan 10,618; India 8,612. Nigeria was the only other nation supplying more than 5000 troops. Figures from *United Nations Peacekeeping*, "Monthly Summary of Contributors of Military and Civilian Police Personnel," May 2009. By January 2010, Bangladesh was only 230 troops behind. It eclipsed its fellow South Asian Islamic nation by 119 as of February; in March, Pakistan was only 16 troops behind Bangladesh. India remained in third place, but Egypt (5466) and Nepal (5171) joined Nigeria (5872) with over 5000 troops. The US had a total of 88. Figures from the UN and can be found at http://www.un.org/en/peacekeeping/contributors/ by clicking the link for the desired month and year.

"If I am ever really in power, the destruction of the Jews will be my first and most important job. As soon as I have power, I shall have gallows after gallows erected, for example, in Munich on the Marienplatz—as many of them as traffic allows. Then the Jews will be hanged one after another, and they will stay hanging until they stink. They will stay hanging as long as hygienically possible. As soon as they are untied, then the next group will follow and that will continue until the last Jew in Munich is exterminated. Exactly the same procedure will be followed in other cities until Germany is cleansed of the last Jew!"[30] At his war crimes trial in Nuremburg, Reichsminister and German labor leader, Robert Ley, was quoted as having said, "We swear we are not going to abandon the struggle until the Last Jew in Europe has been exterminated and is actually dead."[31] In 1939, Heinrich Himmler, head of the SS and the German police told an audience, "We won't waste much time on the Jews. It's great to get to grips with the Jewish race at last. The more they die the better."[32]

Jean Kambanda, who was Prime Minister during Rwanda's Tutsi genocide, said at his war crimes trial that genocide was openly discussed at cabinet meetings and elsewhere. "One cabinet minister," he testified, "said she was personally in favor of getting rid of all Tutsi; without the Tutsi, she told ministers, all of Rwanda's problems would be over."[33] Authorities also used the government-run radio stations to "spur and direct killings both in those areas most eager to attack Tutsi...They relied on [government-run] radio stations to incite and mobilize, then to give specific directions for

---

[30] Quoted in John Toland, *Adolf Hitler*. (Book Club Associates: London, 1977), p.116

[31] *Trial of the Major War Criminals Before the International Military Tribunal*, Vol.3, Nuremberg, 1947, p.36.

[32] Quoted in J. Noakes and G. Pridham, *Nazism, 1919-1945: A Documentary Reader* (University of Exeter Press: Exeter, UK, 1991), Volume 3, p.1055.

[33] Quoted in Mark Doyle, "Ex-Rwandan PM reveals genocide planning," *BBC News*, March 26, 2004.

carrying out the killings (RTLM transcripts: 13, 29 April; 15, 20 May; 1, 5, 9, 19 June 1994).[34] In April 1994, government radio, RTLM called on Hutus to "rise up as a single man," in the "final" war that "would exterminate the Tutsi from the globe ... make them disappear once and for all."[35]

Despite the clear warnings, we stood by while European Nazis murdered six million Jews in the 1940s; while Fulani-led Nigerians slaughtered around a million ethnic Ibos who formed the Republic of Biafra in the 1960s; while majority Hutus murdered almost a million Tutsis in Rwanda in the 1990s; and the humiliating saga continues seemingly without end. Ethnic Arabs are unabashedly still killing non-Arab Sudanese in Darfur; so far over half a million. There have been smaller mass killings too, like when Serbs killed around 10,000 ethnic Albanians and popularized the term "ethnic cleansing" while they did so. In 1988, Iraqi leader Saddam Hussein, a Sunni Muslim, ordered a poison gas attack on Iraq's ethnic Kurds that killed 5,000 immediately and thousands later. And ever since they disposed of their common European colonizers, various tribes and ethnic groups in Central Africa have been slaughtering each other without a break. As we have seen, they all told us what they would do once it was within their power to do so. But we stood by, in the vain hope that the victims' sacrifice would appease the gods of war and spare us and our creature comforts. If there were instances when we did act, we did not do so effectively; certainly not for the millions of dead. And we certainly did not do so in time.

While most of these crimes eventually grabbed the world's attention, it was too late for the victims. Moreover, we waited so long that the criminals did not simply brutalize and murder millions, but they also accomplished their aims of changing

---

[34] Alison Des Forges, "Call to genocide: radio in Rwanda, 1994," in Allan Thompson, editor, *The Media and the Rwanda Genocide* (Pluto Press/Fountain Publishers: London and Kampala, 2007), pp. 41-54.

[35] Quoted in *Ibid.*

the nature of their countries or continents to their own liking. Europe's Jews are slowly but surely dissipating to other parts of the world. Cities like Warsaw and Berlin had prominent Jewish communities before Hitler, virtually none after him. Before World War II, the only city with more Jews than Warsaw with its 350,000 was New York. When the city was liberated in 1945, there were a little over 11,000. Ethnic balances in Nigeria, Rwanda, Sudan, and the Congo have been upset forever. And an independent and vibrant Kurdistan was dead in Iraq until the United States toppled Saddam Hussein in 2003; and even after that war it still has little chance of ever emerging.

When the civilized world eventually does begin its anemic activity, the pattern has always been the same. The United Nations issues proclamations and sends aid to the surviving remnants through its human rights and refugee organizations. Amnesty International (AI), Human Rights Watch (HRW), and others in the human rights business jump on the band wagon and loudly condemn the perpetrators, document the atrocities, and raise money to fund their own aid programs. Several international celebrities take on highly visible roles, and massive protests worldwide give vent to peoples' outrage. But the dead stay dead, and justice for the living remains elusive and hollow.

The pattern is repeating today—even the unmistakable calls to murder. At a 1996 public rally, for instance, former and then-future Prime Minister Khaleda Zia fanned anti-Hindu flames by warning Bangladeshis that Hindus threatened to take over the country. She predicted that if things did not change the "uludhwani,"[36] would soon replace the traditional Muslim call to prayer.[37] Periodic *fatwas* and anti-Hindu messages issue forth from mosques with some regularity. And Islamist groups, often with some official standing make clear

[36] Traditional Hindu wail.

[37] "Bangladesh opposition leader accused of hurting religious sentiment," *Agence-France Press,* November 18, 1996. Also see the following examples. . .

their goal to drive out those who will not convert to Islam and to establish an *iqamat-e-deen*, an Islamic administrated country governed by *Sharia* law.

Despite the rants from mosques and the sort of incitement quoted above from leaders like Khaleda Zia, this really is a *quiet* case of ethnic cleansing not as easily recognizable by the rest of the world. *Jamaat e-Islami* is the most prominent (and probably the most powerful) of those Islamist groups. In its 2001 manifesto, issued in advance of that year's elections, the group states that its preference is to achieve its goals by "peaceful means" and that there is no difference between a Muslim and a non-Muslim.[38] The manifesto and other party documents are laced with high sounding statements about "justice" and "equality," as well as pledges to end poverty, fight corruption, and so forth. Its 2008 manifesto declares, "The aims and objects of Bangladesh *Jamaat-i-Islami* are economic emancipation of the people, ethnic and religious harmony, cultural enrichment, preservation of history and tradition, justice – economic, social and political, and above all to preserve and protect the freedom and sovereignty of Bangladesh. To realise these objectives, *Jamaat* seeks to establish a corruption free, just, equitable and prosperous Bangladesh." Its basic foreign policy principle is "Friendship with all, malice to none." (Nowhere in the manifestos does

---

Anwar Ali And Rafique Sarker, "Villagers see Rangpur arson as persecution," *The Daily Star of Dhaka,* August 28, 2004; in which victims and victimizers cited police inaction with regard to anti-Hindu violence as incitement for individuals to engage in these criminal acts without fear or legal repercussions. Also see "Death threat to Indians," *Cape Argus*, December 6, 2004, in which Hindu "crimes" in the Gujurat communal violence was cited as a reason to kill visiting Indian sportsmen.

[38] The material in this section was taken from the 2001 and 2008 election manifestos of *Jamaat* e-Islami Bangladesh; Jamaat e-Islami, "Election Manifestos, "*Parliamentary Election 2001: 8th National Parliamentary Election of Bangladesh,* http://www.bangla2000.com/Election_2001/ Manifesto_*Jamaat*-e-slami.shtm; and Bangladesh Jamaat e-Islami, " *Election Manifesto 2008: Bangladesh Jamaat-e-Islami," http://www.Jamaat-e-islami.org index.php?option=com_publication&task=detail&info_id=35.*

Jamaat mention how its demonizing statements and actions toward Israel and India are without "malice.")

Jamaat's 2001 manifesto contains an entire section entitled "Right of non-Muslim citizens," promising "All people irrespective of caste, creed,religion... equal civic amenities in respect of citizen's right. Life, property, and honour of non-Muslim population, their religious freedom as well as their civic and legal rights shall be protected." By 2008, it seems that *Jamaat* realized that even having such a section that distinguishes Muslims and non-Muslims indicated its true intention, so its manifesto that year eliminated it entirely. The manifesto simply noted that "Equal religious rights shall be ensured for people from all religions...Measures shall be taken to ensure that people from other [i.e. non-Muslim] religious denominations can perform their religious practices freely." While all of that sounds wonderful, and *Jamaat* would refer to the document as evidence that it has no intention of supporting disabilities for minorities, the reality is far more sinister and the reference to these glowing concepts cynical at best. Even the more "politically correct" 2008 manifesto made its statements about religious equality in between promises to "give preference" to *madrassa* education, provide it with public funds, and to broadcast "Muslim propaganda" (*Jamaat's* words) on publicly owned media.[39]

In a litany that does more to reflect on what can be gotten away with in our time, *Jamaat* makes clear its sectarian and religiously imperialistic intention in language of the moral high ground. "The main objective of *Jamaat*-e-Islami Bangladesh," it said, "is to establish a complete equitable and well rounded social order in the world *on the basis of the Quran and Sunnah* uprooting all sorts of man's oppression over man including the oppressed from the world *through*

---

[39] *Ibid.* All material referenced in the subsequent discussion of Jamaat comes from the same source unless otherwise noted. A *madrass* is a Muslim religious school often for young children.

introducing the law of Allah on His earth." (emphasis mine) Also: "As a primary step to establish an Islamic welfare state, the existing laws of the country will be suitably amended and necessary administrative reforms will be carried out." In other words, seemingly mild changes are only a step toward the establishment of an Islamic Bangladesh rule under *Sharia* law—which necessarily places all Hindu and other Bangladeshi citizens in a second-class, *dhimmi* status. Jamaat has participated in regular elections for years, openly pursuing its goal of establishing Bangladesh as an Islamic state under Sharia law that would be imposed on all citizens of the country, Muslim and non-Muslim alike. Between 2001 and 2006, *Jammat* was even part of Bangladesh's coalition government.

Jamaat e-Islami is not the only Bangladeshi party with that goal, just the most independent. In the run up to the aborted 2007 elections, a fundamentalist party, *Khalefat Andolin Majlis* (KAM), was able to get the "pro-minority" Awami League to sign an agreement that would have allowed KAM to implement *Sharia* law in exchange for its support in a coalition government.[40] Awami's rival BNP was engaged in a more extensive plan to bring *Sharia* to Bangladesh. Accused of rigging the elections, BNP's specific methodology was to tamper with the voter list. Since 2004, South Asian Islamists, including al Qaeda refugees, had been massing in Nepal and an area of India known as the "Chicken's Neck"; just across a porous Bangladeshi border. This would make "stuffing the ballot box" a simple task. It would give the BNP a victory in large part as the reward for extending its coalition with the minority Islamist parties. Had this scheme succeeded, Islamist votes would have been great enough to give *Jamaat* enough power to demand the Law Ministry portfolio in the new coalition government; and that would allow it to implement *Sharia* by fiat. Fortunately, the BNP's overreaching ruse led to

[40] "Hasina's choice of ally criticized," *Al Jazeera*, December 26, 2006.

a military takeover that stopped the elections and the Islamist gains.[41]

It should be noted that in the spring of 2011, Bangladesh's Supreme Court issued its final rulings on a number of constitutional amendments passed under the military dictatorships of General Ziaur Rahman and General Hussain Muhammad Ershad in the 1970s and 1980s.[42] The Fifth and Eighth Amendments were the basis for Bangladesh's caretaker system of government (which serves during a transition period when one party relinquishes power as its mandate expires and holds it until elections are held, generally within 90 days), Islam being made the official state religion (contrary to the original principles of Bangladeshi independence, which included secularism), and, as it relates to this section, religion-based political parties. The court asked the Awami League government to submit replacements for ratification in the Awami-dominated Constituent Assembly. So, essentially, the Awami League had a blank check to submit and assure the ratification of whatever replacements it wanted to pass. On June 30, the Bangladesh Parliament passed new laws that voided the caretaker system, a move that the opposition BNP called political. The status of religious-based parties like *Jamaat* is unclear, but as of yet, they have not ceased operations. There is no sign that they intend to do so, and no credible observer believes that they will quit the political scene, especially given their growing power and bipartisan support. Significantly, the Awami League refused to address the issue of Islam as the state religion.[43]

---

[41] Richard Benkin, "Islamist takeover stopped in Bangladesh?" *World Net Daily*, May 5, 2007.

[42] These final rulings addressed other rulings that were issued as far back as the period of military-backed rule and earlier periods of the current government's rule. See Bangladesh Supreme Court Bar Association http://www.bangladeshsupremecourtbar.com/Fifth_Amendment.php and "Bangladesh SC declares illegal amendment allowing religion in politics," *The Hindu*, February 2, 2010.

[43] "Bangladesh scraps caretaker system, BNP vows to protest amendments," *Jagran Post*, June 30, 2011. Also see "Bangladesh Supreme Court . . .

This is a new kind of ethnic cleansing without concentration camps and mass atrocities.[44] It is what pre-twentieth century Chinese executioners would call *ling chi*: death by a thousand cuts. About 800,000 Rwandan Tutsis were savagely murdered by their neighbors in just over 100 days; six million Jews were exterminated by the Nazis in a little more than six years; the Nigeria-Biafra civil war caused its million plus Ibo dead in about two and a half years; the process that reduced Hindus from one in five Bangladeshis to fewer than one in ten took place unchecked over decades and shows no sign of slowing. Moreover, it is rooted in ideology that finds cover by associating itself with religion. This allows its practitioners to posture their actions as being out of bounds to criticism because they are a matter of religious freedom. It also results in western nations and international bodies failing to address the atrocity for fear of being thought "intolerant" and gives their studied cowardice in the matter some cover.

It is to the everlasting shame of those people and nations who should stop this atrocity that they allow the perpetrators and their allies, both active and passive, to get away with this ruse under the banner of one or another variant of a reflexive multiculturalism. They are the same "good people" for whom Shmuel Zygielbojm searched in vain; the same people whose flaccid and patchwork ideology would have them submit to such nonsense because they care more about avoiding open hostilities on their watch, than they do about *genuine* and lasting peace that eradicates this pernicious ideology.

What about that ideology? Its first and most important premise, which we in the West and elsewhere accept uncritically, is that the world is divided into two camps:

Scraps Caretaker Government System," posted May 31, 2011 at http://newsdawn.blogspot.com/2011/05/bangladesh-supreme-court-scraps.html.

[44] The latter reference is not meant to ignore the "Bangladesh Genocide" of 1971, which saw over two million unarmed civilians, most of them Hindu, massacred by Pakistani troops and local Islamists; but that terrible event was an aberration in this otherwise quiet case of ethnic cleansing and was as intensely anti-Bengali as anti-Hindu.

Muslims and non-Muslims, with the former occupying a position that is unabashedly defined as legally and morally superior. Not so? Consider this. Although I am not a Hindu, I was welcomed as a participant in the great pilgrimage of *Kumbh Mela,* held once every twelve years. Although I am not a Buddhist, I was welcomed to experience a Himalayan temple where the Dalai Lama had recently worshipped. Although I am not a Christian, I was welcomed to Christian holy sites in Bethlehem, Nazareth, Jerusalem, and Rome. As a Jew, I prayed at our holiest site, the Western Wall of our ancient Temple in Jerusalem. One time when I was there, I listened while a group of Korean Christians sang hymns of praise across from Judaism's holiest site. What kind of response would I—a Jew—receive if asked to visit the Great Mosque in Mecca? Or what if I asked to go on *Hajj*? Or even enter Saudi Arabia wearing a *Mogen David* (Jewish Star) around my neck? Would I have been welcomed, or would Muslim leaders consider me unworthy? This is the context that allows ethnic cleansing because it places the practitioners of Islam on a higher plane to which non-Muslims are defined as *ipso facto* unworthy to ascend.

This is a context that sees the world as eternally divided into two classes: *dar al Islam* (the abode of Islam) and *dar al Harb* (the abode of war). *Dar al Islam* refers to all places where Islam thrives, most frequently defined as places under Muslim rule, preferably *Sharia*; that Islam reserves the term abode of ***war*** for everywhere else gives us a pretty good idea of what Islam enjoins Muslims to do. Moreover, the dichotomy has been explained as well as *dar al-Islam* (land of submission [to Islam]) and *dar al-Harb* (destined to be land of submission [to Islam]).[45] No matter how you slice it, the dichotomy is premised on the belief that Islam and Muslims are superior to other faiths and non-Muslims; and the belief that it is a

[45] Majid Khadduri, *War and Peace in the Law of Islam* (John's Hopkins University Press: Baltimore, 1979), pp. 62-6; Cheragh, *The Critical Exposition ...*

Muslim's duty to bring the others under Islam's rule. There have been those apologists who try to obscure that by alleging that as long as Muslims can practice their religion in peace, where they live is not *dar al-Harb*, regardless of who rules it.[46] That is absolute nonsense. Just ask the Israelis whose Muslim citizens enjoy full freedom of religion and more rights than Muslims living in "Muslim" countries. Islam is thriving so much in Israel that the Muslim agency which administers *al Aqsa* mosque on Jerusalem's Temple Mount had to carve out additional mosques under the Mount to accommodate the large number of worshippers—something it never needed to do when the Mount was ruled by Muslim Jordan or Muslim Turkey.[47]

Of course, the apologetics are part of the same ruse that hides a deadly ideology with the cloak of religion. The apologists never define precisely what they mean when they say "practicing Islam in peace," which leaves room for massive amounts of interpretation and is indicative of the duplicity with which Islamists approach the non-Muslim world. Take as an example the United States of America, which by any measure accords full freedom for all people, including Muslims, to practice their religion in peace. But could the United States be *dar al-Harb,* even by this seemingly benign definition of the apologists? The case of American Muslim Sultaana Freeman can help us answer that

---

of Popular Jihad, pp. 163-76; quoted in David Bukay, "The Religious Foundations of Suicide Bombings." *Middle East Quarterly, Fall 2006, Volume XIII, No. 4,* pp. 27-36.

[46] For instance, Murad Wilfried Hofmann, "Muslims As Co-Citizens of the West . . . Rights, Duties & Prospects," *IslamOnline.net,* May 25, 2002, which can be found at http://www.islamonline.net/servlet Satellite?c=Article_C&cid=1158658458905&pagename=Zone-English-Living_Shariah%2FLSELayout#**1.

[47] Richard Benkin, "Modern Destruction of the Temple Mount," *The Bible and Interpretation,* May 2003. Also Ricki Hollander, "The Battle Over the Temple Mount," *Committee for Accuracy in Middle East Reporting in America,* Updated July 6, 2009, http://www.interfaithstrength.com/images/Mount.htm.

question. In 2002, the State of Florida suspended her driver's license because she refused to remove her *niqab,* a full face veil worn by some observant Muslim women that leaves only the eyes visible. In the United States, the driver's license is a very important piece of photo identification, which the state noted in one of the arguments to support its action. That makes it critical for individuals to be recognizable from the picture on the license. Freeman filed a lawsuit against the state claiming that it was interfering with her free practice of Islam; that it was "forcing her to choose between observing her religion and driving." She demanded that the State of Florida give her a license without her having to lift the veil. In 2003, the court issued its ruling.

Even though it found Freeman to be sincere in her beliefs and rejected the state's argument that her rigidity was indicative of a minority belief within Islam; the court still ruled against her. It noted that the requirement to be photographed does not "substantially burden" Freeman's practice of her religion and that Florida moreover makes accommodations for Muslim women by offering them the opportunity to unveil in a private room with a female photographer. She can then keep the license hidden unless or until she is compelled to produce it by a duly constituted law enforcement or other official in the pursuit of authorized duties. The ruling could have ended there, but the court made a point of addressing a larger issue "since [Freeman] also claims that her fundamental constitutional right to free exercise of religion has been impaired." The State of Florida argued that "when religious practices collide with public safety, public safety must prevail"; and the court agreed. The court also took care to note that "it would be foolish not to recognize that there are new threats to public safety, including both foreign and domestic terrorism... Plaintiff's veiling practices must be subordinated to society's need to identify people as quickly as possible in situations in which safety and security of others could be at risk." The court also rejected Freeman's contention that she was singled out as a Muslim, and said that "anyone—Christian, Jew, Buddhist, Atheist" would be accorded the same treatment she received.[48]

The United States has over two centuries of experience and legal precedence of maintaining religious freedom without allowing sectarian laws to impose their authority in the public arena. There is a clear firewall that allows religious laws and norms to predominate up to a certain point when the general laws of the federal, state, and local governments prevail. The Florida case is one example of how that works. Another is the case of Muslim cab drivers who refused to accept passengers at the Minneapolis airport if they were carrying alcohol. They were informed that the practice could cost them their license and that they could face other sanctions because taxi regulations do not allow drivers to refuse to carry any fare paying passengers. The regulations were enacted to assure that drivers would not discriminate against potential riders out of bias. The Muslim drivers claimed that the public regulations did not outweigh Sharia and that forcing them to pick up passengers with alcohol would violate their religious principles. They also refused to carry passengers with dogs, even guide dogs for the blind. On April 17, 2007 the taxicab authorities enacted new penalties in a crackdown of their practice. The first offense would carry a 30-day license suspension, and a second would result in a two-year license revocation (which requires more for reinstatement than a mere suspension).[49]

In another case involving the "Minneapolis imams," several Muslims were taken off an airplane at the Minneapolis airport

[48] Sultaana Lakiana Myke Freeman, Plaintiff v. State of Florida Department of Highway Safety and Motor Vehicles, Defendant. The Circuit Court of the Ninth Judicial Circuit in and for Orange County, Florida; Case No. 2002-CA-2828

[49] "Minnesota's Muslim cab drivers face crackdown," *Reuters,* April 17, 2007. Available at http://www.reuters.com/article/2007/04/17/us-muslims-taxi-idUSN1633289220070417.

when they (with forethought) violated security regulations—that apply to everyone—and got up just before take-off and prayed together. While Northwest Airlines eventually agreed to a monetary settlement to avoid negative publicity, the case represented another confirmation that claims of religious rights do not trump public law or safety.[50]

Does that mean that Freeman, the cab drivers, and other Muslims are *not* free to practice Islam in the United States? According to the interest groups championing the Minneapolis *imams* and cab drivers, they are not. Freeman and her supporters, take the same position. In her case, the court devoted more than half of its ruling to making the point that Islam and any other religion is subordinate to the secular laws of the United States and to setting up a firewall beyond which Islamic (and any other religious) belief cannot intrude. The Florida court also made it clear that Islam deserves to be treated no different than "Christianity, Judaism, Buddhism, or Atheism"—something that might make eminent sense to most people but is in conflict with the *dar al-Islam/dar al-Harb* dichotomy. That bifurcation of humanity in and of itself reveals the ultimate belief system that is at work in the *Islamic State* of Bangladesh. Its Hindus are outsiders in a society that makes a clear distinction between Muslims and everyone else; and holds that the former are entitled to better treatment. As one analyst put it, "Waging war to subjugate non-Muslims,

---

[50] While the US has been pretty consistent in remaining secular without being pseudo-secular, a recent study by the Center for Security Policy analyzed 50 cases that its criteria deemed an attempt to enforce Shariah law in state and appellate courts and found that in at least six of them, the ultimate disposal of the case allowed Shariah to apply. This is not to say that all of those cases involved a serious disagreement between Shariah law and US or state law. "Shariah Law and American Courts: An Assessment of State Appellate Court Cases," *Center for Security Policy,* Washington, 2011. Available at http://www.shariahinamericancourts.com/wp-content/uploads/2011/05/Shariah-Law-and-American-State- Courts-1.3-05202011.pdf.

therefore, is a common sense application of Islam's view of the world."[51]

Constitutional guarantees of religious freedom, which Bangladeshi apologists use to dissuade people from the reality, are subordinate to Islam's legally mandated superiority in Bangladesh—as they are in the *dar al-Islam/dar al-Harb* dichotomy.[52]

The lack of concentration camps in Bangladesh does not equal a lack of atrocities; nor does it mean that the ultimate direction is not the deliberate and violent elimination of an entire people. It does, however, make it more difficult to recognize—which, in turn, makes it easier for perpetrators to continue their murderous rampage. As a result, those who consider themselves the protectors of human rights and have the power to bring serious attention to the Bangladeshi Hindus' terror filled present and horrid future are failing to address *a deliberate and brutal program to ethnically cleanse Bangladesh of its Hindus: by Bangladeshi Islamists who drive it and provide the ideological justification; by "average" Bangladeshi Muslims who carry it out; and by successive Bangladeshi governments, all of whom are complicit in this crime against humanity by refusing to punish the perpetrators and stop the ideology of hatred that provides its engine. Both religion and government thereby together send their people*

---

[51] Jamie Glazov, "*United in Hate: The Left's Romance with Tyranny and Terror.* (WND Books: Los Angeles, 2009), p. 229. Also see, Robert Spencer, *Onward Muslim Soldiers: How Jihad Still Threatens America and the West,* (Regnery: Washington, DC, 2003.) for a comprehensive analysis of *jihad's* reality in Islam.

[52] Three legal tenets remain in force today in Bangladesh, and the current government, despite its empty words, refuses to do away with them: an order stopping money transfers by Hindus, the Vested Property Act, discussed elsewhere here, and the Eighth Amendment to the Bangladesh Constitution that makes Islam the official state religion, gives preference and public monies to Islamic institutions but not those of other religions, and includes fealty to Allah and Islam as basic to all legal actions in Bangladesh.

an unambiguous message that they have no real problem with what the murderers are doing.

* * *

In 1951, after the dust of Partition-era transfers settled, the ratio of Muslims to Hindus in East Bengal was about three and a half to one. Three years after Bangladesh won its independence, the ratio of Muslims to Hindus was still only a little higher than six to one. By 2001, Muslims outnumbered Hindus by a ratio of almost eleven and a half to one.

Bangladesh's Hindu population is dying. This is not opinion or the ravings of an ideologue: It is a fact that cannot be repeated enough times; nor should we stop repeating it until people address it.

> *At the time of India's partition in 1947, they made up a little less than a third of East Pakistan's population. When East Pakistan became Bangladesh in 1971, Hindus were less than a fifth; thirty years later, less than one in ten; and several estimates put the Hindu population at less than eight percent today. Professor Sachi Dastidar of the State University of New York estimates that about 49 million Hindus are missing from the Bangladeshi census. Still having trouble wondering where this is going? Take a look at Pakistan where Hindus are down to one percent or Kashmir where they are almost gone. Take a look at the future of Bangladesh's Hindus if we do not act.*[53]

Bangladesh's Hindu population is dying and no one is doing anything about it. This, too, is not opinion but fact. It is the

---

[53] The trajectory is clear and immutable; no matter that Hinduism pre-dates Islam in East Bengal by centuries; no matter that the land is dotted with Hindu historical and religious sites, although they are being destroyed or left to rot. Population figures taken from *Census of East Pakistan, 1951; Bangladesh Government Census, 1974 and 2001.*. Also see Dastidar, Sachi G., *Empire's Last Casualty: Indian Subcontinent's Vanishing Hindu and other Minorities*. (Firma KLM Private Limited: Kolkata, 2008).

reality that millions live with but only a few others seem to care about; and that is a reality that no one should have to live with. Forty-nine million people! It is a number that boggles the mind; a number larger than the population of all but 23 countries.[54] It is a number so great that people tend to have a tough time grasping its reality, and they thereby fail to recognize the imminent threat. More important for us, however, than the 49 missing million people are the millions more at risk right now. And if we do not take resolute and unbending action soon, those millions will die as well. We cannot do anything about the first group except mourn them and learn from what happened to them. But we *can* do something about the second group. This is the real rationale for our call to action: saving those lives and standing up for what is right. Even though the numbers are greater than those involved in more infamous cases of genocide like Darfur, there is no George Clooney, Angelina Jolie, or other celebrity championing the cause. Even though the numbers are greater than those involved in more famous cases of ethnic cleansing like Bosnia, there are no NATO or US troops fighting to rescue the victims. There have been no declarations from the UN, despite its mandate to stop such atrocities. Its largely misnomered Human Rights Council (UNHRC) and High Commissioner for Human Rights ignore the matter under the leadership of the worst human rights defilers such as Iran, North Korea, and Cuba.

Many victims look to neighboring India and have sought refuge by crossing the border into the world's largest Hindu country. In communist-ruled West Bengal, the Indian state that shares the largest border with Bangladesh, they are shunted from one refugee camp to another, being forced to move

---

[54] China, India, USA, Indonesia, Brazil, Pakistan, Bangladesh, Nigeria, Russia, Japan, Philippines, Mexico, Vietnam, Germany, Ethiopia, Egypt, Turkey, Iran, France, Thailand, Congo, UK, and Italy. These numbers are taken from official national population statistics.

whenever someone wants the land on which they are squatting or simply because their West Bengal overseers have decided that they might profit from the refugees' ersatz homes.[55] Other Bangladeshi Hindu refugees live in virtual garbage dumps in cities like Delhi. The international human rights industry, too, has been silent. A random check of Amnesty International's web site, for example, found pages upon web pages devoted to the United States and especially to its terrorist detention center in Guantanamo, Cuba; but nothing about the Bangladeshi Hindus. People visiting Oxfam International's web site will find story after story about climate change, even more stories complaining about alleged Israeli violations of human rights in Gaza, but none that address real human rights violations in Bangladesh or the oppression of Hindus.

AI and HRW also spend a high percentage of their resources criticizing Israeli democracy and congratulating themselves for defending a few million Palestinian Arabs whose innocence has long been compromised by their commission of some of our era's worst terrorist incidents and by the Palestinian population's consistent support for them.[56] These same Arabs could get along very well with the billions in petrodollars that the Saudis and their other allies can supply from their pocket change. What resources have the Bangladeshi Hindus? I have seen where both sets of people live—Palestinians in Israel and Jordan, Bangladeshi Hindus in India and Bangladesh—and homes of the former look like palaces compared with those of the latter. Yet, the well thought of human rights organizations and international bodies ignore the carnage from Arab terrorism as assiduously as they ignore

[55] The Communist Party of India/Marxist or CPIM enjoyed uninterrupted rule of West Bengal since 1976. Only recently was it finally voted out of power, replaced by Momata Bannerjee and the Trinamool Congress. Exactly how that might change things remains a matter of projection.

[56] In the wake of the 9/11 terror attacks on the US, widespread news reports showed jubilant Palestinian Arabs celebrating in the streets and handing out sweets, a traditional practice to represent great happiness. These were not isolated incidents but general merriment in the disputed territories in Israel.

the carnage being perpetrated against tens of millions of Hindus in South Asia; and as strenuously as they ignore the fact that those terrorists are allied with the very Palestinian terror they champion at the expense of *real* victims in South Asia.

Flushed with passion after meeting with scores of refugees in 2008, I returned to AI's web site and scoured it in search of some outrage—any outrage—over what is so apparent in South Asia; but my search was in vain. Its cover story did indeed express outrage, but over Shiite Muslims being treated "like second class citizens" as described by AI. This is the most important issue on which these self-styled guardians of human rights determined to expend their resources? How many Shiite girls were raped today; how many thrown off their ancestral lands; how many murdered? And how many governments said it was okay? To date Amnesty International has yet to show any stomach for opposing what could be the worst case of ethnic cleansing in our time.[57]

One could advance any number of reasons for their silence. Is it because the victims are Hindu; or the victimizers Muslim? Are they simply moral cowards; or do they just not care? Perhaps it is a case of AI placing ideology above principle, not wanting to offend its leftist coalition partners by straying from their ideological agenda. AI's own history and actions could support any of those contentions. The last time AI, or HRW for that matter, gave the Bangladeshi Hindus even passing mention was in 2006. (Oxfam never has.) In its 2010 report on Bangladesh (the most recent at this writing), AI shockingly did not even mention the oppression of Hindus; a horrid disgrace, that encourages the human rights atrocities those very organizations claim to be fighting![58]

---

[57] A July 2011 search of AI's web site, specifically for Bangladesh, addresses extrajudicial killings, but none against Hindu citizens, the case of an opposition MP, and other matters, but not that of the Bangladeshi Hindus. http://www.amnesty.org/en/region/bangladesh.

[58] It is available online at http://www.amnesty.org/en/region/bangladesh/report-2011.

This is not the first time the world has ignored mass murder in South Asia. Towards the end of the Bangladeshi war of independence—a mere 26 years after the world came face to face with Auschwitz, Pakistani troops and their Islamist allies slaughtered between two and three million Bangladeshi noncombatants, including women, children, and the elderly. Although it is accurate to state that there were Muslim victims as well as Hindus, the latter were victimized way out of proportion to their numbers in the general population. That, in and of itself, should indicate the deliberate targeting of Hindus in Bangladesh, but there is even more evidence that this was not, as some would have us believe, an anti-Bengali atrocity having no religious component but only aimed at killing Bangladeshi independence.[59]

During a 2010 visit to Kolkata, I met with Tathagata Roy, an official of the Bharatiya Janata Party (BJP), India's conservative opposition party. A member of the Bengali Hindu community himself, Roy has devoted much of his adult life to studying its persecution in Bangladesh and Pakistan, demographic changes in West Bengal, and related matters. He told me that there is no doubt that the Bangladeshi Holocaust was largely intended to kill as many Hindus as possible and terrorize the rest. The perpetrators' also hoped to drive most of the remnant across the border into India and force the remainder to convert to Islam.[60] In a book he authored several years earlier, Roy documented the work of the Hamoodur Rahaman Commission. (The Commission took its name from the chair, Pakistani Chief Justice Hamoodur Rahman). It was

[59] Although accurate figures are difficult to come by, there is extensive anecdotal information on top of anti-Hindu and anti-Bengali sentiment among the Pakistanis and their Islamist allies in Bangladesh. See, for example, Peter Hazelhurst, "Dwindling flow of refugees suggests West Bengal border has been closed," *The Times of London*, June 13, 1971; and *Bangladesh Genocide Archive,* which is available online at http://www.genocidebangladesh.org.

[60] Private conversation with Tathagata Roy in Kolkata, February, 21, 2010.

able to recover and produce numerous documents that included written orders to Pakistani troops and their irregular allies to kill as many Hindus as possible.[61] Another author described the method used by the killers to identify Hindus, an ironic reversal of the way anti-Jewish murderers would identify Jews by their circumcisions. "Hindus were sought out and killed on the spot. As a matter of course, soldiers would check males for the obligated circumcision among Muslims. If circumcised, they might live; if not, sure death."[62] This bizarre procedure makes it clear that this was no general Bengali genocide but rather that Pakistanis targeted Hindus no less than the Nazis targeted Jews.

All manner of brutality accompanied the carnage, from mutilation to ritualized gang rape, but the world has chosen to ignore it even now while the victims' descendants cry out for justice and many of the perpetrators are known and could be brought to justice. Compare that backdrop of inaction and unconcern with this. In 1999, only 28 years after these terrifying events in Bengal, NATO aircraft flew over 38,000 bombing missions against Serbian targets when *thousands* of Kosovo Muslims were at risk. Good for them, but here we are another eleven years hence, and no collective body or individual nation has acted to try and save *millions* of Hindus in Bangladesh (or millions more in Pakistan and Kashmir).[63]

---

[61] Tathagato Roy, *My People Uprooted.* (Ratna Prakashan: Kolkata, 2001).

[62] R. J. Rummel, Irving Louis Horowitz, *Death by Government.* (Transaction Publishers: Kolkata, 1977), p. 323; quoted in Mohit Roy, "Illegal Migration and Undeclared Refugees – Idea of West Bengal at Stake," Paper presented at *Migration and Its Impact on Indian State and Democracy,* a seminar at the Department of Politics and Public Administration, University of Pune, Pune, India, March 13, 2009.

[63] Before Bangladesh won its independence, it was known as East Pakistan. What we know as the nation of Pakistan today was then called West Pakistan. In 1965, Hindus represented one in five residents of West Pakistan; today they are less than one percent of the population. The once thriving Hindu community of Kashmir is all but gone.

The mind-numbing consistency of this disparity is glaring to anyone familiar with the situation. To the victims especially, it hardly matters which set of shameful factors are at the bottom of it: anti-Hindu bias; pro-Muslim bias; Petrodollars; moral cowardice and a general reluctance to confront human rights violations; international politics, NGO politics and funding; corruption on both sides of the Bangladeshi border; government denials and cover-ups; Hindus' passivity; their failure to stand up for their co-religionists; the same failure by the world's largest Hindu nation—India; or pseudo-secularism.[64] Wild conspiracy theories abound, as well, most pointing to the intelligence services of India (Research and Analysis Wing or RAW), Pakistan (Inter-services Intelligence or ISI), Bangladesh (Directorate General of Forces Intelligence or DGFI), United States (Central Intelligence Agency or CIA), and Israel (Mossad); none with any evidence to substantiate them.[65]

There likely is a bit of truth to all but the conspiracy theories of them, but attempting to say what that kernel is would be little more than speculation.[66] Most of the refugees I have interviewed believe it is religious bias, something they say they have faced their entire lives. One Indian activist said that fear of terrorist reprisals, the lure of petrodollars, and a rigid political correctness prevent many Hindus from taking a stand against Islamists. But he and others blame "our own nature" as the greatest factor in militating against activism and in tolerating corruption.

We can attribute our tolerance for these atrocities to anything we want, but our conclusions would be academic; for we would be pondering abstract notions while real people

---

[64] Pseudo-secularism refers to the prevailing system in India whereby the desire to be seen as secular results in a false (or pseudo) secularism that advantages non-Hindus.

[65] Intelligence agencies for, respectively, India, Pakistan, Bangladesh, the United States, and Israel.

[66] For one view, see Richard Benkin, "Stop Them Before the Kill Again." *Canada Free Press,* December 26, 2007.

continue to face unrelenting atrocity. This—the murder of millions—should be an issue that leaves no one unmoved. It should not matter to *anyone* that the victims are Hindu and the perpetrators are Muslim. What matters is the death of innocents. That it is part of a greater Islamist *jihad* to cleanse Bangladesh of its Hindu population might help some to see how ruthless that enemy is. It remains mind boggling that this ongoing atrocity does not outrage every decent human being on the planet, regardless of any one of their personal politics or religion. It should, but it does not. I have spoken with quite a few people about this, especially during or before my 2009 mission. We would expect many of these people to stand in the forefront of the fight against this horror.

Yet, almost to an individual they gave a similar sounding response that acknowledged their awareness of the atrocity but ended with some variant of 'let's wait and see.' 'There is a new government in Bangladesh,' they would say in early 2009. 'We should give it time.'

Wait and see? Give it time? Tell that to the victims whose tragic numbers grow every day. We have given them more than 30 years, and they have done nothing to stop the bloodshed. How many more have to die before we tell them, "Time's up"?

As this book is being written (2011), this new government has been in office for over two and a half years. How has that wait and see attitude worked out for those who cling to it? And yet, these individuals and groups continue to at most shake their fists in venues almost guaranteed not to bring about action. *And action is what we need—not empty words—not studied and sterile outrage that is structured to go nowhere—but action.*

What kind of a world do we live in where people say wait and see while another young girl is abducted and raped or while another man is beaten or worse? What kind of a world do we live in where people say wait and see while another family is dispossessed of their tiny plot of land simply because they have refused to convert to Islam? And in what kind of world do those who are charged with helping the helpless and saving the victims, those with enormous resources to do something about this, say that they are otherwise occupied; and we do not call them on it? That they should leave this fight to the likes of me is a disgrace. It has got to change; it has got to change now; and that is the question each of us must ask. Because if *we* do not do it, what hope is there that others will?

* * *

A few important words about Nazis and the Holocaust. Earlier in this chapter and indeed throughout this book, there are references to the Nazi Holocaust against the Jewish people that transpired between 1933 and 1945 but primarily during the Second World War. Quite often, when people encounter references to that unique historical event, they see it more as propaganda than a legitimate comparison. The Nazis and the Holocaust have become international shorthand for pure, unrepentant evil, which makes any such references appear to be hyperbole. Many also do not like the references because their use trivializes the actual event. But to compare two events to one another does not mean to equate them; and it is precisely because the Holocaust was such a singular event that it is pertinent here. Let us be clear that *what is happening to the Hindus of Bangladesh is not the Holocaust; neither is Sheikh Hasina nor any other Bangladeshi leader Adolf Hitler.* Elements of the process unfolding in Bangladesh, however, have precursors in the Nazi Holocaust.

The elimination of the Bangladeshi Hindus differs from the Holocaust in several significant ways. It is not part of the East Bengali social fabric to accept that a "Hindu problem" exists; nor do leaders and citizenry nonchalantly discuss the best methods to resolve it. Mainstream newspapers do not demonize Hindus or describe them as vermin. Bangladeshi leaders do not openly speak of a Hindu-free Bangladesh. The Bangladeshi government, no matter which party is in power, does not expend massive amounts of resources to carry out a program designed to eliminate Hindus, even to the detriment of its national goals. And even during periods of military-backed rule (most recently from 2007-2008), Bangladesh was never a totalitarian state where the constitution was suspended and the nation made subservient to the ruling party. All of these things, however, characterized the Nazi holocaust against the Jews.

The Nazi program of de-legitimization and extermination applied to all Jews equally and (except for some brief and very early exceptions) all at once. That has never been the case in Bangladesh. Hindus serve in the Constituent Assembly (*Jatiya Sangsad*) and even hold cabinet posts. They include prominent professional people and business leaders. The journalist who was my liaison with the current Bangladeshi government and sat with us during our talks is Hindu. Nothing like that could ever happen for a Jew in Nazi Germany or Nazi-occupied territory. Another key difference is that Jews were destined for destruction under the Nazis no matter what actions they took. A Jew could not convert to Christianity and avoid the gas chamber or concentration camps. Nazis held that Judaism was a racial matter that could be disguised but never eliminated by a mere change of religion. In contrast, one of the primary ways in which Hindus are being eliminated is through forced conversion to Islam and the abduction of Hindu women for the production of non-Hindu children. Then why make the references?

The juxtaposition of this epitome of evil (Nazi Germany) with a seemingly benign entity (Bangladesh) on elements of this one point is dramatic. This book does not demonize Bangladesh as a nation, but if this book was about Nazi Germany, it would not hesitate to demonize that nation—and that would hardly be going out on a limb. It does not take anything special to condemn Nazis, but what does take courage and insight is to find and point out legitimate elements today that could have the same outcome for others as the Nazis intended for the Jews: their complete elimination. It is that nuance which creates daylight between the two bodies—between the evil and the apathetic—while also establishing their similarities, that makes the references powerful. No, Bangladesh is not Nazi Germany, and its attack on Hindus is not the Holocaust, but there are at least three chilling similarities; and there is an even more chilling logic to their order.

First, there is no statist ideology that demands the elimination of Hindus in Bangladesh, but there is an ideology that does, and it is growing stronger: radical Islam. Like Nazism in Germany, radical Islam in Bangladesh is contrary to basic traditions among the people but yet flows out of various elements embedded in their history. Hindu-Muslim conflict has a strong historical presence in South Asia just as Christian persecution of Jews did in Europe. Anti-Hindu sentiment has been used to stir emotions among East Bengalis and distract them from other matters, just as anti-Jewish sentiment was used for centuries in Germany. Second, just as Zygielbojm found out to his crushing dismay that the rest of the world was willing to ignore the plight of the Jews in Germany, so too is the world content to look away while Hindus are being brutalized in Bangladesh. The great powers are as silent on this matter as their predecessors were during the Holocaust. The same level of inaction applies to most Hindus today as it did to most Jews in the 1930s; and many read that inaction as evidence that nothing is transpiring as terrible as that which is being alleged. Germany had its Nuremburg laws, which certainly were more extensive and more brutally enforced than Bangladesh's Vested Property Act; both, however, eroded basic rights for some citizens and both were accepted passively by the international community.

Third and perhaps most important, the same intended fate awaits both communities: a Germany free of Jews and a Bangladesh free of Hindus. And if the driving ideologies prevailed, it would be a world free of both. For the victims, nuance matters little. Moreover, that process which started in Germany soon spilled over into neighboring Austria, which had a shared language and culture with Germany. So, too, as later chapters in this book will show, attacks on Hindus have now crossed into the adjacent Indian state of West Bengal, which owns a shared language, culture, and ethnicity with East Bengal, now known as Bangladesh. And make no mistake about it. Just like Hitler with his "territorial demands," these people, too, will not stop with the Bangladeshi Hindus. What happens to them predicts what will happen to us.

The Nazi Holocaust against the Jews, or the *Shoah,*[67] was such a horrific and singular event that it could not help but forever mark those of us—especially Americans and most especially Jews—who came of age in the second half of the twentieth century. This does not mean that we see Adolf Hitlers in every tin pot dictator or disseminator of hate. It does not mean memorializing Jewish victimhood, or even embracing victimhood itself. In fact, it means quite the opposite. It means recognizing the *real* Hitlers as opposed to simple practitioners of hate; and it means a personal and complete commitment to the words that came out of the *Shoah,* "Never again!" "Never again" is first and foremost a

[67] The word, *Shoah,* is the Hebrew term for what is generally called the Holocaust. From the end of the twentieth century forward, the term Holocaust has been cheapened by its use for political purposes. Worse, these political uses are intended to compare the horrible events in World War II—the deliberate and brutal attempt to kill every single Jew—with the Arabs' self-inflicted degradation in the Middle East. Anyone who would see the two as comparable either has no understanding of real genocide or denies that it ever happened to the Jews of Europe. That depraved notion is almost an article of faith in much of the Muslim world where leaders see propaganda as being more important than fact (one major reason for Muslims' degradation and retrograde state, as well as the backward state of most Muslim-majority nations); but appeasers have allowed it to gain currency outside of the "Ummah." That stops here. There is only one exception: the Bangladeshi Holocaust of 1971, in which Pakistanis and Bengali Islamists murdered two to three million Bengali civilians (mostly Hindus) in a deliberate attempt to wipe out a people.

commitment that Jews will *never* be victims again; that we will fight those who attempt to revive those times. It is also a pledge to commit oneself as a moral human being to prevent it from happening again to *any* people. And it is "Never again" that demands we stop the destruction of Bangladesh's Hindus.

The key is putting the three things together: recognizing the signs that were there and ignored in the 1930s, recognizing it for people other than your own, and *acting* on it.[68] For the fact is that although we may yet have no *Gestapo* or *Janjaweed,* running amok in Bangladesh, people are being murdered, raped, and despoiled of their ancestral lands by a Nuremburg-type law nonetheless. I have seen the victims and in one remote corner of Northeast India in March 2009, I stared into the eyes of a 14-year-old Hindu girl as she told of being raped by Muslims because she is a Hindu. There may be no killing fields or crematoria, but the deliberate destruction of Hindu populations in Bangladesh and Pakistan is inescapable. The numbers are inescapable: in Pakistan, one in five to one percent; in Bangladesh, almost one in three to less than nine percent.

And consider. This is Bangladesh! I mean, come on. If we do not have the strength to stand up to Bangladesh—Bangladesh, one of the weakest and most pitiful nations in the world—how can we ever be expected to stand against the real villains on our planet from China and Iran to Al Qaeda? If we cannot stop this atrocity and worse, do not even try to stop it, what kind of world can we expect to follow us? What kind of world can we expect to leave to our children?

We might—*might*—excuse or understand *some* of the people Shmuel Zygielbojm tried to convince. After all, they were busy full-time, fighting a war to save humanity. What's our excuse?

---

[68] Recall the 1992 statement earlier in this book by Tenzin Gyatso, the 14th Dalai Lama "It is not enough to be compassionate; you must ACT." That is the final and most critical component.

CHAPTER ONE AND A HALF

GETTING "IT" OUT OF THE WAY

The importance of this discussion and clarity of the message should be apparent to all who read it—all who read it honestly, that is, and maintain the priorities that all decent human beings share. The world's continued silence in the face of the destruction of millions of Hindus raises it from important to critical. Unfortunately, the context of our times requires a necessary disclaimer. For we often see "respectable" publications giving vent to those who would divert us from recognizing the human tragedy and our obligation to stop it by a reflexive need to ignore the message and instead hurl charges of "Islamaphobia." The issues here are far too important to waste time on the niceties of political correctness and disingenuous posturing that in the end only strengthen the enemies of us all. So let us do it quickly and be done with it.

I am not "anti-Muslim." I am not "Islamaphobic," nor am I a bigot in any way. As related above, I put my life on the line for a Muslim journalist who has no intention of ever leaving Islam or his Muslim-majority country.[69] I could flaunt other credentials as well, including a very heated, public argument with the head of a major Jewish organization in which he contended that the religion of Islam itself was the essence of the threat we face, which is a strategic *cul de sac.* Even if we were to accept the proposition that Islam is the problem, where do we go from there? We have just declared war on more than

[69] More times than I can count, Shoaib has been challenged about remaining a Muslim, but has expressed his faith in remaining one. I also have fielded numerous offers of asylum, all of which he declined.

one-fourth of humanity, telling them that our problem is with their faith and that as long as they adhere to it, they are responsible for worldwide *jihad* and terrorism. So, what is the next step? There is none unless we adopt the values and methods of our enemies—in the name of defending the very values we are casting aside. In addition, the position helps give credence to those among our enemies who try to deny the inherent justice of our war against Islamic extremists.

Moreover, I am not a religious scholar and have neither the information nor the training to make a definitive call regarding the essence of any religion per se; so I will not. I am qualified, however, to speak about consistent actions and patterns of history with regard to the practitioners of any religion and in this quiet case of ethnic cleansing, of Muslims. An honest discussion of this and other topics related to international terrorism and assorted atrocities would be simplistic and incomplete if it did not address Islam, sometimes quite prominently. That 14 year-old rape victim I interviewed in northern Bengal was not raped by random miscreants and, oh yes, she happened to be a Hindu. She was raped *because* she is a Hindu. And the rapists did not savage that child and, oh yes, they happened to be Muslim. They savaged her *because* they are Muslim and recognized their legally favored position in their country. The perpetrators' and victims' religion should be an inconsequential matter that does not concern us. Their religion *should not be important*, but the perpetrators—not we—have *made it important*.

Muslim leaders, religious and secular, by and large have refused to actively dissociate themselves from the perpetrators' identification with Islam. This is the case whether the victims are non-Muslim minorities or other Muslims, especially women. Pious sounding phrases that always include some sort of "but" leave open the door for justifying the terrorists' actions. Nor do pious sounding phrases that never find their manifestation in action qualify as denunciations.

Moreover, I was trained as a social scientist, and learned that if we see a variable common to a series of events, it is contrary to objective investigation to pretend that such is not the case. It is contrary to good science not to identify the common factor and determine why it shows up in that series of, in this case terrorist, events. And in this case, that also means Islam. Come to whatever conclusion objective science points to; but do not cut off knowledge in the name of political correctness.

All of that, of course, is really beside the point. This is not about me; nor is it an academic discussion of Islam. This is about a horrendous atrocity that the world has been silent about for decades. The only reason for this mini-chapter is to dispose of the disingenuous argument of Islamaphobia that almost invariably arises when murderous actions and their Muslim perpetrators are highlighted—especially when those actions are in some way related to their being Muslim; and when Muslim leaders religious and secular either refuse to condemn it or offer only qualified condemnation. That is, they say terrorism is "wrong," but that they understand the "anger" that generated it; or they qualify who is an "innocent" by excluding Israelis, for instance. And it has been demonstrated unequivocally that for decades Muslim clerics and Muslim leaders have given either material support or ideological cover for this murderous *jihad.* By their actions—not by their faith—they have caused the very confusion between ideology and religion that they now cry about when its consequences are manifest.

Again, to be clear, that is not an indictment of Islam itself but of the way that a sizeable proportion of Muslims throughout history have seen their faith and group as privileged and superior to others. If people want to conclude that their actions reflect a failure of Islam itself that is their decision. But those who commit these actions—be they suicide bombers in Mumbai or Middle East *imams* who provide them with ideological cover—they deserve to be attacked, their bigotry exposed, and the failure of their religious and political leaders to stop them highlighted. As Dr. Jamie Glazov, author and managing editor of *Frontpage Magazine,* has written:

> There is a struggle taking place for the soul of Islam at this very moment, and many Muslims who oppose extremism and fanaticism are courageously fighting to bring their religion into the modern world. Individuals such as Canada's Irshad Manji and Italy's Sheikh Abdul Hadi Palazzi, and groups such as Muslims against Sharia and the Center for the Study of Islam & Democracy, are all part of this effort. [70]
>
> [Break]
>
> It will be no easy effort for Muslim reformers to buck nearly fourteen hundred years of tradition. But they do have the power to bring out the tolerant and civilized components of their religion. . .The course of the terror war and the future of freedom are very much dependent on whether or not the voices of reform-minded Muslims prevail. The West has a huge stake in the success of such teachers. . . and must do everything in its power to support them.

In part, Glazov's comments were made as a cautionary tale for Westerners whose leftists have a penchant for supporting brutal "totalist" regimes that wage unremitting and existential war against America and western values. In South Asia, they wage the same war against the *Vedic* teachings and their values; teachings and values that have been inspiring people for thousands of years and have allowed Muslims to flourish in the land of the *Vedas.* Glazov's point also helps explain the "Red-Green Alliance" of communists and Islamists, which is the focus of Chapter Seven.

This mini-chapter, however, is included not only to answer predictable critics once and for all, rather than doing so at multiple points in the book. It is also an artifice that the predictable talking heads of today make necessary in order to dispose of a disingenuous argument that has legitimacy only

---

[70] *Op. cit.,* Glazov, pp. 109-110.

within the context of our day's most cowardly and ridiculous geo-political environment. We can expect it, and we can expect that its impact will be continued tolerance for the killing of Hindus in Bangladesh and other Muslim-majority countries.

Those who fall so easily into that knee-jerk rationalization, knowingly or not, join with the murderers and support their continued atrocities by trying to distract us from taking action to stop them. Those who attempt to discount the information in this book by calling the author anti-Muslim are simply dishonest; they have chosen to be part of the problem, accessories to ethnic cleansing. Their actions are by now a familiar tactic of our enemies and their appeasers to seize the agenda and continue blocking the truth of their own and their allies' activities from becoming known and understood for what they are. In this day and age particularly, the control of information is perhaps the most potent weapon in anyone's arsenal.

Making an author's point of view the issue allows those critics to supplant and ignore the real issue, which is the murder of millions and the jeopardy in which our enemies have placed millions more—and yes, those who do so are our enemies and the enemies of all that is good and decent. They are not unspecified militants; they do not hold a point of view that should be accorded any measure of legitimacy; they do not deserve the same courtesies that we accord those who are not the enemies of civilization.

The late United States Senator and scholar, Daniel Patrick Moynihan of New York is reported to have said, "Everyone is *entitled* to his *own* opinion, but not to his *own facts*." And the facts presented here are inescapable: millions murdered or otherwise brutalized; millions never born as a result; millions more at risk. Is it an indictment of Islam? Neither am I qualified to offer that opinion, nor do I wish to do so. For the argument itself draws attention away from the real issue: the atrocity transpiring in Bangladesh and elsewhere in South

Asia. Do these actions reflect the beliefs of all Muslims? Unlikely; but raising the argument diverts us from the task at hand, which is to stop the killing, to end massive injustice. Asking whether or not it reflects the beliefs of all Muslims is no different than if we were to ignore the Nazi Holocaust by saying, "well, not *all* Germans are like that." To argue otherwise is, whether intentional or not, to argue on behalf of the perpetrators and against the victims.

Those who would make such an argument have lost the vision essential for seeing the threat facing all of us today no less than they have lost a significant helping of basic human decency.

Now that we have cleared away the debris of obfuscation and back door rationalizations, we can move forward to the real issue, having already spent too much time on this necessary disclaimer. Here it is; here is the reality with which we must begin and end: one third, one fifth, one tenth. In 1947, Hindus were somewhat less than one third of East Pakistan's population. In 1971, when East Pakistan became Bangladesh, they were just under one fifth. Thirty years later, they were less than a tenth. It is not happening because of natural demographic processes but because of deliberate effort. The trajectory of those numbers is clear; as it was in Pakistan and Kashmir. Listen to the words of Narain Kataria, President of the Indian American Intellectuals Forum. He has lived in the United States for more than 40 years and is proud to consider that nation his home. ("America has given me freedom of religion and liberty of expression.") But life was not always that way for him and his family because they are Hindu:

> I was living in that part of India which is now called Pakistan. Since I was a Hindu, my life was made miserable by Islamic police and Islamic militia. I was hounded out by Radical Islamists. Many of my friends and colleagues were singled out, chased and brutally killed. Thousands of Hindu and Sikh girls were gang raped by fanatic

> Islamists. More than 10 million Hindus and Sikhs were driven out of the region that is now called Pakistan....In 1947, there were 23% Hindus living there in Pakistan . Today the Hindu population in Pakistan has been reduced to 1% in just 60 years. All the others have been ethnically cleansed.[71]

So, that's it: my final disclaimer. If you think I am Islamaphobic, so be it; but measure your indignation against the murder of millions. Recognize the choice you have to make: either deny the existence of this Islamist attempt to eradicate Bangladesh's Hindu population; rationalize it away; or take action to stop it. Rarely are our choices so clear and so dramatically different in what they say about us and what impact they will have. We can say with almost Biblical certainty that if we do not act, people will continue to be killed, raped, abducted, deprived of their rights; and that a community will be destroyed. And the world will awake one day from its murderous slumber, emerge from beneath its blankets of cowardly rationalization and say, 'How could this have happened,' and 'We didn't know.'

God help us if we do that again!

---

[71] Speech by Narain Kataria to "Rally for Israel," New York, April 25, 2010.

CHAPTER TWO

THE ROOTS OF ETHNIC CLEANSING: HOW DID IT HAPPEN—OR MORE TO THE POINT, HOW DID WE LET IT HAPPEN?

The ethnic cleansing of Bangladesh's Hindus is part of international jihad. It is a direct and imminent threat to the people and nation of India; and an eventual threat to every man, woman, and child on the planet; especially in the United States and Israel. But even if none of that were so, it still would be something horribly wrong that we must oppose with all of our might; for it is destroying an entire people in often brutal fashion and ruining so many innocent lives.

In the aftermath of World War I, the allies created a de-militarized buffer zone between Germany and the West European countries it attacked during the war. This part of Germany was known as the Rhineland; and on March 7, 1936, Adolf Hitler, in open defiance of the League of Nations and the rest of the world, sent German troops across the ersatz border and re-militarized it. The move was an important element in Hitler's overall plans to restore German nationalism and see if the rest of the world would resist his *small* aggressions or prefer instead the safety of what he knew to be a temporary peace. But what no one outside a small group around Hitler and the military knew at the time, was that he had given his troops a secret order to retreat if the French showed *any* sign of resisting the invasion. They did not, and the Rhineland was Hitler's first land grab. It enhanced his status with the German people while gaining credibility for his claims that they were destined to rule over their "faithless" neighbors soon and the rest of the world eventually. By the time the allies finally did resist in 1939, Hitler had grabbed Austria and Czechoslovakia as well, not to mention strengthening his military might, while the rest of the world sat by passively.[72]

For many, reflections on what happened three quarters of a century ago can become tedious; but this example is particularly apt because it refers to a moment in history when humanity had the chance to stop something evil and instead gave it strength. The historical episode also exposes the simple-mindedness of those who use peace as an abstract concept and a slogan to endorse inaction. Of course, the prospect of war is a horrific one, but the behavior of France and the other allies in the 1930s was short-sighted and did far more harm than good. In the name of peace, it merely delayed war and made it far more deadly, which is precisely what is happening today.[73] That same policy of appeasement has been resurrected in the 21st century. Using buzzwords like "constructive engagement" instead of appeasement (which was considered a legitimate strategy back then and not an accusation) will not prevent it from bearing the same bitter fruit than that which came from its pre-World War II incarnation. The attempt by latter day leftists and their fellow traveling appeasers to wrap their cowardice in the banner of peace might win us a brief respite from war but, in the end, will lead only to a more severe, protracted, and deadly one.

Had the French forced Hitler to turn tail and lose face in 1936, history might not have recorded the Second World War

---

[72] William L. Shirer, *The Rise and Fall of the Third Reich* (New York: Simon & Schuster, 1959), pp. 399-405.

[73] Remember the famous quote by George Santayana in *The Life of Reason*? "Those who cannot remember the past are condemned to repeat it."

as the deadliest conflict in history. If the French put up even a token resistance, perhaps to gauge the ferocity or weakness of German will, it could very well have changed the course of history and saved millions of lives. Yet, even if that would have been the result of firm action in 1936, projecting what would have happened remains little more than speculation. Its value is limited—unless we use it to stop us from making the same mistake today.[74] US President Jimmie Carter's misreading and embrace of the 1979 Iranian revolution is an example of repeating that mistake, as is US President Barack Obama's misreading and embrace of the 2010-2011 "Arab Spring." The Islamists' aggression against the Hindus of Bangladesh is, in effect, their Rhineland. The genius of the Islamic strike in Bangladesh rests on the fact that, unlike Hitler's assault on the Rhineland, it has been happening quietly, under the radar if you will. That makes it even more of a litmus test of the world's desire to resist *jihad* than the more infamous Islamist moves in Afghanistan and Somalia, for instance, or even Yemen.

Bangladesh has become one giant Islamist Petri Dish. What we do there will signal to our enemies what sort of action above and beyond words they can expect from us. If we sit by idly while they carry out these crimes, the only thing we will be doing is making them stronger. History and even our individual experiences show unequivocally that rewarding bad behavior only encourages more bad behavior. In this case, the bad behavior is ethnic cleansing—murder, rape, and violent bigotry justified as a means to achieve their overall goal. Call it *lebensraum* if you like.[75]

---

[74] For a light-hearted but serious reference, see Richard Benkin, "Words of Wisdom on Iraq, from Captain Kirk and Mr. Spock," *Jewsweek Magazine,* November 10, 2002.

[75] *Lebensraum* is German for "living space," and was how Hitler justified his expansionist policy, saying that German people needed more "living space" to accommodate its population.

The notion of considering Bangladesh as an important component for overall Islamist aims might seem odd to many, since that country is almost invariably an afterthought in big power calculations about the Indian subcontinent.[76] At a 2009 hearing of the US House Foreign Affairs Committee, Subcommittee on the Middle East and South Asia, Congressman Joseph Crowley of New York, one of four co-chairs of the Congressional Bangladesh Caucus,[77] who has maintained a strong interest in that country over the years, noted, "I have always felt that [the Bangladeshis] have been given less attention than I think they deserve. They have gotten short shrift over the years, even in terms of discussion here at the committee level....You know, being not stuck between but next to rising India and faltering Pakistan, they have been given short shrift....I think they often fall out of sight, or at least it seems to be pushed aside more often than we would like to see."[78] From time to time, I am asked what United States policy is towards Bangladesh; to which I respond, "What policy." Several Washington officials and staff have shared that joke with me, as well. Crowley was questioning the new Assistant Secretary of State for the Bureau

---

[76] Unless otherwise noted, references to the Indian Subcontinent or pre-1948 India include the area that today encompasses India, Pakistan, and Bangladesh.

[77] As of 2009, there were 26 Members of the Congressional Bangladesh Caucus. The two Democrat cochairs are Crowley and Gary Ackerman (NY). They ran the hearing in question. The two Republican cochairs at the time of the hearing were Mark Kirk (IL) and Peter King (NY). (Kirk has since left the House to become one of two US Senators from Illinois.) The other members were: Michael Capuano (MA), William Delahunt (MA), Eliot Engel (NY), Rush Holt (NJ), Sheila Jackson-Lee (TX), Rick Larson (WA), Carolyn Maloney (NY), Carolyn McCarthy (NY), Jim McDermott (WA), Gregory Meeks (NY), James Moran (VA), Jerrold Nadler (NY), Frank Pallone (NJ). William Pascrell (NJ), Thomas Petri (WI), DavidPrice (VA), Silvestri Reyes (TX), Edward Royce (CA), Brad Sherman (CA), Chris Van Hollen (MD), Anthony Wiener (NY) who later resigned in the midst of a sex scandal, and David Wu (OR). Royce was also present at the hearing.

[78] "A Regional Overview of South Asia," Hearing Before the Subcommittee on the Middle East and South Asia of the Committee on Foreign Affairs, United . . .

of South and Central Asian Affairs, Robert O. Blake, and asked whether or not he expected that to change. While Blake answered in the positive, there has been no action to make us believe that his words were more than simply the appropriate answer to a Congressman's question, whether or not there was any truth to them.

Both Crowley and Blake spoke in general terms about the need for more focus on Bangladesh and about efforts by the current, Awami League government to get a handle on Islamist radicalism there. California Congressman Edward Royce, another member of the Caucus, noted however,

> In terms of Bangladesh—and let me just raise a word of caution here, because you [Blake] testified that extremism finds little popular support there. I think this bears close scrutiny because of the *madrasahs* that are opening up. I have spoken to a number of people on the ground, including those in Bangladesh who are monitoring this situation, and they tell me that the Islamist schools there are increasingly radicalizing young Bangladeshis, and that they are proliferating at a particularly fast pace, and, in addition, that those that have been established are, shall we say, some of the most extreme in South Asia. So there should be some focus on that and also on some of the funding that has come in. Reportedly, in the media, it is from the Gulf States in order to fund the types of *madrasahs* we are talking about right now.[79]

In other words, despite the lack of a coherent policy, there are US officials who recognize the growing influence of radical Islam in Bangladesh, which is the most serious driver of ethnic cleansing there. This could very well account for the ambivalent attitude found even among Bangladesh's friends in Washington. They would like to feel unequivocally good about the prospects of a moderate Bangladesh being a trusted friend and ally, but they cannot. This lack of confidence has

States House of Representatives, 111th Congress, First Session, June 25, 2009, Serial No. 111-23, United States Government Printing Office, 2009. Also available at http://www.foreignaffairs.house.gov/111/50634.pdf.

[79] *Ibid.*

prevented cooperation on security matters, limited trust, and has been a bar to more extensive business development, trade, and aid.

In some circles, the empty words will get a polite response; but they have not brought forth anything of substance, no matter how many encouraging promises are made. Many Bangladeshi officials believe that Obama is willing to provide these benefits without any action on their part. Yet, the President recently concluded a trip to neighboring India in which he notched billions in trade deals, and never even stopped in Bangladesh or contacted the government. Similar well wishes by Secretary of State Hillary Clinton did not produce the trade agreements implicit in her remarks.[80]

Thus, the sweepingly positive—virtually Pollyannaish—statements about US-Bangladesh relations that emanate regularly from the Bangladeshi Embassy in Washington and the US State Department, find no expression in action. That disconnect—the fact that there is so much which the United States could do for a truly moderate Bangladesh, but it has not been forthcoming—has been an important tool in fighting Bangladeshi extremism, and as will be seen in later chapters, provides us with important leverage in trying to end the deliberate destruction of Bangladesh's Hindus.

Of all the roots, talons, and tentacles of the crime of anti-Hindu ethnic cleansing in Bangladesh, international *jihad* is the most critical. It is the single element of this crime that enables the others. It provides a justifying philosophy to motivate ethnic cleansing's shock troops and strikes the world's "good people" with a paralyzing fear. They ignore decades of the victims' cries—cries too terrible to acknowledge—and retreat behind a deadly multiculturalism

---

[80] The statements by Bangladeshi officials were made to me in private conversations and emails in 2009 and 2010. In those statements, they also made it clear that this expectation had made them decide not to engage in any action regarding minority rights.

and political correctness. Together, these twin philosophies of weakness are used to excuse these atrocities as some sort of justified Muslim anger; that is, a mere cultural expression that has to be accorded equal respect as any other.

These pernicious rationalizations provide a comforting excuse so these "good people" can enjoy their creature comforts and pretend that their living "in peace" does not come at the expense of innocents. It would be terrifying enough if the Bangladeshi Hindus were the only innocents that they are willing to sacrifice; but they are not. The same lack of moral courage leads those same "good people" to say nothing while—sometimes quietly, sometimes openly—Islamists or Islamist-inspired governments and individuals continue to severely reduce and harass Middle Eastern Christian communities in the name of Islam, even though most of them pre-date Islam by centuries. Islamists and their accomplices ethnically cleansed about 99 percent of Jews in the Arab world between 1948 and 1967. As a result, their ancient communities have all but disappeared. Yet, in all the pious discussions about Middle East peace over decades, no major player has ever raised *that* refugee issue.

In the first few years of the 21st century, Islamists in Kashmir murdered or expelled an estimated 400,000 Kashmiri Pandits. In 2006, Congressman Frank Pallone of New Jersey authored a resolution condemning these murders and ongoing human rights violations against the Kashmiri Pandits. Yet, the Pakistani government and intelligence agency continue to patronize Islamists in the region—and the United States has continued to pour billions of dollars in aid into Pakistan without ever requiring that the Pakistanis take action against these perpetrators of ethnic cleansing. Disappointing but not surprising, the world has done nothing while our supposed Pakistani allies allowed Islamists to carry out a similar program that has reduced their country's Hindu population from almost one in five to a mere one percent. No one—not the United States, not the World Bank, not anyone—has ever conditioned their massive aid to Pakistan on ending the violence, aiding the victims, or even punishing the perpetrators.[81]

The number of Kashmiri Pandits that Islamists murdered is about double that of the number of deaths from the atomic blasts at Hiroshima and Nagasaki combined.[82] Millions of well-meaning individuals march annually to protest those blasts and to mourn those *hundreds of thousands* of victims. But who mourns for the *millions* of *jihad's* victims: victims from every South Asian nation; from Israel; from Arab countries like Jordan, Lebanon, Yemen, and many more; from every North African country from Egypt in the east to Morocco in the West; in sub-Sahara Africa, Nigeria, Kenya, Sudan, Somalia, and more; in Bali, London, and Madrid. Would anyone have the temerity even to suggest that the death toll will not climb higher or the list of places scarred by radical Islam will not grow? By the time it is defeated, *jihad* could well prove to be the deadliest philosophy since the communism of Joseph Stalin and Mao Zedong, mass murderers responsible for killing perhaps 100 million of their own people, in addition to millions more abroad.

---

[81] On March 26, 2003, from the floor of the US Congress, Pallone urged the US to cut off aid to Pakistan after Islamists murdered 24 Hindus (including two children) in Jammu and Kashmir. "There are no words to express the devastation of the Nandimarg massacre and the sad history of the Kashmiri Pandits....I urge President Bush to put more pressure on President Pervez Musharaf to stop Islamic militant infiltration into Kashmir and to end Pakistan's moral and military support to these fundamentalists responsible for the mass murder of the Pandits,... My fear is that U.S. military assistance to Pakistan will then be turned around and used against India, particularly in Kashmir... The president must continue to persuade Pakistan to end terrorism in Kashmir and the U.S. should not be providing military assistance to Musharaf's regime." He also noted that Indian authorities "failed to protect the Pandits" and urged them to do so. Neither country got the message. In 2006, Pallone introduced a Congressional resolution condemning 15 years of human rights violations against the Kashmiri Pandits, saying "The conflict in Kashmir cannot be separated from the global war against terrorism. Over the past fifteen years militant forces, including elements of al Qaeda and the Taliban, have used violence against the Kashmiri Pandits in an effort to institute Islamic rule in this region." House Congressional Resolution 388, however, never got out of committee and died that year.

Is my list all-inclusive? No. Islamist ethnic cleansing is proceeding wherever it is afforded the opportunity by "good people" doing nothing to stop it. We will return to the Islamist roots of ethnic cleansing in South Asia in more detail in later chapters.

Let us be clear, because if we are not, we never will stop the killing: the root cause of it all is Islamist aggression against Hindus. Its justification comes from mosques, media, small and large groups, and government, specifically that Islam is superior and is destined to supersede all other faiths; that Hinduism is inferior, polytheistic, and as such must be wiped out. In 2008, a Bangladeshi Hindu refugee near the India-Nepal border told me that he previously had a small farm in the Dinajpur District of Northern Bangladesh. One day, he said, a chicken of his wandered onto a neighbor's property. When told what happened, he went to the neighbor and asked if he still had the chicken. 'No,' the neighbor said, 'I ate it.' In a distressed voice, the man asked his neighbor why he did it since he knew the chicken was that of a neighbor. 'I did it,' the neighbor replied, 'because you are a Hindu and I am a Muslim, and as such I am doing only what I am entitled to do.' Sometime later, the neighbor and other Muslims drove the man and his family off their little farm, and the police told them to leave Bangladesh.[83]

That sort of violent interaction has so often characterized relations between Hindus and Muslims in South Asia, regardless of how apologists try to dress it up. I recall speaking before a group at American University, and one Muslim student who was born in Bangladesh rose, very incensed, and said that "Muslims and Hindus live in harmony" in

---

[82] There are real discrepancies among the different estimates, but the above statement certainly holds for deaths through 1948, and even the largest estimates of the total number of deaths are lower than the number of Kashmiri Pandits murdered by Islamists.

[83] This is an inexact translation of the refugee's words. It is not far from exact and faithfully renders what the refugee told me. All similarly rendered conversations in this book can be identified by single quotes, as this one is.

Bangladesh and that I was spreading lies. Unfortunately, I had to tell her, being born in Bangladesh made her no more qualified to speak authoritatively about Hindu-Muslim violence today than being born in Philadelphia made me an expert in its current problem with street gangs. Consciously or unconsciously, the student was repeating the standard denial issued by successive Bangladeshi governments and their supporters. And it is a disingenuous denial.

Tensions between Hindus and Muslims on the Indian subcontinent have existed since Islam's appearance there in the seventh century. Periods and pockets of respite from the conflict have been the exception; violence the rule. While many scholars have attempted—with some justification and insight—to attribute this to factors like socio-economic dislocation[84] and political manipulation,[85] to name two, those factors are but the catalysts. They are as necessary as a spark is to a fire. Were it not inter-communal violence, something else would provide the vehicle by which their social tensions would be released. Hindu-Muslim tensions have a life of their own in South Asia, and for whatever effect catalysts might have, they are becoming more violent. Many find this inescapable, and they might be right. As one Indian Hindu said to me in 2009, "You might be able to say that Islam is not the problem from the United States, but when you come here, you see that [the problem] is Islam [itself]."

Hindu-Muslim tensions appeared so endemic to the British that their last act before quitting their colonial role was to divide their territory into two sovereign nations: one Hindu (India) and one Muslim (Pakistan). While some historians with an anti-colonial perspective blame the British for the partition, there is extensive evidence to indicate that Lord Mountbatten

---

[84] James Heitzman and Robert L. Worden, editors. *India: A Country Study.* (Government Printing Office for the Library of Congress: Washington, DC, 1995).

[85] Paul R. Brass, "Organised riots & structured violence in India," *The Hindu,* August 23, 2006.

had little choice but to divide the country.[86] There could be no clearer statement that Muslims and Hindus cannot live together in peace than the Partition. And it is also clear that the idea of partition was a major demand of the Muslim League and its leader Muhammed Ali Jinnah. Mahatma Gandhi acceded to it reluctantly. The resulting two nations (India and Pakistan) and the two religious communities they represent (Hindus and Muslims[87]) within India regularly accuse the other of various atrocities, often reacting with armed conflict. Those tensions and a very tense history marked by violence and communal self-segregation, provide a key undercurrent to ethnic cleansing today.

In 1965, however, something happened that represented a seminal change in those relationships, and it is something that should have caused a loud and sustained international uproar; but it did not.

India and Pakistan fought their second major war that year in their countries' 18 year existence. Although there are those who consider the war something of a standoff in the way of casualties and troop positions at the time of the cease-fire, it was in actuality, a clear Indian victory. For one thing, the war began with a Pakistani operation to wrest control of Kashmir and Jammu from India called "Operation Gibraltar." It was a dismal failure. For another, by war's end the Indian army was very close to capturing the major Pakistani city of Lahore. It was stopped, not by the Pakistani armed forces, but by an imposed ceasefire by the United Nations—a scenario later replayed to stop an Israeli rout of Arab forces in 1973, 2006, and 2009. In those years, and in 1965, the international saviors allowed Muslim forces to avoid a humiliating defeat and create

---

[86] See for instance, Lawrence J. Butler, *Britain and Empire: Adjusting to a Post-Imperial World.* (I.B.Tauris: London, 2002), p. 72.

[87] To be clear, while India is the "Hindu" part of the partition, India is and always has been constituted as a secular state while Pakistan was constituted as a religious (Islamic) state quite explicitly from its birth through today.

their own myths of success, all of which only emboldened them to continue their perpetual warfare rather than seriously negotiate for *genuine* peace in the Middle East or South Asia.

Still, myths only go so far. The truth of the matter was, as *Time Magazine* noted after that war, "apparent to everybody that India is going to emerge as an Asian power in its own right."[88] In fact, that was the case everywhere except Pakistan, where there still was an unremitting barrage of bravado. Once the din of their propaganda machine died down, however, Pakistanis recognized the truth, too. They had not been victorious even, as many of them knew, India was not even at full strength when the war began. Supposed Indian weakness was an integral part of the Pakistani strategy. They launched Operation Gibraltar because they thought they could take advantage of a weakened India following its relatively poor showing in a clash with China only three years earlier.

Pakistan's silly propaganda was based on the same assumptions that seem to inform Islam in general and made their defeat even more humiliating. It was something of an article of faith among Pakistanis that as Muslims, they were strong and brave, and as Hindus Indians were a bunch of cowards.[89] Propaganda emanating from the government and the media and from mosques every Friday continued to feed that contemptuousness for Hindus. So, when the Pakistanis failed to achieve their only stated objective, capturing

---

[88] "Silent Guns, Wary Combatants," *Time Magazine*, October, 1965.

[89] This is similar to what happened to the Arabs after successive defeats at the hands of the Israelis, which they could not reconcile with their assumptions that Muslims were courageous and strong, Jews weak. False reports of successes, an unrelenting Arab insistence of victory in 1973, and so forth all were intended to overcome the realities of their defeats. That 1973 phantom victory is very similar to Pakistan's "Defence Day" holiday that commemorates a non-existent victory in the 1965 conflict. Just as an internationally imposed cease-fire was forced on the Indians as they had a clear field to take Lahore from the Pakistanis who started the war; Israeli troops were on their way to take Cairo and Damascus when an internationally imposed cease-fire saved the Arabs who started the 1973 war.

Kashmir, it attacked their sense of Muslim superiority, as well.[90] They had to do something, and so they retaliated against their own Hindu citizens.

Their act of undisguised retaliation was the *Enemy Property Act* (EPA). Aimed deliberately at its Hindu population, the act empowered the government to declare their land and possessions enemy property and seize it. When Bangladesh won its independence, the new nation re-wrote the *Enemy Property Act* as the *Vested Property Act* with explicit language stating that only the law's title had changed, not its content. In 1965 and again in 1974, the countries of Pakistan and Bangladesh passed laws that were intended to impose disabilities on their minority populations, especially Hindus, that they expected would force them to convert or emigrate.[91] Both the EPA and VPA impose on the Hindus of Pakistan and Bangladesh, the third disability defined in the internationally accepted Convention on the Prevention and Punishment of Genocide, adopted by the United Nations on 9 December 1948. Article II:

> In the present Convention, genocide means any of the following acts committed with intent to destroy, in whole or in part, a national, ethnical, racial or religious group.

The third of those five acts is "Deliberately inflicting on the group conditions of life calculated to bring about its

[90] See, for instance, Aitaf Gauhar, *Ayub Khan: Pakistan's First Military Ruler* (Oxford University Press: Oxford, 1996), p. 328; and Ayaz Amir, "Core issue, my goat," *The Dawn* (Karachi), July 28, 2000. Also see "Indo-Pakistan War of 1965" at http://www.globalsecurity.org/military/world/war/indo-pak_1965.htm.

[91] In Pakistan and Bangladesh, these efforts have been applied to any non-Muslim population. Hindus, by far the largest non-Muslim group in these countries, are the main targets of these acts. And make no mistake about it, these laws were directed primarily against them. Thus, it is to be understood in this book that when the term, "minorities" is used, Hindus are the largest minority and most deliberate targets; but it is in no way intended to minimize the victimization of other minorities. It is merely reality.

physical destruction in whole or in part."[92]

Some terrifying numbers support the proposition that the intention of Pakistan's EPA matches the *Convention's* third element of genocide. When the EPA was passed, West Pakistan's Hindu community was estimated to have been between 15 and 20 percent of the population. Today, Hindus make up a mere one percent; and even that number is dwindling as the remnants of that once significant population started streaming into India in advance of the Taliban.[93] To be sure, Pakistan has imposed a number of disabilities on Hindus and other non-Muslims; but the EPA has been crucial in forcing a demographic change by denying non-Muslims a place to live or the ability to earn a living. The situation is no better in Bangladesh where almost one in five Bangladeshis were Hindu when that country passed the VPA; today the number is well below one in ten.

Imagine for a moment if United States law empowered the government to seize the land and property of non-Christians and give it to Christians; or if Indian law did the same to non-Hindus. Imagine the international hue and cry that—justifiably—would be heard from every human rights NGO and government entity that could afford a fax machine. And imagine the sustained and passionate cries—again justified—of 'Racism, racism, racism,' the loudest likely coming from Americans and Indians themselves. Of course, no such laws exist in the US or India[94], for they are contrary to the basic tenets of both nations and their peoples. But they do not

---

[92] United Nations, *Convention on the Prevention and Punishment of the Crime of Genocide*, adopted 9 December 1948; United Nations Treaty Series, No. 1021, vol. 78 (1951), p. 277. As of 2005, 50 nations were not parties to the Convention. Pakistan and Bangladesh are not among them.

[93] I was in Northern India in March 2009 and was able to confirm this phenomenon directly.

[94] The Pakistani-Bangladeshi law is not to be confused with similar sounding measures in India. There were some instituted at the time of partition to deal with the massive migration that were allowed to expire. To the extent that any governments

conflict with values of freedom and equality in Pakistan and Bangladesh because those values simply do not exist there, certainly when it comes to non-Muslims. The peoples of both nations have had no difficulty having those laws on the books—and widely used—for decades.

The only difference between the EPA/VPA and our imaginary laws in the United States and India is that Pakistan and Bangladesh are Muslim majority countries and the laws place property of non-Muslims up for grabs. Those laws are right in line with the penchant for Islam to divide the world into two separate camps of Muslims and everyone else with the stated belief that the former are superior and the latter are destined to embrace Islam, perish, or live in a degraded and humiliating state.

So here we have blatant and undisguised discrimination against a community solely on the basis of religion, something that is supposed to be an anathema to all decent individuals and nations. Yet, aside from periodic and very anemic statements from one or another NGO—statements never coupled with action or sustained outrage—the world has uttered nary a peep about this blatant form of *de juro* bigotry.[95]

On July 30, 2007, I had a meeting at Bangladesh's embassy in Washington to address the Shoaib Choudhury case and other human rights matters. During the meeting, Bangladesh's

---

or localities have such laws, they are not used as anti-minority measures; Hindus are their main victims.

[95] The VPA should not be confused with temporary laws in India and elsewhere to administer abandoned property during times of massive population transfer. According to Indian attorney Aruneshwar Gupta, the "Administration of Evacuee Property Act," 1950, enabled the Indian government "to allot the property evacuated by the people who left India to those who had to leave their property in Pakistan. There is quite a procedure under the Act to establish the property as evacuee property and to get allotment in your favour, primarily because large number of people who left India, left people behind, who claimed a right in the property and contested that the property was not a evacuee property. In fact the Britishers had a concept of 'Escheat' which was applied by them in India in 1809, where-in-under, if any sovereign died heirless, the property vested in the British."

top representative in the United States, Ambassador M. Humayun Kabir told me flatly that the military-backed caretaker government then in power "has no intention of addressing the Vested Property Act during its tenure"—which at the time he said that was indefinite. More recently, a Bangladeshi military official tried to assuage my outrage by telling me that the VPA was enacted a form of "protection" for the Hindu minority. Neither he nor anyone else present could give me an answer when I responded by asking them just how bad anti-Hindu violence was in Bangladesh if they needed this "protective law" on the books for more than 30 years! (I actually asked, "So are things even worse than I've been told?") I ended up breaking that awkward silence by strongly urging them to come up with a different party line that does not insult the intelligence of the person to whom they say it.[96]

As the year 2008 was about to give way to 2009, the government to which the Ambassador alluded gave way to a new government after the first election in Bangladesh since 2001. The victorious Awami League has historically positioned itself as a left-center party that is sympathetic to minorities, in contrast to its major rival the BNP. The last time the Awami League was in power, it did not put a stop to anti-minority activity or repeal the VPA; but both they and their apologists attributed that failure to limitations that came with being part of a coalition. This time, there were no coalition partners to act as an impediment. The margin of victory for Sheikh Hasina and her Awami League was so large that they did not have to bring others into a coalition in order to rule. Thus, between the Awami League's traditional posturing and its ability to rule without coalition partners, there was a high level of expectation in some quarters that the new government would enact sweeping changes and remove minority

[96] Personal conversation with a group of Bangladeshi officials in May 2008, Washington DC.

disabilities, including the VPA. Well, something has changed under the Awami League. Unlike its predecessor, this government has now *said* it will repeal the VPA. What has not changed is that it has *done* nothing pursuant to that promise.

Here is how the VPA works. As one might imagine, the level of anti-Hindu animus intensified quite a bit in Pakistan during the 1965 war with India. Hindus were associated with an enemy state, India, and that association has been maintained ever since. Consequently, the level of anti-Hindu violence increased; and propaganda broadcasts, articles, and sermons told Pakistani Muslims that they could not count on the loyalty of their Hindu neighbors.[97] Thus, many Hindus fled or were forced across the border into India. It was during all this that Pakistan passed the EPA, which gave the government power to seize the land of *non-residents*; in essence all those fleeing Hindus. To be clear, many (but not all) who returned regained their property, but the effect of the law was to discourage many others from returning to Pakistan. That discouragement was layered on top of other impediments. Whether it was the continuing anti-Hindu propaganda, the state's tolerance for anti-Hindu violence, or just plain fear, many stayed across the border and found that the property they left had been forfeit and distributed to Pakistani Muslims. In East Pakistan, which would become Bangladesh in six years, the same situation pertained until 1974, when the EPA became the VPA under the legal code enshrined by Bangladesh's Awami League government.

One might even find some justification for enacting a law that lets the state seize the land of people who left the country

[97] Since then, several commentators have noted that Pakistani educational institutions perpetuate anti-Hindu and anti-India propaganda through *madrassas*, textbooks, and other curricula. See for instance, almost any of the individual articles in A. H. Nayyar and Ahmad Salim, editors, *The Subtle Subversion: The State of Curricula and Textbooks in Pakistan* (Sustainable Policy Institute: Islamabad, July-October 2003).

and distribute it to loyal citizens; but when the intention of the law is retaliatory and openly discriminatory against a religious minority, as was that of the EPA and its rebirth as the VPA, it becomes an instrument of ethnic cleansing as these two examples demonstrate.

In late February 2009, in the northern Bangladesh district of Dinajpur, local Muslims stormed a small family farm and ordered the Hindu residents to leave. They claimed the land for themselves and started taking objects from the farm and house as if they were their own. When the father of the family protested, the attackers beat him and forced the family off their land. The victims wanted the police to help but they refused, as they do regularly in these cases. Thus, the family fled across the border to Indian state of West Bengal where they had extended family who would care for them. Once they did, the perpetrators and local police who were working with them were able to have the land declared "vested," and make their ownership legal under Bangladeshi law.[98]

On three separate days in March and April of that same year, approximately 400 impoverished Hindus were going about their business in their community in the Sutrapur district of the Bangladeshi capital, Dhaka. Suddenly, according to witnesses, "hundreds of Muslims [and] Awami League operatives" descended on them and demanded they quit the homes where they and their families had lived for the past 150 years. The attackers were accompanied by Dhaka police who justified the seizure under the VPA, and this is how they did it. The land was originally owned by two Hindus, Jogesh Chando and Tarkanath Das, who migrated to India in 1947. Before they did, however, they transferred the land as a gift to the Hindus remaining in Sutrapur. Most of them had been their servants, and this was their way of showing gratitude for years of service to their family.

---

[98] The victimized Hindu family in the incident related their story to me in a small encampment in the West Bengal district of North Dinajpur, March 2009.

As time passed, however, a local Muslim named Mahbubur Rahman came to covet the land. He tried for years to get the land but could not come up with the legal fiction (or necessary bribe money) to pull it off. After his death, however, his brother and nephews determined to do what he could not because they were supporters of Sheikh Hasina's Awami League, which now held power. They used their position to prevail upon police to demand written proof of ownership from the Hindus, which all parties knew they could not provide given their impoverished state and the nature of Partition era transactions. Nevertheless, that was all the government needed to secretly void the Hindus' title using Bangladesh's Vested Property Act. Subsequent appeals to the Dhaka Chief of Police and even members of the Bangladeshi *Sangsad* fell on deaf ears. We will return to this violent action with more damning evidence of the Awami League government's active involvement later.[99]

Unfortunately, these stories are not at all uncommon. As is painfully obvious by the Sutrapur example above, the seized lands have become part of Bangladesh's notorious corruption gravy train, used to woo and benefit officials and hangers on from every major party. Between 2001 and 2006, 45 percent of the spoils went to the right-center BNP, 31 percent to the left-center Awami League. The figures were reversed when the Awami League was in power. Another 15 percent went to various Islamist parties, and the rest to the once-powerful Jatiya Party and others. Even though the Islamist *Jamaat* postures itself as being pristine, it took its share, too. We will return to them and the Vested Property Act in Chapter Six.[100]

---

[99] Richard Benkin, "A Terrifying Existence, "*The Daily Pioneer*, July 21, 2009. Note that before writing this article for a major Indian newspaper, I investigated the incidents and claims thoroughly and confirmed them with multiple sources.

[100] Abul Barkat, *Deprivation of Hindu Minority in Bangladesh: Living with Vested Property* (Pathak Shamabesh: Dhaka, 2008)

Given the foregoing, it can be considered nothing less than the height of arrogance and dishonesty when Islamists, their allies, and their apologists complain that their critics are Islamaphobic for identifying the perpetrators of these atrocities as Muslim. It is at best naïve when liberals and leftists who provide the apologetic fuel for radical Islam and ethnic cleansing complain because we are bringing religion into this discussion—and that we should not. As is clear from an unfettered historical analysis, it was Muslims—radical and otherwise, religious and secular, cleric and politician—who cast this battle as one based on religion. Pakistan's propaganda is anti-Hindu; just as Arab propaganda is anti-Jewish.

This is not about individual Muslims and whether or not they have had second thoughts about the morality of that. Some have, but many have not. It has long been observed that most people do not concern themselves with weighty issues, events around the world, or what might be happening within their own society. Democrat strategist James Carville probably summed up that perspective best during the 1992 US Presidential election between former Presidents George H. W. Bush and Bill Clinton. At first, Bush was considered unbeatable because of the foreign policy achievements during his administration; specifically, winning the Cold War and the first Iraq War. But Carville insisted that none of that would matter to the voters nearly as much as the state of the economy: their personal situations. His phrase, which has become iconic in American politics, was: "It's the economy, stupid!" That is, most Bangladeshi Muslims, like most other people anywhere in the world, are going to be concerned, first and foremost with their own and their family's immediate well-being. Our challenge is to identify the perpetrators and the ideology that animates them without fear of being called names or considered politically incorrect. And we must do that without devolving into the same sort of bigoted worldview that gave life to the EPA and VPA in the first place.

When the British left India in 1947, Hindus were almost a third of the East Bengali population; but things have changed drastically with the rise of a more aggressive and radical Islam, fueled by middle eastern money. In 1971, the newly independent Bangladesh declared itself a secular nation. A short three years later, it enacted the VPA, and less than four years after that, it did an about face and officially proclaimed itself an "Islamic republic," much to the chagrin and horror of its Hindus and other religious minorities who were now pariahs in their own nation. I was at a hearing convened by the US Commission on International Religious Freedom (USCIRF) on the state of religious minorities in Bangladesh in 2006. Throughout the proceedings, people routinely referred to Bangladesh as a "Muslim country," which is objectively correct. But when the audience was allowed to offer comments and ask questions, one Bangladeshi Hindu rose and took umbrage at that description, asking USCIRF if they could understand that "every time you hear that, you feel like an outsider in your own country." Other Bangladeshi Hindus in the audience strenuously expressed their agreement with that sentiment.[101]

The implications of this progression are critical for what was to come. In 1971, the new Bangladesh was very much beholden to India. That nation sent its military to East Pakistan to aid the Bangladeshi rebels and also opened up a second front against Pakistan in India's northeast. Indian troops routed the Pakistanis, without which Bangladesh never could have achieved its independence. At the same time, the power of Islamist parties and groups was at its ebb in post-war Bangladesh. They had come out publicly *against* Bangladeshi independence and rejected the notion of Bengali nationality

---

[101] U.S. Commission on International Religious Freedom, "The Bangladesh Elections: Promoting Democracy and Protecting Rights in a Muslim-majority Country." October 17, 2006. Gold Room, Rayburn House Office Building, Washington, DC.

being the primary basis for identification in the polity; they insisted that it was Islam. During the campaign, Islamists often fought alongside the Pakistanis to try and block independence, and there is extensive documentation linking many of their leaders with the brutal massacre (in cooperation with Pakistani troops) of over three million Bangladeshi noncombatants.

They were not called to account for their actions, however, and Islamists soon re-established themselves in Bangladesh and especially among its officialdom. As they did, Bangladesh moved further and further away from India and its pluralistic beginnings. In a terrible irony, many participants in the 1971 atrocities gained positions of governmental power over survivors of the massacre and the relatives of those murdered. With the rise of an internationalist radical Islam, which began taking root there in the next decade, Bangladeshi Islamists have garnered continuously growing influence even under the present, Awami League government; and perhaps more importantly despite its best efforts.[102] Though a small part of the overall Bangladeshi population, they have entrenched themselves in almost every major institution from education to banking, from the police to the judiciary; and from 2001 to 2006, Islamist parties were members of the ruling coalition. Had the 2007 elections proceeded as scheduled, they would have been so again no matter who won a plurality. Despite Islamists' open and frequent calls for Bangladesh's "Talibanization" including the imposition of Sharia Law, both major parties had agreed to include them in the government.[103]

---

[102] In a February 2011 Dhaka meeting, Bangladeshi cabinet minister, H. T. Imam, who is one of Sheikh Hasina's closest confidants (and a major Awami League figure) emphasized the government's efforts to me. He did this with ostensibly two aims based on the nature of our talks: (1) to convince me that it would be far better for us if the Awami League and not the BNP won the 2014 elections; and (2) to clarify that—despite the lack of results at times—the Awami League and Sheikh Hasina personally are committed to this.

[103] See, for instance, Amin Malik, "The Talibanisation of Bangladesh," *Cobrapost,* August 16, 2005.

Let's be clear about the 1971 "holocaust"

Although the West has no coordinated policy with regard to Bangladesh or the ethnic cleansing that is taking place there, one comparatively well-known incident, noted earlier, is the murder of several million East Pakistanis during Bangladesh's 1971 War of Independence. What happened was so horrible that quite often it is called "holocaust" or "genocide." There is no dispute that it occurred, that two to three million unarmed East Bengalis were murdered and many more brutalized, that it was deliberate, and that the perpetrators were the Pakistani army and East Bengali Islamists opposed to independence. None of that is in question.[104]

There is also no dispute about the fact that the attackers hoped to eliminate or intimidate the East Bengali *intelligentsia* and other leaders that they feared would take a position in favor of Bangladeshi independence. As such, the victims included Muslims as well as Hindus; but long term apologists have with some success spread the notion that the murderous rampage was directed at Bangladeshis in general and not against any minority group, that is Hindus, in particular. To be sure, that accords with the fact that the Awami League, comprised largely of Muslims, was the engine of independence, and that since East Bengal is a Muslim-majority region, any such attacks on political opponents necessarily would find Muslims among the victims.

More to the point, furthering that propaganda is consistent with the Awami League's disingenuous claims of being pro-minority. The propaganda has taken such strong root that so many Bangladeshis believe it uncritically. The Bangladeshi

[104] Shrinandan Vyas, "Hindu Genocide in East Pakistan," *Hindunet.org* and several other internet sources. His own sources include: Department of Planning of the Government of Bangladesh, *Encyclopedia Britannica*, Senator Edward Kennedy's report to the U.S. Senate Judiciary Committee, *Newsweek*, and the *New York Times*.

student at American University, mentioned earlier, made her statements during an address about the ethnic cleansing of Bangladeshi Hindus. The speech was part of the students' observance of "Holocaust Remembrance Week," which commemorates the Nazi holocaust against the Jews.[105] That student insisted that "Muslims and Hindus live in perfect harmony" in Bangladesh; and that there neither was nor is any deliberate targeting of Hindus in the country. This is not only what she believed but more significantly what she has been taught. She also took issue with my identifying the 1971 holocaust as part of the ethnic cleansing of Hindus. Like the apologists noted, she was adamant that Muslims and Hindus were equally victimized.

She was right to the extent that those attacks have hurt the entire population of Bangladesh; that they left the country much poorer for generations by wasting so much of its most precious intellectual resources. But the facts of the 1971 murders do not accord with her insistence that Hindus were not the focus of the attacks. In "Hindu Genocide in East Pakistan," Shrinandan Vyas synthesizes data from several sources to demonstrate that Hindus were indeed the attackers' "primary target."[106]

In looking at Vyas's work, it is important to remember that at the time of the atrocities, Hindus represented no more than one in five East Pakistanis. One would expect then that their proportion of the 1971 victims would be somewhere close to one in five or 600,000; with the other 2.4 million victims being Muslim.[107] Vyas compared East Pakistan's Hindu population reported in 1961with Hindu population figures reported by the

---

[105] Kudos to Josh Jeffries and the Jewish Students Union at American University for recognizing the link between the two and the ethnic cleansing of Hindus in Bangladesh.

[106] *Ibid.*

[107] Even if one were to suggest that Hindus would be more likely to favor independence from a more Islamic Pakistan, especially given the Awami League's

Bangladeshi government in 1974: 9.41 and 9.65 million respectively. He assumed that "in the absence of strife" Hindu demographic forces would be roughly the same as their neighboring Muslims and thereby projected an expected Hindu population of 13.23 million. But that is 3.58 million more than the government's own figures for 1974. The Indian government reports that there were 1.11 million Hindu refugees from Bangladesh during that period, and even subtracting that number leaves a gap of almost two and a half million Hindus that are unaccounted for in these population statistics.[108]

Vyas also notes that roughly 80 percent of the refugees from Bangladesh to India were Hindu during that period. While it is not surprising that more Hindus than Muslims would see Hindustan as a safe haven from the marauding Islamists, the massive exodus indicates that Hindus had that much to fear. While immigrants often report relief if not utter joy in their new nation, few will say that the decision to leave their ancestral land was easy or not fraught with mixed emotions. Muslims who might quit the newly birthed Bangladesh also could expect a large number of coreligionists inside India who would be there to support them and provide them with needed provisions. In fact, India has the world's second largest Muslim population—more Muslims than either East or West Pakistan. And unlike Pakistan, India was a democratic nation that opposed attacks on its minorities.[109]

In addition to these statistics, there is another, anecdotal indicator of the specifically anti-Hindu nature of the 1971 attacks mentioned earlier, as well. Here Vyas quoted a speech

---

seductive promises to end their oppression; it is equally clear that Hindu opportunities for positions of leadership or in academia were limited. Thus, the two factors would largely neutralize one another.

[108] *Ibid.*

[109] *Ibid.* Vyas quotes figures provided in the testimony of the late Senator Edward M. Kennedy to the Senate Judiciary Committee on October 25, 1971.

made on the floor of the United States Senate by the late Edward M. Kennedy. This is from his report of November 1, 1971.

> Field reports to the U.S. Government, countless eye-witness journalistic accounts, reports of International agencies such as World Bank and additional information available to the subcommittee document the reign of terror which grips East Bengal (East Pakistan). Hardest hit have been members of the Hindu community who have been robbed of their lands and shops, systematically slaughtered, and in some places, *painted with yellow patches marked 'H.'* All of this has been officially sanctioned, ordered and implemented under martial law from Islamabad.[110]

Sydney Schanberg, who would later gain notoriety for his compelling reports about genocide by the Khmer Rouge ("The Killing Fields"), covered the events in Bangladesh for the *New York Times.* In a series of syndicated articles, he too noted the anti-Hindu character of the attacks.

> I toured the country by road to see the Pakistani legacy firsthand. In town after town there was an execution area where people had been killed by bayonet, bullet, and bludgeon.... human bones were still scattered along many roadsides. Blood stained clothing and tufts of human hair clung to the brush at these killing grounds. Children too young to understand were playing grotesque games with skulls. Other reminders were the yellow 'H's the Pakistanis had painted on the homes of Hindus, particular targets of the Muslim army.[111]

Toward the end of his article, Vyas plaintively wrote, "The ethnic cleansing of Hindus in Bangla Desh did not end in 1971. Since 1974 to 1981 the Hindu population as a percent

---

[110] "Crisis in South Asia – A report by Senator Edward Kennedy to the Subcommittee investigating the Problem of Refugees and Their Settlement," Submitted to U.S. Senate Judiciary Committee, November 1, 1971, U.S. Govt. Press, pp.6-7.

[111] Sydney Schanberg, "The Pakistani Slaughter that Nixon Ignored," *New York Times*, May 3, 1994.

of total Bangla Deshi population decreased from 13.5 % to 12.2%."[112]

In Sum

It is easy to try and identify one or another party as the villain in this tragedy, and that is what many minority advocates do. For many activists, the twin demons are radical Islamists, both parties like Jamaat and rogue groups, and the center-right BNP. I recall being asked to address a group of Bangladeshi minorities through a conference call on the matter of what strategy should be adopted moving forward. This was shortly after the 2008 election of Sheikh Hasina and the Awami League. Some of the participants were nearly ecstatic and ready to stop their advocacy, convinced that this change of government was all that was needed: just get the bad guys out. That is too easy, and it is wrong.

I counseled them that "now is not the time to fall asleep. You need to press your case with the new government—remind it of how much support they got from you. Several callers, however, cautioned that we should not "antagonize" the new government but "give it time." Of course, we cannot expect significant change to take hold immediately, I told them, but if we do not push for action, it likely will not happen at all.

> Ending the persecution of minorities must be considered one of the first priorities. What is more important than that? And I have one other question: 'this attitude of passivity and let's give them a chance; how well has that worked for the minorities and the victims in the past? Not well. We are sitting by while people are being killed and tortured! So, yes, we must give them some time—but not much or we will see that their words are nothing more than words.[113]

---

[112] *Op. cit.,* Vyas. While we might disagree with some of his specific figures, the direction and conclusion are clear and accord with our own assessment.

[113] Conference call held January 10, 2009, under the auspices of the Bangladesh Buddhist Christian Unity Council and reported in "Repeal Enemy Property Act & Show the Support: Dr. Benkin," *Daily Khabor,* January 11, 2009.

The notion that a new government is the solution to our problems, including some of the more trenchant ones, is ridiculous. Moreover, the Awami League's own history testified against it. When it has had the chance, the party has been consistent in its inaction in stopping minority oppression. It also has participated enthusiastically in the VPA and used its spoils to reward its minions. And unfortunately, my prediction has turned out to be an accurate one. If anything, ethnic cleansing has become more severe since that day in January 2009.

Elites might be fooled by the false BNP-Awami League dichotomy, but most of the common people are not, since they have to deal with the real consequences of both parties and their actions.

"'BNP or Awami League, they are all the same,' says Atiqur, a fruit seller at Dhaka's Kawran Bazaar, next to the plush Sonargaon Hotel... 'Until they go, things cannot improve [and] I think things are going to get a lot worse before it starts getting better.'"[114]

It might be comforting to identify a single cause and therefore an easy solution to the problem, but doing so will not help the victims. In fact, it will hurt them by deluding people into thinking that injustice was the sole province of one particular party and that replacing it with another is all that is needed. No, the ethnic cleansing of Bangladeshi Hindus is now nothing less than the marrow in the Bangladeshi bone, platelets in the blood. Bangladeshi traditions were hijacked long ago by individuals who believed they could benefit personally by opening the door to radical institutions; and they remain hijacked because their descendants—including Bangladesh's leaders—continue to act in a self-serving, corrupt, and timid manner, placing their own interests above those of the nation. The only difference between the BNP and

[114] *Rediff India Abroad,* March 22, 2006.

the Awami League is that the latter will *say* they want to prevent the atrocities. For the victim, the difference is at most one of degree, but not enough to alter the end result if the real problem is not addressed head-on and honestly. Another point should be made, as well. Having spoken with Awami League officials and studied the matter rather extensively, it is clear that the ethnic cleansing of Hindus does not comport with the Bangladesh envisioned by Sheikh Hasina or most of her party's leaders. It does not seem to me, at least, that she really approves of these atrocities or the lack of their prosecution. Yet, they persist—and show no signs of abating despite those beliefs. And for the victims, that is perhaps more chilling than if the government approved of it; for they seem unable to stop them, and it is difficult to imagine a government "better" than the Awami League's at this point.

All of these factors have created a situation in Bangladesh in which severe prejudice is tolerated by those in power. Carrying it to an extreme, even if the government of Sudan has not actually carried out the genocide in that country, its refusal to stop the Janjaweed militia is the primary factor that allows it to happen; and the people in the government know that. Are we looking forward to a time in Bangladesh when severe bigotry turns into genocide because those in power have tolerated its roots and early form; and it has been allowed to proceed unopposed by a timid or uncaring world?

CHAPTER THREE

IMPLEMENTING ETHNIC CLEANSING: ISLAMIST ATTACKS; GOVERNMENT COLLUSION; AND COUNTING ON APPEASEMENT

So, the stage is set. A people—Bengali Muslims—who by tradition and history are relatively gracious and accepting of those who practice other faiths, have become something quite contrary to their values and have turned on their Hindu and other non-Muslim neighbors. A group of self-interested leaders encourage, support, and reward them for it; while a pernicious ideology justifies their acts of ethnic cleansing as furthering the will of Allah.

The ethnic cleansing of Bangladeshi Hindus has intensified in recent years. Although no prominent human rights NGO[115] or the UN Human Rights Commission has taken up this matter; several individual South Asians, some authors and journalists, and a few ersatz (primarily local) organizations have attempted to do something to bring this matter to light. Even a small number of Bangladeshi Muslims, including a fundamentalist Muslim leader, Kazi Azizul Huq, are raising the issue inside Bangladesh. Some military leaders and intelligence operatives inside Bangladesh, along with a few

[115] In 2009, together with Miriam Guttman-Jones of Australia, I founded a human rights NGO, Forcefield, that is among other things, dedicated to ending the persecution of minorities in Bangladesh, especially the most populous, Hindus. Forcefield is a "non-agenda-driven human rights organization"; distinguished from Amnesty International, Human Rights Watch, and others that we believe, are driven by ideology rather than justice. Forcefield can be accessed via the Internet at http://www.forcefieldnow.org.

others, are coming to recognize that it is in their nation's best interests to put a principled stop to this atrocity. Standing against that, however, is the entire Bangladeshi political structure, which militates against such action, and Bangladeshi leaders who lack the will and moral courage for it to find expression in action.[116]

In February 2007, I received a fax from a Hindu living outside of Kolkata. His parents had been forced out of Bangladesh when he was a child, he said, and his family fled to West Bengal. His story is not very different from the ones that many Bangladeshi Hindus have told me, except that Bikash Halder decided that he could not let his own two children or those of his coreligionists grow up in a world no different from the one he knew. Nor could he sleep soundly knowing what was being done to other Bengali Hindus not too far from his own bed. He had heard of me from my previous human rights work in Bangladesh, and took a chance that I would not turn a deaf ear to his plea. His instincts were right on the money, and I am eternally grateful to him for it.

While Bangladeshi representatives were trying to convince the United States and other countries that theirs was a "moderate Muslim nation," they continued to patronize Islamist radicals and even had an Islamist party in the ruling coalition.[117] They also continued persecuting Shoaib

---

[116] It seems that whenever I compliment one or two persons for their work on behalf of minorities, I offend others who feel they deserved a mention. So, let me be clear. This is not an exhaustive list by any means. I have had the pleasure of working with quite a few Bangladeshis—Muslims included—who have put themselves at risk for the sake of justice. (Saleem Samed is the first to come to mind.) *Global Human Rights Defence Fund,* based in The Hague, and *Bangladesh Minority Watch,* especially their primary activist, Rabindra Ghosh, deserve special mention for their tireless and generally unrewarded work. Tapan Ghosh and *Hindu Samhati* in West Bengal also work tirelessly to fight the oppression. The organizations and the people running them deserve our sincere thanks.

[117] *Jamaat* e-Islami was part of the ruling coalition, from 2001 through 2006. Just prior to the aborted 2007 elections, both major parties had signed Memoranda of Understandings that would have brought Islamists into the ruling coalition no matter which of them emerged victorious.

Choudhury for doing nothing more than the work of a good journalist because that work angered Bangladeshi Islamists and their sycophants. We had to expose their lie for what it was. When Bangladesh officials snatched Shoaib in an action inspired and directed by Islamists to silence those voices of anti-Islamist dissent in Bangladesh, they violated basic international tenets of human rights and Bangladesh's own laws.[118] To be sure, even by itself the moral imperative of saving a life was reason to work unceasingly. That this man was imperiled because he dared to speak on behalf of Israel in a Muslim majority and increasingly radicalized country made his case even more compelling. Beyond that, however, the Islamists' actions against him provided us with a real opportunity to expose the truth behind their façade and the disingenuous face that Bangladesh was presenting to the West: the fiction of it being a "moderate" Muslim country.

For a long time, however, no one seemed to notice. After an intense and often acrimonious discussion involving then-Congressman Mark Kirk, then-Bangladeshi Ambassador to the United States, Shamsher M. Chowdhury and me, in the Congressman's Washington office more than 16 months after to "Shoaib's arrest, we succeeded in forcing Shoaib Choudhury's release on April 8, 2005.[119] It was more than a

---

[118] Ironically, the anti-Islamist community in Bangladesh has been at best cool toward Shoaib Choudhury. When he was arrested, not one of them came to his aid, and with latter-day accusations of inappropriate behavior, they have been much more outspoken with their dislike of him, withdrawing whatever grudging support they previously gave at times.

[119] I founded two web sites, http://www.freechoudhury.com and http://www.InterfaithStrength.com. The first one was dedicated to freeing Shoaib Choudhury; the second, once the major site for information about his case, now focuses on several other issues. For information about the Choudhury case, feel free to contact me through http://www.InterfaithStrength.com. At the top of its home page there are two quotes. Shoaib's is, "When my own people abandoned me, my Jewish brother [Richard Benkin] protected me, stood with me." Mine is, "If the Choudhurys were in Europe during the Holocaust, they would have refused to drive the trains [that took Jews to the death camps]." Also see, Salah Uddin Shoaib Choudhury, *Injustice and Jihad* (Blitz Publications: Dhaka, 2007).

year and a half later that Bikash Halder located a Hindu attorney in Dhaka, Advocate Govinda Chandra Pramanik, who I continue to work with and whom I had met in Dhaka the month before Halder contacted me.[120]

The fax he sent me was a plea and a message: Bangladeshi Hindus were suffering and they needed the same principled and unrelenting help that I gave Shoaib Choudhury. I had seen a number of reports about what was being done to these people before receiving that fax, but I had not been involved actively in fighting it beyond some minor protests to the Bangladeshis about their treatment of minorities. I also raised some general questions in speeches I made while in the country. Bikash Halder's contact, however, forced me to delve into the matter. Researching it led me to these inevitable conclusions: (1) The Bangladeshi Hindus were most decidedly under duress, possibly ethnic cleansing; (2) The government of Bangladesh was aware of this and was at best complicit by refusing to take any action against the perpetrators, and often complicit by commission of the anti-Hindu actions themselves; (3) The rest of the world remained silent even when they knew of the atrocity and was done nothing to stop it; (4) The attacks were part and parcel of international *jihad* and as such were not only human rights catastrophes but also battles in the Islamist war against civilization itself.

I often refer to Israel as the "canary in a coal mine." The expression, "like a canary in a coal mine" refers to a practice that persisted into the early 20th century whereby coal miners would bring a canary with them when they went to work down in the mines. Canaries are more sensitive than humans are to the methane and carbon monoxide gases that

[120] Advocate Govinda Chandra Pramanik is with the Bangladesh Minority Lawyers Association, which provided Shoaib Choudhury's legal defense for a time when he could not get other lawyers in Bangladesh to take his case. Often done *pro bono*, the defense was directed by Advocate Samarendra Nath Goswami, a leader of Bangladesh's Baha'i community.

plagued miners. What happened to the canary was a harbinger of what would happen to the miners if they continued to ignore the signs of the deadly substances. Thus, if Israel continues to defeat Islamists, it shows that we can, too. If we sacrifice Israel for the illusion of peace, so too shall we be sacrificed. Czechoslovakia was a canary in the coal mine before the Second World War and at the time of the Communist takeover in Central and Eastern Europe. Kashmir is another one. If we sacrifice Kashmir with the expectations that it will bring peace, expect the same to happen to us. The sacrifice of Czechoslovakia was based on the mistaken premise that the claims Nazis and Communists made to gain our concessions were genuine; that is, when they spoke of specific goals and grievances, that they were being truthful. Not so. Czechoslovakia was only a step toward their ultimate goal of world domination.

Similarly, those who believe we can secure peace in the Middle East by sacrificing Judea and Samaria (i.e., the West Bank) are wrong; and those who believe the sacrifice of Kashmir will bring peace to South Asia are equally mistaken. Kashmir is India's West Bank in that Islamists cannot come out and say they wish the destruction of India in its entirety and expect to be taken seriously as a party to negotiations; in the same way, they cannot come out and declare their intention to destroy Israel and expect anyone to think Israel has any business negotiating with them. We can see this with Hamas, which does say that and is not—at least at this point—being forced on Israel as a legitimate negotiating party (although there are some in the West who would like to do so). In the past, however, both Israel and India have been "encouraged" to make concessions to their implacable enemies without an equivalent demand being made on the latter. Someone will have to remind me when that became negotiation. Islamists in the Middle East and South Asia have made it clear that their demands are absolute and the outcome they demand pre-determined. This is contrary to the very essence of negotiations, which would have two equal parties engage in a give and take that *both* would accept as binding.

So, too, if the rest of the world turns aside while the Bangladeshi Hindus are destroyed by Islamists, it will do the same for others who ultimately find themselves on the Islamist chopping block. Thus, when Bengali Hindus thank me for my efforts, I accept their gratitude but note that I am doing this for my own descendants as well. There is only one moral path to take and that is to destroy the authors of ethnic cleansing: those whose ideology tells them that Bangladesh must be rid of its remaining Hindus and other non-Muslims; and to let the enablers of ethnic cleansing (those who are complicit by action or omission) know that they are liable to get caught in the crossfire.[121]

Islamist Attacks

How severe is the current problem?

It is difficult to get exact figures on the number of Bangladeshi Hindus and their descendants living in India since so much of the movement takes place under the legal radar. Complicating matters further is the fact that there has been extensive movement of economic refugees across the border and deliberate infiltration of Bangladeshi Muslims into West Bengal. Hence it was critical that I go there and see for myself. That trip, which I now repeat at least annually with Bikash Halder and other Bengali Hindus on the ground exposed the full and frightening extent of their condition. My first such trip took place throughout most of February 2008. I visited over a dozen refugee camps (some semi-legal, most

---

[121] Note that for Islamists, the rubric "non-Muslim" contains Muslim minority groups, especially the Ahmadiyya, whose tenets differ from Orthodox Islam in many ways. This is very telling as that tendency remains on the fringes of other faiths, unlike Islam, which are confident and strong enough to encompass numerous subgroups that espouse varying religious principles.

illegal); spoke with dozens of refugees; held private and clandestine meetings with informants; and addressed public forums on the plight of the refugees and what we could do working together.

Numerous refugees testified about atrocities committed by Islamist radicals inside Bangladesh. These included beatings, murders, mutilations, ritualized gang rapes, and forced eviction from their lands. In camp after camp, informants told of one or another relative or neighbor being murdered by the radicals as warnings for Hindus to abandon their property and leave the area. (At some point, their erstwhile neighbors and local officials then verbalized these explicit warnings to them.) Most of the camps I visited were in Northern Bengal, and so the vast majority of refugees had fled from areas in Bangladesh's northwestern or western districts and divisions.[122]

One incident that is becoming more and more common was related to me in almost every colony I visited between 2008 and 2010: the random abduction of young Hindu women and girls. With a numbing consistency, their testimonies would tell of a young female walking by the side of the road. In some cases, she was going to draw water; in others she was on her way to school; and in some, she was just walking on her way to see a relative or friend. Out of the blue, a gang of Muslims would drive up and snatch the woman and then take her to a vacant building or field and rape her repeatedly. In many cases, the women and girls were then forcibly married to one of their victimizers.

In these traditional villages, rape victims often were seen as having shamed their families and were not welcomed back or defended; no honor killings, but most often ostracism. There is

---

[122] Bangladesh is divided into seven divisions: Barisal (6), Chittagong (11), Dhaka (17), Khulna (10), Rajshahi (7), Sylhet (4), and Rangpur (8). Each division is divided into districts, with the number for each in parentheses.

strong anecdotal information to indicate this double victimization has become far less common. When it still happens, however, it plays right into the radicals' calculations because the ostracism process insures that all offspring will then be raised as Muslims in an all-Muslim environment. At the same time, they have stopped a potential source of Hindu offspring from fulfilling that role. The logic is not out of keeping with how radicals target Christians in certain areas of the Middle East and in other traditional societies. It also parallels the practice of Palestinian terrorists. During periods of frequent suicide bombings, they would deliberately target Israeli venues that are populated heavily by women of childbearing age, teenagers, and other young people.

One of the most notorious was the 2003 suicide bombing of Mike's Place, a bar and disco frequented by young people in Tel Aviv; but there were many others. The attack on the popular Mike's Place offered no strategic advantage or other benefits other than its role in advancing the cause of genocide and spreading fear among the population. The same is true with the victimization of these Bengali women and girls. There is extensive statistical evidence to support this, and for anyone to believe that this documented pattern is a coincidence or a "Zionist plot" and not a deliberate and genocidal plan would require the height of naïveté or ingrained bigotry.[123] These actions make it similarly clear by any objective measure that the actions in "quiet case of ethnic cleansing" deliberately target the Hindu gene pool in Bangladesh.

Despite Bangladeshi assurances to the contrary, Hindus and other religious minorities do not enjoy equal rights in that

---

[123] Don Radlauer, "An Engineered Tragedy: Statistical Analysis of Casualties in the Palestinian-Israeli Conflict, September 2000 – September 2002," *International Policy Institute for Counter Terrorism,* Herzliya, September 29, 2002. Also see, for instance, Lee Green, "AP: Palestinian Terrorists 'Shocked' at Killing of Children," *CAMERA: Committee for Accuracy in Middle East Reporting in America,* September 7, 2004.

country to those enjoyed by Muslims. When government representatives point to formalistic laws that guarantee equal rights, I tend to respond by likening them to one of the most beautifully-written documents I ever read; to wit, the Stalinist constitution of the Soviet Union. While it went on about freedom and equality, the circumstances on the ground were anything but free and equal. As German social scientist Ralf Dahrendorf noted, "Without the basis of the rule of law, the constitution of liberty cannot really work; but the basis alone does not guarantee the constitution of liberty."[124] That is, as the citizens of virtually every nation know, the reality of any law is in its implementation, and its implementation by local officials, police, bureaucrats, as well as the reality of power politics, all determine whether the law as written approximates the law as it exists. For Indian citizens, it is how the high-minded principles of secularism morph into pseudo-secularism; for Americans, it is how immigration laws are flaunted by government and business. It is one reason why the pretensions of freedom and equality contained in the Bangladeshi constitution are meaningless in the face of the reality of the law's actual implementation. This principle is expressed in an oft-quoted German dictum Dahrendorf cites: "while constitutional law passes, administrative law persists."[125]

In Bangladesh, administrative law at the local and, as we will see, even higher levels works in reality to rid the country of its Hindu population and increase that of those who practice Bangladesh's official state religion, Islam. In keeping with that duplicity, Bangladeshi spokespersons maintain that their government will defend Hindus and other minorities. The refugees and activists like Rabrindra Ghosh, however,

[124] Ralf Dahrendorf, *Society and Democracy in Germany*. (Doubleday & Company: Garden City, NY, 1967), p. 197.

[125] *Ibid.* p. 196.

report something quite to the contrary. Almost universally, victims would go to the local Bangladeshi authorities for help and protection after an attack or threat only to be turned away. Not one person we have encountered told of receiving any help. Instead, the most common response they received from officials was one to abandon their property and quit Bangladesh. This is a far cry from the role law *enforcers* are expected to play in any civil society. Other people who have faced religious or political persecution in Bangladesh report identical experiences with the authorities. My own experiences with them have been the same: not only are words often empty, but they are frequently spoken with no intention of living up to the pious sounding phrases they contain or fulfilling their commitments. More ominous, there is a good deal of evidence from victims and other sources of local authorities joining in the attacks, participating in subsequent cover-ups, and actively protecting the perpetrators.[126]

Kazi Azizul Huq of the *Khalefat Andolin Bangladesh* said that I needed to take care in accepting stories of Islamist attacks. No doubt, he said, they do occur, but he also asserted that many Hindus have left voluntarily even abandoning or selling their lands. Huq is a fundamentalist Muslim and a good man who supports action to protect Bangladeshi minorities. He and I have engaged in honest dialogue for years in a process that has allowed us to identify the values we share. It also has enabled us to acknowledge the many points of sometimes severe disagreement we have; but Huq and I have "agreed to disagree," as we have put it, which is the hallmark of a civil society.

There is no doubt that, as Huq states, some of the refugees really did leave Bangladesh of their own volition for economic reasons. But it is also clear that most so-called voluntary

[126] We saw that previously with the Sutrapur incident—one of many such examples. And that took place inside the Bangladeshi capital immediately behind a police station. Imagine the lack of regulation persisting in areas under less scrutiny.

transactions by Hindus are rather less than voluntarily; most not voluntary at all. If individuals lack the basic rights and protections that all citizens of society can expect, they do not possess the necessary tools to engage in most activities of their own free will. This is apparent in societal laws criminalizing statutory rape; that is, when one of the participants in a sex act is a minor, the law deems that he or she (usually she) does not have the set of qualities necessary to decide freely to engage in that action. The same principle is often applied to mentally disabled individuals and others whose judgment (as determined by some objective measure like age or intelligence) is too impaired for them to act with free will. For Hindus and other minorities in Bangladesh, their "free will" is imprinted with experiences of seeing others attacked and the authorities refusing to protect them. The experience of the refugees I interviewed was defined by practitioners of that administrative law—local police and other officials—telling them to leave the country rather than defend their homes and families. Their decision to emigrate was undertaken independent of anything we would recognize as free will. The Bangladeshis' reference to formalistic laws is a simplistic and transparent ruse that should not fool anyone; but it does. Because the international human rights and diplomatic communities find uncritical acceptance of the ruse more convenient and easier than challenging it, it has given the Bangladeshis cover for years to continue their march toward an East Bengal free of Hindus.

The refugees told me about attacks going back to a time when Bangladesh was still East Pakistan; then, too, the rest of the world had turned a deaf ear to their cries, a blind eye to their suffering. Providing indirect evidence to bolster these witness accounts, in addition to the objective evidence provided by the steady decline in the Bangladeshi Hindu population, was India's action in passing a succession of laws regarding illegal Hindu immigrants from Bangladesh. I also recall spending a day[127] in a transit camp set up by the Indian government in a town, located in the northeast corner of Uttar Pradesh near the Nepal border, where thousands of Hindu immigrants were processed and given citizenship. But, as the people in the town reported, that stopped decades ago, and the transit camp itself has long been closed.[128]

Except for the few years of respite following Bangladeshi independence, the attacks have proceeded almost non-stop. The victims whom I have met are by no means the only source of evidence for the persecution of religious minorities in Bangladesh. Two organizations with chapters in North America, Europe, and of course South Asia—the Human Rights Congress for Bangladesh Minorities and the Bangladesh Hindu Buddhist Christian Unity Council (BHBCUC)—have been documenting atrocities against Bangladeshi minorities for years. More recently, Global Human Rights Defence (GHRD) and Bangladesh Minority Watch (BDMW) have sent a consistent stream of materials that provide extensive photographic and legal evidence. Collected by Rabindra Ghosh and other activists, their investigations confirm the incidents, the state of the victims, and the studied inaction of the Bangladeshi government. They also have been trying to inform people of the dire situation of their Bangladeshi co-religionists; but there has been no effective response to their pleas. The *Appendix* provides a long list of such incidents that we have been able to confirm. We listed only those incidents we could verify through multiple sources, determine that victims were targeted because they were Hindus, and in which the government of Bangladesh neither acted to protect the victims nor effectively prosecuted the

[127] March 18, 2009.

[128] This information was related to me personally by residents and semi-officials of Hindu refugee organizations in the area. These organizations represent some 300,000 Hindu refugees. Subsequent research allowed me to confirm the presence of a transit camp in that area and the fact that it stopped operating as a way station for Hindu refugees to transition to Indian society and citizenship.

perpetrators. That is not to question the credibility of any sources or to suggest that incidents not listed might not have occurred. The list reflects what we were able to do with our limited resources and from our base in North America.

In a 2009 discussion, I tried to provide some perspective on how structurally embedded the Muslim sense of social superiority is in Bangladesh and Pakistan; that is, in the two Muslim-majority countries carved out of the Indian subcontinent. I asked an audience to consider how likely it would be for Bangladesh to elect a Hindu Prime Minister. We had to ignore the fact that both the Bangladeshi and Pakistani constitutions have provisions that allow Muslims alone to become Prime Minister. Even if that was not the case, however, the thought of Bangladeshis electing a Hindu to run their "Muslim" country was laughable to everyone who considered the question.[129]

"Consider," I said, "that Hindus have about the same numerical strength in Bangladesh as African-Americans have in the United States, and we just elected an African-American President in Barack Obama. When do you think that's going to happen in Bangladesh?"[130]

There are two conclusions to draw. The first is that it is sheer bigotry to enshrine that exclusion into law and disallow anyone except people of one faith to rule a country. It is mind-boggling that while the United Nations and other international bodies hold conferences, pass resolutions, and make firebrand speeches decrying so many activities and national practices that they consider discriminatory; they have never once addressed those countries with laws like the exclusionary laws in Bangladesh and Pakistan. If India, however, excluded

[129] While India has not had a Muslim Prime Minister to date, it has had several Muslim Presidents—the last one being A. P. J. Abdul Kalam who left office in 2007. The current Indian Vice President is a Muslim as well, Mohammad Hamid Ansari. You will not find non-Muslim officials at that level in Muslim countries.

[130] "Genocide we can Prevent," a speech by Richard Benkin to American University as part of the Holocaust Commemoration Week, April 23, 2009.

anyone but Hindus, or United States law had a "whites only" provision for its presidency—which is contrary to the essence of both nations—you can be sure that fighting it would be at the top of the agenda for these same bodies that ignore the exclusionary law in Bangladesh.

This audience of young people separated from Bangladesh by half a world also recognized that even without the de juro bigotry, there was a popular component to the exclusion of Hindus; that is de facto bigotry, even among this Muslim population that is not thought of as being radicalized. That, of course, makes matters worse, because laws can be attributed to the work of nuts or kooks, or the temporary insanity of a radical government for an otherwise non-radical people; but this reveals something quite different and more pernicious. Bangladesh does not have a radical government; nor is it dominated by nuts and kooks. Yet, the popular consensus—that is, the will of the people, if you will—in Bangladesh will not consider the possibility of allowing anyone to rule over their nation who is not a Muslim. Again, the very notion was laughable—to audiences in both North America and South Asia, young and older.

Apologists so easily talk about Islam as a great religion hijacked by a small group of radicals. It is almost a knee-jerk reaction that can be designed only to preempt a charge of Islamaphobia; which repeated again and again is assumed to be fact and not a device. The importance of this quiet case of ethnic cleansing in Bangladesh goes beyond the terrible human suffering it is causing. Bangladesh is not Iran, where *mullahs* have imposed a theocratic Muslim orthodoxy on Jews, Baha'i, Christians, and Zoroastrians, as well as its majority Muslim population. Bangladesh is not Sudan, where a Muslim militia is committing genocide at the government's behest. Nor is it Saudi Arabia, where one cannot even enter the country wearing an amulet or any sign of their non-Muslim faith. And that is precisely why Bangladesh is important.

When the Taliban-run Afghan government destroyed the ancient statues of Buddha, was anyone that surprised? When

Iran periodically prosecutes and often executes Jewish citizens it accuses of spying for Israel, is anyone surprised? When one of Egypt's top "secular" leaders called the Holocaust a lie and 9/11 "made in America," was anyone surprised at this outburst of the misnomered "Arab Spring" of 2011?[131] The fact that the events documented in this book are unfolding in that very "moderate" Muslim nation of Bangladesh makes clear that the comforting retreat about a small minority of radicals is simply a characterization that just does not conform to the facts.

Deliberately Targeting the Gene Pool: Genocide?

Genocide is a very provocative word and tends to be used more for effect and to stir passions, rather than in a deliberate and disciplined fashion. Even though people are being murdered, raped, and despoiled of their ancestral lands by a decades-old law that has been embraced by all Bangladeshi political parties, looking at things objectively, we probably cannot apply that concept to what is happening to Bangladesh's Hindus. In Chapter Two, however, we did point out how the anti-Hindu actions in Bangladesh conform to at least one component of genocide defined in the internationally accepted Convention on the Prevention and Punishment of Genocide; specifically, that Convention's fourth genocidal act: "Imposing measures intended to prevent births within the group."[132]

Don Radlauer conducted an exhaustive study for the world-renown Institute of Counter-Terrorism in Herzliya, Israel. He dissected statistics of Israeli and Palestinian casualties during the Second Intifada (2000-2006). He looked at a two-year period from September 2000 through September 2002 when casualties on both sides their height. So was the number of suicide bombings—the Arabs' primary

---

[131] Ben Birnbaum, "Egypt party leader: Holocaust is 'a lie'," *The Washington Times*, July 5, 2011.

[132] Op. cit., UN, Convention on the Prevention and Punishment of the Crime of Genocide.

contribution to the modern world.[133] "Women and girls account for 31 percent of *all Israelis* killed in the conflict, and almost 40 percent of the *Israeli noncombatants* killed by Palestinians." (emphasis mine) That contrasts with five and eight percent respectively among Palestinian fatalities. That is a significant variance between the two; significant enough to rule out any random causes. It had to be deliberate targeting. Radlauer also found that among Israeli noncombatants under the age of 20—an age range with the greatest number of potential child-bearing years—Arabs killed far more girls than boys. In contrast, boys outnumbered girls among Palestinian noncombatant fatalities in this age range by three to one.[134] This disparity, too, is far too great to be accounted for by random factors. It had to reflect a deliberate strategy on the part of the Islamist forces in the Middle East.[135]

Radlauer further found in his study that Israeli teenagers were killed more than people in any other age bracket. "This high number of teenaged fatalities," he said, "may be the result of suicide bombings, many of which targeted groups of young people."[136] And indeed, as noted earlier with the example of Mike's Place, the popular Tel Aviv night spot, Palestinian homicide bombers[137] quite deliberately targeted places frequented by young people and women of childbearing

---

[133] Op. cit, Radlauer.

[134] *Ibid.*

[135] Radlauer also noted a tremendous disparity in boy/girl ratio of Palestinian victims under 18; viz., 95:5. "'Starting with the ages 11–12, there is a dramatic upswing in casualties among Palestinian boys, but for girls the curve stays low. That tends to indicate that those who were killed did not die in the shelling or bombing of residential neighborhoods,' otherwise the gender distribution of the victims would be the same... most of the non-combatant deaths were at 'sites of confrontation." Radlauer's earlier studies found that deaths of Israeli youth, especially girls, were the result of their being deliberately targeted by Arab terrorists. Erik Schechter, "The Children's Crusade,"*Worldpress.org*. September 29, 2004.

[136] *Ibid.*

[137] Sometimes, we use the term "homicide bombings" as opposed to the more popular "suicide bombings" because the essence of the act is the murder of others not oneself.

years: clubs; markets; shopping malls; pizza parlors; and so forth.

A similar strategy is evident in Muslim attacks on Hindus in Bangladesh. During a three-month-period, January to March 2009, I was able to confirm six separate incidents in which Hindu children were kidnapped, raped, or both. *That is approximately one serious attack on a Hindu child in Bangladesh every other week.* In two cases, the child victim was murdered; and in at least two, raped. None of the families or communities to which these children belonged, save one, reported seeing them since the abductions; nor has anyone else reported seeing them. Still the police have not pursued a case against the alleged perpetrators in any of these incidents, nor have they attempted to retrieve any of the children.

Like many people, I receive regular reports of anti-minority attacks in Bangladesh. While the vast majority of incidents described therein are true, some present veracity problems here in the West where I am trying to raise awareness. For instance, there have been cases where activists and newspapers laced their reports with extensive exaggeration. Moreover, the use of words in these South Asian reports is often different from the way they are used in the West. Reports might describe simple miscreants as terrorists, which is true to the extent that they do terrorize the population, but it is quite different from how it would be understood by my intended audience. The use of words like torture, have different meanings among many South Asians than they do in the West.[138] Thus, the reports might sound exaggerated to the western ear, casting doubt on the veracity of the source.[139] That has required an extensive amount of second and third level verification, re-wording, and the omission of many

[138] I observed this disparity first-hand during a 2010 incident where a South Asian said he was "beaten," but from my perspective he was only pushed. The witness did not mean it as an exaggeration, but it sounded like one to this western ear.

[139] Yet, many accept and report uncritically allegations of Israeli "atrocities" by Arab witnesses.

events that in all likelihood did occur. As I discovered in previous human rights campaigns, not doing this also gives the perpetrators and others who want the issue to go away an opportunity to attack the truth of the entire effort. Moreover, if we are asking a US legislator, human rights attorney, or others to take action, they must be sure that any information on which they act is correct with 100 percent certainty.

In preparing a paper for members of the United States government, I included only those incidents that met all of the following criteria:

1. Two or more independent local sources verified the basic facts of the case.
2. The government did not take action against the perpetrators, but rather allowed them to act with impunity, or even took part in the attack.
3. The victims were Hindu and their targeting not random.
4. The incidents took place in 2009 when the Awami League government was in power.

A couple points need to be made about numbers two and four, not only because of this section but also because the rationale behind them informs this entire book. The exclusive focus on anti-Hindu attacks is not intended to minimize attacks on other minorities in Bangladesh. Bangladesh is indeed a hell hole for all religious and ethnic minorities, but there is a pattern of attacks directed specifically against Hindus that is part of a larger effort to eliminate them as a significant and independent group in South Asia. I have focused on 2009 attacks here (and subsequent attacks as well in the *Appendix*) because apologists, experts, and naïve commentators, have suggested that things have changed with the installation of the Awami League government. That has not happened. Acting as if it has betrays the victims. That simplistic and uninformed falsehood might be supported by ideology, personal investment by international elites, and wishful thinking; but it is not supported by the facts. So far as the nation's Hindus are concerned, the Awami League government is no different than previous Bangladeshi governments. Counting on it acting otherwise has the effect of making inaction in the face of this atrocity somehow acceptable.

Incident 1: On January 1, 14-year-old Subarna Karmaker was walking home from school in Kalapara in the state of Barisal. Several Muslim males led by a local Muslim identified as Jewel, age 22, grabbed her. They forced the girl onto their motorcycle, and fled. Subarna cried loudly for help, but no one came to her aid. Her father went to the police and complained, but was told that they knew of no crime and would not take any action. Subarna remains missing.[140]

Incident 2: On January 15, nine Muslim males went to the family home of eight-year-old Choyon Bairagee in Dumuria in the state of Khulna. They kicked in the door, and forcefully entered the family home. They grabbed Choyon Bairagee and when his mother Aduri lamented, the kidnappers threatened to kill the child if she reported the matter to anyone. They also demanded 20 million taka ransom. The officer-in-charge of Dumuria police station, told newsman that there was no case to pursue.[141]

Incident 3: On February 26, two Muslims, Babul Hossain Zihad alias Zikrul Islam (24) and Md. Razzak Ali (22) abducted 14-year-old Tanusree Roy from her home in Mohadipur in Barisal. According to the girl's father, Rajendra Nath Roy, the girl was taken at about 10 am. In the complaint he filed at the Kotwali Police Station, he notes that the

---

[140] In addition to my own sources inside Bangladesh, this incident was reported by the Bangladesh Minority Watch; Bangladesh Hindu, Buddhist, Christian Unity Council, and the vernacular paper, *Daily Destiny*.

[141] In addition to my own sources inside Bangladesh, this incident was reported by the BDMW, BHBCUC, and the vernacular papers, *Janakantha* and *Daily Purbanchal*.

kidnappers repeatedly threaten to kill him and his family. Despite the matter being assigned a case number on March 2—more than a month after the girl's abduction—the police have taken no action to find her or pursue the perpetrators whom witnesses identified at the scene.[142]

Incident 4: Some time at the end of February, a group of Muslims (as identified by the victim and her family) gang raped a 14-year-old Hindu girl and berated her for being Hindu. She at first said they "chased" her and on further questioning said they "caught her and did bad things to her." This occurred in the state of Dinajpur near Bangladesh's northern border with India. Instead of shunning their daughter and forcing her to return to her victimizer as one of multiple wives, the girl's family took her in. They, too, were victimized by local Muslims who claimed their family farm, and the police said they would not help them. Thus, they abandoned their property and fled—but with their daughter—to Northeastern India.[143]

Incident 5: On March 10, 15-year-old Fulfuli Rani Roy was kidnapped by local Muslims from Dolapar in the state of Rajshahi. Her father filed a complaint with the local police, identifying the perpetrator as Mahabul Islam, the son of Rayaz Uddinbut. The police, however, said that they would not pursue a case in the matter, refusing as well to try and locate and recover the girl. As a result, Fulfuli Rani Roy has not been seen or heard from since, and her father along with others allege that her kidnappers murdered her.[144]

---

[142] In addition to my own sources inside Bangladesh, this incident was reported by the BDMW and the BHBCUC.

[143] The victim and her family related this information to me directly in the North Dinajpur district of West Bengal, India on March 23, 2009. It was further confirmed by a local political leader and a local school teacher.

[144] In addition to my own sources inside Bangladesh, this incident was reported by the BDMW, BHBCUC, and the vernacular paper, *Daily Prothom Alo.*

Incident 6: On March 13, three-year-old Milon Moni Das was abducted by local Muslims from his family's home in Suapur in Dhaka. The family reported Milon's kidnapping to the police that same day, but the police took no action; two days later, a neighbor found the Hindu child dead in some bushes. After the body was discovered, a case was registered at Dhamrai Police station under section 302/201/34 of Bangladesh Penal code. Police then took one Muslim into custody, but released him after intervention by the local Awami League chairman. There has been no further action, and with the police refusing to pursue a case, the perpetrators feel capable of acting with impunity according to locals.[145]

Other attacks in addition to these have been reported, but these six have been verified by my associates on the ground after direct investigations. They help refute those disingenuous or naïve assessments noted above. The current, Awami League government has not brought any relief to Hindus from the consistent persecution they receive in their own country, nor has it changed the government's *de facto* patronization of Islamist radicalism. To be sure, the Awami League did not invent the deliberate targeting of the Hindu gene pool, but it is tacitly supporting what has become a new tradition that defines the life of Hindus in Bangladesh. For instance, in its 2008 human rights report, that reviewed the last year before Awami League rule, the Hindu American Foundation (HAF) cited targeted attacks on Hindus and concluded:

> The gang rape of women and girls, murder, beatings, harassment, kidnappings, attacks on temples, looting of gold and jewelry, and illegal occupation of land constitute the litany of human rights abuses suffered by Hindus, tribal people, and to a lesser extent Christians and Buddhists.[146]

[145] In addition to my own sources inside Bangladesh, this incident was reported by the BDMW, BHBCUC, and Global Human Rights Defence of The Hague.

[146] Hindu American Foundation, *Hindus in South Asia and the Diaspora: A Survey of Human Rights 2008,* p.6. Also see Appendix B, pages 99-121...

Two years later, HAF report reviewed the state of affairs during the Awami League's second full year in power. It cited targeted attacks on Hindus and concluded:

> Hindus of Bangladesh continue to be victims of ethnic cleansing waged by Islamic fundamentalists that include daily acts of murder, rape, kidnapping, temple destruction, and physical intimidation.[147]

Jenny Lundstrom, who is a human rights officer for Global Human Rights Defence in The Hague, is a tireless advocate for putting an end to the anti-Hindu violence in Bangladesh. She notes that according to one source, "200,000 Bengali women were raped with a genocidal motive during the 1971 war."[148] She also refers to "mass rapes of Bangladeshi women in the 1970s and 1980s" as a precedent for using rape to support genocide since then, including cites 1,000 rapes of Hindu women and girls in the immediate aftermath of the 2001 election. That election brought an openly anti-Hindu government to power, including *Jamaat e-Islami,* which advocated imposing Sharia law in Bangladesh and turning the country into an Islamist state along the lines of Iran and Afghanistan under the Taliban, where non-Muslims were killed, driven out of the country, or forced to convert to Islam. Lundstrom's statistics, gathered through exhaustive study, provide the focus of her thesis that rape of minority women in Bangladesh can be defined as a tool for committing genocide[149].

Forced Conversions to Islam

M. A. Khan, founder of the web site, Islam Watch, has

HAF receives numerous reports of atrocities against Hindus and other Bangladeshi minorities and has some rather rigorous standards for verifying them.

[147] Hindu American Foundation, *Hindus in South Asia and the Diaspora: A Survey of Human Rights 2010, pp. ii-iii.* Also see pages 4-17.

[148] Lundstrom, Jenny, *With Intent to Destroy? Rape as Genocide Under International Criminal Law: The Case of Bangladesh.* (Global Human Rights Defence: The Hague, 2007), p. 28 with citation.

[149] *Ibid,* pp. 28-32.

documented a consistent and deliberate historical pattern whereby non-Muslims in areas that Muslims came to dominate were forced to abandon their own faith and convert to Islam. The forced conversion of subjugated populations, according to Khan's research, has been a deliberate and integral component to Islam's growth. He provides particularly compelling evidence that its champions used forced conversions in a religiously-sanctioned attempt to supplant the indigenous Hindu religion throughout the Indian subcontinent.

> Therefore, wherever Muslims made successful inroads, they reduced the Hindu population directly by slaughtering the men in large numbers and taking away the women and children as captives. It indirectly reduced the Hindu populace by rendering the remnant Hindu men unprocreative [sic] by depriving them of childbearing female partners. Since those women became the vehicle for breeding Muslim offspring instead, the final result was a reduction of the Hindu populace and a sharp rise in the number of Muslims. The growing Muslim population was to be maintained by the toiling of the vanquished Hindus, subjected to grinding taxes. This is roughly the same protocol, which Prophet Muhammad had applied to the Jews of Banu Qurayza and Khaybar.[150]

For most people in the developed world, the notion of forced conversion seems to belong to a bygone age and a long discredited mentality; to the Inquisition, Crusaders, and marauding Arab warriors. The sad fact, however, is that like the slave trade and other atrocities we have left in *our* past, forced conversion is alive and well even today. And like the slave trade, forced conversion finds its most welcoming home today in the Muslim world. This should come as no surprise given what we have seen about both political and religious Islam suffused with a mentality that places the entire non-Muslim world on an inferior plane to that occupied by Muslims.

---

[150] M. A. Khan, *Islamic Jihad: A Legacy of Forced Conversion, Imperialism, and Slavery.* (Universe, Inc: New York, 2008), page 102.

In the summer of 2009, the Bangladesh Hindu, Buddhist, Christian Unity Council reported a case of abduction and forced conversion in Bangladesh; and two other human rights organizations, Global Human Rights Defence and Bangladesh Minority Watch also provided information about the incident. All three groups have a history of credibility in these matters, and Interfaith Strength utilized people on the ground in both India and Bangladesh who confirmed the allegations' veracity.

The case involves a Hindu woman named Koli Goswami. According to the BHBCUC report, at least five Muslim perpetrators including a government official broke into Koli's home at 12:45am on June 13, 2009. They engaged in some petty vandalism, but their real target was the 20-year old-college student. They snatched Koli from her bed, and when she tried to alert others by screaming, they threw a cover over her head. The commotion roused several of her family members and others in the area. When they ran to Koli's rescue, however, the home invaders drove them off by brandishing their arms and firing pistols to scare them away.

Koli's uncle, Beraj Goswami, filed a complaint with the Nandail District Police and also identified the alleged perpetrators. One of them has a history of trouble with the law. Touhidul Islam Bhuiya (Sumon), named by Beraj, is currently facing murder charges in a separate case.[151] Under normal and humane circumstances, the very fact of a family complaining about a home invasion and abduction that involved a known felon, would prompt police action and at the very least a serious investigation. Yet, let us recall that in Bangladeshi normal protections and the rule of law are denied to Hindus (available to them only in the form of unkept promises). Thus, police have refused to investigate the complaint or even

[151] Beraj Goswami is the brother of Koli's father, and as the latter is deceased, Beraj is responsible for the family's welfare and would take the lead in this effort in accordance with Bengali traditions.

acknowledge that any crime was committed. Their refusal to acknowledge that a crime was committed, by the way, also allows the known felon Sumon to remain free and to continue committing crimes for himself and in the employ of others with impunity.

When GHRD and BDMW representatives visited the site, police told them, "It is not kidnapping. It is love affairs between kidnapper and victim." Kidnapper? Victim? The violent abduction hardly sounds like a love affair. Yet, Bangladeshi police continue to maintain that position:

- ❑ despite extensive physical evidence of a break-in at the family home;
- ❑ despite the videotaped testimony of the family;
- ❑ despite the lodging of a formal complaint with the authorities by the girl's uncle;
- ❑ and despite repeated requests by the family for the police to help locate and produce Koli.

Moreover, the police do not even dispute the basic facts in this case; namely that a group of Muslim men entered the Goswami home and took Koli Goswami with them. They also admit recovering physical evidence of a struggle when they came to the family home immediately after the crime was reported; evidence including broken light bulbs and other destroyed household items. Yet, they continue to assert that none of this even suggests that a crime was committed; and therefore they have no obligation to investigate the incident further.

The police dispute only the motives of the perpetrators behind the event and assert a prior relationship between Koli and her kidnappers. Those familiar with Franz Kafka's classic novel, *The Trial,* will note the same bizarre logic and no-win situation for the victims here. Since the police have not pursued a thorough Investigation—even to decide that they will *not* investigate the matter—Interfaith Strength conducted an independent investigation of its own.[152]

Interfaith Strength's Bikash Halder led the investigation. He dispatched four men to the family home where they spoke with Professor Goswami. He said that his attempts to recover his niece have met with nothing but corruption, duplicity, and collusion in the crime from the police. When he filed a complaint immediately after the kidnapping, he told our investigators, he expected that the police would take quick action given the serious nature of the crime. It is also an accepted principle in police work that the longer we are from the crime itself, the less likely it is that a missing person will be recovered, at least safely; and Goswami's niece was missing. If they had any real hope of recovering Koli, they would have insisted on taking drastic action immediately.

Instead the police actually obstructed any rescue efforts and treated *him* as the criminal or at least as a nuisance because he had the gall to insist that they act in accordance with their responsibilities and the law. Rather than justice, they offered palliatives with no action, inexplicable delays (about which the Bangladeshi police is expert), and repeated denials that a crime occurred. Still, Goswami persisted, and he refused to relent on his insistence that they produce Koli to clarify what happened that night. At the very least, they owed him that much since there certainly was ample evidence that at minimum we are dealing with a case of unlawful entry into the family home, vandalism, and the discharge of a firearm.

Despite the police's excuses, manufactured obstacles, and threats, he would not back down; for after all in accordance

[152] Interfaith Strength is a loose organization I founded in 2005. Its primary goal is to stop the ethnic cleansing of Bangladesh's Hindus. Interfaith Strength's representative in West Bengal is Bikash Halder, mentioned earlier in this chapter. He has led the organization's efforts in West Bengal and Assam particularly, often doing so despite sabotage and dishonesty from others whose claims to be working on behalf of the Bangladeshi Hindus is belied by their quest for personal gain and lack of effectiveness. Some of them also have falsely claimed to be working for Interfaith Strength in a ruse to collect money from victims—money which neither Interfaith Strength nor its constituents (Bikash and me) have ever had anything to do with; nor have we authorized such action.

with Bengali tradition, he was responsible for the young woman. It was a responsibility Goswami refused to shirk. So, the police finally called him to the station and told him to sit and wait in a room while they recovered his niece. As he waited for the police to return, he came to believe that his persistence had paid off. But it was not to be. When the authorities finally got back to him several hours later, they came with suspect "affidavits and other so-called marriage of conversion documents." Goswami objected that there was no way he or the police could verify that the documents were authentic. Moreover, as the dates on the documents corresponded to times after her abduction when she was presumably being held captive, it was as likely as not that if Koli signed them she did so under duress. The only way to determine their veracity, he insisted, would be for Koli Goswami herself to testify in a safe environment that she signed the documents of her own free will.

Not only did that not happen, but the police and others concocted a bizarre ruse to silence Goswami, end the matter, and foreclose any possibility of Koli's family ever seeing her again. On August 17, 2009, Bikash Halder spoke with Professor Goswami during which time the latter made several accusations against the Nandail police; accusations which the police have yet to deny. He told Halder that the following sequence of events occurred. First, the Investigating Officer agreed to help him in exchange for a 25,000 Taka bribe (about $350 US)—which, by the way is pretty much standard operating procedure among the Bangladeshi police.[153] Once Goswami paid the bribe, the officer told him he would now arrange to produce the young woman and put an end to the controversy. He ordered him to return to the Nandail police station on June 21.

---

[153] In 2004, Sohail Choudhury, Shoaib Choudhury's brother, informed me that police told him the sedition case against his brother would be dropped in exchange for a (much larger) bribe. It made me wonder how seriously these officials can consider the charge or their duties to protect the state against insurrection—give that the charge was sedition!

Goswami did as he was told and returned to the station on that date. According to his testimony, he waited for some time before a police official greeted him and told him to wait while the police retrieved his niece. The wait seemed to Goswami like hours, after which they returned; but it was not with Koli Goswami or any young woman. Instead, they produced an older woman wearing a full Muslim burqa, which of course concealed her identity. She claimed to be Koli Goswami's mother and that her daughter converted to Islam because of a love affair—something Koli's real mother disputed numerous times. Goswami strenuously denies that the woman was his sister-in-law, and cannot even fathom the logic behind the attempted deception; since he most certainly could learn the truth by speaking to the woman he knew to be Koli Goswami's mother. There is a final, rather chilling element to the June 21 meeting: according to Goswami, the local Awami League MP, Retired General Abdus Salam, was present during this episode and threatened him with "dire consequences" should he proceed with the case any further or dispute the conversion.

It is at the very least highly unusual for an individual of the General's stature to be present for that sort of informal session, which raises all sorts of justified suspicions that there was something more here than the immediate crime. The General needs to be grilled about his participation in this; at the very least about what he was doing at the police station at that time. He also should be asked how much he knew about the illicit financial transaction that the police demanded before they engaged in the charade—a charade in which the General participated and to which he gave the government's imprimatur. Finally, there have been numerous attempts made by people in several places around the world to have the Bangladeshi government look into the General's role in this at best questionable incident and to discern his motives for being present. Thus far, they have gone unanswered.

Curiously, while the police did not produce Koli *that* day, they now claim that she was present at a secret hearing held the next. No one from the police or any other arm of the government informed the family about the hearing until after it allegedly occurred. So it is impossible for the family to confirm that their daughter was there or that it even took place. Perhaps the police realized that their previous little ruse did not work. In response to this news, Professor Goswami "protested vehemently" to Naindal officials and told Halder that as a result, "we are afraid we may further be attacked and our adult daughters abducted." Several days later, he again spoke with Halder by phone and reiterated his fears for his own minor daughters' safety as well.

While the government continues to deny that Koli Goswami was forced into apostasy or that she was abducted against her will, certain things are not in dispute: there was a home invasion that involved illegal entry into the Hindu home by several young Muslims; a family's daughter was taken during that illegal action and has not been seen by them since; the alleged perpetrators have been identified and at least one is a known criminal; and the police refuse to pursue a case. We also know that a magistrate and the police have said that Koli converted to Islam. While it is as yet just Goswami's claim that a government official from the ruling Awami League warned the family to stop fighting it; the government has not denied the allegation. Finally, if there was any court involvement in the case, it was held in secret and left no record, which, of course, does not foreclose the possibility of someone producing a fraudulent one that was generated after the duplicity was revealed.[154]

The incident itself is a crime, but as terrible as it is, this and other forms of anti-minority violence and coercion take place

---

[154] Richard Benkin, "Bangladeshi Hindu Abducted, Forced to Convert to Islam," *Weekly Blitz,* October 7, 2009; Richard Benkin, "Bangladeshi Hindu Abducted, Forced to Convert to Islam: Update," *Canada Free Press,* September 11, 2009. Global Human Rights Defence, Case number: 008-GHRD-HRCFBD-009-15, investigated July 3-4, 2009. The case also has been reported and documented by the Hindu American Foundation and Bangladesh Minority Watch, in addition to the organizations already cited.

in countries throughout the world—and in case it has to be said, by Muslims and non-Muslims alike, in countries with and without Muslim majorities. Three specific aspects of anti-Hindu violence in Bangladesh distinguish it from those other incidents and mark cases like the abduction of Koli Goswami qualitatively different from those elsewhere. The first is the action—or inaction—of the Bangladeshi government, which long ago abandoned its obligation to take any responsible action against Bangladeshi *jihadis* or others who perpetrate organized and purposeful anti-Hindu actions. This has been the case regardless of which party holds the reins of power in Dhaka. My own efforts and documentation of government complicity in ethnic cleansing of Bangladeshi Hindus has taken place during the tenures of governments run by the BNP, a civilian caretaker, a military-backed caretaker, and currently the Awami League. None of them has made any principled or effective effort to stop or even slow the destruction of Bangladeshi Hindus; all have benefited from Hindu property plundered under Bangladesh's Vested Property Act; each one is equally responsible for every death and brutalization that occurred during its tenure in office. Each one allowed a system that rewards anti-Hindu violence to operate in full force. Each one is complicit in ethnic cleansing.

The second significant feature of anti-minority violence in Bangladesh is that it is indeed organized and purposeful. None of the incidents related in these pages were carried out by rogue individuals acting on their own behalf or without an organized support system. That support system might derive from Bangladeshi law (like the VPA), its functionaries who really determine what the law is in practice, or from organized *jihadist* enterprises that continue to grow in influence in Bangladesh. Contrast that, for instance, with an event in the United States in 2002. Egyptian Hesham Mohamed Hadayet approached an El Al ticket counter at Los Angeles International Airport and opened fire. He killed two people before a security guard killed him. The FBI ultimately concluded that Hadayet's attack met its own definition of a terrorist action. The gunman was a Muslim and as a Muslim targeted the Israeli airline, as he told the FBI, in an attempt to influence US policy favorably toward the Arabs. But the FBI also concluded that he acted on his own and was not connected to any group. Similarly, in 2006 Naveed Afzal Haq started shooting at the Jewish Federation building in Seattle, Washington. He told police negotiators, "I'm a Muslim American. I'm angry with Israel." He specifically looked for "something Jewish" as a target, he told authorities.[155] All of that made his act a "hate crime," but it was never tied to any group. That is, these two acts do not purport to establish an organized program of anti-Jewish *jihad* in the United States. (While that might have been the case in these two instances, nothing here is meant to suggest that such groups have not been trying to establish themselves within the United States; at this point, however, they do not have the power to make their hateful actions more than anecdotal. That does not mean this will not change.)

Finally, abduction, forced conversion, and other acts of violence against religious minorities in general and against Hindus in particular remain common occurrences in Bangladesh. That is, in contrast to the incidents described above in the United States, the anti-Hindu actions described herein are not random and episodic. They are regular and tolerated. For instance, during January and February 2009 alone, there were anti-Hindu actions including murder, rape, abduction, land grabbing, forced conversion, and religious desecration at the rate of one a half per week. None were prosecuted by the new "pro-minority" government, and some even had state actors participating in the violence or a subsequent cover up.[156]

---

[155] This was reported extensively in local Seattle newspapers and television, as well as on Fox News and other national outlets between July 29 and August 9, 2006.

[156] These actions will be described and documented in these pages. The twelve incidents noted were only a sampling of the many alleged incidents, but for each of

The Koli Goswami incident is another example of how attacks on Bangladeshi Hindus conform to the fourth condition of genocide, as described in the international Convention for the Prevention and Punishment of the Crime of Genocide: "Imposing measures intended to prevent births within the group."[157] Koli Goswami was a promising young Hindu woman. In a few years at most she would have married and borne Hindu children, just as her more fortunate co-religionists will do. She will not, however; her Muslim attackers and the Bangladeshi authorities have seen to that. As a result of their complicity in that fourth condition, any Hindu children to whom she was to give birth will not be born—nor will their children, the next generation, the one after that, and on and on and on for all succeeding generations. To what extent does even this single act of abduction purposely deplete the Hindu population of Bangladesh?

Koli Goswami is not alone in her victimhood. These incidents are occurring at an alarming rate—at least monthly, often several times a month; with no let up since the Awami League has had the reins of power and responsibility for those acts of ethnic cleansing. The victims are young women and girls, sometimes boys, of child bearing years or younger, and either Hindu or Christian. There are too many for anyone to believe their choice as targets is anything but deliberate. As we saw earlier, Islamists have been following this pattern of ethnic cleansing for years in conflicts all over the world. The Israelis happened to aggregate good statistics about it; but it is not unique to the Middle East and South Asia. What Islamists cannot gain on the battlefield because they are militarily weak and morally bankrupt, they try to gain through genocide.

Those professionals who are well-schooled in these things

---

them I was able to verify that they occurred, that they deliberately targeted Hindus, and that the Bangladeshi government either participated or aided the perpetrators in avoiding any prosecution.

[157] *Op. cit.* UN, Convention...Crime of Genocide.

recoil at the use of the word genocide. In part, their reticence is well-founded because the crime of genocide is so horrendous, so abjectly evil, that its overuse will blunt the seriousness of the charge; and we have seen the casualness with which the charge is made. Arab partisans and their sycophants, for instance, frequently refer to Israeli "genocide" of Palestinians, which makes no sense with the Arab population in Israel increasing. They do so, however, not because of any integrity with regards to their use of the genocide charge, but merely in the hopes that sloganeering will be effective in replacing facts on their behalf.

That level of intellectual and moral dishonesty in using it should make us recoil in disgust when we think of Koli Goswami and the other Bangladeshi Hindus. For not a single Arab or Muslim government or organization has recognized the ethnic cleansing of Bangladesh's Hindus by people who carry it out in the name of Islam; they do not even dissociate themselves from these criminals. So we stand united with professionals and others do not want to dilute the concept of genocide through over use. Yet, if we fail to raise the issue, we make it easier for people to miss the seriousness of the threat and of taking the strong moral action that follows from that admission. And because we are competing for the attention of world leaders with partisans have no problem with the disingenuous use of hyperbole, failure to raise the issue helps keep this quiet case of ethnic cleansing off their radar. Our niceties would help condemn more Bangladeshi Hindus to an awful fate.

People can use labels however they wish without making it so; but what should we label a process that oversees the decline of the Bangladeshi Hindu from one third to one fifth to nine percent and less—the same process that is at work in the final days of Pakistan's Hindus?

As we engage in these academic musings, let us keep in mind that at least two other confirmed cases of abduction and forced conversion to Islam in addition to Koli Goswami's were reported in July 2009.[158]

An Anti-Hindu Pogrom[159]

Reports began trickling out of Bangladesh in the spring of 2009 about what can only be described as an anti-Hindu pogrom in the heart of its capital.[160] It was carried out in three stages on 30 March, 17 April, and 29 April. A community of approximately 400 Hindus was reportedly going about its business when, as described to human rights investigators "hundreds of Muslims [and] Awami League operatives," suddenly descended on them and demanded they quit the homes where they and their families had lived for the past 150 years. Witnesses also report that police watched passively while attackers beat residents and destroyed a Hindu Temple.

---

[158] Those of 14-year old Shymoli Rani Mondal of Dinajpur, reported by Global Human Rights Defence; and 17-year old Suvashish Dey of Narayanganj, reported by Bangladesh Minority Watch. It should be noted that Dinajpur is where the 14-year old Hindu girl I interviewed in Northeast India was raped by multiple Muslim men.

[159] *Op. cit,* Benkin "A Terrifying Existence." Thanks to Kanchan Gupta, *The Pioneer's* Associate Editor for his constant support and for his and *The Pioneer's* continued support and willingness to publish the truth that so much of the Indian MSM refuses to follow. My source material had several antecedents. The initial information came from Rabindra Ghosh from BDMW and GHRD, and subsequent material came from both organizations and from GHRD's Jenny Lundstrom. Additional source material came from local human rights groups, including Nagorik Uddyog, Association for Land Reforms and Development, the Dalit Movement in Bangladesh, Bangladesh Legal Aid Services Trust, and to Sohail Choudhury. Numerous articles were run in several Bangladeshi newspapers about the incidents and their aftermath throughout the spring and summer of 2009, including *The Daily Star, New Age, Daily Samakal, Weekly Janmabhum, Weekly Blitz,* and others. The incident was also reported in the Annual Report of South Asia Human Rights, "Status of Minorities in Bangladesh in 2009," which contains numerous other accounts of anti-Hindu violence in Bangladesh.

[160] Pogroms were initially anti-Jewish riots in the empire of Czarist Russia. The attacks were carried out by average (Christian) citizens (Poles, Russians, Byelorussians, Ukrainians, and Lithuanians for the most part), but they were instigated and supported by the entire apparatus of the Czarist government. Since then, the term has been used loosely to describe any attack on religious or ethnic minorities. What makes the term particularly apt in this incident is the

And although every Hindu, as well as the international community, should have reacted with horror and outrage; neither did.[161]

That made it easy for the Bangladeshis simply to deny that anything happened, despite the growing body of evidence that something extremely bad did occur. This tactic of simple denial, as we saw earlier in the Koli Goswami attack, is one that successive Bangladeshi governments have used regularly, and with good effect. It puts the accusers on the defensive and places all responsibility for substantiating the facts on them; and unless someone bothered to snap pictures at the time of the attack, their protestations will carry a lot of weight. Public relations aside, if the denials are so obviously a ruse to us, we must ask why neither the government nor the police would intervene. That takes us back to Islam's bifurcation of the world with non-Muslims considered unworthy of the same consideration as Muslims; and to the record of cowardice amassed by Bangladeshi governments who do not want to offend the radicals. That, in itself, is an indictment against the Bangladeshi government for complicity in these attacks.

The local police captain Tofazzal Hossain declared, "No demolition of temple occurred. There was no temple there, only a few idols." Yet, sources for the charge—Global Human Rights Defence and the Bangladesh Hindu, Buddhist, Christian Unity Council, as well as several local human rights groups and newspapers—are highly credible, prompting a two-month investigation by Interfaith Strength, under the immediate direction of Bikash Halder. It confirmed that something terrible indeed did occur. Perhaps the specifics deviated from the initial, sometimes hyperbolic reports; but while not as sensationalistic, what did happen was far more

---

fact that this anti-Hindu pogrom was also carried out by average (Muslim) citizens, but the entire process was inspired by the government, abetted by it, and the perpetrators were protected by it. It is this unholy wedding of mob action and deliberate government effort that makes it truly an anti-Hindu pogrom.

[161] This is the same attack in the Sutrapur neighborhood of Dhaka alluded to in less detail earlier.

chilling. It reflected a systematic, organized, and ongoing effort extending far beyond the immediate perpetrators; and it leaves no doubt that the Bangladeshi government sanctioned the anti-Hindu action.

Not all of the 400 Hindus in that community were made homeless, contrary to the initial reports, but a significant number were. That certainly is tragic enough, especially since dozens remain so months later. Nor has the Bangladeshi government even bothered to deny that Hindus were beaten *in front of police*, or that some religious desecration occurred *in front of police*. Its representatives simply deny that what occurred was criminal. Has this Bangladeshi government *de-criminalized* attacks on Hindus? We also confirmed that the area attacked was located directly behind the Sutrapur Police Station in Dhaka where it would be easy for police to detect what was about to happen and intervene—if they cared to do so. Moreover, the proximity of the police station combined with most descriptions of police behavior during the pogrom suggests that it is not unlikely that the Awami League government—or at least numerous members of it—had a role in planning and abetting the pogrom; perhaps even colluding with those who organized it to grab the Hindu land.

Additionally, the Hindu Temple that the attackers destroyed—a Shiva Mandir—was located a mere 18 meters from the station; yet, the police did nothing to stop its destruction. *This is not about one terrible event, but about a system of legalized ethnic cleansing that has proceeded non-stop for decades and which places every one of Bangladesh's 13-15,000,000 Hindus at risk.* The Sutrapur pogrom merely provides more evidence that government protestations to the contrary, normal legal protections are suspended for Hindus and other minorities in Bangladesh who are subject to arbitrary actions by the Muslim majority.

The events in Sutrapur were able to take place *only* because of Bangladesh's discriminatory laws, especially the Vested

Property Act, and support at the highest levels for the eradication of its Hindu community. The law provided a legal justification that allowed police to condone the actions, and the existing power structure made sure that it was carried out successfully. We will examine how it does so in Chapter Six, which concerns itself with the Vested Property Act.

Jogesh Chando and Tarkanath Das, both of them Hindu, were the original owners of the land in this area of Old Town Dhaka. Around the time of the subcontinent's partition, Chando and Das migrated to India; but before doing so, they gifted the Sutrapur land to the Hindus living there who decided to remain in that neighborhood of what was then East Pakistan; most of them were their former servants. Although it was a perfectly legal transaction, a local Muslim in Sutrapur, Mahbubur Rahman, tried for years to seize the Hindu-owned property. Fortunately, he was never able to produce the legal fiction that he needed to pull it off under Bangladeshi law. But after Rahman's death, his brother and nephews determined to do what he could not do. Though objective circumstances surrounding the real estate had not changed, they were confident that they could pull off the land seizure because they were supporters of Sheikh Hasina's Awami League, which now held power.

Although the Awami League leaders continue to this day to claim that theirs is a party committed to minority rights in Bangladesh, it supported Rahman's younger relatives' attempt to obtain the land. They colluded with them in supporting the younger Rahmans' (and subsequently the police's) demand that Sutrapur residents produce written proof of their ownership of the land. While that perhaps might seem reasonable and easily resolved in a nation that adheres to the rule of law and maintains official records at local and regional offices, the request was a transparent ruse in Bangladesh. All of the parties knew the poor Sutrapur residents could not provide written proof of ownership, given their impoverished state and the chaotic nature of Partition-era transactions. Nevertheless, with the Awami League in power it was all that the late Rahman's young relatives needed to do. Soon after, the government secretly voided the Hindus' title to the land using Bangladesh's Vested Property Act.

Thus, when the attackers stormed the community they were not alone. As they went from house to house, beating residents and destroying property, the police did nothing to stop them. Instead, several of the uniformed officers accompanied the attackers into the community and announced that the land was being seized under the VPA. The attackers were thereby able to rampage through the community on the three days in question knowing that they would not be called to account for their crimes; and with the police behind them asserted their new title to these properties as they were forcibly ejecting the helpless residents. And even in a twisted system that upholds such things, the police were derelict in standing by while people were beaten and their homes and religious shrines vandalized.

Once the crime itself ended, the police compounded the outrage by refusing to pursue any prosecution in the matter, even though at least three separate crimes were committed: land seizure, beatings, and religious destruction. GHRD and other groups have lodged formal protests and brought the matter to Dhaka's Metropolitan Police Commissioner, but he also "refused to take any action against the perpetrators of crime," according to GHRD's Jenny Lundstrom. Nor did the cover-up stop there. Zakir Hossain, Chief Executive of local human rights group, Nagorik Uddyog, told me that his organization appealed to the Bangladeshi Parliament and specifically to an Awami League MP, Shuranjit Sengupta, but neither he nor his party have taken any action.

All of the Bangladeshi officials I contacted refused to comment on the incident or even acknowledge that a crime occurred, and as of this writing more than two and a half years later, the government has refused to act in this case.[162]

That is, these *enforcers of the law* have become *enforcers of lawlessness*, abetting crimes against minorities and sending a message that Bangladesh is an Islamic State where the law gives Muslims preferential treatment even if it means ignoring elementary standards of justice. It explains how Muslims have been able to seize approximately 75 percent of all Hindu-owned land in Bangladesh.[163] It also means that the reduction of Hindus from almost 30 percent of the population to less than eight percent has been no accident but a deliberate process of ethnic cleansing. If it remains unchecked, that process will rid Bangladesh of its remaining Hindu population in our lifetime. And nobody seems to care; the world's self-appointed human rights arbiters remain shamefully silent.

After my article about the Sutrapur pogrom appeared in *The Daily Pioneer*, Zakir Hossain cited above contacted me very upset. He felt that the article distorted the truth in that he did not believe the attack in Sutrapur was due to any anti-Hindu or anti-minority bias in Bangladesh. Instead, he told

---

[162] *Op. cit,* Benkin "A Terrifying Existence." After Interfaith Strength's investigation and prior to sending the article for publication, I made several attempts to elicit any response from the Bangladeshi Embassy in Washington but was met with a wall of silence. It was my intention to note the Bangladeshi position in response to the charges in the body of the article. I have worked extensively with that embassy and used communication lines previously quite successful in getting messages to the embassy and receiving a response in return. The embassy, however, has not commented on incidents of anti-Hindu violence in Bangladesh from 2009 forward; a period roughly consonant with the installation of the Awami League government in Bangladesh and the Obama Administration (with its new policies in the region) in the United States.

[163] Abul Barkat et. al., *An Inquiry into Causes and Consequences of Deprivation of Hindu Minorities in Bangladesh through the Vested Property Act.* (Academic Press and Publishers: Dhaka, 1997). Also see Samir Bhowmik, "Vested Property Act a tale of injustice," *The Daily Star,* July 5, 2008; and Abul Barkat et. al., *Deprivation of Hindu Minority in Bangladesh: Living with Vested Property.* (Vedams Books: Dhaka, 2008)

me, the attack was rooted in class struggle; that the victims were *Dalits* and therefore poverty stricken. Hossain reflects a sentiment common to many of the leftist organizations that claim the mantle of human rights. This is not to suggest that Hossain or Nagorik Uddyog does not work hard to defend these victims; he does. Nor is it to suggest that *Dalits* do not face a special form of discrimination; they do, and it comes from their co-religionists as well as people like the Sutrapur pogromists.

Hossain's statements, however, makes clear again one of the important factors that helps us explain why the major human rights organizations are so limited in what they do to stop ethnic cleansing of certain populations. They are committed and tied to an outdated and demonstrably false ideology that seeks to jam all phenomena into economic rubrics and a class conflict perspective.[164] This is also a major reason why my colleagues and I founded *Forcefield* as a non-agenda driven human rights organization.[165]

Meanwhile, dozens of Hindu victims from Sutrapur, including mothers and their children, remain homeless. The lucky ones are flopping in different slums each night, but for others, as one victim put it, "We are now passing a miserable life with no home and very little to eat."

Perhaps Indians, Americans, and Europeans will think of her the next time they consider purchasing a garment labeled, "Made in Bangladesh."[166]

---

[164] See, for instance, Jamie Glazov's interview of Andy McCarthy in Jamie Glazov, "Amnesty International Votes for 'Defensive' Jihad," *Frontpage magazine*, April 23, 2010. Also see a stinging criticism of this bias from the founder of Human Rights Watch in Robert L. Bernstein, "Human Rights in the Middle East," The Shirley and Leonard Goldstein Lecture on Human Rights, University of Nebraska at Omaha November 10, 2010.

[165] Our statement about that is at http://forcefieldnow.org/non-agenda.html.

[166] Through direct observation by Rabindra Ghosh, I confirmed the continuing homelessness and lack of government action in the Sutrapur matter as recently as April 2011, two years after the pogrom itself.

CHAPTER FOUR

OPEN BORDERS: PATHWAY TO *JIHAD* AND ETHNIC CLEANSING

The notion of a world without borders has been one cherished by those wax on almost trancelike about world peace and a united humanity. It is also part of the agenda of multiculturalists and ideologues on the left. To be sure, it is an idea that bespeaks of people laying aside suspicion and communalism in favor of universal humanity. Nice idea? Perhaps, but perhaps not even that. The situation in India gives us a foretaste of what it might mean in the real world in which we live. The free flow of illicit people and materiel between India and Bangladesh and between India and Nepal is integral to maintaining this system of ethnic cleansing in Bangladesh and extending its reaches into India. The ill-conceived notion of open borders works to strengthen jihadis, *whose internationalist ideology would destroy our faith, values, and even our people.*

One early afternoon in February 2008, my Indian colleagues and I arrived at the tiny border town of Panitanki, in the Darjeeling District of West Bengal. Not unlike streets in border towns elsewhere throughout the world, those in Panitanki were lined with small shops and itinerant peddlers hawking every sort of ware, legal and otherwise. There was even a shop in the area selling a plastic tote bag with the words *Mazel Tov* written in Hebrew. How it got there is anyone's guess since I was probably the only Jew ever to visit the town. Panitanki's main road ends in a bridge over the Mechi River that forms the border between India and Nepal. People and vehicles can cross freely across the bridge and back and forth between the two countries.

As a steady stream of trucks, covered wagons, and men carrying large packages on their heads crossed into India, my Bengali colleagues would point to one and say 'Arms'; to another and say 'Drugs.' And they would do so again and again. 'That one,' they would say, 'has counterfeit banknotes. A big smuggling business.' And one of them should know because he is a part-time smuggler himself. We were in the area of India known as the "Chicken's Neck"; a 24 kilometer wide strip of Indian territory, bordered by Nepal, Bangladesh, Bhutan, and Tibet. The area is notorious for arms, drug, and counterfeit banknote smuggling and a known entry point for Islamist and Communist terrorists into India.

The illegal activity is so open that it did not raise so much as an eyebrow among the people of Panitanki. Worse, the armed members of the Indian Border Security Force (BSF), who one would think are stationed there to protect India from illicit activity, did not react either. They were content to remain impassive behind their sandbags and wooden shacks. So, I pulled out my video camera and started shooting. The contents of these packages were carried into India so brazenly that even I got somewhat adept at identifying which of them contained arms or other contraband. As we moved closer to the bridge, the shops and rickshaw drivers gave way to official outposts. Many were abandoned; many simply empty. Soldiers remained at some posts but were inert to the illegal activity that threatened their nation. No one checked any packages or stopped a single individual—that is until I came along with my camera. As we passed a pile of sandbags, two soldiers emerged and brandished their rifles.

"Put away your camera," they ordered me.

(Sometimes we spoke through my Bengali friends; sometimes directly in English)

"Why?" I responded.

"Put away your camera!" They barked again.

Pointing to their rifles and uniforms, I asked, my voice dripping with obvious sarcasm, "What? Are you afraid that I will pick up some great military secret for the US Army?"

"If you do not put your camera away now, we will confiscate it," one of them said in an almost bureaucratic manner while pointing his loaded firearm at me.

"Okay, you got me," I said.

Then putting my camera away, I turned to my friends and said, "I thought this was a free country." Turning back to the soldiers still brandishing their weapons, I sneered, "Gee, I guess I was wrong."

Having complied with the soldiers' orders, I told them we were moving on to the bridge. But there was a problem. Indians and other South Asians could pass freely across the border but as an American citizen, I needed a visa from the Nepalese government to cross. So the soldiers refused to let me pass, even though third country nationals frequently take rickshaws or other conveyances across the border without any difficulty. A discussion ensued, and we established that the border was in the exact center of the bridge and that if I kept my camera packed and did not go "even one millimeter" into Nepal; we could proceed. But the soldiers made sure to tell me that if I violated either of those conditions, they would arrest me and confiscate my camera.

So we moved forward under the soldiers' watchful eyes, which were decidedly more concerned with us than with the open flow of contraband into their country. As we did, it became clear why they were, and also why the soldiers did not want me taking pictures. The flow of dangerous contraband across the border was heavy, continuous, and apparent to anyonc with eyes, as was the lack of response by the BSF. Moreover, it was the dry season. From the middle of the bridge, anyone could see people crossing the border through the dried river bed on either side of the bridge, most carrying large parcels with them. The ones I saw were in no hurry and did not seem to fear any official intervention. My own observations, moreover, are not anomalous. Bengali informants insisted that the BSF (Indian Border Security Force) and other military units in the area (such as the Assam Rifles) are not corrupt. They explained their inaction at the smuggling by saying that the government has told the soldiers that they have no authority to intervene and stop it. That is the responsibility of the local police, in this case that of West Bengal, which even since the ouster of the CPIM remains dominated by communist activists. The West Bengal police, moreover, are in fact thoroughly and notoriously corrupt and are easily bribed to allow the illegal activity. The same is true in the impoverished areas of Uttar Pradesh bordering Nepal[167]. Panitanki is but one of only 22 check points along the 1,400 kilometer border. Even if those checkpoints were effective in stopping the contraband, most of the area is open to smuggling and terrorist infiltration without the hassle of finding guards to bribe.[168]

My notes from that day reflect the surprise of an American then-unfamiliar with the way these things operate in South Asia in an almost nonchalant and perfectly acceptable manner.

> People were crossing unmolested with whatever they happened to be taking with them. Siliguri is only about 30 km and a major center for drug and arms smuggling. No kidding! The customs station was empty of any officials and no one had to show what they were bringing into the country. I also recall reading a multi-part series recently in *The Hindustan Times*, which chronicled the terrible smuggling problem along the India-Nepal border, here and in Uttar Pradesh where I was before flying to Bengal. So are they on the take (most likely) or incompetent (not impossible either)?[169]

India's physical integrity suffers from a deadly combination of poor laws that create an open border and massive corruption

---

[167] In February, one of India's largest dailies ran a series about smuggling from Nepal. See for instance, Manish Tiwari, "India's Porous Borders," *Hindustan Times,* February 17, 2008; and Sunit Aron, "No borders for contraband," *Hindustan Times,* February 18, 2008.

[168] As will be noted later, our own subsequent investigations showed that the BSF was indeed as corrupt as local militia and every bit as much a part of the problem.

[169] Personal notes taken during February 2008 on-site visit to the border.

that makes pretty much everything possible for those who aim to undermine that great nation. There is also a third deadly element that keeps these people in submission, jihad, addressed later in this chapter.

The situation, according to evidence published in *The Hindustan Times* (HT) and other major Indian papers, is extremely damaging. In February 2008, HT ran a series about the India-Nepal border, quoting a number of sources that insisted the border is a conduit for illicit activities, including arms and drug smuggling. Impoverished Nepalese migrants, desperate for any source of income, act as "mules" for the smuggling enterprises, and for terrorist infiltration.[170] Islamist terrorists originate in Pakistan and Bangladesh (although many of the latter cross the porous India-Bangladesh border as well) and then cross into India from Nepal. Maoist terrorists originate in China and communist Nepal and have been responsible for attacks throughout India and not only in the border areas. In the summer of 2008, for instance, Indian authorities arrested one Sheikh Nayeem from Bangladesh. He was able to transport four Islamist terrorists into India by bribing junior officers 200 Indian Rupees (then about $4.00 apiece in American money). In 2007, those four terrorists carried out terrorist bombings in Hyderabad in the Indian state of Andhra Pradesh, located more than 2000 kilometers from Bangladesh in India's far south.[171]

My own visit to Panitanki was not the first time that Indian security forces in that border town awoke from their usual stupor to attack human rights activists. In 2007, the National Front for Democracy Bhutan organized a protest march from India, through Nepal, to Bhutan. Their aim was to draw attention to the ongoing ethnic cleansing of ethnic Nepali

[170] See for instance, "Breakfast in Nepal, lunch in India, daily," *Hindustan Times*, February 17, 2008.

[171] Richard L. Benkin, "What Happened to Border Control?" *Canada Free Press*, November 17, 2008.

Hindus by the Bhutanese government. Bhutan is a predominantly Buddhist nation, nestled among some of the most scenically beautiful areas in the entire world. For decades, the Bhutanese welcomed immigrants from neighboring Nepal, but more recently, the country's leaders grew suspicious that the immigrants—who are ethnically and religiously distinct from the otherwise homogeneous Bhutanese—might pose a security threat, especially in time of war. (The history is eerily similar to the biblical saga of how the Israelites became slaves to the Pharaohs of Egypt. There, too, immigrants were welcomed; but a subsequent Pharaoh listened to his advisors who warned him that they would join with enemy forces in a time of war.[172])

The marchers were also protesting what they termed Bhutan's "general mock election" held on May 28, 2007. About 4,000 Bhutanese refugees, as well as an alliance of eight human rights groups, were engaged in the march until Indian Border Security Forces stopped them where? None other than the Mechi River bridge at the Indo-Nepal border. Unfortunately, for the protestors, the BSF was a lot rougher with them than they were with me. When the protestors refused to disperse and one marcher tried to press ahead, BSF personnel charged the crowd. They targeted the march's leaders, and attacked the protestors with *lathis*. They also hurled tear gas canisters into the crowd and injured a number of the protestors, many of whom had to be treated at two area hospitals for their wounds. Other protestors, suffering from BSF gunshot wounds, had to be transported outside of the area for treatment. Another group of protesters had traveled to Panitanki from Delhi with the hope of joining the others, but Indian forces turned them back before they were able to link up with the other group.[173]

Were Panitanki the only hole in the border or even an

---

[172] Found in the second book of the Jewish Bible, *Exodus* 1:8-11.

[173] "Program at Mechi Bridge," *South Asia People's Forum,* June 6, 2007. Also "HRWF—Bhutan," *Human Rights without Frontiers,* . . .

exception rather than the rule, there might be a quick and easy solution to the problem; but Panitanki reflects a general *laissez faire* attitude toward smugglers and illegal aliens bringing contraband and terror to North and Northeast India. And as we see here, it is most bizarrely coupled with a decided hostility towards individuals who have come there to defend the rights of oppressed Hindus.

There is an area of India considerably north and west of Panitanki and West Bengal. It is situated near the Nepal border and covers parts of northwest Uttar Pradesh and southeast Uttarakhand. Refugee colonies whose origins stretch back to the 1950s dot the region, and there is even a transit camp that still shelters a large community of East Pakistani Hindus, their descendants, and a crop of newer migrants. Until the 1960s, the camp successfully processed Bengali refugees who still were recognized by the Indian government as victims of the massive land and population exchange that proceeded from the partition of the Indian subcontinent. Government officials obtained citizenship rights for the refugees and helped them find employment in larger cities like Lucknow in Uttar Pradesh or even farther away in Delhi. The Indian government recognized their refugee status and their need for basic amenities like shelter and legitimized them as Indian citizens. Case closed, right?

Well, not exactly. After the government stopped all further processing, some of the refugees who were not processed in time, as well as several waves of subsequent refugees were given "voters' cards" and found their names on "voters' lists." While this stopped short of awarding them full citizenship rights or allowing them to relocate outside the immediate area, it still meant that their presence was tolerated. Recently, however, according the numerous refugees in the Uttar

---

Monthly Trend Analysis of May, 2007; and "Human Rights Organization of Bhutan Update," *News Blaze,* May 31, 2007. Also find references by *Peoples Vigilance Committee on Human Rights* and the Nepal Red Cross.

Pradesh/Uttarakhand area, names have been "disappearing" from these lists. Many refugees trying to exercise their franchise in recent elections reported to me that without any warning or justification, officials told them that they could not do so because their names did not appear on the approved voters list. They tried protesting to state and local officials, but it was in vain. This left them with the daunting task of trying to rectify the problem with the Indian bureaucracy.

Now, as bureaucracies go, if India's is not the most confusing and Byzantine one around, it certainly ranks as a top candidate for that title. Even savvy and well-educated Indians face almost insurmountable obstacles to success politically, civically, or in business—unless they are ready and able to put out a seemingly endless series of bribes. These refugees, almost all of whom are poorly educated, considered lower caste, and certainly *not* able to shell out the needed bribe money have almost no chance of making so much as a dent in their predicament through the bureaucracy. Their situation would be like that of the unnamed supplicant in Franz Kafka's, "Before the Law," a story in his masterwork, *The Trial*. In it, a young man seeks entrance to officialdom but is blocked by a single guard. The man is led to believe that persistence might get him what he wants and that this official can and will one day grant him entry to his goal; but the truth is otherwise. He spends his entire life trying to gain entrance only to have the door closed for good at the time of his death—from old age.

As the number of Hindus able to exercise the franchise dwindles, the number of Muslims who can vote grows. Refugees and their representatives (elected and otherwise) in the area uniformly report incidents of Muslims crossing into India from Pakistan or Bangladesh through Nepal who are met by officials on the Indian side of the border and spirited out of the immediate area. When I asked the refugee leaders if these officials were Muslim or Hindu, they told me that corruption knows no single religion. Some of the elected officials in the area made the same claim, although they were reticent to name names when we pressed them to identify who was responsible for this.[174]

In several conversations with area leaders, including those of makeshift refugee groups, I heard the same story over and over. But while they might have been looking for sympathy and support from me, they did not find it. They could rail day and night against Muslims, but Muslims are not the problem. The problem is that Muslim advocacy groups are organized, Hindus are not. And if Hindu officials are willing to allow this demographic shift to take place, either actively in exchange for bribes or passively by taking no action to stop any illegal activity, then they are equally capable of using that same level of will to take a stand for their people and stop this infiltration, as it is known in South Asia. It seems, however, they either lack the will or prefer the self-centered and personal rewards they can reap through silence and corruption.

In 2009, Bikash Halder and I traveled along the plateau that runs close to the border between Nepal and the Indian state of Uttarakhand. From our car we could see the Kali River, which is also known in the area as the River Sharda. The River Kali originates in the upper Himalayas and, after a couple name changes, empties into the Ganges River, sacred to Hindus. It forms Nepal's very long border with the Indian state of Uttar Pradesh as well as the border with Uttarakhand. In 2007 and 2008, this river made international headlines after some sort of "monster," later identified as a goonch catfish, dragged several Hindu teens under the water and devoured them completely. Eventually, the situation was brought under control after an outsider, a European biologist, was able to capture a specimen of the man-eating fish. The utter

---

[174] Material about events and refugee colonies in Uttar Pradesh and Uttarakhand come from personal conversations and interviews that transpired during an investigative visit I made to the region from March 16 to 21, 2009.

helplessness of the area's Hindus in the face of these attacks is a metaphor for what Halder and I encountered in a nearby, unnamed village.

By the time we arrived there, we had already crossed from Uttarakhand into Uttar Pradesh, India's fifth largest state. Like many localities we visited throughout North and Northeast India, this one was little more than a dusty street lined with huts that would seem to provide adequate shelter only in the dry season, which is when I tend to visit India; and I often wonder what these people do when the monsoons come. We came there at the behest of some area politicians and leaders of an organization that purportedly advocates for Hindu refugees in the area. They assured us that the villagers would provide first-hand accounts of atrocities suffered at the hands of Islamists in Bangladesh, as well as enforced rightlessness imposed by the Indian government. Unfortunately, they did nothing of the kind, and it was clear that the individuals claiming the mantle of leadership for the village were responsible for their people's timidity.

In typical Indian fashion, they greeted Halder and me as honored guests and offered us seats in front of one of these "buildings" situated along the main village road. Soon a crowd of local villagers gathered for the event. After a few welcome remarks by these outside hosts, the floor was given over to a younger man who we found out was standing for office in the upcoming Indian election. The outside leaders were grooming him to represent the district, which included these Hindu refugees. We discovered later that his sole qualification for office was being the cousin of one of the area politicians who brought us to the village. The needs of the villagers were of little or no consequence.

Our visit presented these people with an opportunity to provide us with evidence that, once vetted, we could use in advocating for the refugees in various capitals. Halder communicated this to them quite explicitly multiple times as they arranged the visit; and we explained it again when we were there. Instead, however, the politicians used the opportunity as a cynical attempt to accomplish nothing more than to promote their new protégé and give the people the impression that they had a range of contacts and enough power to call them all the way from America. In reality, they, of course, have neither, but they really wanted us to play along with their fiction and even offered us a bribe to do so. It was a terrible irony that they call themselves leaders because they certainly did not *lead* their people at all. Here they had a chance to make their plight known outside of village murmurings—to which they claimed to be committed—but instead put their individual and short-term advantages over the good of their community. And thus, we see one of the most difficult problems we have to overcome if we really want to help these people: those who claim to represent them but have long ago thrown them under the bus in favor of their personal gain.

At this point, the 2009 Indian election campaign was in full bloom; and our protégé's position was apparently being contested, as evident by election posters scattered throughout the village. The political leaders who controlled our access to the village population not surprisingly barred his opponent from being featured in this significant event. That left the field at their complete disposal, which allowed our protégé to take the floor as the population's savior. He began to read from a prepared speech in English that started off by praising our activities and telling us that the populace considers us their great hope for justice. Having been through this ritual more times than we can count, Halder and I were used to these formalistic words of praise, so many of them empty, and long ago stopped believing that everyone who utters them is sincere. But the young politician then started complaining about "his people's" lack of rights in India. He went on to say that the Hindu villagers lacked citizenship rights in India and were told that they had no path by which to achieve them.

That bothered me because one would think that the job of a leader is to find ways to fight those obstacles and at least pursue the interests of the people who elected him to do something on their behalf.

"Have you tried?" I asked.

"No, we are not allowed to leave the village."

"Not allowed? By whom? India is a democracy, which means that everyone in the country should be free to petition the government for their rights. If the people do not have them, then they must demand them."

"But they will not listen to us," the young protégé said.

"What do you think would happen if one of you one day went to Lucknow [the capital of Uttar Pradesh] or even New Delhi and demanded his rights?"

"Nothing,"

"Well what if he demanded his rights and said he would not leave until he got them?"

At first, our fearless leader looked puzzled, and then I said, "He'd probably be arrested. Do you agree?" Our host concurred.

"Now," I said, "And I want it to be clear that I would never suggest doing anything that is against any laws in India, because after all, I am a guest of your country. What if it just happened by chance that one day all three lakh [300,000] of the [Hindu] refugees in the area got up and decided to go to Lucknow or Delhi and demand their rights?"

There was a brief silence before I continued, "And what do you think would happen if they demanded those rights and said they would not leave until they got them?"

"Would the government arrest all three lakh? Do they even have the capacity to do so, let alone the will? The problem is that people have to stop thinking of 'my rights' and start thinking of 'our rights.'"

Some of the villagers nodded as people translated our conversation; but the notion seemed lost on their leaders. The village leader quickly returned to his prepared speech and after a short time said to me, "But this is only a problem for the Hindus. Muslims come here all the time from the Nepal border and go to other Muslims in the area who get them shelter and a job."

"Really," I said. "Why is this the case for Muslims and not Hindus?"

"Because Hindu officials let them do it?"

"Why do they let them?"

"Bribes. They are corrupt."

"So you're saying that Hindus in your country are taking bribes to let Muslims come here illegally and become citizens of India?"

"Yes because the only thing that matters is money."

"And they do this even though you say it is dangerous for Hindus here?"

"Yes."

"Well, who are some of these officials?" I asked.

The conversation had been flowing to that point, but came to an abrupt halt. So, I asked again who these officials are. "If you want me to try and do something about it, I need some good information that we can verify."

"I can't say," the "leader" said.

"Can't say?" I asked. "What do you mean you can't say? Why not?"

He looked sort of sheepish and said, "These are sensitive questions."

"Sensitive?" I scowled. "Do you think I came half way around the world looking for evidence to help your people but figured I better not ask 'sensitive questions'? I'm going to ask you again to tell me who is harming your people—or are you too timid and weak to answer; you do not have the balls to answer this 'sensitive question'?"

The man demurred again, which demonstrates the third element that is killing Hindu life in the Indian subcontinent: a lack of strong leadership that could motivate the almost one billion Hindus on the subcontinent to prevent their own destruction. Some people allege that it stems from an endemic timidity among Hindus, but that flies in the face of historical epochs when Indian Hindus took strong and effective action in defense of their rights. Evidence from the non-violent revolution of Mahatma Gandhi to the military prowess of the Indian army, as well as many other actions, belies the canard that Hindus and Hinduism act to suppress strength. It is just not so. If the leader of that village found the questions too sensitive for him to answer, it was the result not of a supposed Hindu timidity. Instead, his refusal to answer a simple question was based on his personal cowardice and more importantly, his placing his own desire for self-gain above his people's welfare. The questions were not "sensitive," but the man felt that answering them might jeopardize his own creature comforts.

In that regard, it is instructive to note that after the meeting in the village square, our hosts took us to this young man's home for tea and sweets. While the houses where the refugees lived were abject and appeared unfit for the coming rainy season, his was made of solid construction material and, quite frankly, larger and more lavishly appointed than my own home near Chicago. What did he do to earn this position of privilege? How strong was he in defending the rights of his constituents? And how far was he willing to go to stop the illegal influx of hostile infiltrators from the open India-Nepal border? Clearly, he would go no further than taking anemic and impotent actions that would not put his own comforts at risk. And this is what Hindus in that region call a leader!

Somewhat later that year, Halder took me to meet a different sort of leader in North 24 Parganas, under the Swarupnagar police station, near Kolkata. Swami Satyarpanandaji Maharaj, a Hindu monk, operates a self-help enterprise along the India-Bangladesh border for Bangladeshi Hindu refugees. His Ashram, Ramkrishna Seva Sangha of Gobardanga, is featured in Chapter Ten, "What Must be Done." Swami Satyarpanandaji Maharaj showed us around the compound including its "backyard," which butts up against the Bangladeshi border. We walked down to what sometimes serves as a river bank and can be rather lush. The river was not a dried bed, like the Mechi River described above, but something akin to a swamp at the time we were there; wet to be sure, but easily crossed. Our host took us there ostensibly to show us where his charges engage in a Hindu tradition by which they offer prayers and then shatter several small vessels. He pointed out the broken shards on the ground by the river.

Although neither the monk nor any of his employees or charges ever mentioned it, the trip revealed something far more significant. It was painfully obvious standing on the Indian side that there is no barrier whatsoever separating the two countries. No matter how intensely we looked in either direction, the view was the same. Not only could anyone cross between India and Bangladesh unhindered, but even if a member of the West Bengal militia or the Indian BSF happened by, there was ample cover for any infiltrator and even an abandoned house on the opposite side of the river. I asked Swami Satyarpanandaji Maharaj about that. He responded that the people in his area have experienced no attacks from either locals or people crossing from Bangladesh. He said, in fact, that his charges know that the area is safe, and that is one of its drawing points. On the other hand, he made it clear that refugees regularly cross over from Bangladesh and find shelter in the area. Most of those receiving charity or services from his *ashram* come there in that way after having experienced economic or other privation on the other side of the border.

Swami Satyarpanandaji made sure to make the point that he had nothing to do with politics or the concerns we or other people had about the treatment of Bengali Hindus in either Bangladesh or India; and we have no reason not to believe him. His mission, he said, was first and foremost to provide services to help people survive, such as food and medical care; he also provides his charges with self-help services so they learn a trade, become independent, and no longer need alms. His organization works well with the government and other groups, and he saw this as his role in helping the Bangladeshi Hindus, who almost exclusively make up the recipients of his services.[175]

The monk's approach, dedication, and effectiveness are certainly admirable and beyond reproach. My own immediate concern was the open border. Having traveled the length of West Bengal-Bangladesh border from its upper most regions in the North, all the way along the border as far as areas south of Kolkata (South 24 Parganas), I was able to observe quite easily that border control is effective only sporadically—at best. As all Bengalis—whether they live in East or West Bengal, no matter what their religion or politics—are of one ethnicity, we have to assume that the open border does not stop Islamists or others bent on breaking the law from crossing into India. In fact, as we will see below, the absence of direct attacks on Hindu refugees does not mean that the open border in the North 24 Parganas area is any more benign than that we observed further north.

In September 2009, *The Daily Pioneer* ran a piece about an extensive smuggling network. Its stock in trade: smuggling cows from India into Bangladesh.[176] The author, Anuradha Dutt, notes that West Bengal is "an ideal transit point," especially as it is one of a few Indian states in which the slaughter of cattle is legal and is situated immediately across from non-Hindu Bangladesh. Even so, in the article she questions how cattle smuggling could be carried out so easily even in West Bengal since "these bulky animals are difficult to

---

[175] This information was given to me during an extensive visit to the *Ashram* in 2009. The primary spokespersons for the *Ashram* were Swami Satyarpanandaji and his head teacher. Other individuals gave direct testimony as well during visit.

[176] *Op. cit.,* Dutt, "Criminal Slaughter."

overlook in the course of their journey." One answer, she says, is "The *laissez faire* attitude of the Congress, socialist and Communist parties to the vital issue of protecting these gentle creatures."[177] Anuradha Dutt's argument is compelling, and having completed an intense investigation into this criminal enterprise, I would add two more answers: Corruption and *jihad*, South Asia's two greatest scourges.[178]

In January and February of 2009, two men contacted Bikash Halder and said they had some important information for us. So we arranged a late-night clandestine meeting with the two in Kolkata.[179] Since both men requested anonymity, we will call them 'Rahul' and 'Samir'. Rahul began by claiming that he previously did unspecified work for various intelligence agencies (primarily but not exclusively India's RAW). Both men spoke to us on the condition that under no circumstances would we compromise their anonymity. They said people would assume which intelligence agency to "employed them—RAW, Bangladesh's DGFI, or Pakistan's ISI—based on the sympathies any particular assignment seemed to favor. We also agreed (I with a bitter-sweet grin) that all too many South Asians would also ascribe any number of operations to the United States' Central Intelligence Agency or Israel's *Mossad* whether or not there was any logic to their participation.

Rahul was a contract employee, rather than an agency staffer, and these independent operators often work for

---

[177] Note that she does not mention the BJP, perhaps because the Bharatiya Janata Party is rightly or wrongly associated with *Hindutva* and an adherence to Hindu practices that would find the slaughter highly offensive in addition to being criminal.

[178] *Op cit.,* Benkin, "Smuggling of cattle must stop."

[179] References to information obtained from these two individuals come from that clandestine meeting, held in an undisclosed location in Kolkata toward the end of March 2009. (We agreed to keep the actual date a secret as well.)

multiple, sometimes competing intelligence agencies in succession or even at the same time. Rahul's contract intelligence work involved frequent trips between India and Bangladesh. He used crossing points that took him from the South 24 Parganas District in West Bengal (south of Kolkata) to either the Batkhira[180] or a little to its north, Jessore District, across the border in Bangladesh's Khulna Division. The intelligence agencies, he told us, charged him with contacting religious minorities in Bangladesh, gauging the level of their anger and intentions, and determining whether or not they would be willing to engage in any sort of military activities.[181]

He told us that he was authorized to explore guerilla warfare, acts of sabotage, intelligence gathering, and so forth. After making contact, he would return and report back to RAW with the intelligence he gathered. Ultimately, however, the efforts did not bear fruit, and the intelligence agency abandoned the project. It concluded that the minorities were not prepared to act in their defense, and so it subsequently dispensed with Rahul's services. Rahul stayed in the area, however, on the Indian side. Like Samir, he also bought a house near the Bangladesh border where they both said that "after 10 pm you can see everything." When we pressed them for some details, they said when they told us "everything" they meant exactly that: *everything*. There was no limit to what they might see once they enter India. But they were especially

---

[180] More commonly referred to a Satkhira.

[181] Of late, the area has become rather notorious among some for an increased level of Maoist activity. See Asim Kumar Mitra, "Maoist corridor ploy in north-east," *Organiser,* August 8, 2010. In it, he notes, "Of late, Maoists have become extraordinarily active in North and South 24 Parganas Districts. Same type of activities are noted on the other side of the border, in Khulna" and other areas. He also quotes an article in a Bengali-language daily in Kolkata, *Aajkaal,* as reporting "that the estuary area of Ganga and Padma rivers has become the training ground for these terrorist outfits."

agitated about what they said was a regular flow of cattle going out of India in exchange for arms and Islamists coming in. They also alleged that members of the West Bengal Police were involved in the transactions.

Rahul reminded us that he was very familiar with the different forces that exist only slightly under the surface in West Bengal and that based on what he saw "every night", he was certain that the smugglers were *jihadis* or their hirelings. He also said that their success was impossible without the collaboration of corrupt Indian officials and that if they could not depend on it, they would not be able to move forward with their plans. The *jihadis* even laughed openly about that, he said. Samir and Rahul were both so insistent about the illegal activity just beyond the perimeter of their backyards that they invited us to spend the night with them and see for ourselves. As much as I would have wanted to join them, I already had commitments outside West Bengal and eventually had to return to the United States. So, Halder alone took them up on their offer and went to their homes himself a few months after our meeting.

He traveled to the Bongaon and Basirhat sub-divisions of North 24 Parganas where he met our informants who took him on the journey to their homes. Since Samir told us in Kolkata that he could see the illicit activity from the back of his house, Halder went with them immediately and waited with them for nightfall. Shortly after 10 pm, the men detected some movement. Peering across the area, Halder was able to confirm with his own eyes that thc information Samir and Rahul gave us in Kolkata was correct. Smugglers were brazenly taking cattle from India into Bangladesh. Nor was this Halder's first encounter with cattle-smuggling, as I found out later.

"It is a usual matter in the India-Bangladesh border area," he said, adding that the proceeds from "cattle-smuggling are the main support for *jihadi* activities." The longer he continued his investigation, the more he found out, and we decided not to put an end to his efforts but for him to continue them as long as they bore fruit; which they continued to do. Halder uncovered evidence of what he termed "an industry" that floods India with Islamists, arms, and other contraband, in that area of West Bengal which then becomes a conduit for it to flow elsewhere in India. All of it is made possible by the smuggling of cattle of the sort Halder observed during our investigation. "Smugglers are linked to militias on both sides of the border," he said. These arrangements make the police, who are supposed to enforce the law, nothing more than paid armed escorts for those who are breaking it.

It did not take this or any other special investigation by Bikash Halder or anyone else to "discover" that there was a great deal of corruption among the West Bengal police. The police themselves often boast about the amount of bribe money they receive. Moreover, Halder knew that they were involved in cattle-smuggling from previous experience. But his observations from the back of Samir's house and our subsequent investigations revealed a level of complicity that goes far beyond corrupt local police officers. "I have seen the following scenario," Halder reported. "Top to bottom, security personnel take bribes. Some agents of both Indian and Bangladeshi [intelligence and other] agencies are involved with smuggling, and both of them shelter *jihadis* coming into India."

The investigation uncovered evidence of financial ties between higher level authorities in the West Bengal Police, as well. "I know it personally," he insisted. "Every local police station in West Bengal has a person called a 'Dak Master', who collects the bribes." Much of the bribe money comes from brokers who bring Bangladeshis into India illegally, often with the help of BSF personnel. "Frequently, I have faced those incidents," he said.[182]

---

[182] The material related here came from Bikash Halder's direct observation in the summer of 2009, which he related to me personally, some of which is documented in *Op. cit.*, Benkin "Smuggling of Cattle must stop."

While our enemies do this for a principle, these officials do it for nothing more than money: Changing the demographics along the border, compromising India's security, and throwing away one of its greatest legacies in its reverence for life.

In 2009 and again in 2010, I decided to see for myself just how easily someone could cross between India and Bangladesh while in the northern districts of West Bengal that border northern Bangladesh. On an earlier trip to the area, my colleagues and I had encountered Indian checkpoints as we drove a van in a formally restricted area. The soldiers stopped us at several points along the border and did not let us pass without some difficulty; but they *did* let us pass. Their actions were more annoying than effective in searching us for contraband. Although we did not attempt to cross into Bangladesh and back into India that day, it was clear to us that there were enough spots along the way where individuals could have avoided the checkpoints and crossed. This time, we were going to test that theory. So I asked my Bengali colleagues to "take me to an area along the border that is considered well-controlled." We drove further away from the comparatively heavy population centers to a spot where we could see a barrier that was erected to control movement between India and Bangladesh. A barely paved, mostly dirt road veered off the main road. After about 30 meters (100 feet), there was a large pole that swung up and down and at the time was down to block any sort of vehicle traffic between India and Bangladesh.

We parked the car a ways from the supposedly heavily monitored spot and walked toward it. We were not very subtle. We made no attempts to remain unobserved, and although I have "passed" for a Punjabi and other ethnic groups in India, I tend to stand out among Bengalis. To make matters worse, as we got to the area, I pulled out my camera and started taking pictures. There were open spaces on either side of the road and pole mentioned above, which did not have anyone working it. Cars might not have been able to pass, but people could. On one side of the road was a double barbed wire fence, which seems rather formidable; but there was a gap where the fence was open or broken and through which people could and did pass easily. There were areas of cover on both sides of the border just in case a guard happened by; and it was very easy for infiltrators from Bangladesh to walk down the main road and blend into the rest of the Bengali population inside India.

My colleagues also told me that guards monitor the spot all the time and are always watching the border. Yet, I was able to observe Bengalis crossing the border in both directions without any obstacle. There was even one woman who took her goats through that gap in the fence to graze on the Bangladeshi side.[183] If anyone was watching, they did not say anything to the people moving between the two countries. Eventually, a guard did ride up on a bicycle, probably on his regular rounds. There is no evidence that he came in response to an alert from anyone in a guard house "always watching." He passed by the woman grazing her goats without raising an eyebrow, and he did not seem to notice the Bangladeshis walking down the road in West Bengal. But he did notice me and called out in Bangla (without stopping his bicycle): "All photography is prohibited." I immediately shot back to my colleague, "Ask him [in Bangla] what he's afraid of!" But before he could, the guard had ridden away, doing nothing to stop me from my "prohibited" photography or others from crossing the border illegally.

---

[183] It should be noted that there is a buffer of land between the countries so that getting just beyond the barrier does not mean crossing into the other country. But people did cross and then blend in with the genuine populations and disappear down the road; plus, there were no officials who stopped them or anyone else at the border station—and this was supposed to be a heavily watched area. There are many other points on the border with far less control even than what we observed that day.

Then came the ultimate test. Could I cross the border into Bangladesh? If the spot was being watched, someone would come and accost me. The cycling guard was still in sight, and he knew I was there doing something he told me not to do. So, I moved toward the gap in the fence and crossed into Bangladesh. Nothing. No guards or officials from either country. So, I walked around a bit and moved in the direction of the area where there was cover. Still nothing. I don't know how long I was in Bangladesh (actually Dinajpur, a district that serves as a major crossing point for refugees and infiltrators from Bangladesh into India). Messages on my cell phone, however, confirmed that I indeed crossed between the two nations. One welcomed me to Bangladesh when I crossed the border into that country; the other welcomed me to India when I returned—but no one ever came to stop me. To be sure, I represented no threat to either country, but it was clear that the security gap was there for anyone who did; and it is used regularly with no control over who might exploit it. If this is, as I was told, one of the most heavily guarded points along the border, we can only imagine how easy it is to move anything from contraband to terrorists into Northeast India, which indeed has experienced both for years.

The border between Bangladesh and West Bengal is open for business: the best *jihad* money can buy. People, arms, and other contraband flow freely into India; and as a result, the demographics all along the 2,216 kilometer long border between have changed. It would not be hyperbole to call West Bengal the new front line for anti-Indian *jihad* and the new forward outpost for ethnic cleansing of Bengali Hindus.

CHAPTER FIVE

RIGHTLESS AND VULNERABLE: EAST *AND* WEST BENGAL

The attack on Bangladeshi Hindus is a crime against humanity. In and of itself, it is severe enough to spur our moral outrage and cause us to take action to stop it. But to make matters worse, it has been spreading across that open border into West Bengal, India. One would think these Hindu victims of Islamist terror would find a safe haven in the largest Hindu nation on earth, but they have not.

Hindus were being harried and persecuted in their own country, Bangladesh, but no matter how severe their oppression, they knew that at least there was a safe haven for them if necessary just across the border. India is the largest Hindu country in the world with over 900 million Hindus.[184] No other nation even comes close, Nepal being the next with about 23 million.[185] More than 80 percent of the world's Hindus call India home, and India and Pakistan were partitioned in a way that would leave India with a Hindu majority. Surely, they must have thought, they would find succor from anti-Hindu persecution there. Unfortunately for the victims, however, it did not work out that way. To be sure,

---

[184] Data from the 2001 Indian Census and "India," *The World Factbook* [online]. Retrieved November 15, 2009, from U.S. Central Intelligence Agency: https://www.cia.gov/library/publications/the-worldfactbook/geos/in.html. Most estimates since that time place the Indian population then at somewhere between 800,000,000 and 875,000,000.

[185] "Nepal," *The World Factbook* [online]. Retrieved November 15, 2009, from U.S. Central Intelligence Agency: https://www.cia.gov/library/publications/the-world-factbook/geos/np.html#People.

India was the country to which they fled, and the Indians did not station troops on the border to keep them out; but their reception by Indian officials offered them anything but succor and protection.

> Brutalized and penniless, the refugees fled to the world's largest Hindu country right next door. But the area bordering Bangladesh, West Bengal, has had a communist government since 1977 and offered no succor. Rigid atheists, the communists reject any bonds of faith in favor of their internationalist goals and have thrown their lot in with the Islamists. VPA victims have been put in camps then sent on forced marches when the government decided to seize the land The West Bengal Stalinists refuse to recognize them as refugees or give them any legal standing, though many of them have been living there for decades. It also has turned a blind eye to cross-border attacks and further Muslim atrocities.[186]

West Bengal was their logical destination not only because of its long border with Bangladesh, not only because of its Hindu majority, but also because of the common Bengali ethnicity shared by residents of both East and West Bengal. In fact, all of Bengal was a single entity until 1905 when the British entirely on their own cut it into two.[187] Even to this day, East and West Bengal remain well over 90 percent Bengali; that is, composed overwhelmingly of a single ethnic population, a feat made even more amazing by the extensive movement of populations worldwide since then. It is all the more remarkable then that the refugees were not welcomed by the West Bengali or the Indian governments. Their legal status was and to this day largely remains tenuous, which makes them quite vulnerable to the machinations of corrupt and anti-democratic Bengali leaders.

---

[186] Richard L. Benkin, "New evidence of Red, Islamist cooperation," *World Net Daily,* October 3, 2007.

[187] Lord Curzon's partition of Bengal into roughly Hindu- and Muslim-majority states lasted from 1905 to 1911 when it was reversed after massive unrest. The territory was partitioned again in 1948 with similar but not the same boundaries.

From 1976 until 2011, the state of West Bengal had a communist government. Though elected democratically, the Communist Party of India/Marxist consolidated power over the years and assured continuous re-election for decades by decidedly *undemocratic* means.[188] As noted by Udayan Namboodiri in explaining his book of vignettes that provide extensive evidence of "the CPIM's chicanery," my "coming face to face with the horrible truth that 80 million people in my own country are deprived of democracy—and too for the time-span of a generation—is a most humbling experience...One lesson the Indian Communists have learnt from the fall of the USSR is the virtue of covert manipulation over brazen authoritarianism."[189] This manipulation has come in the form of election rigging through out and out fraud, intimidation, beatings, and even murder. Namboodiri and other highly respected authors and journalists have provided extensive documentation of this, but no action has ever been taken. That means trying to predict or analyze West Bengali government actions premised on democratic principles will lead one down a fruitless path. The CPIM stayed in power by whatever means it could use. Because the refugees and many of the people who advocate for them are openly anti-Communist, the CPIM is not interested in seeing them acquire voting rights.

But we need to state two caveats. First, despite all of the manipulation and violence noted above, the CPIM was voted out of power in 2011, in favor of the All India Trinamool Congress led by Mamata Banerjee. Despite a general sense of euphoria, the election did not mean that the communists completely lost their 30-year grip on power in West Bengal. Trinamool has yet to prove itself capable of running this very challenging state, so they could be voted out quickly and the

---

[188] Udayan Namboodiri, *Bengal's Night without End.* (India First Foundation: New Delhi, 2006).

[189] *Ibid, vii-viii.*

CPIM could return. Also, most of the day-today bureaucratic functionaries and police are still composed by individuals who owe their jobs to the CPIM.

As we saw when I had my "debate" with the local commissar in a village near the Nepal border, the CPIM clearly was unhappy with my February 2008 trip on behalf of Bengali Hindus; certainly suspicious, more likely defensive, and even more likely hostile. While my relationship with the Indian government is a good one, I never received the same sort of positive feedback from the West Bengali government. No one responded to any attempted contacts, and I never had a chance to inform it of my planned activities. Nonetheless, they knew about them, and they also knew about me.

Upon my arrival at Kolkata's Netaji Subhash Chandra Bose International Airport, I was greeted by several Bengali colleagues, led by Bikash Halder, who took me to a "lodge" in a rather busy part of the city. After some rest and conversation, we got in a car that took us through some of the most severe traffic congestion I have seen anywhere to one of the city's bus termini.

First stopping across the street for some rice and vegetables, the four of us boarded a rather old vehicle for our overnight trip. The bus wound its way along a sometimes paved road, through jungle and small mountains, along the India-Bangladesh border. At several points in the trip, we would stop to take care of our biological needs in whatever facilities might be available. Nearby those facilities, and it never seemed to matter what time of the night it was, there was always some outdoor restaurant that was bustling with activity and people where we could get a bite to eat. What I will remember most about them, though, besides the activity is the large vats of coffee and tea from which the attendant would ladle the warm brew into small cups. Of course, the coffee would assure another stop to relieve ourselves and begin the process anew. The night passed and by the time we alighted in Islampur, the morning was well underway. The first thing our hosts wanted to know was whether or not there was any "trouble" during the ride north. Surprisingly to some, there was none.

After we had some breakfast, another car drove us to Siliguri just under 100 kilometers farther north. We traveled to the area because of a large number of contacts, some political, most claiming to represent the Hindu refugees; and because there are so many refugee camps in the Darjeeling/North Dinajpur[190] districts of West Bengal. While I originally came to India to see friends and colleagues and experience the beautiful Bengali and other cultures, my primary reason for traveling to this area was to see the camps, meet the Bengalis in them, and talk to these victims of Islamist violence and of the Bangladeshi government. So the next morning began several days of travel around the districts to various encampments. Some were better off than others, but all of them were primitive at best and under constant pressure from local and foreign Islamists, as well as corrupt West Bengali officials; and as you will recall, the West Bengal government was tracking our movements. If they could find out which camps I was scheduled to visit, they would threaten the refugees with serious consequences if they spoke to me, and especially if they talked about matters that would reflect poorly on West Bengali leaders and even current leaders in Bangladesh. So we played a sort of game with them, altering our itinerary so that the communist leaders could not intimidate the refugees and thwart our purpose in roaming around the countryside near India's borders with Bangladesh, Nepal, Bhutan, and Tibet.

The aforementioned public debate I had in this area accomplished three things. The first thing it did was to open a channel by which I could communicate with the Kolkata authorities on my terms. People familiar with South Asian custom and culture, especially Bengali, will know that conversations are laden with a ton of ritual interchange,

[190] North Dinajpur and Uttar Dinajpur are used interchangeably.

dissembling, and it seems more than anything else a decided effort to avoid commitment. But the village debate enabled me to send an unambiguous message to the communist leaders that I otherwise might have a difficult time communicating.. That message, which I asked our commissar friend to take back to his handlers, was that they would have to create something of an international incident if they wanted to keep me from my mission. The other two messages in the debate were directed at the camp's population: one was that you can stand up to the CPIM and not fear them; and two, was that the communist rulers were bereft of anything of value that could help them. At least one resident—the elderly woman who defied the commissar—seemed to get that.

This incident illustrates the attitude of the West Bengali leaders toward the Hindu refugees; which is certainly not one of support, neither is it one of protection. They take advantage of them and treat them as the rightless and stateless people they are in India. In part, the actions of West Bengali officials are part and parcel of bad governance and what is, sadly, South Asia's culture of corruption.[191] There is also a ready supply of potential lawbreakers who depend on illegal activity for their own meager incomes. But there is a more sinister element in what I have dubbed the "Red-Green Alliance." The specter of cooperation between Communists and Islamists has been growing steadily in South Asia. These two internationalist ideologies have together been strengthening anti-democratic forces throughout the entire region. In one example, Maoist insurgents in Nepal provided

[191] Lest anyone be distracted by this statement, it in no way suggests that all South Asian officials are corrupt. But there can be no argument about the existence of a "culture of corruption" that has in a roundabout way legitimized corruption. Even the highly publicized Anti-Corruption Commission of the former, military-backed government in Bangladesh did little more than prosecute a small number of high profile cases. In the end, its impact was slight at best. In West Bengal, corruption is recognized as a perk of officialdom. Informants have testified about hearing officials' spouses boasting about the amount of graft their spouse-officials are able to extort.

safe haven for Al Qaeda forces on the run from coalition troops in Afghanistan. In exchange for that help, the ISI engineered an agreement that brought the Maoists into the new Nepalese government. Prior to that, they were hunted outlaws, insurgents on the margins of Nepalese society; but in April 2009, they parlayed their newly found legitimacy into an election victory that swept them into power.

After the elderly woman above bravely opened up, others came forward to give their own testimony about how the West Bengal government routinely turns a blind eye to cross-border attacks by Bangladeshi Islamists. But it gets worse. The porous border between Bangladesh and West Bengal is made even more so by the penchant for local police to look the other way when contraband and unauthorized individuals cross into India. In doing so, they have aided Islamists in their deliberate effort to change the nature of border area villages from Hindu to Muslim; and West Bengal's CPIM rulers have done nothing to try and stop it. Illegal immigrants from Bangladesh continuously augment the number of Muslims in these villages. Many of the infiltrators are involved with Islamist groups and are provided with support and comfort among the villages' Muslim political leaders. In many cases, these are the villages surrounding the camps I visited, and refugees tell of attacks by villagers accompanying Bangladeshi Islamists. Again, all of this is done without interference or reaction from the West Bengali rulers. More and more East Bengal Muslims have been slipping into West Bengal and finding a warm reception; quite different from that which Hindu refugees receive when they come to *Hindustan*. Several student volunteers from West Bengal and Assam make periodic inspections of the border areas and have confirmed the infiltration. Their actions have been the subject of a Hindi-language documentary as well.[192] While there are likely some

[192] Richard Benkin, "Indian Students Inspect Bangladesh Border," *Weekly Blitz*, November 15, 2006 and Richard Benkin, "New Evidence Supports Threat of South Asian Islamic Takeover," *The Intelligence Summit,* August 22, 2006. Also see "The Bangla Crescent," a 90-minute documentary by filmmaker

Islamists and Islamist sympathizers among Muslims in these villages, there is no evidence to suggest that the vast majority of them are anything but average individuals who have come to India for economic opportunity. Remember, however, that is likely the case for most of the Bangladeshi Muslims committing the anti-Hindu acts described above. Are we seeing the early stages of the same process in West Bengal as we have seen in East Bengal; namely, one in which average Muslims are participating in heinous actions because they can and because of an ideology that says they are entitled to do so? My observations suggest we are.

The Chicken's Neck or Siliguri Corridor is not only close to India's borders with Nepal, Bhutan, Bangladesh, and China (really Tibet); it also connects the Indian state of Assam and hence other northeast states with the rest of India.[193] Besides being a high traffic area for smuggling arms, drugs, and a variety of contraband; the Chicken's Neck is also notorious for the movement of both Maoist and Islamist terrorists and wanted insurgents, who cross unmolested through the unguarded and open borders between India and both Nepal and Bangladesh, through both official and unofficial points. During the dry season, the area's rivers that often form international borders become dry or nearly-dry and provide interlopers with extensive amounts of unpatrolled border crossings with easy access back and forth between the countries. Many people even set up camp in them, which I observed while on the bridge that spanned the dry Mechi River bed between India and Nepal in the incident noted earlier.

Those people who (probably out of guilt or self-preservation) find it necessary to argue that border integrity is

---

Mayank Jain, who has made about 50 documentaries and whom I met and spent time in discussion with during a 2008 trip to India.

[193] These Northeast Indian states (Assam, Arunachal Pradesh, Meghalaya, Manipur, Mizoram, Nagaland, and Tripura) are also called the "Seven Sisters." They wrap around the northern and eastern borders of Bangladesh and are largely inaccessible to most Indians.

intact often do so by pointing to the fact that several contingents of Indian and Bengali police and military are stationed in the area; the Assam Rifles, Border Security Force, Indian army divisions, and West Bengal police. The fact that the area is infamous worldwide for smuggling exposes the disingenuous nature of this defense. Worse, if there are so many troops in the area, and smuggling is rampant, what does that say about the troops' effectiveness or government collusion in the smuggling? Many of them remain in their barracks, despite the fact that every local child can identify the contraband entering their country. A traveler riding through the area will notice troops in large and small transports moving along the roads seemingly without any purpose or any end in sight to their aimless travels.

On December 4, 2010, a division of the Kolkata High Court, including Chief Justice Jay Narayan Patel, criticized the West Bengal government and police for not implementing "the National Police Commission guidelines framed by Justice Savarwal of the Supreme Court, in the matter of security surveillance." It also blasted the government for remaining silent about it and noted that it took a lawsuit brought before them in the name of Jasobanto Rakshit to bring the matter to light. In a lame defense, the state responded that the security guidelines were not implemented because of "objections by senior officers." No doubt they feared for their ill-gotten income. Chief Justice Patel scored the government for failing to protect the common people against the growing terrorist threat and said that West Bengal has become a "safe haven for the subversive terrorist elements."[194]

Although several of the longer term Bangladeshi or East Pakistani Hindus living in these areas have found a path to legitimacy or semi-legitimacy; most have not. The people I met inhabit various ersatz dwellings along the border area

---

[194] This was in the matter of PIL (Public Interest Litigation) WP 1882w/2009, Jasobanto Rakshit vs. Union of India & ORS.

that include abandoned railway stations, roadside huts, and other makeshift communities. Some appear somewhat stable; many do not. But even the best dwellings seem secure enough only for the dry season and vulnerable to the elements during seasonal monsoons. Bengalis, however, are quite adept at living under the most abject circumstances. Creature comforts seem to have little meaning to most whom I have met. It is not their poor dwellings or poverty but their lack of legal standing that makes the refugees vulnerable to manipulation by many forces in the area; and people are skeptical that things will be any different under Trinamool than it was under the CPIM. The local police and other functionaries that they see have not changed.

According to several witnesses, the authorities are aware of the illegal communities and tell the residents that they will be allowed to remain only if they do as they are told. In some cases, refugees testified, they are ordered to attend pro-CPIM rallies. In others, a number of them said, they were told that they would receive voter cards, but that the CPIM would fill them out. Any objections by the refugees would result in severe reprisals. Similarly, many of the refugee children are allowed to attend local schools—but again, only insofar as the community cooperates with the authorities and are allowed to remain in the area. At times, however, the land on which they are squatting simply becomes desirable to someone else. It might be one of the authorities, a relative, or someone who is willing to give local officials more in bribes than the refugees can afford. When that happens, the refugees are told to leave and find other dwellings on their own. I saw that for myself when I went to visit one group of refugees living in a cluster of huts by a northern Bengal roadside, only to be told that they had just received that order to vacate their dwellings. They were not sure where they would end up, but commented that there are many areas of abandoned huts alongside Bengali roads. They believed they would find something—until someone else desired that plot of land. When I asked about appealing to local authorities about this, they shrugged that their lack of legal status makes such appeals impossible.

The Kolkata-based Hindu Youth Forum (HYF) has compiled a list of anti-Hindu attacks inside West Bengal for the period 2007-2008.[195] HYF representatives met with me in March 2009 in Kolkata and testified that there were far more incidents reported than the ones listed in their paper, but the facts of these cases were so apparent that they were able to confirm their accuracy even with their own limited resources. They also reported several 2009 incidents, as well, and stated without hesitation that "Muslim fundamentalists" continue to attack Hindus with impunity in West Bengal. Below is a sample of 2008 attacks HYF was able to verify.

- In April, 15 Muslims abducted 19-year old Durga Singh from Kolkata's Shibpur tram depot. They took him to a remote area in South 24 Parganas where they "slashed choppers all over his body and mistaking him to be dead threw his unconscious body by the roadside." Durga had to be treated in two separate hospitals where he received 88 stitches and nearly died. This happened after he protested the actions of one Ramzan Ali (already at the time wanted for extortion, abduction, and murder) and a group of Muslims who would "molest [Hindu] girls" in Kolkata's Ghoshbagan area. The West Bengal government did not file any charges in this case.[196]
- In June, a large mob of approximately 5,000 Muslim fundamentalists, "compris[ed] mostly of Bangladeshi infiltrators", attacked a major religious gathering of Hindus at one of their holiest sites at one of the pilgrimage points of Gangasagar in West Bengal. They

[195] "A Survey of Hindu Human Rights West Bengal 20076-08," Presented by the Hindu Youth Forum to the *Greater Hindu Assembly*, 27-28th December, 2008; Chennai, India.

[196] *Ibid.* p. 7.

outnumbered the pilgrims by 25 to one, and focused assaults on women and children, sending about 15 to the hospital. When the other religious pilgrims barricaded themselves in a building, the attackers tried but failed to break in so instead turned their fury on a nearby temple to the goddess Kali, which they desecrated. Even though the West Bengal police were themselves the target of the rioters, they amazingly did not charge any of them. But in a move reminiscent of Nazi Germany, which would charge the Jewish community when they were attacked, the West Bengal government arrested 15 of the religious pilgrims "under several sections of the Indian Penal Code for inciting communal disharmony, while the perpetrators roam Scott free."[197]

- In July, four Muslims in the village of Lakshmanpur, located in Murshidabad, beheaded a Hindu man for marrying a Muslim woman. Twenty-seven year old Shailendra Prasad was working as a day laborer in Mumbai when he met and married Murnira Bibi, who was working there as domestic help. The two, along with their son, went to Lakshmanpur where Murnira introduced Shailendra as her Muslim husband. Eventually, he gave himself away with a sudden cry, and so was brought before a local village court, which in this case was comprised exclusively of "very orthodox Muslims." The Shalishi court sentenced the man to beheading for the "crime" of marrying a Muslim woman. The government of West Bengal had legitimated local Shalishi courts as a way for the poor to settle their legal disputes without incurring the high costs involved with regular costs. The government's move was never intended to treat with capital offenses, let alone give legal force to decisions made contrary to the law of the land. Moreover, the government

[197] *Ibid.* pp.7-9.

eventually withdrew the bill that would have empowered the Shalishi courts. Yet, the West Bengal government, even up to "the Chief Minister," determined not to interfere. As the HYF noted, "While such cases of gross human rights violations in Pakistan or Bangladesh or even in [the Indian states of] Bihar and [Uttar Pradesh] attract international human rights activists, the numerous such incidents of [West] Bengal simply go unreported."[198]

- In July, Arka Banerjee, a Hindu, was set ablaze for marrying a Muslim woman. In this instance, the perpetrators sought out and traced Banerjee to his home in the Kolkata suburb of Haroa. They seized his wife, Rehanna, and their young son Aryan at gunpoint. Banerjee made it clear that he knew they would be taking his family to his in-laws' home in the town of Baduria. But they responded by threatening him with "dire consequences if he dared to set foot" there. After several attempts, he managed to get there but was beaten. Then, his brother-in-law Manirul dumped a can of kerosene on him and set him on fire. After running through the streets ablaze, Banerjee was admitted to Baduria's hospital. Police arrested Manirul but soon let him out on bail and never renewed the prosecution. No one else was ever charged in the incident either.[199]
- In October, Hindus were in the midst of celebrating one of their most important holidays, Durga Puja. "Religious fundamentalists...cut off the power supply and vandalized the *pandal*[200] and hung up the severed leg of a cow." Locals gathered at the site of the religious desecration and demanded that police arrest

[198] *Ibid.* pp. 9-10.

[199] *Ibid.* p. 10.

[200] A *pandal* is a temporary religious structure set up by Hindus during Durga Puja to venerate the goddess Durga.

> the culprits—who made no attempt to conceal their identities. Instead, they arrested "26 protestors including four women... for agitation over the issue." The incident occurred in West Bengal's South Dinajpur district, located in the northern part of the Indian state.[201]

HYF has drawn on reports from numerous newspapers, periodicals, and web sites, as well as its own investigation to document these and several other incidents. It summarized its findings to the Greater Hindu Assembly by noting that "The cases of such human rights violations in West Bengal, regarding freedom of religion and freedom of expression are pretty similar to those in Bangladesh...it is sheer irony that it is in this very cradle of secularism, the universal principles of human rights are being violated every day"; an irony they attribute to massive corruption at every level from the local constables to the top of the West Bengal government.[202]

Brutalized and penniless, these Hindu refugees once fled merciless attacks by Muslims to the world's largest Hindu country. But the communist leaders and motley array of local officials in West Bengal, their nearest destination for refuge, reject any bonds of faith. Either they do so as communists because of their atheistic philosophy and internationalist goals; or it is simply a matter of personal gain and greed. They label any stance in favor of these *Hindu* refugees "communal," and have thrown their lot in with the Islamists, who can provide them with far more in graft than they would ever have if they just took home their salaries. VPA victims have been put in camps then sent on forced marches in their supposed haven and the West Bengal Stalinists refuse to recognize them as refugees or give them legal standing. They have turned a blind eye to cross-border attacks and the accompanying Muslim atrocities.[203]

---

[201] *Op, cit.*, pp. 11-12.

[202] *Ibid.* p. 15.

[203] *Op. cit.*, Benkin, Stop Them before they Kill Again.

Dr. Sachi Dastidar of the State University of New York says the problem is as much political as moral. The Communists fear being voted out of power if the strongly anti-communist victims are granted citizenship. He also noted, in West Bengal, "Many state officials are Bangladeshis [but only] Islamist approved Bangladeshis are given safe haven in West Bengal." In Bangladesh, many party members and other apparatchik are among the major beneficiaries of the VPA, and they are the very people who are charged with overturning that law.[204] None of the parties who are responsible for taking action are doing so; nor are they even addressing the complicity of the West Bengal government.

- ❑ The national Indian government maintains a hands-off policy toward that state.
- ❑ The Indian government has not signed the international conventions that would require it to accord the victims refugee status, which would entitle them to both material and legal benefits.
- ❑ Neither has the United Nations recognized them as refugees and does not even have a presence—official or unofficial—among them.[205]
- ❑ No major international human rights group has ever addressed the situation in West Bengal, and they have rarely addressed the situation in Bangladesh. When they have it has come in the form of anemic statements with no action. Amnesty International, for instance, has called for "international human rights monitors in Israel and the Occupied Palestinian Territories," but none in East or West Bengal.[206]

---

[204] Private communications with Professor Sachi Dastidar of the State University of New York, Old Westbury. December 2007.

[205] In February 2011, I visited several refugee camps in India with my colleague and co-founder of Forcefield, Miriam Guttman-Jones of Australia. One of the things that shocked her and about which she commented profusely during the trip and upon returning to Australia, was the total absence of the UN among people we saw living in deplorable conditions. As she noted after some of our interviews with the refugees, they "never even heard of the UN."

[206] *Op. cit.,* Benkin, "Stop Them before they Kill Again."

Deganga: A Case Study for Hindus in West Bengal

While the following incidents do not necessarily involve Hindu refugees from Bangladesh, it says a great deal about the reality of life for Hindus in West Bengal. For three days in September 2010, anti-Hindu violence wracked the Deganga area in North 24 Parganas, only 40 kilometers from the West Bengal capital of Kolkata. Even after the violence subsided, Hindu residents continued to fear renewed attacks, which could have been the attackers' intention all along. West Bengal BJP member Tathagata Roy visited the area twice since the violence began and noted, "This was a well-thought-out, well-executed pogrom whose objective was to terrorize the Hindus no end without committing any major crime beyond arson. The ultimate intention can only be to cleanse the area of Hindus with a view to totally Islamize the area." While Indian troops ultimately stationed themselves on the area's main road, they did not follow pogromists into the nearby villages and settlements where they were able to do a great deal of damage with impunity.[207]

Along with human rights activists Tapan Ghosh, Animitra Chakraborty, Amitabh Tripathi, and Miriam Guttman-Jones, I went on a fact-finding mission to Deganga five months after the pogrom. What I found there was chilling.

> The first home we stopped at foreshadowed what we would encounter pretty uniformly. The owner of the land, an elderly Hindu woman, spoke with us but was afraid to give her name for fear of reprisals (something repeated by our other informants in the area). Since the violence, her Muslim neighbors have become more aggressive, boldly encroaching on her small plot of land, which has been in the family for generations. Near the perimeter, in fact, they had erected a wall on which was painted a star and crescent to represent the fact that the land was now under Muslim control. Our witness said that her neighbors have made no secret of their intention to push her out of the

---

[207] Richard L. Benkin, "Ill winds that blow through Deganga," *The Pioneer,* October 21, 2010; and Benkin, "Deganga Intifada," *New English Review,* October 2010.

> region, and lamented that the authorities have been no help. She fears more violence. As we spoke, her Muslim neighbors congregated around the land and made a menacing show of watching the woman. At the second home, we were greeted by a mother and her young daughter who told us that not more than two weeks prior, neighbors threw part of a cow carcass in their yard. This is not only a serious form of religious desecration for Hindus (and illegal in India), but it also has been used to intimidate them elsewhere, suggesting that they might be next. The authorities told her that they would not intervene and that she had to work it out with her Muslim neighbors; but according to Animitra Chakraborty of Hindu Samhati (a Hindu self-defense and renewal organization), "they were in no mood to talk." As a result, the woman is seriously thinking of taking her daughter and moving out of the area.[208]

As we stood on that main road where troops were once deployed, Tapan Ghosh waved his arm to indicate a market down the road. He told us that "all the Hindu shops were looted and then burned" to the ground; clearly a religiously based attack as no Muslim properties were harmed. The community has re-built most of the brick homes and shops that were destroyed, but it has not been able to re-build the people's sense of safety. Every Hindu with whom we spoke said the women of the house could not go to market or anywhere else without harassment and threats of sexual assault. Their children could not attend school because of the threats. The police? They refuse to take any action, and most people in the community are thinking about leaving.

One exception was a group of young Hindus who stood by a *Mandir* that was rebuilt. They told us how Muslim attackers first urinated on the Hindu deities and then destroyed them, as well as the temple itself. But they vowed to "stay and fight," and we got a sense of what they are facing. As we have come to expect, a crowd of Muslims gathered menacingly nearby, and at one point, a Muslim vendor set up shop (illegally) in

---

[208] Richard L. Benkin, "Deganga Intifada – Update," *New English Review*, March 2011.

front of the temple. He began hanging out leather shoes, which was a deliberate act of religious desecration. Some Hindus objected, and tempers on both sides flared. Some of my colleagues and I intervened and calmed tensions. The next day, however, the vendor repeated the action and several Muslim residents started attacking some undefended Hindus.[209]

Unfortunately, the situation in Deganga is being repeated throughout West Bengal. Hindus in the Howrah area testified to regular intimidation and attacks by Muslims and showed us a temple that was destroyed in another deliberate act of religious desecration. Residents and advocates complained to the West Bengal police, but they took no action. (In fact, the only evidence of action we saw was when a pair of lawmen accosted us.) The most poignant testimony came from a woman in the village of Norit. She told us how five weeks before our visit, Muslims abducted her 22-year-old daughter, and she has not been seen since. Various relatives and community members have gone to the police numerous times, but the police refuse to get involved.

These examples and others sometimes involve Bangladeshi Hindus, sometimes not. Nevertheless, they demonstrate just how dangerous it has become for Hindus in certain parts of that state, especially those where Hindu refugees from Bangladesh might try to find a safe haven.

Muslim growth in Northeast India

On February 15, 2010, I sat in a cab while it made its way through a traffic-clogged Kolkata to the office of Bimal Pramanik. He is trying to help poor Hindus of West Bengal by running a program of micro-credit, similar to the one for which Bangladesh's Mohammed Yunis won the Nobel Prize. He is also a very influential researcher and director of the Kolkata-based Centre for Research in Indo-Bangladesh Relations.

---

[209] *Ibid.*

Bimal Pramanik has spent the better part of his professional life studying various aspects of the India-Bangladesh relationship. He is also a sought after expert on population changes in West Bengal and various related matters who is quoted periodically in *The Times of India* and other major newspapers and journals. We had a very frank conversation in which he noted his serious concerns about the undeniable and decades-long pattern of demographic changes in West Bengal (and Assam). My Indian colleague Amitabh Tripathi, founder of the South Asia Forum and a tireless activist in the fight against radical Islam, arranged the meeting and was a key participant in that 2010 discussion as well.[210]

Pramanik, who was born and grew up in what was then East Pakistan, is familiar with traditional relations among Bengali Hindus and Muslims as well as how much they have changed in recent decades. He fought to help liberate his country in its 1971 War of Independence, but left after Sheikh Mujibur Rahman's assassination in 1975. He eventually settled in Kolkata.[211] While many Indians complain about "Muslim infiltration" from Bangladesh, Pramanik is more concerned about its deliberate nature. He called it "Bangladeshi

[210] Amitabh Tripathi, along with Australian Miriam Guttman-Jones , and me, is a board member of Forcefield, the human rights organization dedicated to, among other things, stopping the persecution of minorities in Bangladesh. He is responsible for opening numerous doors for me in official and unofficial Indian circles, supporting my missions there, and furthering our effort to protect the Bangladeshi Hindu refugees in India. Together, he and I are making significant inroads into the traditional silence imposed by traditional politicians, academia, and the media on numerous topics from this noted demographic change, to attacks on Hinduism in India, to the rabid persecution of Hindus in Bangladesh, Pakistan, Kashmir, and elsewhere.

[211] In 2009, Pramanik told *The Indian Times* about the "mayhem in the country" after Sheikh Mujib's assassination, including the infamous "Dhaka Central Jail killings." "Five ministers of the Mujib government, who had refused to attend the swearing-in of the new cabinet, were killed... I had to go underground. For four months I kept moving from one place to another before finally sneaking out of the country to India. I might have been killed otherwise." "'History has come full circle' Mujib Bahini," *The Times of India,* November 20, 2009.

infiltration with Pakistani ideas... trying to 'Pakistanize' the entire region." Many Bangladeshi Muslims now in India, he said, are practicing a more "Arabic" dominated culture rather than their traditional South Asian culture and that if they return to their South Asian roots, communal conflict "will be reduced."[212] In that regard, Tripathi referenced South Asia Forum's findings about the growth of Wahabi influence in Bangladesh.

In 1905 then again in 1947, Bengal was divided into a Muslim-majority entity (Bangladesh, previously East Bengal and East Pakistan) and a Hindu majority entity (West Bengal state within India). While the two areas maintain those same religious majorities, the second half of the twentieth century saw the Muslim proportion of West Bengal's population rise by 25 percent and its Hindu population decline by almost nine percent. You will recall that in the same period, the proportion of East Bengal's Hindu population declined by almost three-fourths, while the Muslim share of its people rose by more than one-third. Those significant shifts do not happen as a result of natural demographic processes, and the trends have continued into the 21st century. Pramanik noted that while Muslim population growth in West Bengal was nearly 35 percent between 1981 and 1991, it was only 25 percent in the same period in Bangladesh. "How can there be such a wide difference in growth rates between the two countries, particularly when awareness about family planning is even less in Bangladesh? Pramanik asks. "This can only be explained by the illegal immigration from across the border."[213]

[212] These statements were made in our interview in Bimal Pramanik's Kolkata office on February 15, 2010.

[213] The raw figures come from the Director of Census Operations, West Bengal, and were noted in Nirmalya Banerjee, "Muslims mushroom in 3 Bengal districts," *The Times of India,* June 24, 2005. They also are cited and analyzed extensively in Bimal Pramanik, *Endangered Demography: Nature and Impact of Demographic Changes in West Bengal 1951-2001.* (G. C. Modak: Kolkata, 2005). The statement from Bimal Pramanik is also from the same *Times of India* article.

The South Asia Research Society conducted an exhaustive demographic study of population trends in West Bengal since 1941, with particular emphasis on the decade 1981 to 1991. It found:

> Even after the emergence of Bangladesh as an independent country in 1971, however, the march of refugees to West Bengal appeared to be ceaseless. Nevertheless, there is one great difference in the patterns of migration before and after 1971. In the days of Pakistan, nearly all refugees coming to West Bengal were members of the minority communities in East Bengal (East Pakistan), viz. Buddhists, Christians, and Hindus. In the Bangladesh era, however, in addition to the forced migration of members of minority community (the overwhelming majority being Hindus) to West Bengal, there has been large-scale voluntary infiltration of Bangladeshi Muslims (forming the majority community in that country) to West Bengal and other parts of India.[214]

The study contrasts government population projections that were based on factors of fertility and mortality with actual population changes in the decade. They also parsed the remaining figures to account for internal Indian migration, as well as the influx of Hindu refugees from Bangladesh. In the end they were unable to explain the discrepancy that remained without recourse to voluntary Muslim infiltration from Bangladesh, about which they note both the governments of India and West Bengal periodically express concern.[215]

Bimal Pramanik released his exhaustive study of population changes in East and West Bengal in 2005, tracing the changes that occurred in the critical period between 1951 and 2001. Its beginning point, almost four years after independence was formally recognized on the Indian subcontinent and so the figures cited for that year reflect conditions that pertained after the major population transfers, agreed to as part of the

---

[214] South Asia Research Society "Population Explosion in West Bengal: A Survey," in Sita Ram Goel, editor, *Time for Stock Taking Whither Sangh Parivar?* (Voice of India Books: New Delhi, 1996)

[215] *Ibid.*

subcontinent's partition, had essentially been concluded.[216] The intervening 50 years between the study's start and end points encompasses a host of major events, including several wars between the two countries and the emergence of an independent Bangladesh out of what was initially East Pakistan. The period also encompasses the rise of radical Islam as a major international player and so also several decades of efforts by radical Muslims to implement their designs.

Differential growth rates between Hindus and Muslims in Bengal are startling. In Bangladesh, the Hindu population grew from about nine to eleven million, or 23.16 percent; while the Muslim population grew from 32 to 111 million, or 244.68 percent. Some of the academics and government officials with whom I have discussed this disparity have attempted to explain it by saying that, regardless of the reasons that propelled them, many Hindus simply decided to move to India as it is a Hindu-majority country with greater economic prospects than Bangladesh; in other words, that the population shift has been driven by "economic refugees." My immediate response is that calling them economic refugees ignores the serious problems that caused the economic dislocation. That

---

[216] After successfully defeating the British in the period immediately following World War II, the Indian factions under Mahatma Gandhi broke into two major camps, one favoring a unified independent state, and the other demanding two separate states, divided on the basis of religion. It should be noted, however, that the demand for partition came from Muslim leaders who had formally made the demand more than a decade earlier; most notably the Muslim League under Mohammad Ali Jinnah. Thus, Pakistan was formally incorporated as an Islamic State, while India has always maintained its status as a secular state. In determining how the partition would be made, in accordance with the "Mountbatten Plan" as ratified by the British Parliament, "Hindu" and "Muslim" states to be incorporated into India and Pakistan respectively. Additionally, two major states were partitioned: West Punjab became part of Pakistan and East Punjab became part of India; and West and East Bengal became part of India and Pakistan respectively. The status of Jammu and Kashmir remained unresolved, sparking the first India-Pakistan war almost immediately in 1947 and several wars (declared and undeclared) since then. Estimates of the number of people who participated in these population transfers range from 15 to 25 million, and at least another million were killed in sectarian violence that accompanied them.

is, whether it was seizure of assets under the Vested Property Act, religious discrimination, or persecution, chalking it up to economic factors ignores the more important forces behind it. And if it was simply a matter of Hindus and Muslims reacting to the same economic forces, we would expect it to be reflected in population figures for the Indian state closest to Bangladesh and whose population is composed of the same ethnic group, namely West Bengal. So what do we see? West Bengal had about 19 million Hindus in 1951 and 58 million in 2001, an increase of 198.54 percent. Its 1951 Muslim population of approximately five million Muslims grew to more than 20 million in 2001 or by 310.13 percent.[217]

Moreover, Pramanik's study indicates that during this period the Muslim growth rate exceeded that of Hindus in each individual district of West Bengal, with the exception of Kooch Bihar, a small district sandwiched between Bangladesh and Bhutan. He was unable to provide figures for Uttar Dinajpur, Dakshin Dinajpur, North 24 Parganas, South 24 Parganas because they were not incorporated until decades after 1951; but in all four cases, the Muslim growth rate exceeded the Hindu growth rate for the 1991 to 2001 period.[218] These latter figures should be given even greater significance in light of the fact that these districts, as noted throughout this book, receive large numbers of Bangladeshi Hindu refugees, trying to escape persecution. Population patterns in Kooch Bihar, however, are very instructive. Its growth rates between 1951 and 1981 were skewed by the large influx of Bangladeshi Hindus refugees. According to Pramanik's study, those initial population transfers (i.e., Hindus migrating from East Pakistan to India) continued in this district well after 1951. Then, he notes, "a good number of Hindu refugees, who had crossed over to this district during

---

[217] *Op cit.* Pramanik, *Endangered Demography,* pp. 131-132.

[218] *Ibid.*

the nine months of Bangladesh Liberation War in 1971, did not return to newly independent Bangladesh. As a result, from 1951 to 1981, a continuously high growth rate of Hindu population is observed." Pramanik also notes that during the same period there was "no notable out-migration of Muslim population to East Pakistan or Bangladesh." Yet, a "massive Muslim infiltration from Bangladesh" to Kooch Bihar took place from 1981 forward.[219] And in fact, during the last decade of Pramanik's study, Muslim population growth exceeded the Hindu increase by one third.[220] Pramanik also conducted separate studies of four districts that border Bangladesh: Uttar Dinajpur (also comprising the former districts of West and Dakshin Dinajpur); Murshidabad, Nadia, and North and South 24 Parganas. He noted a situation of "unabated infiltration," especially during the final two decades of his study, and he also documented a pattern of increased crime in these districts as the Muslim infiltration became more prominent.[221] His findings conform to anecdotal information I have gathered in three years of direct fact-finding in these areas, most particularly Uttar Dinajpur and North 24 Parganas. They help quantify frequent testimony by Bangladeshi Hindu refugees of an increased pattern of attacks on their ersatz colonies by combined forces of Bangladeshis and Muslim from surrounding villages; which would help explain the noted increased rates of murder and other violent crimes. In a more anecdotal way, we saw the impact of this as we drove through and stopped in villages near the border. These once mixed Hindu-Muslim localities are now all or almost all Muslim. It is also sad to note the disappearance or abandonment of the once ubiquitous roadside Mandirs or Hindu temples that has accompanied this population shift.

The prolific Pramanik summarizes the demographic changes in West Bengal in a way that indicates what is in store

---

[219] *Ibid,* p. 24.

[220] *Ibid,* p.133.

[221] *Ibid,* pp. 61-118.

for Hindus living in that state, as well as the darker motivations behind the phenomena noted in this book:

> In the nineteen eighties, planned migration from Bangladesh conformed to the *lebensraum* theory [RB: Hitler's justification for territorial expansion and the seizure of "non-Aryan" assets; specifically that Germans needed more "living room"], which was encouraged by Indian Muslims in the border States under the protection and patronization of some political and social forces of India's Eastern and North Eastern region. This continuous infiltration from across the border is slowly and steadily changing the demographic pattern in the border areas, especially in the States of West Bengal and Assam... which is threatening our secular polity and national security. *This is a religio-cultural process taking place in a geographical space considered to be strategically important. Thus, the emergence of Bangladesh has created in the North-Eastern States of India certain conditions conducive to Islamisation.* At least three factors, facilitating the process of Islamisation, are obvious...a secular political environment...the appeasement of aliens for the purpose of garnering votes... [and] a weak, undefined and unorganized secular frame.[222] [emphasis mine]

The basic theses of this book are that we are facing a deliberate human rights atrocity in the ethnic cleansing of Bangladeshi Hindus, that it is part of a wider movement that we can group under *jihad*, and that we as a civilized people are failing miserably at identifying at combating both. The processes Pramanik observed have only increased in ferocity in the nine years since he observed them; certainly as confirmed by the continuous observation and testimony by and to me and my associates as we scour the countryside of Northeast India. Clearly, if the so-called civilized world does not take action soon, it will awake one day wondering "how it all could have happened." Time is running out—for the victims and for us.

---

[222] *Ibid.* p.13.

CHAPTER SIX

BEYOND BELIEF: BANGLADESH'S VESTED PROPERTY ACT

Scholars, journalists, activists, and others have an almost knee-jerk tendency to praise Bangladesh's beginnings as a secular nation and trace its slide into Islamist domination from the 1975 assassination of its founding father, Sheikh Mujibur Rahman. That praise is warranted—but only to a limited extent, for secularism and any semblance of democratic ideals were in their death throes long before Sheikh Mujib was.

Without an appeal to democratic ideals, the nation of Bangladesh never would have come into being. The essential complaint of those who agitated for independence was that the nation's wealth and power were concentrated in West Pakistan and among its dominant Punjabi, Pashtun, and Sindhi ethnic groups. The Bengalis of East Pakistan—whether Muslim or Hindu—were in effect second-class citizens with a disproportionately smaller part of the nation's wealth. As Hiranmay Karlekar notes, "The central leadership of the [Pakistani] Muslim League treated East Bengal almost as a colony. As it is, there was a basic inequality in the relationship between the eastern and western wings. The bureaucracy and the armed forces were overwhelmingly dominated by West Pakistanis." He also notes that the West Pakistanis appropriated "the entire foreign exchange earned by East Bengal," as well as such things as sales tax receipts.[223] Umar Badruddin added that "in major policy-making decisions, or in

---

[223] Hiranmay Karlekar, *Bangladesh The Next Afghanistan?* (Sage Publications India: New Delhi, 2005), pp. 39-40.

actual execution of policies, East Pakistan did not have any effective say."[224]

In other words, the setup was simply not fair, and in the formulation of these and other writers and international officials, that unfairness gave the Bengalis—Muslim and Hindu—the right to revolt.

In 1971, Pakistan's military rulers allowed the country to hold elections for a democratic government. The results showed the chasm that now existed between East and West Pakistan. In the West, the Pakistan People's Party (PPP) won 85 seats; it won no seats in the East. In East Pakistan, the Awami League won all but two seats; it won none in the West. The election results would catapult the Awami League to power and make Sheikh Mujibar Rahman the Prime Minister. The ruling General Yahya Khan backed openly by the PPP and its leader Ali Bhutto refused to hand over power. Sheikh Mujib was taken in chains to a West Pakistan prison. In March, Ziaur Rahman, who later founded the BNP, declared an independent Bangladesh and the revolt was underway.

Thus, the revolution was able to rally internal and external support based on the claim that it would create a decidedly non-communal Bangladesh with equal rights for both majority and minority populations. Born on the basis of Muslim communalism, Pakistan was the villain and the revolutionaries were a clearly non-communal alternative. It was a clarion call for a united Bengal ethnic group regardless of religion. It was no surprise, then, that when Pakistani shock troops, along with East Bengali Islamists attacked unarmed civilians they murdered both Hindus and Muslims, although as noted earlier, the victimization of Hindus was often deliberate and in significantly greater proportion to its percentage of the East Pakistani population.

There was another factor that made a philosophy rejecting Hindu-Muslim conflict almost obligatory for the new nation of

[224] Umar Badruddin, *The Emergence of Bangladesh: Class Struggles in East Pakistan (1947-58)* (Oxford University Press: Karachi, 2004), p. 12.

Bangladesh: that nation would not have achieved its independence without the arms and blood of the Indian armed forces, Hindu and Muslim. India's early support for East Bengali rebels, known as the *Mukti Bahini*, caused enough concern in Pakistan for the latter to launch a pre-emptive strike against India's western border on December 3. It failed miserably and was a turning point in the war. Prior to that, the East Pakistani population was suffering, and about 15 percent of it had fled to India. But in response to Pakistan's action, Indian Prime Minister Indira Gandhi threw the weight of her nation behind the rebels and declared war. Four days later, three Indian corps crossed into East Pakistan, liberated Jessore, and prepared to take Dhaka. They routed the Pakistani troops who then found themselves attacked from their other side by almost three full brigades of *Mukti Bahini* and an untold number of irregulars. Pakistan tried to fend off India by launching more attacks on its western border but to no avail. On December 16, 1971, Pakistani forces in East Bengal surrendered to the Indians and became the largest group of POWs since World War II.

Given those two factors—the active and bloody opposition to Bangladeshi independence by parties like *Jamaat* e-Islami, and India's critical role in winning independence—it should not surprise anyone that Bangladesh was born a secular and democratic nation that guaranteed rights for all religious and ethnic groups, much after the model on which India was constituted in 1947. It took power with a commitment and philosophy that discouraged Hindu-Muslim violence. Unfortunately, in what came to be the *modus operandi* of all subsequent Bangladeshi governments, those noble sounding words were never matched by action. It is popular to portray the early days of the new Bangladeshi republic as some sort of democratic and secular Nirvana; and that things started to go wrong only after the assassination of Sheikh Mujibur Rahman.

Known as the father of the nation, and more affectionately *Bangabandhu*, Mujib led the Awami League to victory over the Pakistanis and their sympathizers; and yes, it is the same

Awami League that is in power again. He is also the father of Bangladesh's current Prime Minister, Sheikh Hasina Wajed. Mujib became Bangladesh's first Prime Minister in January 1972 and was assassinated on August 15, 1975 at the age of 55. Although the nation was born with a commitment to move it away from its Pakistani past—a past tainted with a lack of democracy, poor governance, and growing ties with political Islam—that began to change rather quickly.

And it started with Mujib himself. In what has proven to be a terribly misguided policy, he attempted to forge some sort of unity in the nation by seeking to mollify Islamic fundamentalists. He revoked the ban on the Islamic Academy, which was imposed in 1972 after it was identified as a breeding ground for pro-Islamist and pro-Pakistani sentiment and guerilla activity. He also banned the production and sale of alcohol as well as all gambling in the country. All of these were major demands of Bangladeshi Islamists and they set Bangladesh on a path toward a level of official Islamization. Mujib's actions favored those elements in the new nation that had actively opposed its independence and at the same time imposed a *de facto* second-class status on its Hindu population, which sacrificed greatly for Bangladeshi independence.

On January 25, 1975, in the face of growing opposition to his rule, Mujib declared a State of Emergency in Bangladesh and was named "president for life." That's right. The man revered as the spirit of Bangladeshi democracy and freedom outlawed any presidential elections during his lifetime. Following that move, he engineered a ban on all political parties except for the one created by his supporters, and accepted "extraordinary powers." Like all tyrants, he used those powers to have his opponents arrested. So much for the myth of Bangladeshi democracy![225]

---

[225] Raman, B, "Bangladesh: A Bengali Abbasi Lurking Somewhere?" *South Asia Analysis Group,* April 23, 2001; Maniruzzaman, Talukder, "Bangladesh in 1975: The Fall of the Mujib Regime and its Aftermath." *Asian Survey 16:2*, February 2006.

While the process of making Bangladesh officially an Islamic nation began under Sheikh Mujibur Rahman, Islam was not declared the nation's official religion until sometime after his assassination[226]; the same can be said for using Islam to promote anti-Indian sentiment, which is now something of a hallowed Bangladeshi tradition. *In 1974, Sheikh Mujibur Rahman presided over something that was to mark his country for decades as a place that is antithetical to religious equality and even become the funding mechanism for Bangladesh's ethnic cleansing of its Hindu population.*

That year, the party over which he presided had an absolute majority in Constituent Assembly and controlled every executive and judicial post in the nation. It was on Sheikh Mujib's watch and under his control that the Awami League dominated Constituent Assembly ratified Bangladesh's new constitution. That process began with a review of the existing Pakistani laws that were in effect when the Bangladeshi War of Independence erupted. For each law individually, the new leaders had to make a choice. Would it remain a law in the new nation of Bangladesh; or would it be rejected and no longer be in force? They rejected many of them as incompatible with the principles of equality and religious freedom that animated their nation's fight to be born. Oddly, when it came to the openly anti-Hindu Enemy Property Act, they passed on eliminating it. Instead, they simply re-named it the Vested Property Act. Mujib himself issued an executive order making it official that the former Pakistani law was now a Bangladeshi law, too.[227]

---

[226] That happened with the Eight Amendment to the Bangladeshi Constitution, passed in1988 under the dictatorship of General Hussain Muhammed Ershad. When Sheikh Mujib's daughter and the current Prime Minister, Sheikh Hasina was handed a golden opportunity to repeal it in 2011, she decided not to do so.

[227] Rabindranath Trivedi, "The legacy of enemy turned vested property act in Bangladesh." *Asian Tribune*, May 29, 2007. You can also find a wealth of information about this at my own web site, at two locations:

http://www.interfaithstrength.com/VPA.html and

http:/www.interfaithstrength.com/Alert3b.html.

Though one can accuse Mujib of betraying the principles of the revolution that brought him to power, the world's acceptance of this law and refusal to address it as the openly anti-Hindu law that it is, represents a far greater betrayal. Consistent and principled opposition to such an abomination and its disregard of equality and human rights would have nipped this quiet case of ethnic cleansing in the bud and perhaps helped move Bangladesh in a direction away from the grip of Islamists. If donor nations made the VPA's repeal a condition for the aid that it has poured into the country, the history of this sad nation would have been very different.

In Chapter 2, I asked the reader to imagine what would happen if the United States, Canada, Italy, or any other country with a large Christian majority had a law that empowered the government to seize the land and property of non-Christians and then distribute it to Christians of their choice. Or what if India had a law that empowered its government to seize the land and property of non-Hindus and distribute it to Hindus. You probably cannot imagine such a thing existing in any of these countries. But that same law does exist in some countries with Muslim majorities. Bangladesh's Vested Property Act allows the government—which in reality means corrupt politicians and petty functionaries supported by the government and Bangladeshi law—to seize the homes and farms of innocent Hindu citizens and distribute them as graft to their cronies. The "vested" property most often is a modest plot of land that had been worked by Hindu families for generations, perhaps centuries.

If any of the countries mentioned at the outset had such a law directed at non-Christians, the rest of the world would call it racist, and rightly so. In today's political climate, there no doubt would be charges of Islamaphobia, too. We can bet that the United Nations would pass angry resolutions, with its members acting oh so outraged as if they had not looked the other way for decades when countries and ideologies they favor maintain such laws. They no doubt would clamor for the Security Council to take more direct action or if it did not would say that it exposed itself as anti-whatever they call it at the time. We would be surprised if the world's leading human rights NGOs did not make this an important cause and feature it prominently in publications, web sites, and public appearances. And all of them would be correct in doing so. If the world allowed itself to be riveted for weeks over some cartoons in Denmark, it is only reasonable to expect a matter such as this to occupy our attention for as long as it takes to end it.

"Racism! Racism! Racism!" Every one of them would cry. And you know what? I believe the loudest cries would come from Americans and Canadians, Italians and Indians, or the citizens of whatever democratic country had such a law. The reason is that we simply do not do that sort of thing precisely *because* we are free societies. But the nation of Bangladesh, along with Pakistan, has such a law. They have had it for decades and never repealed it or even left it to wither and die unused. While the VPA has been in force for over three decades, the EPA has been in force for over four having been passed in 1965 after Pakistan suffered another embarrassing defeat at Indian hands. Unable to take out its vengeance on India, the Pakistani government attacked its own Hindu citizens by passing that retaliatory law which allowed it to declare certain citizens (read Hindu citizens) enemies and confiscate their property. The law was openly anti-Hindu, and matched the open and nationally supported rhetoric at the time, as well as the prevailing national sentiment all of the time even to our day. The nature of anti-Hindu sentiment and rhetoric among the Pakistani population is transparently racist[228] since it persisted when Hindus were almost a fifth of the population and continues with Hindus now a sad and powerless one percent.

[228] I know that the term, "racist," is not formally accurate when applied to this religious group that shares ethnicity with the various Pakistani and Bangladeshi ethnic groups, but it is used here because its meaning is immediately recognized, as opposed to a concocted term like, "religionist."

Despite the empty rhetoric of their leaders, Bangladesh and Pakistan are not free societies. In Pakistan, even the myth is only promoted periodically, most recently with the 2008 election of the Zardari government, which the world's talking-heads-in-the-sand, lead by US President Barack Obama and Secretary of State Hillary Clinton, were committed to posing as some sort of democracy opposed to radical Islam. Since those halcyon days for the appeasing soft left, Pakistan has participated in several terrorist attacks against both the United States and India, supported by official bodies such as the ISI. Neither Pakistan nor Bangladesh has ever been free in reality; and that commitment to a lack of freedom is what enables their leaders to identify a minority group of their citizens (Hindus) and suspend normal legal protections for them. It is that national and religiously-supported ideology that allows their citizens to live with that for decades without finding it repugnant.

Well, that is their problem, and it has been from the day they became independent nations. But what about the rest of us? How can we live with it? Perhaps we are witnessing the outrage noted above from the UN, Amnesty International. Surely, we must also be reading about it in *Le Monde*, *The Times of London*, and *The New York Times* and other "great" newspapers; and hearing about it on the *BBC, CNN,* and *Fox News.* Aren't we? Let us listen together for the outcry. What, you don't hear anything? Perhaps we are just not listening hard enough; so listen again. Still nothing—nothing from the UN, nothing from Amnesty International, nothing from Human Rights Watch, nothing from the plethora of entities responsible for the prevailing *zeitgeist* of *Muslim victimology.* That is the prevailing and politically correct belief of our time that somehow the only real problem is that Muslims are somehow the victim of discrimination by non-Muslims.[229]

[229] One example of how this political correctness trumps fact for those who subscribe first and foremost to the world view it demands was in Bill O'Reilly's November 23, 2010 interview with entertainer Whoopi Goldberg on Fox News. When Goldberg complained about "kids being beat up because they're Muslim,"

What rot! And if we are at all in doubt about that, find anything akin to Bangladesh's Vested Property Act in a non-Muslim majority country.[230]

We should not be surprised. All of those entities are consistent only in their agenda-driven inconsistency. When have they ever taken unequivocal stands against the institutionalized bigotry practiced so openly in the Muslim world? When have they taken effective action against at least two countries that do not allow non-Muslims to be citizens—or even allow foreigners to practice their non-Muslim religions openly?[231] But with regard to the VPA and EPA, we must ask more pointedly why we have heard nothing from the government of India, which is *the* Hindu nation and should be the foremost defender of Hindus abroad. Why have we as yet heard nothing from my own United States, which is committed to defending religious freedom—by our own laws—wherever it is under attack.[232]

O'Reilly cited FBI statistics for 2008 and 2009 that showed hate crimes against Jews in the US to be almost nine times that against Muslims. Goldberg would have none of it and said simply that she did not believe that was the case. Of course, she provided nothing other than her own feelings to support her contention—and even admitted that she had nothing to support her contention except how she felt.

[230] This imbalance extends beyond Bangladesh's Vested Property Act. That law was nothing more than a renaming of the same law that remains in force in Pakistan, the Enemy Property Act. Similarly, the world "guardians" of human rights have been silent about the official ban on non-Muslim religions and religious artifacts in Saudi Arabia; the fact that Jews are not even allowed into that country; the fact that by law Jews cannot become citizens of Jordan; the fact that Islam is taught to all students in Egypt, but the teaching of Christianity (including to Christians) is outlawed; and many more forms of discrimination against non-Muslims. Also consider that in Saudi Arabia, Qatar, Iran and Sudan, the law specifies the death sentence for a Muslim who converts to another religion. Imagine if a non-Muslim state specified death to any member of their majority religions that converts to Islam. The hue and cry—not to mention the disingenuous appeals to equality—would be deafening; yet, when Muslims do it to others, the silence is. And just to be comprehensive and to anticipate the cries of the anti-Israel pack, there is no such law in Israel regarding non-Jews, and its Supreme Court has weighed in on that several times.

[231] Saudi Arabia and the Maldives.

[232] The International Religious Freedom Act, passed during the administration of President Bill Clinton, requires the United States government to consider . . .

What we must understand is this: *The Vested Property Act is legalized racism and legalized thievery.* The fact that the Bangladeshi government has refused to repeal it, let alone compensate the victims, makes it quite clear that it is not interested in developing a society that allows freedom and equal protection under the law for all of its citizens. The force with which it has been used has been the same no matter which party has held power in Bangladesh. In fact, as noted above, the VPA was ratified into law by none other than the Father of the Country and his allegedly democratic party. All parties upheld this terrible law and benefited from the spoils proportionally. We have been equally silent about it and ignored the fact that the only impediments to its repeal are bigotry and corruption. There is no justification for its continued presence.

When Bangladesh passed the VPA a mere three years after victory in its war of independence, it had to be slipped through quickly and quietly with an avalanche of other laws in the hopes that no one would notice its ratification of bigotry into law. Thus someone hit on the idea of changing its name while wording the law to make clear that the VPA's substance was no different from its Pakistani forebear. After all, Awami League politicians then and now try to maintain the fiction that they care enough about Bangladesh's non-Muslim minorities to take effective action that would protect them. Good politics, you know, and the minorities continue to fall for it hook, line, and sinker. Moreover, when the law was passed most Bangladeshis still appreciated the fact that their independence was possible only because the Indian military played the major role in that war, horror of horrors, some even knew that Israel was one of the first countries to extend the new nation recognition and support.

While the act has been used against other religious and

...religious freedom issues when formulating foreign policy. Yet, the government has never required Pakistan or Bangladesh to repeal this openly anti-Hindu act as a requirement for aid or any other sort of support.

ethnic minorities on occasion, only Hindus have faced a consistent and organized effort to use the law to eliminate them from the Bangladeshi polity. Hindus are the VPA's real targets. Professor Abul Barkat of Dhaka University undertook the most authoritative study of the VPA and concluded that by 1997, 40 percent of Hindu families in Bangladesh had been affected by it and more than half of all Hindu-owned land already had been confiscated under the act. Much more land and many more Hindus have been affected in the fourteen years since then. So, there is no doubt that the VPA is a critical ingredient in ethnic cleansing. The fact that the percent of Hindus in Bangladesh has been cut in half concurrent with the act is evidence of those even more sinister, ethnic cleansing, motives behind the law.[233]

The VPA is so clearly immoral that the question of its being an outrage to every decent human being should not even be a legitimate topic for discussion among civilized individuals. There is no justification for it, and every Bangladeshi should be embarrassed by it. Trying to make a case for it is like trying to justify Holocaust denial. Holocaust denial is the genocide embracing attempt by people, including Iran's President Mahmoud Ahmedinejad—to say that the Nazi slaughter of Europe's Jews never happened. Some appeasers in universities and elsewhere are now trying to say that holocaust denial is merely another point of view that is a legitimate topic for study. Nonsense! It is a supremely bigoted lie; members of my family who survived the Holocaust can testify to that. Other members of my family who did not survive it would do the same if they could! Trying to justify the VPA is a racist lie, too.

According to Barkat, only about 0.4 percent of the Bangladeshi population shares in the spoils of the VPA, all of them connected to one political party or another. During the period of his original study, at the time of Awami League

[233] *Op. cit.*, Barkat et. al., *An Inquiry into Causes and Consequences of Deprivation of Hindu Minorities in Bangladesh through the Vested Property Act.*

control, Barkat found the following breakdown of who got the seized property:

Awami League	44%
BNP	32%
Jatiya Party	6%
Jamaat-e-Islami	5%
Others	13%

Barkat's breakdown during BNP control was:

BNP	45%
Awami League	31%
Jamaat-e-Islami	8%
Jatiya Party	6%
Others	10% [234]

In the two periods, according to Barkat's study, the percentages of seized property for the two major parties flip flopped depending on who held power, with their proportions varying by only one percent. Additionally, in both periods, the same 24 percent of the spoils seemed to be reserved for the other, minor parties. Coincidence? Hardly!

Bangladesh has long been known for its massive and endemic corruption. These figures make it clear that this is not even a principled form of bigotry but nothing more than legalized plunder for dishonest politicians. That blood money seems to be the real reason why Bangladeshis refuse to repeal this racist law. Various Bangladeshi officials like to call Israel "apartheid" and take a political position in which the government tries to pretend it is morally superior to the Jewish state. The passport regulations they uphold deprive its citizens of the right to travel to Israel where they might find out that things as portrayed by their government do not conform to reality. These same individuals, however, along with their

---

[234] *Ibid.*

minions grow fat by stealing ancestral Hindu lands and expelling their Hindu citizens.

Trying to defend the indefensible can make Bangladeshi representatives look especially foolish and lessen both their credibility and respect in foreign capitals. In 2008, I spoke with Bangladesh's Military Attaché at its embassy in Washington. Brigadier General Khan Md Nuruzzamen and I had several talks both in public and private regarding the persecution of Hindus in his country and the case of journalist Salah Uddin Shoaib Choudhury.[235] During that conversation with officials at that embassy, I addressed the VPA saying that I simply found its existence "beyond belief." I also told him that, while as a private American citizen, I cannot speak for the government or make any promises, he could rest assured that I would continue to do everything in my power to block any legislation or directives that would award Bangladesh trade benefits or any other advantages so long as it had this openly discriminatory law that fuels the ethnic cleansing of his nation's Hindus. The VPA's unjust and cynical nature was so patent, I said, that I had to know how they can maintain it and still call Bangladesh a democratic and religiously tolerant society.

"No, no," the General responded. "The Vested Property Act was actually passed as a protection for minorities."

And though I waited for some logical contortions by which he was going to explain that incredulous statement, none was

[235] As noted above, Salah Uddin Shoaib Choudhury is a Bangladeshi Muslim who was arrested and tortured for 17 months after he exposed the rise of radical Islam in his country and especially its use of *madrassas* to spread its hate among an otherwise open and tolerant population; urged Dhaka-Jerusalem relations; and advocated genuine interfaith understanding based on respect and religious equality. I made numerous trips to the Bangladeshi Embassy to win his freedom, block re-incarceration attempts, and keep him publishing free and unfettered, which he is.

forthcoming. So we sat there for perhaps a full minute of silence while I stared dumbfounded into his eyes before saying, "Now, that's crap and you know it." I was smiling when I said it, but just to make sure no one misunderstood my reaction to his response, I very genuinely advised him, "General, do yourself a favor and never respond that way to anyone in this city. We're not stupid and your answer makes it seem as if you think we are."

This individual held a position of responsibility, and as a member of the military, really did speak for the military-backed government that ruled Bangladesh at the time. This military man was otherwise a reasonable fellow, but I wanted him to know that it also makes Bangladesh look tragically ridiculous and begs a question for anyone listening. Okay, if that's the case, why do Hindus need that much protection in Bangladesh; and from whom? Later in private conversations, others there admitted that the General's comment was disingenuous and probably would not be repeated by anyone from the embassy. One embassy veteran admitted that the VPA "is a black law and must be repealed." Several others at the embassy agreed.

Later in 2008, I met with then- Ambassador M. Humayan Kabir at the embassy and demanded from him that the VPA be repealed forthwith. He responded by telling me in a rather canned fashion that "the current [caretaker] government has no intention of addressing the Vested Property Act during its tenure," as, he said, the matter was too complex. "Complex?" I asked. The Vested Property Act is undisguised racism and brings nothing but international disrepute on Bangladesh. "Oh, and by the way," I said, "no one—not even the Awami League's toadies in the press—were taken in by their disingenuous Vested Properties Return Act, which was nothing more than a cheap stunt to win votes in an election year."

The VPA is so beyond the pale of what decent nations subscribe to that its continuation has other, serious consequences for the people of Bangladesh—almost none of whom derive even a single Taka from the VPA. For instance, Bangladesh has been struggling for years, and with no success, to obtain tariff relief and other trade benefits from the United States, one of its principle garment customers. To be sure, its failure has been due to a number of factors, but one big one is the VPA; and all of them are in some way related to the same practice of curtailing freedoms and supporting the persecution of minorities and dissidents. Bangladesh's continued enforcement of the VPA is also at odds with US law that would block any such treaties and agreements because of it. The VPA could be a similar obstacle to agreements with Canada, the European Union (EU), and other countries, as well as the World Trade Organization.[236]

One would think that if human decency cannot move Bangladeshi leaders to do the right thing, perhaps self-interest would. We do know that the current government has more flexibility to act than the previous, corrupt regimes ever did, and their immediate (military backed) predecessors had a much clearer perception of the realities facing Bangladesh. Whether they do act, however, remains a matter of speculation. What is not speculative is that if they fail to act and the VPA remains, the losers will be all Bangladeshis—Muslims as well as Hindus and other minorities. And the world will remain silent no longer.

This is not about one terrible law, however. It is about a system of legalized ethnic cleansing that has operated non-stop for decades and which places every one of Bangladesh's 13-15,000,000 Hindus at risk. For what does it say about a nation and a people that they could sit back and tolerate a law that targeted a minority of their fellow citizens as worthy of nothing more than victimization? What does that say about the vaunted harmony in which Bangladeshi Hindus and Muslims

---

[236] The EU, US, and Canada are the three largest importers of Bangladeshi goods.

supposedly live if it has been so easy for the majority (Muslims) to suspend normal legal protections for millions of their (primarily Hindu) neighbors and subject them to arbitrary actions by that majority? For if they are capable of doing that to other Bangladeshis simply because they are Hindu, what else might they agree to accept?

That is the real lesson of the Vested Property Act: not one bad law but a society that has devolved almost from the beginning to a besmirched and degraded level that says to neighbors who do not share its beliefs: "To hell with you." The missing piece of that puzzle, of course, is that we non-Bangladeshis let them do it; have allowed it to proceed along its devastating course without so much as a whimper—even while we feign outrage at something, anything else. For shame!

The existence of the VPA is not merely fodder for academics and legal scholars. Testimony by Hindu refugees in India has confirmed that it takes the form of a deadly reality almost daily. Moreover, the 2009 anti-Hindu pogrom in Dhaka discussed earlier would not have occurred were it not for Bangladesh's discriminatory laws and support for the eradication of its Hindu community. As noted above, the VPA provided the pogromists with a legal fiction justifying their actions. We even noted that police were present at the time of the attack and allowed them to go on because the seizure of property was legal under the VPA; the police even cited it. But the VPA does not only uphold *injustice* by its very existence; it also allows individuals to pervert the rule of law in Bangladesh for their own material purposes. Recall that the Sutrapur land was originally owned by two Hindus, Jogesh Chando and Tarkanath Das, who gifted the land to their Hindu servants when they emigrated from Pakistan to India. It was a perfectly legal transaction, and the owners had the right under the law to dispose of their own private property in any way they saw fit.

The transfer, however, frustrated the designs of those who expected the population transfers to make the land left behind available for the taking. Almost from the day of the partition there was a sense of Muslim entitlement to lands that were now part of the Muslim political entity. That sense of entitlement trickled down to the populations, making the seizure of non-Muslim lands an ever more common occurrence. Mahbubur Rahman's attempts to take possession of the Sutrapur land over several decades were merely a common manifestation of it. What his connected brother and nephews did after his death demonstrated that success ultimately depended on one's role in the multi-layered system of corruption in Bangladesh. It also made it clear to everyone who wanted to see that nothing had changed with Sheikh Hasina and the Awami League's return to power. The police dutifully played their supporting role in subverting the law, and when some groups complained, the party in power played its part in quashing any effective protest. The Sutrapur incident also demonstrates how the VPA subverts property rights in Bangladesh. It substitutes graft and corruption, not to mention out and out bigotry, for the law and the free market. It replaces the right of individuals with the supremacy of the central authority.

After telling me that "the current [military-backed caretaker] government has no intention of addressing the Vested Property Act during its tenure," Ambassador Kabir explained that doing so would exceed its mandate, which was to bring order to the country and pave the way for free and fair democratic elections. Less than two months before it gave up power to a democratically elected government, however, it took a step that no elected government in Bangladesh ever did. And the subsequent elected government did everything in its power to let it die a quiet death.

On November 6, 2008, the High Court division of the Supreme Court of Bangladesh issued a "Rule Nisi" with regard to "instructions issued in the contents of presidential order 29 of 1972, act 45 and 46 of 1974, ordinance No. 92, 93 of 1976 [that is, the Vested Property Act and subsequent clarifications]; and *Arpita Sampatty Protapyan Ain* 2001 and circulars [that is, the sham Vested Property Return Act]." It declared those laws and their enhancements "in contradiction with the fundamental rights and the charter of declaration of Independence of Bangladesh, 10 April 1971," and ordered the government to show cause why they should not be declared to be *ultra vires* the constitution; that is, contrary to the constitution of Bangladesh and therefore null and void. The Rule Nisi also ordered the government to state why the properties so far incorporated in the list as Enemy [Vested] property should not be returned to the title holder/successor/legal possession holders "and or such other or further order or orders passed as to this Court may seem fit and proper." The court ordered the government to respond within four weeks of October 28, 2008.[237]

In short, the court forced the government to justify the continued existence and use of the VPA, as well as any reason why property seized under it for the past 35 years should not be returned to its rightful owners. And the military government did something extraordinary. It chose not to provide that justification and let the deadline pass. Now to be sure, as is standard operating procedure in Bangladesh, when the due date for a response came and went, the court did not take any action. In countries that have an independent and relevant judiciary, the passing of that date would have automatically meant that the court would declare the laws in question unconstitutional. If we hearken back to Ambassador Kabir's statement that the interim government would take no action on the VPA and that doing so would exceed its charter and *raison d'être*, the lack of action by the military-backed government all seems consistent with proper procedure.

The Supreme Court, however, was under no such

[237] Salah Uddin Shoaib Choudhury, "Vested Property Act being scrapped in Bangladesh." *Weekly Blitz*, September 10, 2009.

restriction. The interim government could have provided any number of legal artifices to justify the law and prevent or delay change by the next elected one, but did not. In what bounces between irony and tragedy, but remains squarely within the realm of hypocrisy, the world's democracies and self-styled arbiters of what should be continuously condemned that government and inaccurately called it a military dictatorship. They issued pious statement after pious statement demanding that it give up power and waxed poetically about how wonderful its successor, the Awami League, would be for all the people of Bangladesh. Yet, this military-backed regime struck a blow for minority rights in Bangladesh that no other government ever did: not Sheikh Mujibur Rahman, not the previous Awami League government, not any other government that advertises itself to be a champion of Bangladeshi minorities. Those two governments, especially Mujib's, were critical players in the institution and implementation, indeed the very existence of a Vested Property Act in Bangladesh. Yet, the international community's self-proclaimed moral leaders praise them and look the other way while their Hindu citizens are dying under their watch. The military-backed caretaker went as far as its charter (under the constitution) allowed it to go and set the table for the incoming Awami League to remove this stain from Bangladesh and choke off the economic octane that fuels this quiet case of ethnic cleansing once and for all.

Handed that gift, Sheikh Hasina and her Awami League did something decidedly un-extraordinary: they ignored the impact of the Rule Nisi and allowed the VPA to continue in force. They have assured the rest of the world time and again that they are the one true guarantor of minority rights in Bangladesh, but have so far taken a pass on this gift presented them by the outgoing government. It has not even come close to taking any action. In April of 2009, Hasina told visiting Vice Admiral of the French Navy and Commander of Joint

Forces in the Indian Ocean Gerard Valin that her government would repeal all of the country's "anti-minority" laws—openly admitting for the first time that the nation she presides over in fact has anti-minority laws. But she has not been true to her word more than two years hence.[238]

In 2010, I received an email from a Bangladeshi Hindu living in England that read:

> Bangladesh's "secularism" is a hoax. My late father's land and property at Chithalia, Kushtia, Bangladesh and my late mother's property in Pabna Town, Pabna, Bangladesh have been confiscated as "enemy property". I gave details with documentary evidence to High Commissioner of Bangladesh in London in 1981 for compensation and have been reminding them since. During Hasina's first spell, I met with her High Commissioner in London and again gave all details but the so-called "secularist" Hasina did nothing then or even now. There are thousands of Hindus like me. I took up the issue with Indian government. I was advised to go to Bangladesh to sue the Bangladesh government. What a solution! Salman Rushdie, a Pakistani/British national can recover his paternal property in Simla [Pakistan] but a Hindu like me whose parents migrated from Bangladesh has no chance to recover any property either in Pakistan or in Bangladesh.[239]

By the end of 2009, the government retained over three million acres of Hindu land, treating it as vested property, according to a consortium of human rights and research organizations. The group also dismissed as unacceptable the Awami League's 2009 Vested Property Return Act, especially because it contains no provision to return the land to its "genuine owners." According to Tobarak Hossain, who spoke at the gathering of these groups, "influential people with the connivance of local land officials had occupied these lands."

---

[238] "Govt to ensure minority rights, CHT peace treaty: PM," *Daily Star [Dhaka]*, April 30, 2009.

[239] Email from Sunil Kumar Pal, August 2, 2010.

He also said that "the land officials themselves illegally occupied a large portion of the vested property."[240]

The current government has thrown another obstacle in the way of redressing the grievance of the VPA. While the researchers claim that it holds over three million acres, the government admits to only 650,000. In part, that could be because they and their predecessors have given most of the land they seized to individuals. But it also means that even if the government finally landed on the side of justice and repealed the VPA, it would be neigh impossible for an equitable redress if those despoiled of their property made a claim. Claims will far exceeded what the government alleges it has to return; and at that point, the entire process would come to a permanent standstill. None of the VPA's seizures would ever be nullified. Injustice would reign in Bangladesh forever and ever.

Clearly, the roots of Islamic radicalism, which is the source for this quiet case of ethnic cleansing, go far deeper than the assassination of Mujib in 1975 or the tenure of the Bangladesh Nationalist Party, even with its Islamist coalition partners. None of Bangladesh's major actors can escape their share of culpability for the creeping stranglehold of radical Islam on their country. But Sheikh Hasina and her current Awami League government are carving out an especially guilty role for themselves because they are passing on a historical chance to strike a blow for real change and for a type of justice that has so far been absent in Bangladesh. The events of the last quarter of 2008—the final days of the military-backed government—have given the Awami League and Sheik Hasina a ready-made device to end the racist Vested Property Act; the grandfather of all anti-minority legislation, a system by which the Awami League has filled its coffers and bought supporters. Thus far,

---

[240] "30 lakh acres of land vested property," *Daily Star [Dhaka]*, November 27, 2009.

its answer to this historic call is a resounding "No,"which suggests that only external pressure from a morally outraged civilized world holds out hope for ending the ethnic cleansing of Bangladesh's Hindus and the expansion of Islamist power that threatens us all.

As long as the VPA continues in force, justice for Bangladeshi Hindus is a chimera. We might be reminded of the 1960 American film *Inherit the Wind*, in which a schoolteacher was charged with breaking a law that prevented him from teaching his conscience. The prosecutors and the court insisted that its sole function was "impartial administration of the law." But the movie's Clarence Darrow-like character, Henry Drummond, played by the great American film actor Spencer Tracey, disagreed. "I say that you cannot administer a wicked law impartially. You can only destroy, you can only punish. And I warn you, that a wicked law, like cholera, destroys everyone it touches."[241]

The VPA, an especially wicked law, is one piece in the larger puzzle of radical Islam's growing stranglehold on Bangladesh. Its 1974 passage, along with the 1988 ratification of the eighth amendment to the Bangladeshi constitution that made Bangladesh an Islamic state, are taking this South Asian country down an inexorable path to ethnic cleansing and Islamic supremacism. What does that bode for the future of the Bangladeshi Hindus?

As of 2008, there were 22 countries that declared Islam to be the official State religion; seven of them (Afghanistan, Bangladesh, Iran, Mauritania, Pakistan, Saudi Arabia, and Yemen) were officially Islamic States as well. An additional three countries, while not officially Islamic used *Sharia* law to administer justice. The impact on their non-Muslim populations could not be more striking:

---

[241] *Inherit the Wind,* 1960, Stanley Kramer Productions.

Country	Current percent Muslim	Previous Percent Muslim
Afghanistan*	99.7%	99% in 2002
Algeria	98.0%	98% in 2002
Bahrain***	81.2%	95.28% in 1965
Bangladesh*	89.6%	85.4% in 1974
Brunei	67.2%	60.3% in 1960
Comoros	99.0%	98% in 2002
Egypt	94.6%	92.9% in 1966
Indonesia**	88.2%	87.5% in 2002
Iran*	99.4%	98.4% in 1956
Iraq	99.0%	95.5% in 1965
Jordan	98.2%	93.6% in 1961
Kuwait***	95.0%	94.08% in 1965
Libya	99.9%	97.2 in 1964
Malaysia**	60.4%	50.4% in 1970
Maldives	100%	100%
Mauritania*	99.9%	n/a
Morocco	99.0%	98.7% in 2002
Oman	>95%	****
Pakistan*	96.3%	85.9% in 1951
Qatar**	77.5%	n/a
Saudi Arabia	100%	100%
Somalia**	99.9%	n/a
Tunisia	99.5%	98% in 2002
UAE***	76.2%	96.1% in 1968
Yemen*	99.9%	****

(*) Indicates an Islamic State

(**) Indicates a state where *Sharia* is implemented but Islam is not the official religion

(***) Indicates Gulf States, all but one of which has seen a drop in the percentage of Muslims. The reasons are a small population combined with numerous immigrants and immigrant workers that flocked to the Gulf with the oil boom.

(****) Data not available but a significant Jewish population fled or was expelled after 1948 and 1967.[242]

As the above table makes abundantly clear, modern societies that have made Islam their official state religion—and certainly those like Bangladesh and Pakistan that have declared themselves to be Islamic States—show a clear and unmistakable pattern of eliminating non-Muslims from their midst. In more than half the states listed, their non-Muslim populations have essentially disappeared. This is what comes from enshrining religious supremacy and religious degradation into the law. Contrast this with two other states located in the same region as many of the countries on the above chart that have recognizable religious majorities. But neither country—Israel or India—have declared Judaism or Hinduism respectively to be the official state religion; and thus the population figures for both reflect *increased* diversity not less, as we saw with the Muslim countries above. Between 1970 and 2008, the percentage of Israel's population that is Jewish actually dropped from 85.4 percent to 75.5 percent; while its Muslim population increased in percentage from 10.9 to 16.8.[243] During the decade, 1991-2001, India's Hindu

---

[242] Population figures are from Tracey Miller, editor, *Mapping the Global Muslim Population: A Report on the Size and Distribution of the World's Muslim Population; World Fact Book,* United States Central Intelligence Agency, Washington, DC, 2002; Houssain Kettanni, "Muslim Population in Asia," *Proceedings of the 2009 International Conference on Social Sciences and Humanities.* Singapore, October 2009; and Houssain Kettanni, "2010 World Muslim Population," *Proceedings of the 8th Hawaii International Conference on Arts and Humanities.* Honolulu, HI, January 2010.

[243] Central Bureau of Statistics, *Statistical Abstract of Israel 2009.* State of Israel, 1991-2010. I used 1970 figures as the starting point—even though using earlier figures would have been more dramatic—because they would reflect a stable situation following any dislocation after the 1967 War.

population grew by 20.3 percent, contrasted with Indian Christians who grew by 22.6 percent and Indian Muslims who grew by 36.0 percent.[244]

In Bangladesh, there might be pro-minority rhetoric and formalistic legal provisions, but the rhetoric has never been back up by actions, and the legal administration subverts the provisions' high sounding principles. The reality is that the VPA is a transparent element in the elimination of Bangladesh's Hindu population. And while the Bangladeshis have been generous enough to signal their intentions of the fate they want for their Hindus, we have failed to act in a moral way or even in our own self-defense.

Should anyone still harbor doubts about the ultimate impact of allowing a discriminatory law like the VPA to exist, they might listen to this word of warning from another people who tried to live with their own social and legal de-legitimization. As Nazism took hold in Germany and Jews had to face the first anti-Jewish laws and actions there—in a period where there were as yet no concentration camps or killing fields—many German Jews fought attempts by some to take on the Nazis and their anti-Jewish actions and initial laws. They thought it best to keep their heads down and "weather the storm." In the end, they prevailed, too: long enough to see the folly of their inaction and accompany those who wanted to fight on the long boxcar ride to death camps in Poland. According to one scholar of the period, the problem was that despite the evidence before their eyes, Germany's Jews had faith that "so long as there were 'laws,' they could live under them on the assumption that one can live under any law."[245]

For holocaust victims in the 1940s and victims of ethnic cleansing today, recognizing the true danger is much more

---

[244] Census of India, 2001, Data on Religion, Office of Registrar General, India, New Delhi, 2001.

[245] Nora Levin, *The Holocaust.* (Schocken Books: New York, 1973), p. 60.

difficult without the perspective that history provides those of us who are not in the midst of the maelstrom.

Today's Bangladeshi Hindus are in possession of clear historical evidence that passive acceptance of *any* law which takes away the rights of a minority will do nothing but encourage more and ever increasingly severe laws aimed at delegitimizing and ultimately ridding the country of that minority. So, take heed and remember that George Santayana quote from *The Life of Reason,* "Those who cannot remember the past are condemned to repeat it."

CHAPTER SEVEN

THE RED GREEN ALLIANCE

"The founding fathers of the Constitution of India overlooked the fact that civilization was a delicate thing. It can be smashed any time by a barbarian from outside or, worse, bled to death from within by the saboteur...One distinguishing characteristic of the Indian national temperament is its willingness to forget and forgive. But in its interface with two specific quarters, Islamic fundamentalism and communism, this has turned out to be a weakness." Udayan Namboodiri[246]

In May of 2008, a little noted meeting of tremendous significance took place in the South Indian state of Kerala. The participants were leaders of several communist and Islamist groups. Although all of them were devoted to the destruction of the Indian nation as we know it, the meeting was held openly. According to one of the meeting's Islamist leaders, Nazaruddeen Elamarom of the National Development Fund, it was the first open and public meeting of "Naxalites and Muslim groups for building a common strategy." In fact, the meeting generated a joint Maoist-Muslim platform and a pledge that "the rest of the fight would be fought together."[247]

Despite its importance, however, the meeting was almost entirely ignored by India's print and broadcast media. Even the most thorough review of the web sites and archives belonging to any of India's major newspapers will be undertaken in vain; a similar search for any record of it among

---

[246] *Op. cit.,* Namboodiri, p. 435.

[247] Cithara Paul, "Maoists, Muslim fundamentalists to fight 'state terror' together." *Indian Express*, June 13, 2008.

that country's broadcast media again will come up empty. With the exception of a lone posting on the *Indian Express* website, there was no mention of it at all in the India media, let alone those of other countries. While disappointing, it is far more frightening than it is sad, because this alliance of revolutionary communism and Islamism is further developed—and deadlier—in South Asia than anywhere else in the world.

In fact, this murderous association between South Asian Islamists and Communists—which I have dubbed the *Red-Green Alliance*—has been operating at least since 2004; and I have been writing about it since 2006. (Recently more articles are appearing about it from other sources, as well.) Why such silence about the Kerala meeting and other Red-Green events? There has been some hard analysis but far more speculation. Conspiracy theories, which surface whenever any political or economic subject arises in South Asia, abound in this case as well: the threat of Islamist terrorism as the price of exposure; the power of oil wealth used to blackmail people in keeping things quiet; India's cult of pseudo-secularism and political correctness; anti-Hindu bias; and more. Such explanations might have some kernel of truth to them but are far more entertaining than incisive. Dr. Jamie Glazov, on the other hand, has given us something better. He examined the way those whom we might call the "soft left" continued to hide evidence of mass murder in Stalinist Russia, Communist China, and elsewhere. The soft left dominates the media, academia, and the ruling party in India today and has for decades. While they have a difficult time engaging in the crimes common to these regimes, they seem to have no such difficulty overlooking them when committed by others who share their basic philosophy. As Glazov writes:

> As the historical record shows, the Left would do this over and over again. Every time the elements of Stalinism were uncovered in the current favorite communist paradise, the Left would simply redirect its emotional and intellectual devotion to a new, identical experiment, where the same ingredients would lead inevitably to yet

> another bloodbath. This would go on until today, when al-Qaeda and Hezbollah fill the void left by the collapse of communism [as a ruling philosophy].[248]

That is, even while the soft left would be quite genuine in saying that terror attacks, violent purges, and such are wrong; its incumbents have a penchant for somehow justifying them if they see that they have been carried out to reach the same utopian goal for which they pine. Communism's supposed goals of human equality and helping the downtrodden do that for them; so do Islamists' alleged goals of (their own but nobody else's) religious freedom and reclaiming what they allege is theirs. Both groups are also anti-Western, set their actions within a context of anti-colonialism, and claim that their movements will bring about a paradise on earth that will be the best of all possible worlds for "the people." That ever-elusive "people's paradise" appeals to leftists in academia and the media often without regard to the means used time and again in its service, because it mirrors their own philosophies.

Even so, for many people, the very notion of an alliance among communists and Islamists is a difficult concept to grasp. Could any two groups be as different as they are?

> An alliance between Asian Maoists and Islamists might seem far-fetched. Al-Qaida and its ilk, after all, won their stripes fighting communists. Moreover, its fundamental religiosity is diametrically opposed to the enforced atheism of the leftists. But evidence reaching Indian intelligence and others confirms such an alliance. Whether it is merely a marriage of convenience or the basis for a new world order with separate spheres of influence the two groups are united in their mutual quest to stamp out free choice and anyone remotely supportive of United States and Western values.[249]

Yet, for the well-known socialist Member of the British

---

[248] *Op. cit.* Glazov, p. 38. Glazov's book, *United in Hate,* does an excellent job of delving into the conceptual and other details uniting communism and Islamism, especially from Chapter Nine onward.

[249] Dr. Richard L. Benkin, "Unholy alliance of Reds, jihadists," *World Net Daily; Joseph Farah's G2 Bulletin;* November 6, 2006.

Parliament, George Galloway, it does not seem odd at all. He said that such an alliance is not only possible but also "vitally necessary and I think it is happening already."[250] No less an expert on *jihad* than the late Osama bin Laden agrees. He told *Al Jazeera* in 2003 that, "the interests of Muslims and the interests of the socialists coincide in the war against the crusaders."[251]

While on the surface the two groups might seem fatally opposed to one another, deep down inside they actually are quite in sync. Glazov notes, for instance, that communism "had a profound influence on the godfathers of Islamism, notably Sayyib Qutb, Egyptian Muslim radical and Muslim Brotherhood theorist; Pakistani Sayyid Abul A'la Maududi, a chief architect of the present-day Islamic resurgence; and Ali Shariati, a philosopher who helped lay the groundwork for the Iranian revolution".[252] Beyond that, members of free societies like the United States, India, and Israel make a serious mistake by focusing on Islam the religion and ignoring political Islam's essential nature as a movement similar to the old adversary, communism.

> Because we are free societies and must remain so, we blanch at the thought of identifying any religion with something so heinous as wanton murder. While that is to our credit, one of the most effective ways we can deal with our enemy ***is to stop giving it the status of a religion***. Using the dichotomy offered by American scholar, Dr. Daniel Pipes, we must recognize that Islam is a religion that has roots going back to the seventh century. ***Radical Islam*** is not a religion but a millenarian ideology with roots as far back as the 1920s. A religion seeks to transform its adherents in an image that is pleasing to God. The ideology of radical Islam seeks to transform the entire world in its image, and as dictated by its own warped interpretation of the religion, Islam.[253]

---

[250] Iraq News Network, "Galloway Calls for Global Unity between Islamic and Leftist Forces," April 25, 2005.

[251] *Al Jazeera* TV, February 12, 2003.

[252] *Op cit,* Glazov, p. 102.

[253] Richard L. Benkin, "Challenges before India and Israel and areas of co-operation." Address by Dr. Richard L. Benkin to South Asia Forum, March 8, 2009, Constitution Club; New Delhi, India.

And from Daniel Pipes himself, perhaps the foremost analyst of radical Islam and related phenomena, as well as one of the great minds of our age:

> [Radical Islam] is totalitarian in nature. It turns Islam from a personal faith into an ideology, into an ism. It is the transformation of a personal faith into a system for ordering power and wealth. Radical Islam derives from Islam but is an antimodern, millenarian, misanthropic, misogynist, anti-Christian, anti-Semitic, triumphalist, jihadistic, terroristic, and suicidal version of it. It is an Islamic flavored totalitarianism.
>
> Like fascism and communism, radical Islam is a compelling way of seeing the world in a way that can absorb an intelligent person—to show him or her a whole new way of seeing life. It is radically utopian and takes the mundane qualities of everyday life and turns them into something grand and glistening.[254]

Pipes has upset many who are otherwise allies of his in the war against radical Islam by distinguishing between Islam the religion and Islamism the radical ideology, in fact noting that the latter has more in common with Marxist-Leninism than with the religion itself. Yet, it is an important distinction and one worth making so we are clear that we do not see all Muslims as our enemies; that is, *we are focused on behavior not religion.*

Still, most people have a tough time imagining an alliance between groups with the clear and apparent differences that communists and Islamists have. Glazov, however, goes beneath those surface differences and has identified at least four basic characteristics that the two groups share and which have been present in any of their manifestations: puritanical rigidity, hatred and persecution of Jews, which he calls "an indispensible element in the leftist-Islamist romance,"[255] a death cult that worships "martyrdom" for the cause, and:

[254] Daniel Pipes, "Radical Islam vs. Civilization," *FrontPageMagazine.com,* February 1, 2007. The quote is from the text of a debate between Dr. Pipes and London Mayor Ken Livingstone, London, January 20, 2007.

[255] *Op. cit.,* Glazov, p. 156.

> Like fascism and communism, Islamism sublimates the individual into the collective whole, making it virtually impossible for individuals to take any real action to fix a societal problem.... To attempt to change or reform this system is perceived as blasphemous.[256]

And that is the key to understanding why the Red-Green Alliance is no mystery at all: focusing on specific beliefs of radical Islam or communism only distracts us from seeing the logic that connects the practitioners of both political philosophies.

Udayan Namboodiri, quoted in the beginning note of this chapter, has seen both communists and Islamists up close and as a Bengali Hindu has lived with the consequences of their actions. He has witnessed a steady and burgeoning growth of the Red-Green alliance and the cooperation of Islamic radicals and communists, especially West Bengal's Marxist rulers. That first-hand experience has convinced him that while cooperation is indeed tactically advantageous for both groups, the basis for it rests more solidly on their mutual opposition to democracies and to freedom for anyone who does not espouse their philosophies, whether religious or secular. Those familiar with the philosopher Eric Hoffer will recognize in the leaders and followers of both groups what he called the "true believer": "man of fanatical faith who is ready to sacrifice his life for a holy cause." [257] That is, neither communists nor Islamists have any doubt that their movements must prevail over all others for the good of humanity; and for such a just and noble cause they are willing to justify even the most unjust and ignoble behavior. True believers of both groups firmly believe that the principles underlying their ideologies are destined to become the basis for a new world order. It is a moral imperative, and they each have a moral obligation to bring it about; moral at least in their own formulation.

---

[256] *Op. cit.*, Glazov, p. 132-133.

[257] Eric Hoffer, *The True Believer: Thoughts on the Nature of Mass Movements.* (Harper & Row: New York, 1951), p. xiii.

The Red-Green alliance then is indeed a marriage of convenience, *a temporary and tactical alliance that has nothing to do with the content of the two philosophies, only their mutual opposition to the prevailing one (i.e., democracy and freedom).* The followers of each component, the Red and the Green, believe that the ultimate triumph of their own millenarian philosophy will come in a battle that destroys these erstwhile allies; not an uncommon phenomenon throughout history. While the Hitler-Stalin Non-Aggression Treaty of 1939 is the most obvious, we saw the same sort of thinking more recently when the United States armed Iraqi strongman Saddam Hussein in his long war with the Islamist Republic of Iran that caused over a million fatalities, then later invaded Iraq not once but twice, eventually ousting Hussein and seeing him executed by Iraqi leaders.

In June 2008, West Bengal's communist leaders arrested a Hindu nationalist by the name of Tapan Ghosh[258] after he convened a workshop with at least 180 participants on the "contemporary social and political scenario." In an attack that was clearly planned in advance with the connivance of West Bengal authorities, a mob supposedly acting out of spontaneous outrage descended upon the workshop while loudly denouncing it as "communal." According to local informants and others, as well as press accounts, the mob was comprised of "6,000 Muslims." West Bengal police were already present when they attacked since they had been monitoring the workshop (for what has never been clear). Yet, they made sure not to intervene and allowed the one-sided attack to transpire. What does it say about the priorities of that West Bengal government that allocates its time and attention to "monitor" its own citizens' peaceful gathering, yet sits by passively while those same citizens are attacked? Under the CPIM at least, legal and peaceful assemblage of citizens who disagree with the state's Red-Green ideology are not tolerated,

[258] This was not an isolated incident, and the West Bengal communists arrested him again in 2010.

while law breaking Islamists are. Quite a few workshop participants were injured, some even hospitalized. Yet, in a move reminiscent of almost every totalitarian regime, police arrested Ghosh, accused him of inciting the mob that disrupted the workshop and attacked him and his colleagues; and then denied him the opportunity even to apply for bail.[259] Witnesses testified that during the attack attackers shouted *Allaho Akbar*, a favorite Islamist slogan, and *Inquilab Zindabad*,[260] a popular communist shout.[261]

Sanjay Upadhya is another analyst of the South Asian scene. He, too, has written about the growing alliance of communism and Islamism there. Despite the obvious differences, he notes, the South Asian variants of the groups "clearly have much in common." Their philosophies and propaganda rely heavily on a professed disdain for Western culture and for capitalism, and they share a "utopian internationalism." They also glorify death in the service of the group's ultimate aim as "an act of piety." In other words, South Asian practitioners of the two philosophies are committed to a planned and dictated way of life that obliterates concepts like nation and ethnicity. Upadhya calls Islamists and Communists "strategic pragmatists" with "a history of joining hands with unlikely allies to destroy the primary enemy of the day." In that regard, he cites Stalin's alliance with America and

---

[259] In the summer of 2010, Tapan Ghosh toured several cities in the United States. In a *Mandir* outside of Chicago during that tour, I spoke with him, and he confirmed the facts of this case as noted here.

[260] "Allaho [or Allah] Akbar" means "Allah is great," and is almost always the phrase called out by suicide bombers and other Islamists just before carrying out their terror attacks. "Inquilab Zindabad" is a Hindi phrase that means "Long live revolution." It was originally popular by forces trying to win India's independence from Great Britain. In recent years, however, it has become the standard cry for Indian Maoists, originally popularized for the Indian left by the Hindustan Socialist Republican Association.

[261] Amitabh Tripathi, "Red-green alliance against Hindus." *Weekly Blitz,* June 25, 2008.

Britain to defeat Hitler, and the *jihadists'* alliance with the United States to drive the Soviet Union out of Afghanistan.[262] That Upadhya is a Nepalese journalist is especially relevant as he and his nation experienced the consequences of the alliance directly, as is evident below.

Less than a month after the September 11th terrorist attacks on the United States, American and allied troops landed in Afghanistan with the immediate goals of expelling Al Qaeda as a military force, destroying its safe haven there, and ending the reign of their partners in crime, the Taliban. By 2003 NATO troops had effectively destroyed the terror group's infrastructure and base of operations. From there, the Islamist terrorists moved to Pakistan's tribal belt where troops loyal to strongman General Pervez Musharaf disrupted their comfortable network of hiding places, at least for quite some time. While Osama bin Laden's terrorist organization responded in part by decentralizing, the group still needed a safe base of operations; but Afghanistan was crawling with coalition forces, Pakistan was no longer a safe haven due to Musharaf's need to show the United States he was a reliable ally, and the U.S. was in the Middle East with the terrorists having no idea where they would strike next. Where then might that safe haven be located?[263]

Besides the U.S. presence in the Arab world, there were other tactical and strategic considerations that made the Middle East less appealing for their base of operations at that

---

[262] Sanjay Upadhya, "Islamist-Communist Alliance in South Asia: Hyperbole or Hazard." *World Politics Review*, November 1, 2007.

[263] Former Pakistani Prime Minister Pervez Musharaf since has admitted that much of the US aid his country received was diverted for use against India. In order to do that, however, he had to keep US leaders convinced that he really was their ally. He also had to maintain a perpetual balancing act to keep his population from seeing him as a US puppet and an enemy of Islam, viz., the radicals who already had a chokehold on Pakistan, its institutions, and its people. See BBC News, "Musharaf admits US aid diverted," September 14, 2009.

time. The Middle East is on everybody's radar screen, and it would be difficult to disguise an effective build up of infrastructure at that time. Besides, these terrorists operate most effectively when democratic forces lose sight of them. The area is also quite a distance from their former base of operations, and it would be difficult if not impossible to cross the thousands of kilometers efficiently or without being detected. Nor is the terrain of the Middle East conducive to a clandestine build up with its flat plains and open desert that make hiding difficult. They also would find themselves within the sites of Israeli intelligence, which makes covert operations essentially impossible.[264]

South Asia, on the other hand, offered them the cover of mountains, rough terrain, and inaccessible villages; and South Asia stands at the gateway to the rest of Muslim Asia, where almost four-fifths of the world's Muslim population lives. The Arab street was already sufficiently radicalized and its social institutions thoroughly corrupted by Islamist ideology. Muslim Asia on the other hand, excluding the Arab world and Iran, was not as thoroughly in the Islamist camp and represented both a challenge and opportunity for Islamists.

The terrorists seem to have found their answer in an unholy alliance with South Asian ultra-leftists who are very active in the region and a force to be reckoned with. In fact, Maoists already had control of several areas in the region where they had been carrying out long and bloody insurgencies. As early as 2004, a US official in the Himalayan nation of Nepal commented, "Al-Qaida's nest in Afghanistan and Pakistan has been destroyed. The birds are looking for a new home."

---

[264] Since that time, Al Qaeda has built a notable base of operations in Yemen, but times have changed. A lot of focus has shifted from the Middle East to South Asia with the winding down of America's Iraq operations and President Obama's exclusive focus on Afghanistan. The Yemeni center has not supplanted those in South Asia but has augmented them. It has proven to be a more convenient point from which to launch terrorist attacks against the West. And although Israel's intelligence is just as good, if not better, the US and other in the West seem not to be utilizing it as well, certainly since Obama's shift in US-Israel policy.

He suggested that Nepal, where he was stationed, might be that home. The official was commenting on a statement earlier in the month by the United States ambassador to Nepal Michael Malinowski. Ambassador Maliknowski said that the United States was concerned that "areas in Nepal don't get out of control, don't become a vacuum where terrorist groups can move into and use Nepal for whatever." When asked if he was referring to Al Qaeda, Malinowski answered in the affirmative.[265] These official and anonymous musings were based in part on a growing state of turmoil in the tiny nation, which the Americans believed made Nepal an easy mark for the Islamists. They believed that the ongoing and decades-long insurgency by Nepalese Maoists against the constitutional monarchy, which had claimed over 13,000 lives already, might have made Nepal even more vulnerable. The population was restless; and social and political control was starting to break down, especially outside Katmandu, the capital.[266]

On Feb. 1, 2005, Nepal's King Gyanendra threw gasoline on this smoldering fire when he seized absolute power. He dissolved the Constituent Assembly, sacked the prime minister, and claimed that the action was necessary for the government to fight the Maoist rebels effectively; that is, necessary for protecting his people. But if that was his intention it completely backfired because it caused an immediate reaction by his people in the form of extensive social unrest in Katmandu, which had largely been spared the effects of the insurgency before then. Quelling that domestic unrest now became Gyanendra's number one priority. This forced him to divert limited government resources and efforts, previously aimed at stopping the rebels, so he could prosecute an internal police action against his own people. The unrest

---

[265] Sudha Ramachandran, "Nepal: A new nest for al-Qaeda?" *Asia Times online*, May 6, 2004.

[266] The above material and most of what follows can be found in, *Op. cit.*, Benkin, "Unholy alliance of Reds, jihadists."

intensified with over a year of street clashes that involved a plethora of different groups from human rights activists to leftists seeking to impose a communist dictatorship on Nepal and depose the monarch. With continuous street violence and the government fighting to maintain its power base, border control was non-existent; and Nepal had become a target too tempting for the Islamists to ignore. According to a 2006 article in the Indian newspaper, *The Pioneer*, that cites Indian Intelligence as its source, "Faced with grave internal crisis, Nepal provides the kind of environment that suits a terrorist outfit like the al-Qaeda."[267] The earlier warnings of that unnamed U.S. official seemed prophetic. On April 20, 2006, the king ceded the powers he grabbed, but it was too late. Earlier that year, according to reports from Indian intelligence, Al Qaeda terrorists already were operating in several Nepalese towns.[268]

Now what is particularly interesting about Al Qaeda setting up house in Nepal is the fact that Nepal is more than 80 percent Hindu and most of the rest of its people are Buddhist.[269] This hardly qualifies Nepal as the next Islamic republic. It was clear that Nepal could be no more than a way station for them and not another Afghanistan. The alliance with the left could be nothing more than that temporary marriage of convenience; a tactical move rather than a true marriage. What might their real target be once they feel safe enough from coalition forces to venture forth? There is an answer. If one continues the line stretching from Afghanistan through the mountains of Pakistan, then terrorist-controlled parts of Kashmir and across the Indian-Chinese frontier into Nepal; we come to Al Qaeda's

---

[267] Pramod Kumar Singh, "Time to neutralise terror camps in Nepal: Intelligence," *The Daily Pioneer*, April 15, 2006.

[268] In 2006, I began receiving private communications about this from several sources, and found further confirmation of the Indian intelligence in the *Daily Pioneer* article noted below.

[269] Nepal has the world's second largest Hindu population, and Muslims make up about four percent of its people. United States Central Intelligence Agency. *World Factbook: Nepal.*

real Shangri La: the world's third largest Muslim-majority country, Bangladesh.

While the rugged terrain and remoteness of the areas provided the Al Qaeda operatives with most of the protection they needed, Indian intelligence claims that they also received needed help from another quarter sympathetic to Al Qaeda's Islamist aims: the Pakistanis. Additionally, the Kashmiri region in question is controlled in large part by three major terror groups all aligned spiritually and politically with Al Qaida. As the terrorists were making their way toward Bangladesh, the chaos in Nepal only worsened.[270]

That gave this unholy alliance of Communists and Islamists its opening. With regular violence in the streets of Katmandu and massive social unrest pretty much all over the country, the Nepalese authorities had little time or effort to expend on border control. According to reports from Indian intelligence, individuals from Pakistan's Inter-Services Intelligence approached the Maoist insurgents with a request to provide their Al Qaeda allies with save havens in Nepal. The deal itself, according to the reports, was brokered out of the Pakistani embassy in Katmandu. The Islamist terrorists were safe, and the communist terrorists got a strong regional ally in return. As their reward, after the king ceded his emergency powers in 2006, the Maoists were made part of Nepal's government, a feat they were unable to accomplish on their own. Even India had to accede to this reality and sign off on it.

So, at the same time that we were counting on—and funding with US tax dollars—Pakistan's soldiers to destroy Al Qaeda, its diplomats and intelligence agents in league with revolutionary communists, played a key role in saving it. As a result, those Al Qaeda forces today still menace the world's

[270] *Op. cit,* Benkin, "Unholy alliance of Reds, jihadists." Also for further analysis about the Red-Green alliance in South Asia, especially its presence in Nepal, see Richard L. Benkin, "Leftist-Islamist cooperation in Asia," *World Net Daily,* August 19, 2006; and Richard L. Benkin, "Why is Al-Qaeda in Nepal?" *Weekly Blitz,* June 17, 2006.

third largest Muslim country, a mere stone's throw from Nepal; and they almost succeeded in a bloodless coup in 2007 as a result.[271] This level of cooperation is being replicated throughout the area that lies between Iran and China—where one in every four human beings lives. And the Obama Administration seems to have just discovered to its surprise Pakistan's double game.

The communist party is almost non-existent in Bangladesh, yet machinations of the Red-Green Alliance almost transformed that country into an Islamic state whose people would live under *Sharia* law. In October 2006, as directed by the Bangladeshi constitution, the ruling Bangladesh Nationalist Party handed over power to a caretaker government at the end of its five-year term. The caretaker formalized the schedule for national elections to be held the following January. Almost immediately the opposition Awami League began accusing the BNP of rigging the January vote. The charge was not given a lot of credence at first, given what several have called Bangladesh's "zero sum" political climate in which the two major parties (and especially their two leaders) will do almost anything to sabotage the other. It was not long, however, before the charge could no longer be dismissed so easily as evidence of real fraud by the BNP continued to mount; and soon, the international community was convinced that the election would not be free and fair.

When I arrived in Dhaka on January 7, 2007, I was greeted with the sight of widespread unrest in the streets of the capital and soon the sound of Awami League leader Sheikh Hasina Wajed enjoining her followers to "close down the country." What really struck me—and had to strike any other western observer as bizarre—though, was that I also arrived to hear every single western democracy demand that the elections *not* be held; too bad they did not do the same thing in Gaza. This had to be an event unique in history: democracies telling

[271] *Op. cit.*, Benkin, "Islamist takeover stopped in Bangladesh?"

a nation not to hold elections. They soon got their wish. Three days later, the military gave the civilian government an impossible ultimatum: fix this within 24 hours or they will step in and do it. Realizing the impossibility of the demand as well as the military's true motive in issuing it, the government had no choice but to resign; within hours, the military took over the country in a bloodless coup. It was to hold power in Bangladesh—as a temporary "caretaker"—for the next two years. But let us delve deeper into what happened.

Bangladesh is a democracy that will always remain uncomfortably ripe for an Islamist takeover unless or until there is an internal dynamic among its major parties to recognize that Islamists, not their political opponents, represent a clear and present danger to themselves and to the country. Bangladesh is a democracy, and the Islamists intend to use the democratic process to assume power and then destroy it—just as Hitler did in Germany, Chavez did in Venezuela, and Hamas did in Gaza. In fact, in the year leading up to the 2007 elections, their power was growing. During a 2006 conversation in Washington, then Bangladeshi Ambassador to the United States Shamsher M. Chowdhury continued to hew to the government line and told me that my concerns were unwarranted, that "the Islamists are weak." He predicted that Jaamat e-Islami, the Islamist member of Bangladesh's 2001-2006 government coalition, would lose its share of government power in the 2007 elections. Reality, unfortunately, predicted quite a different scenario that did not include the Islamists' ouster from any coalition government; quite the contrary.

In advance of the January elections, both major parties had entered into agreements with Islamist parties that favored the imposition of *Sharia* law on the Bangladeshi population. Those agreements pretty much guaranteed that whichever party won the January elections it would be bound to implement *Sharia* as the law of the land. Moreover, conditions for most Bangladeshis remained severe, and they lacked confidence in either the BNP or the Awami League. Despite some progress in alleviating it, poverty remained widespread, and there was no sign that either party had offered them much hope of anything better. Infrastructure was (and still is) inconsistent at best even in the capital. It is rather primitive in many cases; and the nation remained the first or second most corrupt country in the world by every international survey.[272] Islamist bombings had rocked the country in late 2005, and leftists fomented widespread labor unrest in 2006. It was so severe in May of that year that it forced the government to deploy the paramilitary Bangladesh Rifles. They eventually quelled the unrest but at the cost of well over 100 casualties.

As the elections drew nearer, the political parties continued to snipe at each other without either of them offering the voters any positive program to suggest that their election would alleviate their suffering. Their essentially negative campaigns only succeeded in eroding their popular support further, and a number of voters with whom I spoke expressed their frustration at both the BNP and Awami League. For many Bangladeshis, the Islamist option was becoming more attractive every day. At the very least, it seemed to many a legitimate option. Consider, too, Bangladeshi officialdom and the media continued to lionize Palestinian Arabs who faced many of the same problems with their own corrupt and unresponsive government. And what did they do about it?

---

[272] On a 2007 flight from Tokyo to Chicago, I sat next to an official from McDonald's whose primary job was to scout out locations for new restaurants in Asia. As we chatted, I remarked to her that I had seen her company's restaurants throughout that continent—from the Middle East to the Far East; everywhere but Bangladesh. Given the fact that Dhaka's population was around seven million, I wondered why. (In fact, the only recognizable fast food restaurant I saw in the capital was one Pizza Hut.) She told me that she had looked into the possibility and I was unlikely to see any McDonald's in Dhaka any time soon. Infrastructure was bad and in some cases virtually non-existent, water supplies unreliable, electricity spotty at best with regular blackouts, labor with a penchant to strike or just not show up, and so forth—not to mention the rampant corruption that interferes with getting anything done.

On January 26 that same year, they chose that Islamist option; ignoring Hamas's hate-filled platform and promise of a brutal and repressive regime to grasp what they hoped was a lifeline that would save them from Fatah's corrupt and chaotic rule. It appeared that Bangladeshis might be ready to do the same. And even if they decided otherwise, the Islamists had a pretty fool-proof Plan B.

When the dust settled over the 2007 election scandal, it became clear that the core of the BNP election-rigging scheme lay in their manipulation of the "voter lists." Those lists determine which citizens are eligible to vote, would be used by officials at the polls to verify that, and allow the individual to cast his or her vote. The above-mentioned events in Nepal had brought large numbers of foreign Al Qaeda forces to Bangladesh's doorstep. More to the point, their new proximity to more remote polls in Bangladesh gave the terrorists the ability to send in their own voters to stuff the ballot box; and that is exactly what would have happened had the BNP scheme succeeded. As noted in Chapter Four, Bangladesh's borders are porous; so porous that even an amateur like me has been able to pierce several of them with impunity. With a wink and a nod from complicit BNP officials, and a few petrodollars for the ubiquitous corrupt border guards, droves of Islamists could slip quite easily into Bangladesh and cast their votes "legally" with the help of those doctored voters lists.

Although both parties had signed agreements to bring Islamists into their governments should they win the 2007 elections, Islamists could expect an easier rise to the top with a BNP victory. That party had an extensive history of cooperation with practitioners of radical Islam, and even made them part of its 2001-2006 ruling coalition in the form of *Jamaat e-Islami*. A BNP victory was likely the best vehicle for their peaceful takeover. In that coalition, *Jamaat* controlled the less powerful portfolios. Our own sources inside Bangladesh stated that strong Islamist cooperation with the BNP election fraud, as well as increased votes for *Jamaat* and other fundamentalist parties, was likely to give Islamists the Justice Ministry portfolio. Control of the Justice Ministry would enable the Islamists to start imposing *Sharia* law in the country by fiat. All it would require is periodic directives to courts throughout Bangladesh. Were it not for the military's 2007 intervention, Bangladesh might today be a nation under *Sharia* law with an even darker record of its treatment of non-Muslims.

As noted earlier, the communist regime that ruled West Bengal for decades still remains a force with an overriding interest in maintaining the status quo even to the extent of strengthening Islamist activities in the state. One way we saw that was in the government's attempt to prevent me from finding out the truth about the persecution of Bangladeshi Hindus, including those living in West Bengal today. I am not the only anti-Islamist activist they have targeted; the only difference between me and the others is that the West Bengal communists did not physically attack me.

On October 5, 2007, Indian communists with ties to that government did attack an anti-Islamist activist in West Bengal, who has been working to help Hindu refugees from East Bengal. According to witnesses, Bimal Sarkar was "brutally attacked by CPIM criminals at Dinhata in Cooch Bihar District." Sarkar is president of the Bharatiya Refugee Front, "and the major pillar of our [anti-Islamist] activities in North Bengal."[273] The attack on Sarkar was particularly significant because his attackers felt connected enough to carry it out in broad daylight and in front of a government building. Their confidence was justified; no member of West Bengal's Communist government or police stopped it. Witnesses—who testified on the condition of anonymity for fear of reprisals—report that eleven party members beat Sarkar "with sticks and other lethal weapons," breaking his nose and causing

[273] Testimony about the attack and the individual were given to me directly or through Bikash Halder. Many are part of the article cited below.

numerous lacerations. Sarkar had to be taken to the Tufangang Sub-Divisional Hospital where his wounds were treated; and after several hours, he was released but ordered to consult a specialist to prevent permanent damage to his nose.

Sarkar's first trip, however, was not to the doctor. It was to the local police station where he filed a complaint. In it, he named the local Communist Party secretary and the head of the party's "Youth Front" among his attackers. Bikash Halder continued to interview witnesses to the attack He asked them if they thought the government was likely to act on Sarkar's complaint and try to bring the attackers to justice. The informants were skeptical, with more than one remarking that the government would do nothing because "they are Pro-Chinese."[274]

Bimal Sarkar is part of a growing though fragmented resistance to the increasing power of radical Islamists in South Asia. In 2008, we met in northern Bengal and accompanied each other to several refugee camps where we gathered evidence of the refugees' plight and the oppression that forced them out of Bangladesh.[275]

The year 2008 also saw an uptick in Communist violence in

---

[274] West Bengal has been under communism for so long that one can detect what we might call a "communist culture" there, so entrenched are its elements; as can be seen in these notes from a meeting in Kolkata, February 16, 2010: "Amitabh [Tripathi] and I went to meet with a very prominent and aged director, Biyush Gangooly. As Amitabh noted, even prominent individuals live in modest circumstances here. Under the communist regime, it is considered almost a crime to appear comfortable. This is another reason why West Bengal has not had much in the way of capitalist investment. The situation last year with the Tata Nano plant resonates with what is happening with Obama and health care. The Tata plant was bringing a great many jobs with health care and other benefits to a rather poor state. The communists, however, put up roadblocks and had public protests almost daily. So Tata pulled out and re-located in Gujurat. I remember reading an article in the *Daily Telegraph*, about a female employee who lamented her loss of health care benefits from this employer. Other former employees were left without services that they now had to hope the state would provide."

[275] Richard Benkin, "Communist Thugs Attack Anti-Islamist Activist in West Bengal." *Asian Tribune*, October 18, 2007.

West Bengal and other areas of India that are close to or share a border with Bangladesh.[276] Intelligence agents operating in those areas "traced the source of the additional firepower the Maoists have acquired" to Bangladesh. In particular, they said that Indian Maoists have been waging a bloody insurgency in that part of the country and elsewhere and that they used the additional weaponry "to renew violence in the eastern part of the nation." (These Indian Maoists are called Naxalites.[277]) India's *Daily News & Analysis* reported that those same agents traced the arms to the violent Bangladeshi Islamist group, HUJI.[278] They concluded that HUJI and the Naxalites "forged a quid pro quo understanding... and set up shelter pockets across the border." Members of India's Border Security Force have alerted authorities along the two countries' long border to be on the lookout for "possible attempts by the most wanted Maoist guerillas to cross the border with the help of HUJI agents" to take shelter there. Others have reported the same sort of understanding and cooperation between the two internationalist groups for some time.[279]

The BSF has increased its patrols in the southern part of the

---

[276] There had been a split among Indian communists in 1967. The West Bengal rulers are from the more established Communist Party of India/Marxist; they are not part of the violent Communist Party of India/Maoist.

[277] The Naxalite movement can be traced to the Indian Communist Party's 1967 split. Naxalites are associated with the more radical faction in the split. The group began its activities in Communist West Bengal but was never favored by the government there. Since then, it has branched out to operate in 22 Indian states throughout the subcontinent. Per figures collected by the South Asia Terrorism Portal, Naxalites accounted for 1326 Indian fatalities between 2005 and 2009. In 2008, I entered the village of Naxalpari in West Bengal. Located in the stretch of Indian territory between Nepal and Bhutan and just south of Sikkim, Naxalpari was the site of a 1967 communist uprising that gave birth to the violent Maoist movement. It is the town where the Maoist group got its start and from which it took its name. While there are an estimated "millions of [Naxalite] sympathizers" on whom the communist cadres count, neither they nor the Naxalite organization itself evident in its founding town when I was there. I did meet with a large group of Bangladeshi Hindu refugees living in the village, though.

[278] Harkat ul-Jihadi Islami.

[279] Sumanta Ray Chaudhuri, "Is Huji powering Maoists?" *Daily News & Analysis*, October 29, 2007.

state, especially in the districts of Nadia, and North and South 24 Parganas, where it believes the greatest danger of infiltration lies. Unfortunately, the additional manpower and attention did nothing to hamper the success and expansion of this Red-Green alliance. In fact, the terrorist groups have found ways to work together despite these patrols. In one reported instance of cooperation, Maoists gave the Islamists "the high-intensity explosive Neogel-90" that they coveted; and in exchange the Islamists gave them the use of "the terror outfit's network in Nadia and South 24 Parganas" so it could extend its stronghold.[280]

It is no coincidence that the Islamist-Communist meeting in May 2008 took place in Kerala, one of three Indian states that have had communist governments for some time. The other two, West Bengal and Tripura, are both in India's Northeast.[281] The silence of India's print and broadcast media is rather baffling, however, especially since representatives of both groups have been carrying out terrorist attacks throughout the country for decades. One wonders if the silence was because there is some substance to the persistent charge that India's media suffers from a leftist bias and a timidity that militates against their reporting on any matter that might offend the large and active Muslim minority. While there is hardly sufficient space for a thorough explanation of this charge, the lack of media coverage for significant events like the Communist-Islamist strategy session in Kerala is not isolated. Media silence regarding the ethnic cleansing of Bangladeshi Hindus replicates it. With the exception of *The Daily Pioneer,* major English-language print and broadcast media in India have ignored the issue. When activists like me attempt to make people and institutions aware of the carnage in Bangladesh, we find that we often are met with skepticism.[282] That skepticism is particularly strong outside of India where I am

---

[280] *Ibid.*

[281] *Op. cit,* Paul.

[282] Almost tongue in cheek but with a good deal of seriousness, I once asked if my sources of information were that much better than those of major news

regularly asked, 'Well if it is such a terrible atrocity against Hindus, why do we hear nothing from India?' the assumption being that if any entity would be outraged at the atrocities and feel obliged to defend the attacked Hindus, it would be India—*the* Hindu nation. Early in 2010, I met with a renowned and impeccably credentialed human rights organization—and one whose actions merit that reputation. Their initial reaction was first and foremost skepticism and a challenge to provide the objective information that will overcome it. The group's long history of consistent and principled human rights efforts was a major factor leading to this book and the research that went with it.

Is there a leftist or more appropriately a "multiculturalist" bias in the Indian media? I believe it is blatant; and since there is a world of literature debating the subject—ranging from outraged denial to outraged accusations of anti-Hinduism—this discussion will suffice with three examples of blatant bias of which the author has direct knowledge.

In March 2009, Varun Gandhi, candidate for the Indian *Lak Sabha* and the great-great grandson of Mahatma Gandhi, was arrested for "hate speech" by the state government of Uttar Pradesh. The press portrayed him uniformly as a "communalist" who was out to spark a religious war between Hindus and Muslims. They never said what that "hate speech" was because, they said—and this was so bizarre for anyone who lives in a society that allows free speech and supports a free press—doing so would make them liable to arrest for the same offense. So the public received a great big "trust us" from the media. I recall watching panel after panel on Indian television about the matter, and every single one of them was

---

organizations; for if I was aware of these things, either they were not and my sources are better, or they were and have suppressed the news. For an article that explores this question with regard to the lack of reportage on the death of a truly moderate Muslim (that is, one who does not require us to accept bigotry as the price of dialogue), see Richard L. Benkin, "Are my Sources Better than CNN's." *Canada Free Press,* February 8, 2009.

stacked heavily with participants who vilified Varun. In one instance, a panel member said that by his speech, Varun was guilty of "killing hundreds." Her statement was so extreme that even the host suggested that she did not mean that literally. But the panelist insisted she did, and neither the host nor the other panelists took up the matter again.

Longtime activist, Kolkata resident, and expert on India, Francois Gautier noted that the "tragedy is that the Indian press does not play its role, because not many mainstream newspapers or television channels complained when Varun Gandhi was in jail, while [convicted terrorist] Madani, a criminal who has the lives of 60 innocent people on his hands, was free and standing for MP" without media comment.[283] What one could not tell from the media was that many Indians were galvanized by Varun Gandhi and his successful resistance to the concerted attempts to demonize him. On the day he returned to Pilibhit (the Uttar Pradesh town from which he was running for office) to challenge the authorities to arrest him or let the matter drop, the roads into town were lined with hundreds of thousands of Indians who cheered him. Media coverage tended to minimize or discount the popular reaction. Nor did the media cover the fact that Varun was elected to parliament by a huge margin even while the rest of his party experienced a crushing defeat.[284]

Just a month earlier, there was another revealing incident. The editor and publisher of West Bengal's oldest and most prestigious English-language newspaper, *The Statesman,* were arrested under Section 295A of the Indian Penal Code. Ravindra Kumar and Anand Sinha, editor and publisher

---

[283] Francois Gautier, "While traitors are unhanged, monks suffer, "*The New Indian Express,* April 26, 2009.

[284] The above comments were based on direct observations and experiences of mine in India during the month of March 2009. This included extensive interviews with random people on the streets of various cities, rural populations, and others; as well as hours of watching Indian news television programs. The incident involving the panel member was on the IBN-CNN network.

respectively, were charged with "deliberate and malicious acts intended to outrage religious feelings" for reprinting an article from the British newspaper, *The Independent.* In the reprinted article, "Why should I respect these oppressive religions," its author Johann Hari took issue with religions in general that he felt were rigid and attempted to impose their mandated way of life on others.[285] He had the misfortune of counting Islam among those religions and so *The Statesman's* reprint led to protests and even riots that paralyzed parts of Kolkata. Indian Muslims demanded action, claiming that the journalists insulted their religion and its prophet, Mohammed. The government responded predictably in a knee-jerk fashion with the arrest.

Now, anyone who is familiar with the British media knows that its members will assiduously avoid writing *anything* that might be interpreted as being offensive to Muslims. Hari's article was no exception. The fact that the rioting was so severe, at one point causing *Statesman* staff to barricade the building's front entrance and be escorted by police in and out of it by a side door, indicates how rare it is for an Indian publication to publish anything even as mild as the Hari article with regard to Muslim sensibilities. The West Bengal government further reinforced the media's self-censorship by signaling that it would arrest journalists when what they write is merely *perceived* as offensive whether it is or not. And finally, except for a few mild protests from European outlets or Indian media with European parents, the media did not join in a principled defense of their colleagues and freedom of the press.

At the end of March that same year, US President Barack Obama delivered his long-awaited "Af-Pak" policy speech. If one counted on the Indian media to provide comprehensive news and commentary on how the Indian people reacted to it, he or she would have been sorely disappointed. While the

---

[285] Johann Hari, "Why should I respect these oppressive religions?" *The Independent,* January 28, 2009.

media virtually drooled over the attention Obama gave the subcontinent, individual Indians (including past and current members of the military and intelligence communities) were outraged. Many whom I interviewed said what this analyst told me, that Obama "lived up to his middle name [i.e. the Muslim name Hussein] by showing the face of a pro-Pakistan US policy." Obama's call to seek out "moderate Taliban" and negotiate a peace—a major element in the policy—was met with a combination of outrage and derision at the president's naiveté. Yet, these reactions were absent in the media accounts, which focused instead on the formal and polite compliments issued by the government in New Delhi.

More telling was the fact that just hours before Obama's speech, a suicide bomber detonated his explosives and himself in a mosque located in the Khyber region near the Pakistan-Afghan border, destroying the mosque and killing almost 200 worshippers. Most media reported the incident briefly and reported that it was a signal to Obama that peace would not come easily. While that might be true, almost no outlet reported the fact that several security sources had evidence that the attack was the work of one of those potentially "moderate" Taliban groups that had entered into the sort of agreement Obama said should be a model for peace. There was an almost total blackout on more information, and no English-language media even mentioned it. One Hindi-language channel reported that the group's spokesman said that by the attack it was abrogating the treaty because "it is against the will of Allah to fight for Sharia only in Swat Valley, that all of Pakistan must be under Sharia." That is, the treaty was nothing more than a temporary inconvenience which they felt free to scrap at any moment.[286]

Returning to the assiduously ignored Red-Green powwow in Kerala, given their power base there, the Maoists were the logical driving force behind this conclave. The most

---

[286] Richard L. Benkin, "Obama Afghan-Pakistan Policy Already Unraveling." *American Thinker*, March 28, 2009.

prominent leftist group was South India's Porattom. According to Minority Watch, Porattom is linked to banned leftist and Islamist terrorist groups; including the Students Islamic Movement of India (SIMI) and National Democratic Front, a radical Muslim group accused of having similar links with the banned Islamic Sevak Sangh. The Porattom leader who convened the meeting said, "Maoists and Muslims share the similar plight of being the victims of the state terror. The best way to eliminate anyone who raises his voice against the wrong doings of the State is to brand him as a Naxalite. Similar is the plight of Muslim brethren. Whenever and wherever there is a terrorist attack, the community as a whole is brought under the eye of suspicion. Every Muslim is being treated as a potential terrorist. It is in this background that we have decided to join hands to combat this state sponsored terrorism."

A Muslim leader of the meeting, Nazaruddeen Elamarom of the National Development Fund said pretty much the same thing. He claimed that Maoists and Muslims suffer from "state terror" more than any other people in India, and called them the government's "favourite whipping boys." He also provided those who doubt the likelihood of such an alliance with yet another rationale for it: that the government accuses both groups of being "anti-nationals. And this is the common thread that connects the two." Moreover, Nazaruddeen made certain to describe that strategy not in his own group's religious phrasing, but in a leftist, class conflict perspective. They would, he said, concentrate on fighting "the upper caste ruling elite forces of Hindutva and imperialism who have the agenda of hunting down Maoists and Muslims."[287]

The world's worst human rights abusers, especially Islamists and leftists, have appropriated the language of human rights to disguise their anti-human rights aims and confuse liberals and democracies. Islamists and leftists alike long have used the tactic of branding their victims as victimizers and their murderous behavior as somehow

[287] *Op. cit.*, Paul.

principled self-defense of their presumed "people." Adolf Hitler justified his actions as self-defense—defending the German people from "treacherous Jews" or the anti-German machinations of other nations as manifest in the draconian Treaty of Versailles, imposed upon Germany after the First World War. In his June 22, 1941 speech, for instance, announcing Germany's invasion of the Soviet Union, Hitler said, "The alliance between these nations [Germany, Japan, and Italy,] was therefore only an act of self-defense against a threatening, egotistical world coalition of wealth and power."[288]

The corruption of the concept of self-defense allowed Hitler and his followers to justify genocide and the murder of the most defenseless, children; which is where it comes uncomfortably close to what we are seeing in Bangladesh.

> If only one country, for whatever reason, tolerates a Jewish family in it, that family will become the germ center for fresh sedition. If one little Jewish boy survives without any Jewish education, with no synagogue and no Hebrew school, it [Judaism] is in his soul. Even if there had never been a synagogue or a Jewish school or an Old Testament, the Jewish spirit would still exist and exert its influence. It has been there from the beginning and there is no Jew, not a single one, who does not personify it.[289]

His propaganda films portrayed Jews as vermin that had to be exterminated or else they would pollute a healthy German society. So, too, we have seen instances in which *imams* and other Muslim leaders take a similar tone with regard to Hindus and other *kaffirs*.

All of this falls neatly into the *modus operandi* of the Red-Green Alliance; nor is it the first time that this association has

---

[288] "Der Fłhrer an das deutsche Volk 22. Juni 1941," in Philipp Bouhler (ed.), *Der grodeutsche Freiheitskampf. Reden Adolf Hitlers,* vol. 3 (Franz Eher: Munich, 1942), pp. 51-61.

[289] Robert Wistrich, Hitler's Apocalypse, p. 122; from a conversation with Croatian Foreign Minister General Kvaternik, July 21, 1941.

played a terrible and critical role in world events. Ion Mihai Pacepa was an intelligence officer during the reign of communism in Rumania. During those decades, the various intelligence agencies behind the Iron Curtain worked closely with and took their marching orders from the Soviet KGB. Pacepa has since revealed that the KGB saw the Islamic world as a:

> Petri dish in which we could nurture a violent strain of America-hate. Islamic cultures had a taste for nationalism, jingoism, and victimology. Their illiterate, oppressed mobs could be whipped up to a fever pitch. Terrorism and violence against America would flow naturally from their religious fervor. We only had to keep repeating, over and over, that the United States was a "Zionist country" bankrolled by rich Jews.[290]

Pacepa also has testified that "the PLO [Palestine Liberation Organization] was dreamt up by the KGB, that its Palestinian National Charter (which remains in force today) was drafted in Moscow, and that the first Palestine National Council's 422 members all were "handpicked by the KGB." The Rumanian secret service "was responsible for providing the PLO with logistical support," and the East German intelligence branch (Stasi) and the KGB armed it. He said that communist intelligence agents were working openly in at least four Arab countries: Egypt, Syria, Iraq, and Libya. But two years after these states were humiliated by Israel in the 1967 Six-Day War, the Soviets embarked on a new strategy:

> In 1969, the KGB managed to catapult [Yassir Arafat] up as chairman of the PLO executive committee. Egyptian ruler Gamal Abdel Nasser, who was also a Soviet puppet, publicly proposed the appointment. Soon after that, the KGB tasked Arafat to declare war on American "imperial Zionism."....Arafat claimed to have coined the word "imperial-Zionism," but in fact Moscow had invented this battle cry many years earlier, combining the traditionally (sic) Russian anti-Semitism with the new Marxist anti-Americanism.[291]

---

[290] Ion Muihai Pacepa's comment in "Symposium: The Terror War: How We Can Win," *FrontpageMag.com,* November 15, 2004; quoted in Glazov, p. 153.

[291] Jamie Glazov, "From Russia With Terror," *Frontpage Magazine,* March 1, 2004.

We can only imagine how different history would have been—not to mention the present and foreseeable future—if the Red-Green Alliance did not spawn and maintain the Middle East conflict and work overtime to make sure all efforts at peace would be futile.

Thus, this alliance of communists and Islamists is not new; its roots stretch back decades with no break. It is not new, just under reported. It is not new, just more prominent (though still under reported). It is not new, just more deadly (though still under reported by the major media and international talking heads).

Thus, it behooves us to listen again to the words of the leader of the radical leftist group, Porattom, at the Kerala conference. "Maoists and Muslims share the similar plight of being the victims of the state terror. The best way to eliminate anyone who raises his voice against the wrong doings of the State is to brand him as a Naxalite. Similar is the plight of Muslim brethren....It is in this background that we have decided to join hands to combat this state sponsored terrorism."[292] Several analysts have identified the growing alliance among Islamists and the left, but they have not applied it to the populous and volatile area of South Asia.[293] The short-lived German-Soviet Alliance allowed the German-Japanese-Italian "self-defense" Axis to launch World War II, which resulted in the deaths of up to 78 million people.[294] With almost one out of every four human beings living in South Asia, how many deaths might we expect if this unholy, Red-Green alliance is not stopped and stopped now?

---

[292] *Op. cit.,* Paul.

[293] For instance, *Op. cit.,* Glazov, *United in Hate*; and David Horowitz, *Unholy Alliance: Radical Islam and the American Left.* (Regnery: Washington, DC, 2004).

[294] Estimates of World War II deaths vary greatly, and the sources are many. Whether one uses the lowest estimate of 50 million dead or the high estimate of 78 million, the reality is that this unholy alliance from the last century plunged the world into hell and snuffed out the lives of tens of millions of people.

CHAPTER EIGHT

WOMEN: DOUBLY VICTIMIZED; DOUBLY STRONG

"Female refugees are those with the inner strength to force both Indians and Bangladeshis to secure their people's safety and their legal status. We could be witnessing a bottom up power revolution far more widespread and grassroots than anything represented by the female heads of state; something that might be signaling a real transformation in gender relationships in South Asia." Richard Benkin[295]

In February 2008, I visited over a dozen and a half refugee camps along the volatile India-Bangladesh border; and often in the proximity of Maoist and Islamist camps. Some were tolerated as semi-legal, most not even that. Speaking out against their conditions can be a life and death decision for these refugees who lack any legal status and the protections that come with it. This means that when the West Bengal government sent out its thugs to threaten people with serious reprisals, should they reveal its secrets to me, the refugees knew that the consequences would be real and significant. Thus, in an example cited earlier, consider what it would take for someone to defy that threat. In that village near the Nepal border, the threat was having the desired effect. With the local Commissar staring at anyone who stood up to talk, the refugees spoke freely about atrocities that occurred some years back in Bangladesh but would become mute when I asked about crossborder attacks by Bangladeshi radicals

[295] Richard L. Benkin, "South Asia's Irrepressible Women," *Weekly Blitz,* June 25, 2008

today. It took one brave woman to break that wall of silence. She stood up, looked the communist official in the eye, and said, "I'm not afraid of anybody," and proceeded to describe the frequent violence the refugees still face in West Bengal.

How many people are so afraid of being thought politically incorrect that they do not even have the courage to call out someone who makes an offensive, anti-Hindu, or racially insensitive remark in casual conversation or social interaction? How many people let it pass thereby extending their tacit approval to it? How many people stand in silence for fear of what? Discomfort? Being thought impolite? Now think about what this woman risked by standing up for justice in defiance of a repressive government with one of its representatives right there.

In another camp, a group of young girls were especially adamant about their pride in being Bengali and their determination to help others regain the same. One of them told me how she wanted to be a schoolteacher and teach young Bengalis their history and culture so they will demand the same rights others have. The common thread linking these two incidents is that the people who had the courage and determination to take a stand publicly—and to make a difference for their people—were women. These women spoke out in potentially dangerous situations while their male counterparts remained silent. In some of the camps I visited men were my major informants; in others, women were the ones who testified to Islamist violence. That tended to intrigue me as our image of rural Hindu societies is one in which women occupy a decidedly lower status than men.

The above vignettes contrast sharply with the stereotypical image of South Asian women. They are not passive. They are strong and brave enough to take action—seemingly more so than their male counterparts in the camp. Yet, South Asia is losing a tremendous resource in them. And their bravery also stands in contrast to the special atrocities they face every day in both Bangladesh and their ersatz havens in India.

One story men and women both told me repeatedly involved abductions of young Hindu women in Bangladesh. They might be walking by the road or on their way to school when groups of Muslims would force them into vehicles, carry them off, and then rape them. The attacks were abominable, but the victims also had reason to believe they might be victimized again; this time by their own people who would not let them return home where they were thought to have shamed their families. In fact, they often had no choice but to remain with their victimizers and even bear them children.[296]

One (ideology-driven) argument is that Hindus were not targeted specifically by Pakistani troops and Bengali Islamists during the 1971 "Bengali holocaust" that accompanied Bangladesh's War of Independence. The fact that there were Muslim victims, too, only makes sense given the preponderance of Muslims in the country and the fact that the revolt was essentially a revolt of one group of Muslims against another. As we argued earlier in this book, it does not however, refute the argument that Hindus were targeted *as Hindus, not merely participants in the revolt.*

Hard data on the numbers of Hindu women raped or abducted during that period are difficult to come by due not only to the chaotic situation pertaining in the country during that time of revolution, but also because good data were always—and to some extent continue to be—elusive in East Bengal/East Pakistan/Bangladesh. A statement by the American author, Susan Brownmiller, that in 1971, Hindus and Muslim women were raped in proportion to one another "reflecting the population of Bangladesh" does not appear compelling and merely contributes to the often-leftist driven effort to downplay the importance of religious and ethnic identity as determinants of action and emphasize economic or

[296] These stories were told to me with a numbing repetitiveness by refugees in North and Northeast India. For numerous examples of targeted anti-Hindu violence during the current, Awami League government's tenure, see this book's *Appendix*.

political factors.[297] Virtually every other credible source from that year makes it clear that Hindus were particular targets of the Pakistani army and their Islamist allies; and that the precipitous decline of the Hindu population in Bangladesh during and immediately after the war provide further confirmation. Moreover, in the ongoing ethnic cleansing of Hindus in Bangladesh, Hindu women have always been specific targets for violence, including rape. Their objectification as a means to attack Hindu men and the entire community has, as Jenny Lundstrom notes, "proven more effective than murder."

Numerous examples in this book's *Appendix* help demonstrate that rape and forced conversion of young women continue to be used widely against the Bangladeshi Hindu community. As noted by the Hindu American Foundation in its 2010 report:

> Violence against women is a common weapon used to intimidate and harass minority communities across the world. It has similarly been used in Bangladesh as a means to attack Hindus. For instance, in the period immediately following the 2001 elections [of the nationalist BNP government], approximately 1,000 Hindu women and girls were raped....The *systematic* kidnapping, rape, and murder of minority women, particularly young Hindu girls, continued in 2009....Rapes and kidnappings of Hindu girls are often accompanied by forced conversions to Islam (emphasis mine).[298]

Its report the following year noted no substantive change:

> Violence against women is a common weapon used to intimidate and harass minority communities across the world. It has similarly been used in Bangladesh as a means to attack Hindus....For instance, in the period immediately following the 2001 elections [of the nationalist BNP government], approximately 1,000 Hindu women and girls were raped. The systematic kidnapping, rape, and murder of minority

[297] Susan Brownmiller, *Against our Will: Men, Women, and Rape.* (Simon & Schuster: New York, 1976), p. 81.

[298] "Hindus in South Asia and the Diaspora: A Survey of Human Rights 2009," Hindu American Foundation, March 21, 2010, pp. 13-14.

> women, particularly young Hindu girls, continued in 2010. Rapes and kidnappings of Hindus are often accompanied by forced conversion to Islam.[299]

While HAF noted a reduction in the total number of incidents under Awami and called it "encouraging," the organization still recognizes that violence against Hindus, and especially Hindu women, remains a serious problem in Bangladesh that is not being addressed by the Awami League, citing Lundstrom. "In Bangladesh," she wrote, "gang rape has become a major tool of political terror, forcing minorities to flee and has proven more effective than murder. The victims have all been women belonging to either of the ethnic/religious minorities. Neither little girls nor pregnant women and the elderly are spared."[300]

Lundstrom's insight that rape is more effective than murder is central to understanding that these attacks on Hindu women are in essence tools of political terror. They are not about sex; they are about asserting religious privilege and dominance. The female victims are not the rapists' targets: their male family members and religious community are. The pattern has been cited numerous times throughout this book and has special significance within the context of rape and female (especially Hindu female) rightlessness. Government complicity in this process is the critical glue that holds it together and without it, the process breaks down entirely.

One of the most important functions for the head of any household is the ability to protect its other (physically and socially weaker) members. In traditional (and even less traditional) societies where the heads of households are overwhelmingly male, there is a sexual component to that function. (Take note that "sexual" does not refer to the

---

[299] "Hindus in South Asia and the Diaspora: A Survey of Human Rights 2010," Hindu American Foundation, May 25, 2011, p. 11.

[300] *Op. cit.*, Lundstrom, *With Intent to Destroy? Rape as Genocide under International Criminal Law: The Case of Bangladesh.*

physical act of lovemaking but to gender roles or acts of *violence* that assume the guise of that same act. The same holds true for the use of the term throughout this discussion.) If a man's spouse, mother, daughter, or some other female family member can be taken at will and raped, it is a statement that the man cannot protect "his women." If it happens again and again, the statement grows stronger and more powerful in its effect. And if there is a clearly discernable pattern that the victims are from one ethnic or religious community (i.e., Hindu) and the victimizers from another (i.e., Muslim), it takes on a more intense dimension. Sociologists in fact have long noted that the more discernable social dimensions that parties to any conflict share in contrast with those individuals on the other side, the more severe the conflict.[301] Thus, the rape of Hindu women by Muslim men seemingly at will is a statement to Hindu men that they lack a basic ability that define what a man is.

In a civil society, the government has an obligation to protect those citizens who are not able to protect themselves and their families; hence, the criminal law and law enforcement apparatus. As we have seen, however, the Bangladeshi government has refused to live up to that obligation with regard to Hindus. It does not matter which political party is in power, nor does it matter whether the government representative is local or national. The male head of the household's only option for protecting its members is to flee to a society that will protect them against rape. It is also his only option for regaining his status as a man. Once the Hindu family flees, its property is forfeit to the state under the Vested Property Act, to be awarded to whichever crony the state desires—often the very Muslims who victimized the Hindus and forced them to flee for their own protection. In that way,

[301] See the work of Georg Simmel, often called the "father of conflict sociology," especially, Georg Simmel, *The Web of Group Affiliations.* (The Free Press: New York, 1955).

Lundstrom's statement about rape being "more effective than murder" becomes very clear: rape more than murder will force Hindus to leave their homes in Bangladesh and more effectively furthers the elimination of Hindus in that country. The effectiveness of rape as a tool for ethnic cleansing, however, goes away as soon as the Bangladeshi government steps into its role and punishes the rapists, thus protecting and preventing future victims.

There is another aspect to the use of rape as a weapon: the objectification and rightlessness of women, in this case, Hindu women specifically. Incidents such as the one involving Koli Goswami, reported in Chapter 3, show clearly how this works. When Koli was taken from her bed and kept from her loved ones, it was a statement that she was not in control of her life or movements; her abductors were. When the police summarily dismissed the incident as a lover's quarrel, they refused to consider than anyone other than the male perpetrators had anything material to say. More generally, the use of rape and abduction against women *as mere devices* in the pursuit of larger goals places women in the role of objects without laws or parameters that would protect their individual rights. Why Hindus in particular? Because no group of Muslim women or the female (Muslim) Prime Ministers have objected to their sisters' objectification or even today do anything to change it.

I encountered a chilling indication of how this objectification of Hindu women and its link to Islamization has spread to West Bengal in February 2011. On February 17 in the late morning, I entered a rural village in the Gangooly district of West Bengal. While there, my colleagues and I were asked by the women in the village to meet with them and listened to their testimony. Several indicated a covered area nearby and one woman told us through a translator, "When the women go there to bathe, Muslim men and boys from nearby villages make places from themselves [indicating a raised area] and look at the women in their nakedness." They station themselves on an adjoining raised area and watch the nude women. Sometimes, they would laugh loudly and call out to them.

When representatives of the Hindu community complained to Muslim elders in the area, the young men and boys told the women that they are there for the "enjoyment" of the Muslim males; that is, have no say in the matter or right to any modicum of modesty or privacy. None of the Muslims disagreed or have attempted to stop this behavior. Local police have told the two communities to "work out their differences" but will not intervene or sanction the Muslim males, again confirming that these women have no right to demand that their personhood be respected.

These events were confirmed by all of the dozens of women present.[302]

The earlier report on 20-year-old Hindu college student Koli Goswami's ordeal demonstrates the Bangladeshi government's deep involvement in the victimization of women, despite its female Prime Minister. It also shows how the major media, human rights groups, and women's rights groups have abandoned Bangladeshi Hindu women. Even young women like Koli Goswami, who have broken out of old, restricted roles in an effort to chart a new course for Bengali women, can so easily be turned into non-persons without any protections from the law or activists.

As noted earlier, many facts in the case are not in dispute: Five Muslim men broke into Koli's family home at 12:45am on June 13, 2009. The home is in Ghosai Chandura, located in the district of Dinajpur in northern Bangladesh; there were clear signs of both vandalism and a struggle; whether as a ruse, which police allege, or as part of a kidnapping, as Koli's family insists, when the young woman cried out for help, the men over powered her and covered her mouth to muffle her

[302] This was told to us at a general village gathering on February 17, 2011. Accompanying me were Miriam Guttman-Jones and Amitabh Tripathi of Forcefield and Tapan Ghosh and Aminatra Chakrabarty of Hindu Samhati.

scream; then, they carried her away. Her family has not seen her since. To most Westerners, stories like this strain credulity. It simply is not within the realm of their experience. That means when presenting these incidents in Washington, to feminists, and in other venues, allegations alone are insufficient to resonate. Moreover, the Bangladeshi government's predictable denials actually seem more plausible than incidents themselves.[303]

When the police told human rights activist Rabindra Ghosh and other GHRD and BDMW representatives on site, "It is not kidnapping. It is love affairs between kidnapper and victim"; it gave them leave not to protect the young woman. It also enabled them to define Koli not as the victim of a violent crime but simply a "wayward lover"; no one whom they have to find and save. In their formulation, she and her "boyfriend" cooked up this fake crime so she could taste forbidden love. Given the position of superiority Islam enjoys in Bangladesh, such an elaborate and violent ruse hardly seems necessary. Yet, the police continue to insist on that as a justification for their inaction in fighting the abuse of women. As noted earlier and elsewhere in this book, normal legal protections are suspended for Hindus and other minorities in Bangladesh. Evidently, that is doubly so for minority women.

Abductions, rape, and forced conversion of young minority girls is on the rise under the current Bangladeshi government; prosecutions are nonexistent. The case of Koli Goswami is but one of many sad examples. To indicate the extensive nature of the problem, here follows only six of many examples that exist: the first two from HAF's 2010 report,[304] the next two

[303] The information in this chapter about the abduction of Koli Goswami has been taken from two articles in which I reported our findings: Richard L. Benkin, "Bangladeshi Hindu Abducted, Forced to Convert to Islam," *Canada Free Press,* August 11, 2009; and Richard L. Benkin, "Bangladeshi Hindu Abducted, Forced to Convert to Islam: Update," *Canada Free Press,* September 11, 2009.

[304] "Hindus in South Asia and the Diaspora: A Survey of Human Rights 2010," Hindu American Foundation, May 25, 2011, pp. 11-12.

from BDMW and GHRD[305], and the final two from my own investigation and confirmed by multiple sources.[306]

- Indrani Sikdar (18) was abducted on January 17, 2010 while she was on her way to Eden College in Dhaka. Her father, Gopal Sikdar, complained to the Tejgaon police, who said his daughter was with Asif Shakil. They then warned him not to file a complaint. That same day, Indrani Sikdar called her sister-in-law crying and asking to be rescued. She reported that she had been abducted by Asif Shakil (24) and others. After Gopal Sikdar again asked the police to help recover his daughter and they refused, he contacted BDMW for help.
- Deepa Rani Kundu (23) was kidnapped by a group of Muslims on March 14, 2010 while going to the Youth Training Centre at Pal Para. Deepa was an honor student at the Government Azizul Hoque College, Bogra district. Her father asked the officer-in-charge at the Bogra Sadar police station to rescue his daughter, but instead of taking the immediate action warranted in this sort of case, he told him to just file a complaint. When the police did not follow up on the complaint, he tried again in vain to get them to act. He then filed a case with the Women and Children Repression Tribunal and named five perpetrators, no action has been taken by any official body to recover the young woman or arrest the perpetrators.
- Nipa Banarjee (17), a Hindu school girl, was kidnapped December 1, 2010 in Dinajpur on her way to a class in computer training. Four identified Muslim perpetrators incapacitated her brother, who was

[305] Material sent to me in two email communications from Rabindra Ghosh and supported by the Bangladesh Minority Watch.

[306] See Appendix II.

accompanying her, and shoved the young woman into a micro bus. Her parents have asked the police to help recover their daughter, but the police have taken no action to recover her or question the perpetrators (identified by several witnesses and newspapers). When BDMW's Rabindra Ghosh agreed to help them and contacted the police, the latter told him that they were "not always bound by law for arresting the perpetrators on the request of human rights activist." The police superintendant also told Ghosh to stop his inquiries.

- Shika Rani Roy (15), a Hindu school girl of Durgapur Palashbari Upazila of Gaibandha, was kidnapped on October 25, 2010 at about 2:30am while she was on her way to the outhouse. Several Muslim men, led by one who had been making lewd advances to her for some time, grabbed her from behind, covered her mouth, and abducted her. Despite the family's complaints, the police have taken no action saying that the perpetrators are still on the move and they are helpless.
- Beauty Biswas (5) of Gach Baria, Narail in Khulna was taken at night and raped by Badsha Mollah, a 27 year old Muslim. The girl was left unconscious and bleeding from her vagina, and the family found her assailant trying to strangle the child. Despite media coverage, BDMW involvement, and evidence including witnesses and pictures, as well as the perpetrator's previous criminal history, the police have taken no action.
- Class IX student Anju Rani Das (16) of Patuakhali in Barisal was taken from her older brother's custody by eight identified Muslims, who took her to a Muslim dominated area, Kaina, where all eight gang raped her in turn. She also was assaulted and her belongings looted. The area police superintendent has admitted

> that the incident occurred, but the police nevertheless did nothing more than question two of the eight perpetrators, releasing them with no charges.

This has not stopped in 2011, which has at least a half dozen confirmed cases of Hindu women being raped and abducted within the first five months of the year.

The purpose of this chapter, however, is not to recount the litany of violent attacks on Hindu women; there are enough sources for that information. It is instead to demonstrate the continuous evidence of inner strength that I have seen again and again among Hindu women in the refugee camps and other places in West Bengal near the India-Bangladesh border; it is the tremendous loss we experience by denying these women their right to thrive and even lead; it is perhaps another source of strength that will help bring an end to the ethnic cleansing of Bangladeshi Hindus. The number of attacks on Hindu women is greater than those in this book's two Appendices, and include those which very well could have happened but were not confirmed sufficiently for inclusion, and those which the victims do not report, whether out of fear, shame or the belief that nothing other than their further victimization is likely to come of it.

This deliberate attack on the Hindu gene pool as a strategy proceeds with a wink and a nod from the Awami League and silence from the international community. It is neither new nor unique; but it demonstrates that Bangladeshi Hindu women are in danger even beyond the frequent use of rape as a weapon of war. Reviewing the Koli Goswami case, it is clear that the (male) kidnappers took action, as did those (males) who likely paid their way; the (male) authorities took action; and so did her (male) uncle, Professor Goswami. The women, however, were nothing but pawns—objects in the battle for South Asia's future. We might never know Koli Goswami's fate, but we do know that she will not be a model for other Bangladeshi Hindu women wanting change; that she will not contribute any insights that will help her people break away from their role as victims; that she will not contribute to the Hindu gene pool and succeeding generations of her people.

We have noted a quiet strength among Bengali women that should betoken a revolutionary change in gender roles. We noted that in the elderly woman who spoke out in front of the menacing West Bengal commissar; we noted that in the young refugee near Nepal who wishes to become a schoolteacher and teach her young Bengali cohorts to have pride in who they are and demand the same rights that others have. And we have seen it in young women in Bangladesh like Koli Goswami, a promising young college student, and 17-year-old Nipa Banarjee, kidnapped on her way to a class in computer training. Beyond the injustices done to these women, these and other incidents reinforce retrograde beliefs that women are incapable of independent action; and they stand as warnings to Bengali women not try to break out of their traditional roles or attempt to stand in contradiction to the misogynist ascendency of radical Islam.

In March 2009, a group of NGOs addressed a UN panel that was to investigate violence against women and girls in Bangladesh. "Often harrowing in their depictions, the panelists detailed abuses of Hindu and Buddhist women and girls in today's Bangladesh solely on account of their religions. Pressure to convert to Islam, the use of rape as a tool for humiliation and the Vested Property Act that dispossesses Hindus of their properties were among many issues discussed," according to the Hindu American Foundation, which participated in the panel.[307a]

Former HAF Public Policy Director, Ishani Chowdhury, described Bangladesh as "a land spiraling to a path of

[307a] "HAF Joins Prominent Bangladesh Human Rights Groups at United Nations Panel: Highlight Abuse Against Minority Women in Bangladesh," *Hindu American Foundation,* March 6, 2009. Available at http://www.hafsite.org/?q=media/pr/bangladesh-hr-un-panel.

intolerance for non-Islamic faiths, lack of respect and justice towards its female population and the inability to coexist in an ever shrinking global village." She went on to cite several examples of young girls gang raped or kidnapped because of their non-Muslim faith. Her examples were taken from 306 specific incidents documented by the HAF.[307b]

In the two years since this damning evidence was presented, the UN has taken no action.

Despite that, feminist groups, who should be the most vocal opponents of this inaction over this victimization of women in Bangladesh, have offered neither help nor shared outrage. Major human rights groups have been silent as well; and governments around the world have taken no action. Perhaps they remain wedded to the forlorn hope that the election of the Awami League government would bring needed change for the mass of Bangladesh's Hindus living outside of the major cities like Dhaka and Chittagong; a hope proven empty time and again with that government's tenure about half over with no action on the matter.

These outsiders can help, and should if they still wish to claim the mantle of justice. Their support can give hope to young women like those mentioned in this chapter; can tell them that they are not alone; can let them know that the hell in which they live is the exception to what is right, not the rule. But that is all we can do. For change to be real, it must come from the Bengali Hindus themselves. During my first visit with the refugees in Northern Bengal, something happened that would define my efforts and what my goals are. I was in a camp not far from the borders of Nepal, Bhutan, Bangladesh, and Tibet/China, speaking with a gathering of Bangladeshi Hindu refugees and asked them: "What do you want me to do?" Their answer, expressed by one individual: "We want you to give us our rights." I thought a moment and responded:

[307b] *Ibid.*

"You don't want me to 'give' your rights, because if I can give them to you, I can take them away. You want to demand and take those rights. They're yours and not mine to give."

That notion, however, would seem especially alien to women in and from the society these refugees left and where their forebears lived for centuries. According to the United Nations,

> Hindu women in Bangladesh are reported to suffer greater gender discrimination than Muslim women due to existing legislation that governs the religious community. Hindu women do not have any legal rights to inherit property and as no formal registration of Hindu marriages is required, Hindu women do not have the legal right to divorce.[307c]

That is, because Bangladesh is formally an Islamic State, in which the name of Allah is inserted into most legislation, the nation's laws govern a Muslim population; minority communities are expected to pass their own laws.[308] Hindu marriage, for example, is a purely religious affair with no standing in law, and Hindu marriages are not even registered with the state. That makes for rightless women if something goes wrong in the marriage. As one Awami League official noted during the rule of its arch-rival, BNP, "Hindu laws need to be reformed in our country. But the free democratic environment that is needed for the reforms has not properly developed yet."[309]

Islamists and Communists actually did Hindus a favor because they have overturned a social order that bred a Bengali Hindu population known for passivity, especially in Muslim dominated Bangladesh and the lands surrounding it. Women in that order held to an especially submissive role, from which they only rarely were allowed to depart and then

---

[307c] UN High Commissioner for Refugees, "Chronology for Hindus in Bangladesh," *RefWorld,* Published in 2004; last updated 2011.

[308] *Ibid.*

[309] Shanchita Sharma, "Hindu women in Bangladesh Suffering for absence of marriage registration," *Daily Star,* June 27, 2004.

only within the bosom of their families. But the radicals turned that order on its head, emasculating the men and leaving many women with no effective protector. Hence the sort of incidents noted above in which women and not men spoke out in dangerous situations to get some degree of help from the world outside of their rural societies.

Now from Nepal, not very far from some of those villages in Northern Bengal, comes another remarkable story about South Asia women speaking out. In 2008, Nepalese Communists took over the government after a parliamentary election propelled them to power. Not too long before, these same Maoists were carrying out a brutal insurgency that had caused over 15,000 deaths in the impoverished Himalayan country. Through an arrangement with Pakistani intelligence, Maoist rebels provided safe havens for Al Qaeda troops on the run from coalition forces in Afghanistan. In exchange, the Pakistanis secured them a place in Nepal's emerging coalition. With their transformation from a radical insurgency to a political party both recent and tactical, Nepal's new communist rulers have been systematically destroying both opposition and individual rights in that country.[310]

Journalist Niraj Aryal writes in *Telegraph Nepal*, "It was in the district of Dailekh-Nepal, women folks took to the topsy-turvy *Ghodeto* and *Godeto* (Horse and Foot trails) protesting against the Maoists' atrocities." He made sure to add, "No male counterparts as of then had the courage to protest against the Maoists." Aryal also notes that in the bloody days before the communists got their rebel feet in the constitutional door, it was women in the Nepalese countryside who worked as "underground party cadres or even carried weapons

[310] Beyond its implications for the people of Nepal, this is the same transformation that many Europeans (largely but not entirely on the left), as well as people like former US President Jimmie Carter, are urging for Hezbollah in Lebanon, Hamas in Gaza, and the Muslim Brotherhood in Egypt. It also predicts and mirrors Barak Obama's search for "moderate Taliban."

in the Peoples' Liberation Army fighting against the age-old discrimination and bravely resisting the State led high-handedness."[311] His point was not that women favor a particular political faction but that they have had the strength and courage to take dangerous stands. There was danger from the monarchy then, and there is extreme danger now that the Maoists have taken power. According to the South Asian Terrorism Portal, "Maoist atrocities" are coming in from all over the country.[312] In some cases, it appears Nepal's new rulers are exacting a brutal revenge on those who previously opposed them, especially in the countryside. Yet, these women stood against that tide.

Sharada Silwal, an official of Nepal's Sancharika Samuha [Women Journalists' Association] told Aryal that women now comprise about a third of the nation's Constituent Assembly, while previously they were only about five percent. Aryal quotes Silwal as saying, "Above all women's inherent rights must also be well drafted in the new constitution...the women legislatures must be careful to not let the patriarchic mindset prevail in the Nepali politics that may finally get reflected in the new constitution."[313]

Bangladesh, India, and Pakistan all have had female heads of state, but their examples of female leadership never translated in a way that affected the lives of most South Asian women. In fact, it is quite the opposite. While their actual terms in office can be judged independent of how they got there; all of them owed their positions to their relationship with a man: Indira Gandhi (India) to her lineage from the Gandhi/Nehru line; Benazir Bhutto (Pakistan) to her father and former Prime Minister Ali Bhutto; and Bangladesh's two *begums,* to their

---

[311] Niraj Aryal, "Women on Top," *Telegraph Nepal,* May 30, 2008.

[312] The online portal has an array of documents pertaining to the situation in Nepal:
http://www.satp.org/satporgtp/countries/nepal/document/index.html.

[313] *Op. cit.,* Aryal, "Women on Top."

father (Sheikh Hasina Wajed to Sheikh Mujibar Rahman) or husband (Khaleda Zia to Ziaur Rahman). Interestingly, with the exception of Nehru, all of those men were assassinated.

Do the women of South Asia offer the greatest hope of stopping these atrocities, whether those against women in particular or against Hindus in general? It appears from the incidents in the camps that the strength for such an upheaval exists. It is also clear that while the old patriarchal values that have suppressed female initiative for generations persist; the chaos imposed on the community by Islamists intent on destroying it have also destroyed those old norms. With each human rights visit I make to South Asia, I encounter more and more women—Bengalis and others—breaking free of those restrictions. I meet them in the camps, yes, but also on college campuses throughout the region where many are prominent in our efforts to organize South Asians. They are taking more significant roles in media, both mainstream and alternative.

It seems that the revolution is building. The most significant element still lacking is support from the outside world that should have been forthcoming long ago.

CHAPTER NINE

JIHAD AND THE GOALS OF ETHNIC CLEANSING

"Democracies never get it quite right, always responding to tyrannies too late. In 1936, Nazi troops crossing into the Rhineland had secret orders to retreat at the slightest sign of resistance; but it was only Hitler's first land grab so we let it go." Richard Benkin[314]

It is difficult to say this but quite often when I tell people about the ethnic cleansing of Bangladesh's Hindus, they react in a way that pretty much says, *'That's a shame, but so what.'* Many of my fellow Americans have asked me why I concentrate on things half way around the world when there are so many people in need here in the United States. I tend to answer them in two different ways. The first answer is that atrocities are terrible whether committed near or far; whether on people 'like us' or not like us; and opposing them is integral to the way we Americans understand the world and our role in it. Perhaps contemporary Americans carry an additional burden because we are so often considered the leader of the free world. Despite contemporary economics and the chattering of the international elites, as well as our dedicated foes, we remain the great beacon for the oppressed that still draws millions to our shores to escape persecution, lack of opportunity, and thwarted potential. Yet, leader though we came to be, we sat on the sidelines with the lesser lights of this world while millions of Jews in Europe, Ibos in Biafra, Tutsis in Rwanda, and how many others were brutally murdered.

---

[314] *Op. cit.*, Benkin, "Stop Them before they Kill Again."

That moral answer must always come first; it demands that position of supremacy in our hearts and minds.

Americans and others, however, need to hear a second answer as well. 'Do you really believe,' I ask, 'that what is happening to the Hindus of Bangladesh will have no impact on us? That if we turn away while Islamists drive Hindus out of Bengal, their ancestral homes and perhaps all of India, that *our* enemies will not be strengthened and come after *our* children next? Connect the dots,' I tell them. Is it any coincidence that the world's most volatile and dangerous regions are violent because of attempts to drive out, convert, or murder their non-Muslim populations: Israel, Lebanon, and the rest of the Middle East; Chechnya and cities like Malmo in Europe; Malaysia, the Philippines, parts of China and Thailand in East Asia; and Afghanistan, Kashmir, Pakistan, and now East and West Bengal in South Asia? Still not convinced?

Okay try this. Hebron is a city near Jerusalem and the location of one of Judaism's holiest sites, the Cave of Machpelah. Hebron had a continuous Jewish presence in from the time that the Jewish Patriarch Abraham purchased a plot of land there almost 4000 years ago until 1929. In that year, Hebron and vicinity's entire Jewish population was either massacred or driven out in an anti-Jewish pogrom by Arabs. Every mosque and imam in the region incited and supported the atrocity:

> House to house, they went, bursting into every room looking for hiding Jews. Religious books and scrolls were burned or torn to shreds.... Jews were variously beheaded, castrated, their breasts and fingers sliced off and, in some cases, their eyes plucked from their sockets....The carnage went on for hours, with the Arab policemen standing down – or joining in. Blood ran in streamlets down the narrow stone staircases outside the buildings. House to house, room by room, the savagery was repeated....Not a single victim was simply killed. Each was mutilated and tortured in accordance with their identities, the specific information provided by local Arabs. The Jewish man who lent money to Arabs was sliced open and the IOUs burned in his body. The Jewish baker's head was tied to the

> stove and then baked. A Jewish scholar who had studied Koranic philosophy for years was seized, his cranium cut open and his brain extracted. Another man was nailed to a door. Some 67 Jews were brutally murdered.[315]

In 1967, Israel reclaimed the area. Prior to that reclamation, including the period of the Jordanian occupation, which began in 1948, Jews were barred from the area, and thereby deliberately prevented from paying homage or praying at this very holy site. Israelis, now able to return to Hebron for the first time since the pogrom, observed that almost four decades after the 1929 massacres, traditional Jewish amulets, or *mezzuzot*, were still affixed to many doorposts.

Some years later, as the Arab population concentrated in the city itself while Jews lived in the surrounding areas like *Kiryat Arba,* people observed that the *mezzuzot* had been removed, but one could still see their outlines on the doorposts. Eventually, Israelis in the areas saw that the doorposts themselves had been replaced, especially as the conflict between Jews and Arabs in the area became ever more intense and there was a decided attempt by Arabs to deny that Jews had any title to the area; thus their effort to erase all trace of the ancient Jewish community in Hebron. And now after the Arabs essentially falsified the historical record, the world has the utter gall to call the descendants of the victims "settlers" and those of the attackers the rightful owners![316]

How does that happen? Simple. Islamic leaders, religious and lay, come in two kinds: those who have an agenda and will push it with religious fervor; and those lacking courage, insight, or both and will tacitly approve of the others by never unequivocally objecting to their actions. Part of that agenda is to erase the extensive non-Muslim history in the Middle East

---

[315] Edwin Black, *The Farhud, Roots of the Arab-Nazi Alliance during the Holocaust* (Dialog Press: Washington, DC, 2010), pp. 205-206.

[316] Also see Richard L. Benkin, "The Modern Destruction of the Temple Mount," *Bible and Interpretation*, May 2003.

and South Asia that pre-dates Islam. It is integral to their cynical effort at de-legitimizing non-Muslim claims to territory and holy spots, and any attempt for non-Muslims to assert a moral authority backing their presence. In 2000, my family and I ascended Mount Nebo in Jordan—the place where Moses watched the Jewish people cross into Israel after their 40-year journey from Egypt and where he then died. My wife noticed that there were both Christian and Muslim commemoratives on the site but no trace of anything Jewish—which she found odd since she and everybody else she knew associated Mount Nebo most strongly with Judaism. So she asked our guide why that was so, to which he replied dismissively, "There are no Jews in Jordan." The history of Hebrews on the east side of the Jordan River goes back to biblical times, thousands of years before Mohammed was even a gleam in his father's eyes. Yet, with a dismissive flourish of his hand, our guide felt justified in their "right" to erase Jewish history in the region. Take a peek at the Jewish holy sites in Hebron and elsewhere on the west side of the Jordan if a *judenrein*[317] Arab state ever takes hold there.

Moreover, a spineless international community gives cover to Islam's "historical jihad" by complying with its demands, and if facts get in the way, they will ignore them. In 2010, the Islam toadying United Nations organization, UNESCO (United Nations Educational, Scientific and Cultural Organization), declared that Rachel's Tomb just outside Bethlehem was "a mosque." It was an affront to Jews everywhere and to the integrity of an historical narrative. For never before, outside of marginal screeds made with no evidence to support them, was the site considered to be anything but the burial site of the Jewish matriarch and holy to Jews.[318] Shortly thereafter, some Muslims tried to take things

[317] Literally, "Jew free" in German. Judenrein was the term Nazis used to spell out their goal for German, Europe, and ultimately the entire world. It is how they would report that they accomplished that goal in particular areas.

[318] Hillel Fendel, "UNESCO Erases Israeli Protests from Rachel's Tomb Protocol," *Arutz Sheva (Israel National News),* November 1, 2010.

further by declaring that there was no Jewish connection to the Western Wall of the Temple in Jerusalem—the holiest site in the Jewish religion. To compound matters, the Palestinian Authority (PA)—with no historical evidence to support the ridiculous Muslim claim—declared it to be its holy writ.[319]

After the Holocaust, Jews determined that they would never be victims again, and with the State of Israel as their model, have held to that vow, defeating the far more numerous *jihadis* who wish to return Jews to their former status as victims. They have continued to defy UNESCO's bigoted resolution declaring Rachel's Tomb an Israeli "national heritage site" (along with the Cave of Machpelah). The lesson is important not only for Jews because the process is not unique to the Middle East. It is happening on the Indian subcontinent as well. It began under the Muslim Mughals after their conquest and subsequent rule of the subcontinent that lasted for centuries.[320] The same ideology (and its supporters) responsible for atrocities against Bangladesh's Hindus and for other human rights travesties, advance their ethnically-cleansed version of history that pretends millennia of history before Islam in South Asia simply never existed. The same

---

[319] From the world's greatest (non-Jewish) expert on the Temple Mount and its archeology, see, Leen Ritmeyer, "PA Declares 'Western Wall Was not Jewish' until 16th Century AD," *Ritmeyer Archeological Design,* November 23, 2010; http://www.ritmeyer.com/2010/11/23/pa-declares-western-wall-was-notjewish-until-16th-century-ad/.

[320] The Mughals ruled most of the Indian subcontinent from their bloody invasion in 1526 to their demise which began with the death of Emperor Muhiuddin Muhammad Aurangzeb Bahadur Alamgir I in 1707. They were Indo-Arabic Muslim rulers responsible for overseeing massive, forced conversion of many in the Indian subcontinent to Islam. They oversaw some voluntary conversions as well, often for social and economic reasons. The last Mughal Emperor was deposed by the British in 1857. Prior to that, however, with British rule progressively supplanting the Mughals and religious tolerance re-taking hold, the Mughal grip on the subcontinent's population weakened considerably. I use "re-taking" because religious tolerance was an essential element of Hindu-ruled society prior to the Muslim takeover.

appeasers repeat their falsehoods as if they were true. These are the same people who lock on to the politically correct version of history and international events whatever it might be, and assiduously avoid those pesky facts that get in the way. A great example of that is the Ram Temple. What is that, you ask? The site about which I am referring is usually referred to as the Babri Mosque by the mainstream media and most "respected" international organizations. Located in Ayodhya in the Indian state of Uttar Pradesh, the Babri Mosque became the most popular mosque in the area until 1992 when it was destroyed in riots that left 2,000 dead. The standard narrative is that the mosque was an original construction commissioned by the first Mughal emperor, Zahir Uddin Muhammad Babur in 1527. That, however, is patently false. Muslims, revisionist historians, and the fearfully politically correct in academia and media have advanced a periodic drumbeat to rebuild the mosque on the same site; however, they do *not* want people to know that the Babri Mosque was built on land holy to Hindus for centuries before Islam ever came to the subcontinent.

As late at 1986, the *Encyclopedia Britannica* noted that "Rama's birthplace is marked by a mosque, erected by the Moghul emperor Babar in 1528 on the site of an earlier temple"; an entry that is mysteriously absent from post 1986 encyclopedias.[321] Moreover, the Archaeological Survey of India's excavations found "a massive structure just below the disputed structure and evidence of continuity in structural activities from the 10th century onwards up to the construction of the disputed structure (Babri Mosque)."[322] That is, in order for the mosque to be built, the invading Mughals had to destroy an ancient and religiously significant Hindu *Mandir*. Yet, because the Babri Mosque incident has become a *cause*

[321] "Ayodhya," *Encyclopedia Britannica*, 15th edition (Encyclopedia Britannica Inc.: Chicago, 1986).

[322] "Proof of temple found at Ayodhya: ASI report," *India Abroad,* August 25, 2003.

célèbre for Muslim radicals and their supporters, that history is being denied and ignored. This instance of politically correct revisionist history supports contemporary *jihad.* This is because acknowledging that the mosque was built to destroy a Hindu holy site, sheds an uncomfortable light on the cynical claims that re-constructing the Babri Mosque there is a matter of justice. In fact, those claims support the opposite position, one of injustice, which is why even the suggestion of that pre-Islamic history is demonized as somehow Islamaphobic.

Acknowledging that Muslims deliberately built their mosque on the Hindu holy site is an extremely uncomfortable recognition for those who are trying to whitewash the "religiously imperialistic" nature of Islam's history. The point needing emphasis this is that there is extensive evidence to cause scholars and others to question the standard narrative, regardless of whether or not one believes in the Muslim or Hindu version. Those individuals and institutions considered to be the standard bearers of accepted knowledge and academic discourse have not flinched from questioning the narratives of other faiths or the veracity of non-Muslim holy books, on much flimsier bases. Yet, many—both Muslims and their politically timid fellow travelers—would find our suggestion that they treat Islam, the Quran and Hadiths, and as well as standard Muslim narratives with the same scrutiny they treat their cognates from other faiths and peoples nothing less than Islamaphobic. Can we guess why these revisionists fear such objective inquiry? *It is because the Ram Temple episode and so many others are part of a grander scheme for global jihad and Muslim imperialism. The same can be said of the effort to drive Hindus from Bangladesh first and the rest of Bengal after that.*

In 2001, the ultra-fundamentalist Muslim leaders in Afghanistan destroyed the massive sixth century statues of the Buddha in their country because, they said, they were blasphemous. An explanation that is in keeping with their Taliban philosophy, however, suggests that they destroyed the giant Buddha statues because they were reminders of an ancient and pre-Islamic past that has been relentlessly oppressed out of existence in Afghanistan. Again, real history is suppressed to serve the goals of *jihad,* which threatens everyone who reads this book: vulnerable populations like the Bangladeshi Hindus, of course; targeted nations like India, Israel and the United States, to be sure; and Muslims as well, who can count more dead from *jihadists* than anyone else.[323] Standing by while Bangladesh's Hindus, Israel's Jews, or Middle Eastern Christians are sacrificed to appease the Islamists will do as much to protect the appeaser as sacrificing the Czechs did to keep Nazi and communist imperialists from pursuing those British and French appeasers.

The problem is not confined only to westerners and non-Hindus. It has been a gargantuan task to get other Indians, including other Hindus, to recognize the atrocities committed against their co-religionists in Bangladesh and their own government's failure to take action even when the victims stream into India for help. Immediate action is needed to save their very existence, but those same Indian authorities continue to turn their backs on them. As I once remarked at a 2008 press interview in Lucknow, Uttar Pradesh: "If I were an Indian Hindu, I would be ashamed that an American Jew had to come half way around the world to stand up for the Bangladeshi Hindus."[324]

In the end, of course, no amount of sacrificial lambs or revisionist history will satisfy evil regimes. History is littered with corpses that the rest of the world threw at the feet of violent oppressors in the vain hope that their sacrifice would save the hides of those who sacrificed them. That was not only cowardly and immoral, but wrong and self-defeating as well. Ask the people of what was then called Czechoslovakia.

---

[323] Richard Benkin, "Al Qaeda's War on Islam," *Arabs for Israel,* 2005; http://www.interfaithstrength.com/images/WAR.html.

[324] Statement made to various members of the Indian press following addresses to students and faculty at Lucknow University, February 20, 2008.

It happened to them not once but twice, most infamously in 1938. British and French officials signed the notorious *Munich Pact* with Adolf Hitler that gave him title to the Czech "Sudetenland," where a large ethnic German population lived. Those ethnic Germans and the fascist state that claimed to represent them refused to live in a larger polity with others—something which we are experiencing today with many Muslim populations in western nations like the United Kingdom (where they are yet a minority) and eastern nations like Bangladesh (where they are a majority). The Munich Pact was signed on September 30, and Hitler was in Prague the following March 16, having gone much farther than the small territory given him under the Pact. In 1948 it happened again as western powers remained passive while communist Czechs, backed by Soviet troops that had massed on the country's borders, staged a coup that routed non-communist forces in Czechoslovakia. Did appeasement in Munich stop Nazi expansionism? Did passivity to the Czech coup stop Soviet expansionism? Of course, neither did. How about the lack of action against the Communist Chinese whose naked aggression removed Tibet from the world map? Tibet: you remember that country? It was swallowed up by China over five decades ago, and there are no talking heads calling that an "occupation."

The fact is that the imperialism of powers like Nazi Germany, Soviet Russia, and Communist China is rooted in their governing ideologies and cannot be satisfied by throwing them one or another land or people. Those and similar states and entities are fired by their desire to spread their totalitarian ways of life across the world. Feeding them a sacrificial lamb only makes the fires grow. Or put in a way that every parent knows, rewarding bad behavior only encourages more bad behavior.

All of which brings us to our current millenarian ideology, radical Islam, and to Daniel Pipes. The lifelong scholar of Islam has noted that we in democratic nations falter because we see radical Islam within the framework of religion; that is, we get stuck on the "Islam" part. As such, we give any cowardly authorities who might want one—whether we call them appeasers, multiculturalists, or liberals—an excuse to minimize the threat that this ideology poses. Because they fear stepping on politically correct memes or being called "communal," they can posture as morally strong individuals while implementing a morally bereft policy. On December 1, 2001, Pipes wrote that "there is a growing inclination on the part of non-Muslim politicians, journalists, and others to assert that Islamism—or at least a vague hostile ideology—not 'terrorism,' is the enemy, and to acknowledge that this includes a war of ideas as well as one of violence. This recognition is vital; just as a physician must identify and name a disease before being able to treat it, so too, a strategist must identify and name an enemy before defeating it."[325]

That inclination might have been dominant at the time Pipes wrote that—less than two months after 9/11—but it was before the international effort to demonize anyone who identified the attackers as Muslims was in full swing. Pipes, however, was already aware of that effort, noting on the day after Islamist terrorists attacked the United States, a "a contrary current, that of disassociating Islam from the problem, or pooh-poohing radical Islam as a threat, should not be ignored"; and Pipes has continued to update his list of infamy with more and more examples, especially from the administration of Barack Obama.[326] Unfortunately, the latter tendency seems to have taken over in academia, the media, and in most western governments, with President Obama using the power and moral suasion of the United States to further their appeasing goals. And that is now a major impediment in the fight to stop

---

[325] Daniel Pipes, "Calling Islamism the Enemy," Daniel Pipes Blog, www.danielpipes.org, December 1, 2001; updated June 19, 2010.

[326] Daniel Pipes, "Not Calling Islamism the Enemy," Daniel Pipes Blog, www.danielpipes.org, September 12, 2001; updated May 15, 2010.

ethnic cleansing of Hindus in Bangladesh. This is not to accuse Obama and company of deliberate complicity in ethnic cleansing, but the philosophies of appeasement and multiculturalism that they champion militate against efforts to identify the problem and the perpetrators and to defeat them. Obama's culpability is akin to how former Harvard President Lawrence Summers described the impact of anti-Israel advocates: "Serious and thoughtful people are advocating and taking actions that are anti-Semitic in their effect, if not their intent."[327] That is, while not their intention, the ethnic cleansing of Hindus necessarily follows from the defeatist positions they support.

As noted in the last chapter, Pipes has provided the rest of us with a clear and easy-to-follow dichotomy between Islam, the religion and radical Islam the totalitarian philosophy. ***Islam is a religion*** that has roots going back to the seventh century. ***Radical Islam*** is not a religion but a millenarian ideology with roots that stretch back no further than the 1920s. A religion seeks to transform *its adherents* in an image that is pleasing to God. The ideology of radical Islam seeks to transform *the entire world* in its image, and as dictated by its own warped interpretation of that religion. This is not about territorial demands, whether in the Middle East or South Asia, because there are no limits to them. Territory is not their goal, and no territory will satisfy it. As Pipes has written, "the struggle is ultimately one of ideas and armies, not of law enforcement or religion. As in World War II or the Cold War, the ideological enemy has to be defeated, followed by a rebuilding of the societies in which the ideology took hold."[328] Once we understand the essential nature of our enemy, the course of action becomes unmistakable.

---

[327] Speech by Harvard President Lawrence Summers at Harvard Memorial Church, September 17, 2002. Quoted in Patrick Healy, "Summers hits 'anti-Semitic' actions," *Boston Globe*, September 20, 2002.

[328] Daniel Pipes and Graham Fuller, "Combating the Ideology of Radical Islam," *Washington Institute for Near East Policy,* April 10, 2003. Also see Daniel Pipes, *Militant Islam Reaches America* (W.W. Norton: New York, 2002).

> Ostensibly, property disputes, in Palestine, Kashmir and elsewhere are the justification for Islamic terrorism. Will peace be established if Palestinians are given the territory they want and Kashmir is handed over to Pakistan? It is more than likely that such concessions will only whet the appetite of Islamic fundamentalists.[329]

The foregoing should have provided some perspective on my statement earlier that Kashmir is India's West Bank. Our enemies are not interested in Kashmir or the West Bank per se. If they were, they could have had a Palestinian Arab state on the West Bank any time between 1948 and 1967; but they did not create one—did not even ask for one from the occupying powers, Jordan and Egypt. They never criticized either country for "the occupation," as they do Israel, but instead always called for *Israel's* total destruction. They realized, however, that calling for Israel's destruction was not going to win friends and influence people to their cause. So after the Arabs' humiliating defeat in 1967 they focused on the fictional occupation. That is called *incrementalism* in international politics. Get that (West Bank) first then move on to your greater goal (Israel), which is what Hitler did when he secured the Sudetenland from England and France before grabbing the rest of Czechoslovakia; what Stalin did in securing the agreements with Roosevelt and Churchill at Yalta.

Similarly with Kashmir, it would be tough finding open international support for a naked call to destroy India. Such a rallying call might even awaken Indian leaders and others to the true nature of the threat they face. Calling for "justicc" in Kashmir, however, is far more palatable, and can provide cover to democratic appeasers who never would agree to naked aggression without that subterfuge. Can anyone "say with a straight face that resolving the land dispute over Kashmir will get the terrorists to say, 'Okay, I'm satisfied' and

---

[329] P. V. Indiresan, Dealing with Terror," *The Hindu,* September 15, 2001 (four days after 9/11).

stop murdering people?"[331] That is also what is happening on India's eastern frontier with the ethnic cleansing of Bangladeshi Hindus. Does anyone think that the Islamists will be content with the elimination of *East* Bengal's Hindu population and not take their holy war further into *West* Bengal and perhaps the rest of India? Of course, not; the spread of this deadly *jihad* to West Bengal has been underway for some time already.

Perhaps most significantly, our enemies are also learning that they can count reliably on our silence—or as several of them have put it to me, our "moral cowardice"—to help them create a *fait accompli* that will lead them to hegemony over parts of what is still India. To combat this, we must give heed to Dr. Pipes' warning. As democracies we are committed to protecting religious freedom; and that noble and necessary commitment clouds our understandings of what we need to do. We must fight and defeat radical Islam, not because of the Islam part but because of its commitment to impose a totalitarian way of life on the rest of us, as Dr. Pipes had emphasized.

> We blanch at the thought of identifying *any* religion with something so heinous as wanton murder. While that is to our credit, one of the most effective ways we can deal with our enemy ***is to stop giving it the status of a religion....*** To the extent that apologists treat radical Islam as a religion, they actually undermine the very institutions they believe they are upholding with their craven appeasement.... A millenarian ideology never says 'Enough' until it has sated its insatiable appetite. The millenarian ideology, radical Islam, is much closer to other such ideologies like Marxist-Leninism and fascism than it is to the religion of Islam. And we know that the only way those two ideologies stopped expanding was when free societies ***stopped them.***[332]

Whether they still live in Bangladesh or have fled to West Bengal, the lives of these Bangladeshi Hindus are in danger—

[331] *Op. cit.* Benkin, "Challenges before India and Israel and areas of co-operation."

[332] *Ibid.*

but so are the lives of anyone who does not fit into the utopian view of radical Islam: Hindus and Jews, certainly; Sikhs, Bahais and Ahmadiyyas, as we have seen; Christians and Buddhists, too, have suffered already. Let us also recognize the danger faced by those Muslims who have stood against the radicals and those who have tried to bring their faith in line with the modern and free world. As horrible as the ethnic cleansing of the Bangladeshi Hindus and the accompanying atrocities are—and they are vile—they are a key element in a much greater *jihad* that is being waged by radical Islam against civilization itself. India and Israel happen to be the primary and immediate target, but they are merely "the canary in a coal mine." Recall that as long as coal miners heard the canary singing, they knew they were okay, but when the singing stopped, it directed them to take action; and if the miners ignored the bird's reaction, they soon would be felled themselves.

What happened to the canary? Did it die or get safely to the surface? Well, no one really cared, did they? And that is why the metaphor is so apt when used in reference to the canaries in today's geopolitical coal mine. There are talking heads right now who believe that if only Israel did not exist, Islamist radicals would be content to live in their own world and stop attacking others; and they thus support policies that in reality mean Israel's doom. They refuse to see that what happens to Israel—or more to the point what the rest of the world allows to happen to Israel—is only a sign of what will happen to them, too. In their quest for a way to flee from the danger that radical Islam represents, they urge us to slay the canary whose presence can save them by alerting them to the imperative of protecting themselves from the noxious gas of Islamism and eventually destroying it.

India is no less a primary target than is Israel. Hindus are no less vilified than are Jews. Islamists have made Kashmir an international human rights issue in the hopes that people will be craven enough to sacrifice it in the vain hope of satisfying their blood lust. Do you see a pattern: the Sudetenland and Czechoslovakia; the West Bank and Israel; Kashmir and India? We can add another, the Bengali Hindus; for as their fate goes, so goes the fate of all India and ultimately the rest of the world. Our enemies—and make no mistake, that is what they are—have been trying to chip away at the legitimacy of India's 1947 partition into a secular state (India) in which a minority Muslim population remained and flourished (growing from about ten percent of the 1951 population to at least 17 percent today); and a state with Islam as its official state religion and policy driver (Pakistan) in which a minority Hindu population has been harassed almost out of existence, falling from almost 20 percent to about one percent in the same period.[333]

It is a total mystery how nations and organizations that call themselves moral are not struck by this disparity and do not find it to be a primary consideration in understanding and resolving conflict and human rights violations in South Asia. Consider: one nation secular and protective of religious freedom, the other openly favoring one religion over all others and supporting a history of disabilities against those other faiths; one nation where the minority grows and flourishes to the extent that many of their leaders assume that they will become the dominant faith there one day, the other where minorities have been depleted and persecuted; one nation that continually offers concessions and dialogue, the other rigidly adhering to its maximalist demands. And yet it is the second nation in all these instances that complains of being the victim and more amazingly to whom the rest of the world pays heed.

What is Mughalistan?[334]

Mughalistan refers to a single Muslim nation that would

[333] Figures are from 2001 Indian census (cited earlier) and 1998 Pakistan Census (updated July 19, 2010). Also see, Moorthy Muthuswamy, "India's Future: Trend should be a Friend," Paper No. 876, *South Asia Analysis Group,* December 31, 2003.

[334] Also spelled Mughalstan.

stretch continuously from Pakistan to Bangladesh, linked by large pieces of what is now northern India. Kashmir, would be part of it, of course, but so would all or part of Punjab, Haryana (the state that borders Delhi), Rajasthan, Uttarakhand, Himachal Pradesh, Uttar Pradesh (India's most populous state), Bihar (the third most populous), Jharkhand, West Bengal (the fourth most populous), and Assam. All currently have large Hindu majorities.[335]

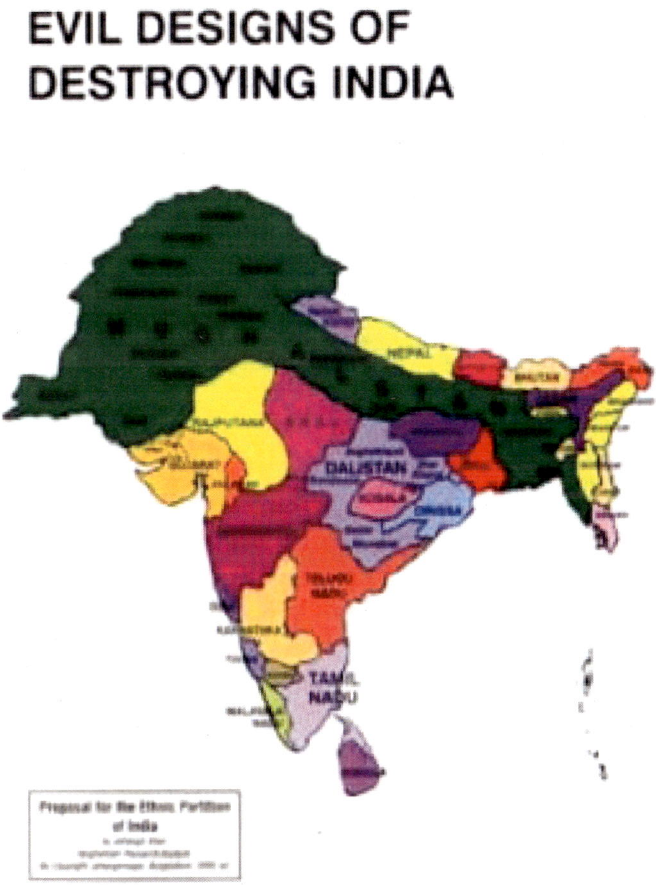

[335] The following map was reprinted from "Greater Pakistan: Mughalstan," *Hindu Janajagruti Samiti.*

Many credible individuals question the notion of Mughalistan as a specific design or element of Islamist policy, and whether Mughalistan is an articulated element of Islamist policy is uncertain. What is certain, however, is the expansionist nature of Islamism. What is certain is the philosophy that India—with its 20 percent Muslim population—must be "reclaimed" and placed under Islamic rule as it was in the pre-British days when Muslim monarchs ruled India after their predecessors conquered it in an invasion far bloodier than anything the British ever carried out on Indian soil. This discussion of Mughalistan, then, could refer to a real aim of Islamists or it could be a metaphor for what Indians can expect from Islamist imperialists. While we would be naïve to deny that dreams of a Mughalistan have taken hold among many in South Asia, the following discussion should be understood in that context.[336]

Mughalistan, as a goal, is one element in a greater "new world order" envisioned by Islamists (just as another partition of Israel is). It would be part of a greater Muslim nation contiguous with other Muslim nations that would form an impregnable bloc for radical Islam and include, in addition to Mughalistan: Afghanistan, the Muslim majority nations of the former Soviet Union, and onto Iran, Turkey, and the Middle East and beyond into Africa. It could extend its reach eastward from Bangladesh to areas that already have Islamic insurgencies like Thailand and the Philippines, and Muslim-majority states with Islamist movements like Malaysia and Indonesia. Thus, the notion of a great Muslim *ummah* is in its essence expansionist—like those of other totalitarian and violent regimes.

The Pakistan-based terrorist group Lashkar-e-Taibi, widely believed to be responsible for the 2008 terrorist attack on Mumbai that killed at least 173 people, published a pamphlet

---

[336] For an alternate but equally chilling scenario, see the following YouTube video produced by Muslims, "Pakistan's new map INSHALLAH." Available at: http://www.youtube.com/watch?v=oZouu5nZll4.

that declared India, Israel, and the United States "existential" enemies of Islam. It also listed eight reasons for pursuing *jihad*: "1) to eliminate evil and facilitate conversion to and practice of Islam; 2) to ensure the ascendancy of Islam; 3) to force non-Muslims to pay *jizya*[337]; 4) to assist the weak and powerless; 5) to avenge the blood of Muslims killed by unbelievers; 6) to punish enemies for breaking promises and treaties; 7) to defend a Muslim state; and 8) to liberate Muslim territories under non-Muslim occupation."[338] Territories under the last category include most of Southeast

[337] Tax paid by non-Muslims for the right to live in Muslim nations. It gives them formal protection by the Muslim ruler—much like protection rackets run by organized crime—and formally defines their inferior legal and social status as *dhimmis*.

[338] Markaz al-Dawa wal-Irshad, "Hum Jihad kyun Kar rahe hain? (Why Are We Waging Jihad?);" quoted in Husain Huqqani, "The Ideology of South Asia Groups"; in Eric Brown, Hillel Fradkin, and Husain Haqqai, editors, *Current Trends in Islamist Ideology Volume I* (Hudson Books: New York, 2005), pp. 24-25.

Europe, Spain, parts of France, and India because it was conquered by Muslim imperialists and became part of the Moghul Empire. Thus, they all are "lost territories" that must be returned to Muslim rule. The idea of a "right" to a Mughalistan, then, is not out of keeping with the rest of Islamist ideology—or, in fact, with some basic tenets in Islam that we noted in Chapter One.

So whether or not Mughalistan per se is a specific goal of all Islamists, the notion of Mughalistan grows out of and is supported by the Islamist ideology described throughout this book, and as we saw in the Lashkar statement, is consistent with Islamists' ultimate goals. Another aspect that makes this particularly dangerous: incrementalism. Islamic rule over the entire Indian subcontinent is consistent with the mandate to "return" previously Muslim ruled territories to Islamic rule. It resonates with a large and committed group of true believers.

But in the arena of international politics, are they openly calling for India to join the caliphate? No; but they *are* calling for a Sharia-ruled Kashmir. Next, it will be areas of India with large Muslim populations—perhaps first given elements of Sharia law then placed under Sharia in its entirety; after that, they might be joined with other Sharia ruled lands. While at the moment, the section of India where this is heard the most frequently and the loudest is Kerala in the south.[339] The faint calls coming from areas envisioned in a Mughalistan no doubt will grow more strident if Islamists are given the other incremental victories. So after Kashmir, Kerala, and Mughalistan, how far a leap is it to the entire subcontinent? Call Islamists a minority, but their impact on events and the attention we give them hardly suggest minority status. If they are victorious, there is no doubt that more and more Muslims who are not necessarily Islamists will opt to support their more

[339] Private conversation with former Indian MP and two-time cabinet minister Dr. Subramanian Swami, July 23, 2010; Niles, IL. Dr. Swami and I had previously shared a podium in New Delhi in 2009.

radical co-religionists.[340]

The idea of Mughalistan first appeared in a 2000 article by Samar Abbas, in which he advocated further partitions of India to separate the Hindu and Muslim communities.[341] Referring to the proposed trifurcation of Kashmir, Abbas wrote, "In fact, the peaceful partition of a region beset by ethnic-based conflicts can actually prevent much unnecessary blood-shed, and provide a lasting solution to age-old historical disputes."[342] He goes on to propose a greater Muslim state that connects the Muslim-majority states of Pakistan and Bangladesh taking much of Northern India with it. Abbas talks eerily of a "final solution" to the Hindu-Muslim problem (the same terminology employed by the Nazis) and cites the racist and miniscule fringe group in the United States, Americans for Self-Determination, as his model.[343]

"Perhaps the Hindus may wish to set aside 12 per cent of the territory of the Indian Union for the Muslims, who form 12 per cent of the population and hence could claim to have a 'right' to 12 per cent of the land. This land would sensibly comprise the already Muslim-dominated and historically Islamicised regions of northern UP (Rohilkhand, North Oudh) and northern Bihar (Seemanchal), where Hindus already live in fear of Muslims."[344]

Abbas is using a tried and true ruse that all imperialistic tyrannies have employed: describing their imperialistic aims

---

[340] In fact, based on the testimony of numerous Muslims in Bangladesh and India, that is already happening as the Obama administration appears weak and ready to cave into Islamist demands.

[341] Samar Abbas, "Kashmir: Autonomy Demand," *Economic and Political Weekly*, Vol. 35, No. 49 (Dec. 2-8, 2000), p. 4360.

[342] *Ibid.*

[343] Americans for Self-Determination calls for the United States to be divided into Hispanic, Black, and White nations—something that would weaken the United States and therefore something that the *jihadists* would favor. It should be noted, too, that Americans for Self-Determination is so miniscule and unknown among the US population and it ideas are resoundingly rejected by Americans—or at least would be if they were serious enough to be part of any dialogue.

[344] *Op. cit.*, Abbas, "Kashmir: Autonomy Demand."

not in terms of the expansion of their power base (which others would easily reject out of hand) but in moderate sounding words ("perhaps Hindus may wish to set aside"). Of course their goals are anything but moderate. In fact, they could be the poster child for radical Islam precisely because their author tries to strike a moderate tone while advocating Islamist expansion. First, let us recall that the Indian subcontinent was already partitioned into Hindu and Muslim regions in 1947. Calling for a second partition—which is what he is doing—smacks of Islamist incrementalism that eventually will call for a third, fourth, and further partitions. Islamists will not be satisfied until the entire subcontinent falls under their sway. Second, he speaks of Muslims' "rights" to the land they claim.

The first implication is that Muslims should not live any place where the rulers are not Muslim and that the character of the nation is not Muslim. (Again, we see the ideology noted earlier of Islam's division of the world into Muslim-good and non-Muslim-bad categories.) It is a shame that Europeans will not take heed of this call and instead continue to see their Muslim population grow and claim their "rights" to an autonomous territory within Europe. The second implication is that *only* Muslims have that right; for he did not call for a similar land distribution for the Hindus in Pakistan or Bangladesh, both of whom made up far more than 12 percent of their respective nations' population in the recent past. And third, he refers to "historically Islamicized regions" in India—without considering whether they became that way voluntarily or through coercive means, how such regions would be determined and by whom, or what the affected populations—both Muslim and non-Muslim—might think.

Abbas goes on. "The Muslims all across the rest of India could then migrate to that region, whilst Hindus would then comprise the sole ethnic group in the remaining 88 per cent of India. This migration would be a peaceful process spread over several years, with both communities slowly migrating to regions wherein they dominate, avoiding blood-baths. At the ground level, I would like to point out that this process is already at work in many parts of India."[345]

That was also the plan in 1947, but things did not work out that way, as the sanguine Abbas suggests. Many areas in both new nations contained mixed Hindu and Muslim populations. Only the Muslim nation found a way to solve that "problem"; namely, by casting out their Hindu populations. India, on the other hand, being a democracy and actually protects its Muslims, sometimes many suggest to the detriment of the majority Hindus. Hence, there is no "need" to partition Pakistan or Bangladesh. Their non-Muslim populations have been largely eliminated and are continuing to be so. That is why Abbas can justify focusing on India without considering the Muslim nations. Neither does he address how he might convince Muslims who are about one in four in the far southern Indian state of Kerala to migrate "peacefully" to Uttar Pradesh in the North or West Bengal in the Northeast. He does not even come close to suggesting how non-Muslims, who comprise about three of four West Bengalis, would decide to leave their ancestral lands for Hindustan.[346] Contrary to what Abbas sees "on the ground," there is no migration to communal areas as he suggests. For instance, between 1991 and 2004, Muslims *increased* their share of the Kerala population by almost two percentage points.[347] So if at some point in the future those Muslims demand their own state in southern India, would the nation be partitioned again, based on those Muslim "rights"?

The most widely repeated explanation of the Mughalistan concept comes from the web site, *Bengal Genocide.*[348] Detractors and some supporters of the site and the reality of Mughalistan as a concept often get lost in the details of the

---

[345] *Ibid.*

[346] *Op. cit.,* 2001 Indian census.

[347] Biju Govind, "Increase in Muslim population in the State," *The Hindu*, September 23, 2004.

[348] *Bengal Genocide,* "Pakistan-Bangladesh plan a Mughalistan to split India," http://www.bengalgenocide.com/mughalistan.php.

argument—an argument that can be quite persuasive. For purposes of its inclusion here, however, *Bengal Genocide's* ability to tie it to the imperialistic aims of international *jihad* is what makes the discussion particularly compelling. It cites Osama Bin Laden's call for creating a "Greater Pakistan to 'liberate' the Muslims of India from the Hindus." It also notes how groups from areas surrounding India have formally declared the importance of creating an "undivided Islamic nation in the Indian subcontinent." These groups include the one led by "Dawood Ibrahim (who executed the gruesome 1993 Mumbai bombings), Jamaat-e-Islami, Lashkare-Tayyaba, Jaish-e-Mohammad, and Hizbul Mujahideen." It sites similar support by groups within India including "Students Islamic Movement of India (SIMI) and Indian Mujahideen [who] are working in tandem with the aforementioned organizations to waged (sic) Jihad against the Hindus of India." The site notes that

> In its "holy war" against India, the Lashkar-e-Tayyaba has openly declared Hindus to be the "enemies of Islam" who should all be converted or killed [and] has repeatedly claimed through its journals and websites that its main aim is to destroy the Indian republic and to annihilate Hinduism. Jaish-e-Mohammed has vowed to "liberate" not just Kashmir, but also to hoist the Islamic flag atop the historic Red Fort after capturing New Delhi and the rest of India.
>
> SIMI has championed the "liberation of India through Islam" and aim to restore the supremacy of Islam through the resurrection of the Khilafat (Islamic Caliphate), emphasis on the Muslim Ummah (Islamic) and the waging of Jihad on the Indian state, secularism, democracy and nationalism—the basic keystones of the Indian Constitution—as these concepts are antithetical to Islam. The Indian Mujahideen... refer to notorious Islamic conquerors of India (Mohammed bin Qasim, Mohammad Ghauri and Mahmud Ghaznawi) as their role-models, refer to Hindu blood as "blood to be the cheapest of all mankind" and taunt Hindus that their "[Hindu] history is full of subjugation, humiliation, and insult [at the hands of Islamic conquerors]".
>
> The Indian Mujahideen's emails warn the Hindus to "Accept Islam and save yourselves" and or else face a horrible fate:- "Hindus!

> O disbelieving faithless Indians! Haven't you still realized that the falsehood of your 33 crore dirty mud idols and the blasphemy of your deaf, dumb, mute and naked idols of ram, krishna and hanuman are not at all going to save your necks, Insha-Allah, from being slaughtered by our [Muslim] hands?"[349]

Note that the names of Hindu deities are purposely spelled in lower case. This is a common practice by this ilk with regard to groups it denigrates and religions it seeks to delegitimize.

This is the ultimate goal of Islamists, and the widely cited piece in *Bengal Genocide* does a good job of tying the Mughalistan concept to ongoing anti-Hindu actions by Islamists on the subcontinent. They note prominently in that context the ethnic cleansing of East Bengali Hindus and accompanying demographic changes to West Bengal. What is happening to those Hindus is little more than a step along the way to the goal of Islam's imperialist spread across all of South Asia and ultimately the rest of the world. The Hindus of Bangladesh are an obstacle, and the Islamists want to eliminate them, just as they do to Jews and Christians in the Middle East.

Islamists have made a decided effort to discredit the notion of Mughalistan, even tie it to Hindu nationalism and discredit that. Yet, even those polemics fail to include any information that rebuts the sited material showing how the Mughalistan concept fits with the greater, imperialist goals of these various Islamist groups.[350] And as noted, while the idea of a Mughalistan does indeed exist among many, the importance of this discussion is not the Mughalistan notion per se but the ultimate goal that Islamists hold of "re-taking" the entire Indian subcontinent, of trying to do so through incrementalism, and of cloaking their desires in *faux* human rights or moderate language. The rest of us: *Beware!*

---

[349] *Ibid.*

[350] S M Rahman, "The insidious Indian propaganda," *Pakistan Observer,* January 18, 2010.

Red-Green Mughalistan

There is an alternate scenario, which is perhaps even more frightening because it could be happening already as part of the Red-Green Alliance. When India was partitioned, and East Bengal was incorporated into Pakistan, it left a chunk of territory as part of India but largely cut off from it. This area comprises the Northeast Indian states known as the "Seven Sisters," and they all are located to the east of Bangladesh: Arunachal Pradesh, Assam, Manipur, Meghalaya, Mizoram, Nagaland, and Tripura.[351] Some states are Christian-dominated, some Hindu, and two of them even contain elements of the Bnei Menasha, a group of indigenous people who practice Judaism and consider themselves to be descended from the ancient Hebrew tribe of Menasha.

The separation of these states from the rest of India is quite different from the way the two US states, Alaska and Hawaii, are cut off from "the mainland." Nothing but friendly or benign territories (Canada and the Pacific Ocean respectively) lay between them and the rest of the US. Quite to the contrary, except for a brief period after the Bangladeshi War of Independence, the land between the Seven Sisters and the rest of India has been quite hostile (Bangladesh, China, Myanmar; while the small border with Bhutan is a bit of an exception, recall that the Buddhist dominated nation has been engaged in the brutal expulsion of its Hindu population for quite some time). The Mughalistan map above does not foresee these states (save a part of Assam) as being within the Muslim nation's borders. Mughalistan, however, would cut off these states even more than they are now; and it is difficult to see how they possibly could survive this partition of the subcontinent.

---

[351] Meghalaya and part of Assam are actually sandwiched between Bangladesh's north and Bhutan.

So, while not on the Mughalistan map, they could end up being part of that entity, simply because their survival after yet another partition of the area is simply unsustainable. They are too weak, too small, and too dependent on their ties to the rest of India. But their becoming part of Mughalistan is not the only endgame they might face.

China has laid claim to the largest and easternmost of these Indian states, Arunachal Pradesh. In 1914, India's British rulers signed the Simla agreement with what was then the independent nation of Tibet and fixed their common border on what became known as the McMahon Line. That has been the demarcation line between India and China ever since the latter seized Tibet in 1950. China held power over Tibet when the negotiations that ultimately established the McMahon Line began. Chinese troops had maintained direct control of the Himalayan nation from 1910 until 1912 when the Dalai Lama returned to Tibet and expelled them. In 1913, he declared Tibet to be independent in a formal proclamation. With that conflict still unresolved, the Chinese agreed to the treaty line between India and Outer Tibet, but refused to agree to the proposed border between Outer Tibet (independent) and Inner Tibet (still in Chinese hands). So they stormed out of the talks and refused to recognize the Simla Agreement and the McMahon Line that was incorporated into it.

Today, of course, the British are gone and so is an independent Tibet. The Chinese, however, are using that disagreement from almost a century ago as a pretext for laying claim to a large portion of Arunachal Pradesh. Not unlike the Islamists, they are playing the "European colonialist" card to stake their claim. The Chinese insist that the area is and always has been a part of Tibet/China and that those Europeans had no right to draw boundaries in Asia. To complicate matters further and indicate that this is much more than a simple land grab, Arunachal Pradesh has enormous and as yet untapped resources of hydro-electric power. The burgeoning economies of India and China both could sorely use that resource. For the

most part, China has been rather surreptitious about its claim, certainly in comparison to those made by the Islamists; but just as they are about everything they do, here too the Chinese are deadly serious and will not relent until they have Arunachal Pradesh and its vast resources in their hands. Earlier, we documented the growing importance of the Red-Green alliance in this part of the world. So in the complex and often sinister world of international politics, it is not inconceivable at all that the two forces would reprise their successful unholy alliance that worked so well for them in Nepal.

Several matters are not in doubt: Muslim-ruled nations (especially Pakistan and its ISI intelligence service) are hostile to India and want to weaken it; Pakistani hostility toward India has never abated. The Islamic State has even directed several terrorist attacks against its neighbor.[352] Moreover, elements of the Indian Muslim population with Pakistani support and encouragement have become more vocal in their demands for separate rights and even autonomy.[353] It is also clear that Communist China is an unrelenting expansionist power that has grabbed control of several territories it considers historically part of China and covets others.[354] Making matters even more volatile, India and China are emerging Asian giants—both economically and politically—whose interests often clash; and China has been getting closer to Pakistan at India's expense.[355]

In exchange for the support of Muslim nations (and the invariable silence of Europe and others as a result) for China's claims; the communist giant and its allies would support Muslim claims to Mughalistan. After all, China had no

---

[352] Pakistani involvement in the November 2008 terror attack on Mumbai, for instance, is well-known and well-documented despite its denials. For further perspective and examples, see "Benkin: Chicago Terror Suspect Cased Sites For Pune Attack," *The Iconoclast,* February 14, 2010; "Benkin: Pakistan breaks off India talks on Mumbai attacks," *The Iconoclast,* February 8, 2010; and Amol Sharma and Tom Wright, "Terror Charge Mars India-Pakistan Talks," *Wall Street Journal,* July 15, 2010.

[353] Former Sahara TV news producer and on-air personality, Madhuri Singh is probably the most fearless journalist in India. In 2008, 2009, and 2010, she shared some of her experiences with me. In one instance, she investigated the imposition of Sharia law on a village near Delhi, how after her report the Indian government took action, and how after the government left Islamist leaders reverted back to Sharia law. In another, she showed me her interview of a Muslim man who had fathered 50 children to that point (all of whom were on the public dole in India) and was explicit in telling her that his motive was to increase the number of Muslims to help them become the rulers in India.

[354] The former group includes Hong Kong, Macao, and Inner Mongolia in addition to Tibet. The latter includes Taiwan, part of Kashmir, and Arunachal Pradesh.

[355] In 2010, for instance, the Chinese and Pakistanis signed a nuclear cooperation pact that begins with sending two new nuclear reactors to the Islamic nation. Besides being a deliberate and open attack on Indian interests ("playing the Pakistan card," as one observer calls it), the agreement was a clear counterweight to India's 2008 nuclear agreement with the United States.

compunctions about swallowing up Tibet; Nepal has now joined the league of communist nations; and Myanmar, which borders Arunachal Pradesh, is one of China's closest allies. It makes for two solid, continuous and contiguous blocs (with the exception of Bhutan, which easily could go the way of Tibet). Recall, too, the consistent support for Islamist expansion in West Bengal by the communist rulers of that Indian state, and the 2009 unity meeting of communists and Islamists in Kerala. Add to that the Red-Green cooperation in Nepal, and the alliance for an Islamist North and Northeast India alongside a Communist Chinese Arunachal Pradesh is already in place and merely awaits the right set of circumstances to bring down the executioner's ax. Think about it!

West Bengal, however, is the key. Cross-border attacks are not uncommon, and Islamist infiltrators from nearby Bangladesh now dominate many of the villages surrounding the camps where the refugees are forced to live. For years, operatives from Pakistan and Bangladesh have been working with Indian Muslims for changes in the demographic balance in the states of a future Mughalistan, especially West Bengal, Assam, and Uttar Pradesh.[356]

The plan is really simple. Place a virus in a hapless cell. The virus is the cult of radical Islam; the hapless cell is Bangladesh. Make sure it is a virus that is capable of destroying the cell—which we are seeing consistently that it is. Even the most apparently antithetical government must pay homage to the virus and for fear of alienating it. And in order for this process to remain unrecognized by the international anti-virus software, the host must appear reasonably functional for its an impoverished and needy people. As the virus grows in power, allow it to spread slowly to other cells, in this case India's West Bengal.

Ignore it at our own risk and that of our children.

---

[356] Recall the figures presented earlier in Chapter Five: Rightless and Vulnerable: East and West Bengal.

CHAPTER TEN

WHAT MUST BE DONE

The only purpose for everything that has preceded this chapter is in fact this chapter. The only reason to meet is to act, and the only reason to act is to win!

What if you found yourself in Nazi Germany in the 1930s, or more recently in Darfur? You might have looked around and thought, 'Something's wrong. Something's terribly wrong. You can see that. I'm afraid that something really bad is about to happen, and no one seems to be doing anything to stop it.' Knowing what you know now, what would you have done? Gone about your life, pretending that you didn't see what you saw? Or would you do everything in your power to stop the impending atrocity and save the lives of so many innocent people? Would it have mattered if you were not Jewish or African? We here today do not have to guess at what our answer should be. We have the lessons of history. Because of the Holocaust and what happened in places like Darfur, we know what will happen in South Asia because it is about to happen again.

But if there has been any consistency in this quiet case of ethnic cleansing, it has been non-action; certainly non-action by the Bangladeshis to stop it and non-action by the international arbiters of good and evil even to recognize it. Yet, the non-action of those who want to stop this crime against humanity has been far more destructive, and it plays right into the *jihadis'* hands. Instead of taking action, we attend conference after conference and seminar after seminar, with everyone feeling oh so good about themselves, only to see the same people shaking the same ineffective fists at the same enemies. We need to stop shaking our fists and do something! Insanity has been defined as doing the same thing over and over again expecting different results. That is, no matter how much we "care," whatever people have done thus far has not worked. If we are to save the lives of our brothers and sisters, we have to think and act strategically—and, why not, our enemies do. Having a "conference" or writing an angry rant on Facebook has no value in and of itself. In fact, things like that can do more harm than good if all they do is make author, reader, or attendees feel better about themselves. Our enemies have counted on that inaction for decades and continue to do so. That has to change, and it has to change now if we are to save this beleaguered population.

Shmuel Zygielbojm took action. He committed suicide to protest the inaction of western nations while the Nazis murdered his fellow Jews. "By looking on passively upon this murder of defenseless millions," he wrote, "tortured children, women, and men; [the western nations] have become partners to the responsibility."[357] He acted out of despair, and his suicide ended up saving no one; but he took that action only after trying others unceasingly for years, something most of us have yet to do.

The Bangladeshi Hindus might not be at the point of genocide right now, but if we do nothing to stop the Islamists, they will be—and not as far in the future as the complacent people assume. Already there are documented atrocities with a clear goal of ethnic cleansing and international imperialism; but no one is taking effective action. Shall we sit by idly or engage in the same ineffective fist-shaking that has characterized most activity thus far?

If our resolve would lead us to fight against this quiet case of ethnic cleansing, we must be aware of a sad and at times

---

[357] *The Last Letter From Szmul Zygielbojm*, The Bund Representative With The Polish National Council In Exile, May 11, 1943. Yad Vashem Archives, O-55 (Yad Vashem The Holocaust Martyrs' and Heroes' Remembrance Authority: Jerusalem, 2004)

frustrating reality with which we have to deal. In my initial trips to India, I had a very difficult time understanding the lack of action among Bengalis, especially those who were living free and with full citizenship rights in the world's largest democracy, India. I did not understand why so many people used flowery words as nothing more than a thin veneer atop person interests. I certainly understood the despair and powerlessness that led to inaction among the refugees; and my heart went out to them. I had a more difficult time understanding other Bengalis who could take action but did not; and I was incensed that those who claimed the mantle of leadership on this issue and for this population were almost exclusively concerned with their personal pretensions and parochial power struggles to the exclusion of their people's interests.. As my 2008 journal notes reflect, I faced a regular refrain to the effect that the people were "afraid" to do whatever it was that we requested. I noted these comments from Siliguri in northern Bengal.

> I had a bit of a snit, but one that was important to have at some point. Earlier just before we left for the camps, I spoke to the Secretary of a major organization here for Bangladeshi Hindus (INR?). I was made to understand that the meeting they were to arrange in Assam had been canceled for the reason that "people were afraid because the Islamic radicals said they would kill anyone who goes." I explained to him that I understood the people but that if the answer is always that the people are scared, then nothing will change. It is not that they are scared it is a failure of leadership.[358]

A few days later, "I determined to write a book, *Bengal's Shame*, which essentially exposes the plight of the people... that Bangladesh oppresses them, India ignores them, and they are victimized again by those who say they are helping them but do quite the opposite." On the final day of that 2008 trip, my Bengali colleagues took me on a little tour of Kolkata—a time to relax and take in all that I had seen and heard in the

[358] Personal notes made at the time of my visit to India, February 23, 2008.

previous weeks. It was very nice of them, and when we visited the stately Kolkata public library, it put me in mind of the Rod Taylor character in the movie version of H. G. Wells' *The Time Machine*. This time traveler from the distant past wanted to know more about his new contemporaries and was told that they had books he could read. Thrilled, he asked to be taken to them because they would tell him all about these people. When, however, he found that the books had been untouched for centuries and crumbled in his hands, he said, 'They do tell me about you.'

The books did not crumble in my hands in the Kolkata library, but I found that the ability of people to access any book—even just to read—was so fraught with restriction, denial, and delay that it told me a great deal about this government and the people. Moreover, the original building was a beautiful structure from British colonial days, but I was prohibited from taking any pictures of it, even from the outside. The bureaucracy, the Byzantine rules, the obfuscation, the government's role as a barrier between the people and their history: that was a failure of leadership, too, but of a different kind and one that would prove to be just as formidable and obstacle.

In subsequent trips and interactions, I came to accept these realities and the challenge they pose to those of us who want to stop the oppression that the victims face through no fault of their own. If I allowed the frustration to overwhelm me, I would be no different from those individuals who turned with ease to the excuse about the people being afraid.

Quite often, Hindus both in India and the Diaspora will lament the fact that their people are passive. This is not the case only in Bengal but elsewhere in India and among Indian-Hindu-Americans. In fact, one of the frequent refrains I hear from that community is that we Jews—unlike Hindus—are so strong and have been able to fight off *jihadis* and others bent on our destruction. When that happens, I inform my audience that until fairly recently, "we Jews" were thought as passive as

Hindus consider themselves to be.. We, too, lamented the fact that others pushed us around; but it changed for us, which means that Hindus' supposed "passivity" can change, too. It means that their observed passivity is not an essential element of what it means to be Hindu.

On March 5, 2009, I was asked to address a group of attorneys at the Indian Law Institute across from the Supreme Court. The topic they wanted me to address was "Jihad: The Jews' response, Lessons for India." As my personal diary from that day records:

> I made sure to say that the situation in India is not the same as elsewhere, but that the one ingredient that changed things for the Jews was attitude—letting the *jihadis* know that we were not going to lay down and just take it from them. Three Muslim infiltrators were planted to disrupt the meeting, which often happens when I speak anywhere in India. But when they interrupted my talk with anti-US and anti-Israel screeds, I gave them back what they gave and more. I was especially clear with a Middle Eastern history lesson to show that "there can be no doubt that the root cause of the entire Middle East conflict is the refusal by Arabs to accept a viable Jewish state in their midst." One tried to impugn the US, but I essentially answered his conspiratorial nonsense quickly and did not get off track (again something they try to do—hijack our agenda and substitute their own). Then when they tried it again a little later, a remarkable thing happened. The assembled Hindus got angry and started opposing the Muslims, such that they had to leave dispirited, defeated, and looking foolish. As I said to one of the *jihadis*, "You guys start this shit then cry when your nose gets bloodied. Well, it's not going to work!" It was really quite a donnybrook and left a lot of people motivated to work, I think because they saw that Hindus are not necessarily passive as people say and that they do not have to roll over for *jihadis* and their supporters.[359]

For Jews, certainly the creation of the State of Israel had much to do with our transformation, if you will, as did the nature of inclusion in the United States of America. But at two Hindu

[359] Personal notes from trip to South Asia 2009.

Mandirs outside of Chicago, I also spoke about a specific effort by Jews:

> Some of you might remember that during the 1970s and 1980s, you could not pass a synagogue anywhere here that did not have a large sign reading, "Save Soviet Jewry." The Jewish community undertook a massive and relentless effort to save our co-religionists suffering terrible persecution in the USSR. It was massive. We gave to every synagogue and organization we could, involved ourselves in letter writing and pen pal efforts, and so much more. Some members of our community risked their own freedom to smuggle religious books into Russia. And in the end, we got over a million Jews out of there to safety, primarily in the United States and Israel.

I also told them that those Jews—now adults—who were part of that as children (because we really organized in our religious schools) gained a strong sense of identity as Jews that they will never lose. Could saving Bangladeshi Hindus do the same thing for the Hindu community?[360]

So, what do we do?

First of all, we must stop looking for somebody else to stop the violence. Instead, individuals need to challenge themselves and ask: Knowing that the Bangladeshi Hindus are being brutalized and worse, what kind of person am I if I do not do everything in my power to help them? Basic human decency demands that we stop this evil, and that requires one crucial element: *that each and every one of us accept personal responsibility for putting a stop to the ethnic cleansing of the Bangladeshi Hindus.* You will recall that the most successful cases of genocide and ethnic cleansing occur when average citizens commit heinous actions that they otherwise would not dream of committing. The converse is also true: this attempt at ethnic cleansing will be a failure if *average citizens commit heroic acts to prevent it, actions they otherwise might have thought themselves incapable of taking.*

---

[360] Personal notes from discussion following addresses at Hindu *Mandirs* in Lemont and Grayslake, Illinois; April and June 2010.

If, at the same time, we stop the spread of international *jihad*, good for us. Doing so will prevent the brutal murder of so many others, as well as the ethnic cleansing (or dare we say genocide) of additional non-Islamic communities. We certainly can expect that confounding the Islamists and their fellow travelers' desire to kill or convert the Hindus of Bangladesh will upset their well-laid plans. Regardless, the key to success is personal responsibility. It is lying in bed every night—when we are alone with our thoughts in the dark before falling asleep—in distress over the terrible things that are being done to people just like us while we remain comfortable and safe in our homes. It is waking every morning with thoughts about what we can do to help those people. It means accepting personal guilt so long as the atrocities continue, and relieving ourselves of it only when they stop.

But while necessary, that commitment alone is not enough. We cannot allow our personal agonies to paralyze us. We need to take them and use them to move us to principled and organized action; action that will continue without end despite setbacks and despite frustration; action that must come coordinated from the combined efforts of principled westerners and South Asians. There are several specific actions that should be taken on behalf of these victims of apathy in the face of passionate hatred. Which ones and in what order are not as important as our unending commitment to fight this fight to the very end without ceasing. We should be outraged by now at what is happening to the Hindus of Bangladesh; and so should the rest of the world. And we should be doubly outraged that so few people share our outrage. I am just an individual with a day job. I am not a professional intelligence officer, full-time human rights activist, or journalist. Yet, I have been able to uncover the atrocities referred to and analyzed in this book. I have been able to determine who the culprits are, including those who claim to be something other than what they are in this atrocity.

So, ask yourself, are my meager resources that much better than those of, say, CNN; or the AP, or Reuters, or *Al Jazeera*? Are they more formidable than those of the *New York Times*, the *Times of London*, or any other great news organization or newspaper in the world? Are my resources better than those of all the great intelligence agencies in the world, friend and foe alike, America's Central Intelligence Agency, India's Research and Analysis Wing, Britain's Secret Intelligence Service (SIS, formerly M16), or countless others? Or am I better informed than the President of the United States, India's Prime Minister, or the Secretary General of the United Nations? The point should be clear. Unless you believe that I really do know things that none of these people or institutions do, it means that they, too, know about it but either do not care enough to stop it or believe that other things are more important than saving millions of lives.

In 2005 and again in 2007, former US President Bill Clinton expressed regret over his failure to take action on the Rwandan genocide.[361a] Clinton called it a "personal failure" and should be commended for his admission and the awareness it demonstrates. But what of other world leaders who sat on the sidelines while almost a million Africans were murdered; of those leaders who continue to ignore or justify their inaction in Armenia after World War I, Nazi Europe, Biafra, or more recently the Congo and Darfur; or while Middle Eastern Christians continue to be ethnically cleansed? Given that history, can anyone believe that this "guy with a day job" has uncovered things that all of these great world leaders and media somehow missed?

And take note that I included our greatest potential allies, India and the United States, among that roll of shame. We might understand why nations like China and Iran have no

---

[361a] "Clinton Expresses Regret Over 1994 Genocide," *Los Angeles Times*, July 24, 2005. "His big regret: not acting in Rwanda," *Boston Globe*, December 11, 2007.

problem sitting by while millions are killed. China's greatest icon, Mao Tse-tung, was the 20th century's most successful mass murderer—and he won that dubious distinction despite competition from people like Adolf Hitler and Josef Stalin. The government of Iran has gone on record supporting terrorism and international *jihad* and has never hesitated to kill its own citizens, let alone others. The United Nations and the nations of Europe, to name two other culprits, both have a long and storied history of inaction in the face of tyranny. No surprise there, either. But that there is no action from India or the United States should engender rage—yet also the hope that they might change, something that we cannot expect from the other nations and governments mentioned.[361b]

Thus, there is no option for us but to adhere to those high standards for verifying every scintilla of evidence and making the matter so blatant, so public, that no credible leader can ignore it and still maintain a façade of moral integrity. Connect with people like Rabindra Ghosh in Bangladesh, who has personally investigated the atrocities and is periodically attacked by government agents for it; with Tapan Ghosh in West Bengal, who has verified incidents among Hindus (both Bangladeshi refugees and others) in that Indian state; and with my Interfaith Strength colleague, Bikash Halder, who is the man responsible for my involvement in this issue and who had dedicated himself to protecting his people. Connect with the few human rights groups that are trying to fight this quiet case of ethnic cleansing: with Global Human Rights Defence in The Hague, Netherlands; with Bangladesh Minority Watch in Bangladesh; and with Forcefield, based in the United States with a sister organization in India.

The time for polite protest has long past. People are being murdered; people are being pauperized as their ancestral

[361b] There have been signs among European leaders of late, however, to suggest that their response to moral outrages could change, as well, although changes in that respect remain a minority opinion.

homes are brutally stolen for them; and the nations that should be expected more than others to support them are just letting it all happen. Damn right, we're outraged! Any inconvenience or discomfort such outrage causes pales into insignificance compared to what the victims are facing day after day! Americans like me have learned since childhood that our nation speaks for the voiceless, stands side by side with the oppressed, and is the moral leader of our world. Failing to fight the ethnic cleansing of Bangladeshi Hindus belies all of that.

As an American, I look to my country first for solutions. After all, we have a history of providing them—from defeating fascism and communism, to stopping ethnic cleansing in the Balkans and the Middle East. Moreover, as I have traveled to different parts of the world, I have been told again and again that whenever people are looking for someone to champion their cries for human rights and stop those who are oppressing them, they look to one place. It is not Europe, the UN, Saudi Arabia, India, or China—certainly not our loudest critics, Iran, Cuba, and Venezuela. They look to the United States of America. Since 2009, many of those same freedom fighters have told me that they wonder if the United States is still the reliable ally it once was, given our more recent record of weakness and inaction in the face of clear human rights violations. It is time to engage the United States in this effort, so we can regain the moral high ground that many believe we have lost.[362]

Before doing so, however, recognize that very few Americans know much about Bangladesh, let alone what is happening to the Hindus there; and during this time of economic distress and anxiety over the future, neither do they care very much about events in that puny country half way

---

[362] While this book focuses on US inaction in South Asia, many people in the United States and abroad thought a real watershed was during the popular protests against the Iranian mullahs. People were astounded that France took a stronger stance than the US; and most people believe that the lack of support b the Obama administration gave Iran's theocratic and brutal dictators a green light for their violent crackdown on the protestors.

around the world. Our mainstream media almost never mentions Bangladesh other than to report some natural disaster, and most Americans will take that as a sign that nothing important is happening there. And that is a shame because average Americans have always been the incredibly charitable and personally touched when informed of human rights and other disasters. (When I was in India, on the other hand, it seemed that everyone knew what was happening to Bangladeshi Hindus, but no one was taking action to stop it.[363])

Whenever you start talking about Bangladesh here, however, it is not long before people start looking at their watches. Sometimes, they will listen if you tie it to international *jihad* or talk about how it has spilled into India, which Americans recognize as important; and some people will be motivated by the human rights drama. Regardless of what gets their attention—and getting their attention can be quite a formidable hurdle—success still requires a strategic and relentless effort to get Americans and American authorities to recognize the problem that we face. It means that we will be competing for their attention with a plethora of issues, domestic and foreign. That does not make them "wrong," just more difficult to get to on this issue. It takes a practical, deliberate approach. Simply expecting people to recognize, *'Oh, this is the right thing to do,'* is not going to work for the Bangladeshi Hindus.

We first have to know what our goals are, and we need to be specific. Of course, we want to stop the ethnic cleansing of Hindus in Bangladesh, but what does that mean specifically? In other words, what actions will put an end to it:

- ❑ Prosecuting and punishing the perpetrators of these actions to the fullest extent of the law in Bangladesh.

- ❑ Prosecuting and punishing government officials, including police, who cover up these anti-Hindu

[363] "American Jew fights for Bangladeshi Hindus," *The Times of India*, February 20, 2008, page 3.

crimes to the fullest extent of the law in Bangladesh.

- ❑ Making forced religious conversion a crime in Bangladesh.
- ❑ Fulfilling Sheikh Hasina's promise to repeal anti minority laws, including the repeal of the Vested Property Act and returning all seized property to its rightful owners, or if they choose, providing them with just compensation.
- ❑ Empanelling and empowering a commission composed of Hindu community leaders, jurists, and international monitors to process the return of seized property and to determine owners and just compensation; and enforcing the commission's decisions.
- ❑ Repealing the Eighth Amendment of the Bangladeshi constitution, making Islam the official state religion, as recommended by the Bangladeshi Supreme Court.

These are six easy to define and measure demands. Some require changes in the law; some merely require enforcing the law. Moreover, with little exception, these demands are not asking a truly free country to do anything that is not in line with basic human rights and decency. Refusing to do so (whether outright or more in the manner of Bangladeshi governments, by offering words without action) is a clear statement by the Bangladeshis that they do not wish to join the community of decent nations. And other nations have to tell them that.

Prosecuting and punishing the perpetrators of these actions and government officials who cover up these anti-Hindu crimes. It is an unfortunate fact that minorities face attacks in pretty much every society, some more than others, some frequent and others isolated. This is a dodge that perpetrators of anti-minority violence (including members of the Bangladeshi government) have used to neutralize any attempt to address their actions; that is, that the accusations are unfair even if the substance is true because we can point to attacks on minorities in the accuser's own country. That might be true, but no society can—or should—regulate every action of every individual within it. The critical question is when it happens, does the majority population have a problem with it; and the best measure of that is what the government does in reaction.

When Hindu students were attacked in Australia in 2010, the government went after the perpetrators with a vengeance. In the United States, crimes against any minority are considered just that, crimes; and the state will punish you to the fullest extent of the law; but not in Bangladesh. The incidents catalogued in Appendices I and II are all examples of Bangladeshi government complicity through inaction. It is that inaction which separates what is happening to Hindus in Bangladesh from isolated crimes against minorities elsewhere: they are carried out with the implicit approval of the government and by extension the Bangladeshi nation that has not demanded that politicians end this pollution of their country.[364]

Even for the majority population, the rule of law has limited authority in Bangladesh. For minorities—and especially Hindus—its effectiveness if far more the exception rather than the rule. As the University of Rajshahi's Md. Awal Hossain Mollah noted, "In true and real sense there is no rule of law in Bangladesh today. Law in Bangladesh follows a course of selective and discretionary application. Institution[s] and procedures required for ensuring rule of law also are no[t] effective in the country."[365] In and of itself this is a serious issue for Bangladesh, despite efforts by some elements of the

---

[364] In 2009, I was presenting a case against Bangladesh to USCIRF at the end of which a key staff person (who was leaving the Commission) pulled me aside and told me that USCIRF staff believe me, but that the key that would enable them to act is documenting *government* complicity, in this case inaction when it had a responsibility to its citizens to act.

[365] Md. Awal Hossain Mollah, "Rule of Law in Bangladesh: An Overview," Paper presented to the Department of Public Administration, University of Rajshahi, Bangladesh.

judicial community to strengthen the rule of law. It is not, however, a justification for allowing the continued ethnic cleansing of the Hindu minority. Effective law enforcement never foresees punishment of every crime committed in a society; but by effectively punishing those whose crimes become known, the government provides a deterrent that will stop others from committing the same crimes. A high profile prosecution of the perpetrators of the anti-Hindu pogrom in Sutrapur, for example, regardless of government position, party affiliation, or other status would go far in sending a strong message to those who believe Hindus can be brutalized in Bangladesh with impunity.

Many people worldwide hoped that the Awami League's return to power at the end of 2008 would mean government defense of minorities and the rule of law; but it did not. "The people who believed those pledges still face the same conditions they had to endure under the past military regime. Ordinary people, who dreamed of a new era, are frustrated by the unlawful actions still practiced in the country."[366]

Make forced conversion a crime in Bangladesh. The courageous journalist Saleem Samed, who had to flee his country because of his human rights efforts, reported in July 2011 that "Bangladesh's chief prosecutor Ghulam Arif Tipu detained senior Jamaat-e-Islami leader Maulana Delwar Hossain Sayedee and accused him of "crimes against humanity, looting, arson and forcible conversion to Islam."[367] While this was an effort limited to those who planned and carried out war crimes during the 1971 War of Independence, it was the first time a Bangladeshi government listed forced conversion as a crime against humanity, in fact as any crime at all. As forced conversion has been a prominent tool in the

---

[366] Rater Zonaki, "Still no rule of law in Bangladesh," *UPI Asia,* May 19, 2009.

[367] Saleem Samad, "Bangladesh press war crime charges against Islamic leader," *eBangladesh,* July 12, 2011; available at: http://www.ebangladesh.com/2011/07/12/bangladesh-press-war-crime-charges-againstislamic-leader/.

ethnic cleansing of Hindus, the Bangladeshi government should be encouraged to translate this recognition into law—which can be done without reference to Islam or any other religion and thus avoid the potential political fallout it fears.

Fulfilling Sheikh Hasina's promise to repeal anti-minority laws, including the Vested Property Act and return all seized property to its rightful owners. (Repealing the constitution's Eighth Amendment would be part of the same effort.) This is a straightforward demand that rests on the Bangladeshi Prime Minister's own admission, as we saw earlier. She is the one guilty of duplicity, and she is the one who can reverse that and absolve her government of that guilt. Demand that she identify such laws and begin—again with a deadline for completed action—their repeal. This is related to the same rule of law issues, and the courts can be her greatest ally. They already have shown a willingness to act as such, and the Bangladeshi constitution's promise of equality for all citizens demands that action. As she implements the changes she promised to bring about so long ago, she would do well to utilize the services of noted international legal scholars on human rights (such as Irwin Cotler of Canada and Ved Nanda of the United States) and noted Bangladeshi legal scholars, many of whom have been fighting for the rule of law in their country for decades.[368]

The most obnoxious of these laws is the VPA, and its repeal has to be a nonnegotiable demand, given its instrumentality in driving ethnic cleansing. Repeal will eliminate the financial rewards for anti-Hindu violence, demonstrate the current Bangladeshi government's commitment to ending both the atrocities and its complicity, and will provide genuine relief to the victims. The trap we must avoid, however, is the long-standing pattern of accepting mere words without action from the Bangladeshis.

---

[368] Richard L. Benkin, "Commentary: More empty words from the Bangladeshi government," *Weekly Blitz,* September 16, 2009.

As noted above, the Supreme Court and the Awami League's super majority in parliament make nullifying this "black law," as more than one Bangladeshi official described the VPA to me, easy.[369] All it requires is that donor nations and trade partners demand it as a condition for continued contributions and cooperation.

The next step is more complicated—but not too complicated to implement. Over the past several years, I have spoken with VPA victims, living both legally and illegally in India primarily. Many of them have stated unequivocally that they would not return to Bangladesh even if given the chance. They fear for their lives and those of their families. They are convinced that they are forever unwelcome in Bangladesh at both official and popular levels. Response to the Supreme Court's 2008 rule Nisi noted above, should provide victims with the option of receiving their stolen property or accepting a fair payment in lieu of it. The government needs to set up a real commission, comprised of its members as well as Hindu leaders and human rights activists like Advocate Rabindra Ghosh to implement the return under specific conditions (perhaps even monitored by international legal authorities) with specific deadlines for satisfying all victims.

The Bangladeshis have demonstrated that they will not do any of this simply because it is the right thing to do. Were that the case, it would have been done a long time ago—and certainly in early 2009 at the latest. As noted previously, there is no internal dynamic that would move the Bangladeshi government to change things. Those who claim that Sheikh Hasina's Awami League government will be able to change things significantly enough to stave off disaster are as hopeless as those who believe negotiations with the Iranian mullahs have a chance of being productive. The Awami League factors political risks and possible physical dangers in considering

[369] It is unfortunate, but several Bangladeshi officials have spoken to me at various times and in various places, but only on the condition that neither they nor their locations be revealed.

their actions; and in their defense, Sheikh Hasina and her supporters have been the targets of Islamist violence.

Arguments based on notions of justice, of right and wrong, have never had any effect on any Bangladeshi government, including this one. We have to use arguments based on self-interest. Moreover, Bangladeshi leaders are used to begging for scraps from the table of donor nations, especially the United States and Europe. They are pros at giving those donors verbal reassurances of what they are going to do without ever having to do them. That means those arguments about self-interest must:

1) Be powerful enough to leave no doubt of the devastating impact that any sanctions would have;
2) Leave no doubt that they will be applied if the Bangladeshis do not take severe and immediate action by a specific date; and
3) Open the door to expanding the war against radical Islam in Bangladesh.

And with all due respect, we are talking about Bangladesh, after all, not China or Iran. Bangladesh is a nation with such an array of dependencies and vulnerabilities that finding a way to force an end to the atrocities is not difficult. The only way the brutality will stop is if some outside force "convinces" the Bangladeshis to stop it. Those who thought that the current Awami government has that internal dynamic learned that their "give them time" approach did nothing but increase the tally of victims. Giving it any more time now will ensure even more brutalities.[370]

Those Bangladeshi vulnerabilities are called "pressure points," and given the volume of those dependencies and vulnerabilities, it is baffling why the West has not done this already. If anything, conditions in Bangladesh have worsened

---

370 "Repeal Enemy Property Act & Show the Support: Dr. Benkin," Worldwide conference call of BHBCUC, *Daily Khabor*, January 11, 2009.

of late, which provides us with a real opportunity. Given domestic politics, corruption, and the dissembling nature of Bangladeshi leaders when addressing those other countries, however, we need to identify the pressure points that make the government especially vulnerable so that their application forces it to stop tolerating *jihad-inspired* ethnic cleansing; that is, we must identify actions that will have immediate consequences so that the option of tried and true stalling tactics will not be a viable one. There are at least seven pressure points.

1) The economy is desperately in need of international assistance;
2) The economy is desperately in need of international investment and joint ventures;
3) The economy is dependent on exports, especially readymade garment exports to Europe, Canada, and the United States;
4) The economy is dependent on the monthly payments received by 10,000 or more UN peacekeeping troops from Bangladesh;
5) The country and the economy is dependent for what it does receive on its continued ability to portray itself as a "moderate Muslim nation";
6) Ultimately, the country is dependent on outside protection against Islamist radicals who have attacked the country and the current ruling party several times;
7) The country and economy are dependent on international agencies ignoring its shameful history of human rights violations.

Success on even one or two of the above pressure points could be enough to end the ethnic cleansing of Bangladesh's Hindus and strike a serious blow against the spread of radical Islam in South Asia—a process that we have seen is now making its way through Northeast India. The ongoing silence and inaction of international bodies and individual nations has been the principle obstacle to ending that atrocity. That is, the history of the East Bengali people is not such as to make the ethnic cleansing of Hindus and other minorities something organic or inevitable. It has come because both internal and external authorities have allowed radical Islam to take a greater and greater hold on that nation and drive this *unnatural* stake into its heart. We allowed it to happen, and we can stop it.

The great American jurist and first Jewish Justice of the US Supreme Court, Louis D. Brandeis, once said, "Sunlight is said to be the best of disinfectants."[371] He used it in connection with the notion of transparency, and we understand it to mean that if people are forced to confront the reality of atrocities like these, they will do something about it. The government of Bangladesh and the forces of violent *jihad* continue to benefit by the lack of "light" on their anti-Hindu assault. It allows the international powers that be to ignore the matter and focus on pretty much anything else. We need to correct that. It is also clear that South Asian realties have somehow impeded area governments from taking the lead in defending the defenseless and giving voice to the voiceless. Americans, on the other hand, do not have those same domestic political situations or have to concern ourselves with any such "realities" and instead can live up to the ideals of freedom and justice that are at the core of who we are as a nation and people. But we cannot—and should not—do it alone.

When I speak to other Americans about the Bangladeshi Hindus, I often hear: *'Well, if things are as dire as you say they are, why are we not hearing anything from the Hindus themselves; or what about India?'* It is a pretty powerful argument. We can understand if the refugees and other victims do not feel empowered to speak out, but we also know that there are many who can. There is a large NRI (Non-Resident Indian) population making waves throughout the world, but

[371] From "What can publicity do," *Harper's Weekly*, December 20, 1913.

never about this issue. Why? More to the point, there are plenty people inside India who can raise their voices through various legal means and let the government and media know that they will not stand for the continued murder of the Bangladeshi Hindus; that if they are not listened to today, they will return tomorrow, and next week, and next year, and so on and so on and will do so until their anguished cries become too loud to ignore.

It took little more than that sort of notoriety to rouse consciences over Darfur, and in an earlier era Biafra. Unlike those African populations, Indians can boast prominent members in positions of power and influence throughout the world. For instance, the governors of two US states (Louisiana and South Carolina) are both of Indian descent; not to mention prominent entrepreneurs and innovators like the Hindu inventors of the Pentium processor or one of the leading candidates to succeed American tycoon and pundit Warren Buffet[372]. Take note, too, that the genocide in Darfur would not have grabbed the world's attention as it did were it not for celebrity George Clooney. Why can't that work for this issue? Refusing to be silenced about what is happening could stir celebrity activists like soon to be Hindus Brad Pitt and Angelina Jolie, or Hindu Julia Roberts whose notoriety would shine that disinfecting light on these atrocities.

India has long been recognized as the world's largest democracy. When the subcontinent was partitioned on a religious basis, Indians determined that they would never become a theocracy or compromise on their essential values that call for a free society for all of its citizens. While that has sometimes taken on bizarre forms—as our references earlier to pseudosecularism noted—even they represent a sincere effort on the part of Indians to maintain that commitment. For instance, travelers on their way to Indira Gandhi International

---

[372] The governors are Bobby Jindal and Nikki Haley respectively; the Pentium inventors are Vinod Dham and Ajay Bhatt; and the potential successor to Buffet is Ajit Jain.

Airport will notice that they first pass a special terminal built for and used exclusively by Muslims on their way to the *Hajj* in Saudi Arabia. This religious event takes place annually—for five days—and for the rest of the year's 300 plus days, this special terminal sits dark and unused. The entire population of India bore the burden for its construction. In budget after budget, they also allocate significant funds to be used as subsidies for Muslims to visit Jerusalem's Al Aqsa mosque. Yet, their budgets do not allocate a single rupee for Hindu refugees in West Bengal who live in a legal netherworld and an economic underworld.

The only way that disparity will change is if Indians themselves change it. Every Indian has a number of elected representatives. If they are like politicians everywhere else, there likely are some who can be motivated with appeals to justice; and there likely are a larger number who are concerned first and foremost with securing votes and responding to those issues that concern a large number of their consitutents. If you have a representative among the former, then make your clear appeal for the moral duty to stop ethnic cleansing of Bangladeshi Hindus; and if the message is either not received or not heard, make it again—and again and again and as many times as it takes to make it clear that we are facing a moral catastrophe of immense proportions. If your representatives fall into the latter category, you still need to make your appeal in the same relentless way. But it is critical for him or her to understand that there are a number of voters for whom this will be a major factor in their election decision. The more voters who can write, telephone, or even visit the elected official, the greater impact they will have. But the key is for that person to recognize that advocates for Bangladeshi Hindus will never stop; never even slow down. As one member of the US Congress described my success there, "Dr. Benkin is just someone who refuses to take 'no' for an answer." There is nothing special about me, and what I did is nothing that anyone else cannot do!

Ultimately, it is the Bangladeshi government and nation that must act; no one is going to send in troops, cut off relations, or boycott Bangladeshi goods. From the point of view of the Bangladeshis, however, there are some real consequences that they will suffer if they do take the needed moral action. The most significant is fear of angering Islamic radicals. At the very least, it would cost them at the polls. They would be called un-Islamic in the mosques and accused of standing in the way of Islam's fulfilling its long held dreams. Opposition candidates would seize upon the charges and amplify them. Worse still, the offending party could become victims of terror attacks, something we noted Sheikh Hasina has faced before. We also saw (Chapter Six) that the VPA has become part and parcel of the Bangladeshi system of political patronage. As Dhaka University's Professor Abul Barkat demonstrated, it is part of a *system* that all parties use to shore up their followers' support. Politicians who dismantle that system are going to anger a lot of people who have gained tangible benefits from it. On the other hand, they see no concrete benefits from principled action. Justice itself is evidently not much motivation for politicians in Bangladesh.

There is, however, a narrow window of opportunity that likely will grow narrower and ultimately slam shut. In February 2011, I traveled from Silchar in Assam to the Bangladeshi capital of Dhaka to meet with Bangladeshi cabinet minister, H. T. Imam. He is a political leader of the Awami League and a very close confidant of Sheikh Hasina's, who I was told was behind the request for me to come there. They wanted to meet with me because the Awami League is aware that the next election (2014) is not as far away as it seems. Like all political entities, they are concerned about their re-election; and to their credit, they realize that their best chances will come from the people seeing concrete achievements, especially in areas of their immediate concern. In general, that means their material well-being; or as political advisor James Carville famously told his candidate (former US

President Bill Clinton), "it's the economy stupid." Imam made it clear that an Awami League victory is in the interests of the United States and others; certainly more in our interests than the BNP's return to power, he said. The best way to further those mutual interests was for those parties to help the Awami League so that Bangladesh's citizens recognize real improvements in their lives, and attribute them to the ruling party before they cast their votes. That means more trade, technological assistance, investments by US corporations, joint ventures, and especially help with improving the outmoded and inadequate Bangladeshi infrastructure.

I responded—as I always do—that I do not represent the United States government or any other government and cannot make decisions or commitments for them; but I will pass on the information to people who can, which I have done. But I also made it clear that I would strongly urge anyone with whom I speak not to do anything based on words alone; that they must demand action first, or as we have seen time and again, the action will never materialize. In that context, I also raised the issue of the Bangladeshi Hindus and told Imam that it is "going to have to be addressed."

To its credit, the Awami League was not looking to manipulate the people, offering bribes, or looking for mere smoke and mirrors; it wanted to help its people in concrete ways as the path to re-election. To their detriment, however, we have had numerous communications since then in which the Bangladeshis have asked me to make introductions for them in Washington and otherwise take specific actions. I told them that while I could do it, I would not as we had agreed on certain actions in Dhaka, but they have so far not lived up to their commitments—*and just to be clear, those actions had nothing to do with money or with personal gain for me.* I am not so vain as to presume that mine was the only route that the Bangladeshis have taken toward getting the things they want. Evidently, at this point, they still feel they can get those goodies without taking action as I require in exchange. Good luck with that, but their intransigence has made me more emphatic about our sticking to our principles: In order to save the Hindus of Bangladesh, we must make the Bangladeshis recognize that complying with basic human decency and taking concrete steps in that regard are the only things that will get them what they need.[373]

The United States is Bangladesh's third largest trading partner, and the one serious lobbying group in Bangladesh is the Bangladesh Garment Manufacturing and Exporting Association. In 2008, the United States imported $3.74 billion worth of goods from Bangladesh—or 26.5 percent of all of that country's exports. Making that even more powerful is the fact that Bangladesh had a $3.25 billion trade surplus with the US that year. For perspective, that's an amount equal to 30 percent of Bangladesh's entire national budget. Now imagine what it would mean to the Bangladesh government if that number dropped—or what it would mean for all the people of Bangladesh if it grew![374] Do you see the power that we have?

When I first encountered Bangladeshi officials in Washington many years back, their number one goal was to win a Free Trade Agreement with the United States. Not only has that not happened thanks to a lot of good people committed to human rights and free expression, but during that time there have been several legislative attempts to give Bangladesh some sort of tariff reduction to increase its exports to the United States. We have been fortunate enough to defeat all of them on human rights grounds, despite the efforts of Bangladesh and its lobbyists.[375]

---

[373] These discussions took place in H. T. Imam's office in Dhaka on February 21, 2011.

[374] "Background Note: Bangladesh," Bureau of South and Central Asian Affairs, US Department of State, May 24, 2010.

[375] In one 2008 attempt for instance, Senate Bill 652, the Bangladeshis sent no lesser a light than Nobel laureate Mohammed Yunis to urge its passage. Although he was greeted with the respect due a man of his accomplishments, the bill never even got out of subcommittee, let alone to the Senate Finance Committee, where it was buried.

In November 2010, voters of Illinois' Tenth Congressional District elected Robert Dold as their representative in Washington. Even during his campaign, he and I spoke about the need to take a strong and definite human rights stand in defense of the Bangladeshi Hindus. When I showed the future Congressman evidence of their oppression, you could tell he was moved personally; thus very shortly after taking office, he joined the Tom Lantos Human Rights Commission in the United States House of Representatives (TLHRC). The TLHRC is unlike any other Congressional committee in that it is voluntary and, unlike every other Congressional body, is not structured with a majority party Chair and a minority Ranking Member; but with two co-equal chairs. The commission is named after its co-founder Congressman Tom Lantos, the only Holocaust survivor ever to serve in the US Congress, who also served as co-chair of the commission until his death in 2008. Lantos' co-founder, Congressman John Porter represented the same district as Dold does and served on the TLHRC until he left the US House. Porter's successor, US Senator Mark Kirk who preceded Dold as Congressman from the Illinois Tenth District, also served on the Commission until he left Congress. The mission of the TLHRC is to "promote, defend and advocate internationally recognized human rights norms in a nonpartisan manner, both within and outside of Congress, as enshrined in the Universal Declaration of Human Rights and other relevant human rights instruments. In particular, the Commission shall:

- ❑ Develop congressional strategies to promote, defend and advocate internationally recognized human rights norms reflecting the role and responsibilities of the United States Congress.
- ❑ Raise greater awareness of human rights issues among Members of Congress and their staff, as well as the public.
- ❑ Provide expert human rights advice to Members of Congress and their staff.

- ❑ Advocate on behalf of individuals or groups whose human rights are violated or are in danger of being violated.
- ❑ Collaborate closely with professional staff of relevant congressional committees on human rights matters.
- ❑ Collaborate closely with the President of the United States and the Executive Branch, as well as recognized national and international human rights entities, to promote human rights initiatives in the United States Congress.
- ❑ Encourage Members of Congress to actively engage in human rights matters." [376]

On July 28, 2011, however, Dold did something that exceeded even my hopes and changed forever prospects for the Bangladeshi Hindus. On that date, he rose to make a brief speech in support of HR440, a bill calling for the appointment of a "Special Envoy" to promote religious freedom in the Near East and South Central Asia.[379] In justifying the need for the Special Envoy and United States leadership in this critical area, Congressman Dold began by saying, "Since 1947, 49 million Hindus in Bangladesh have gone missing." He went on to offer the Congress more evidence of the atrocity perpetrated against Hindus in Bangladesh. Instead of speaking in general terms about "minorities" or "extremists," he addressed this issue of anti-Hindu persecution in Bangladesh specifically and forcefully; and he cited it as a reason for US action. That had never been done before in the United States Congress.

This is particularly important because our opponents—both those who are perpetrating these atrocities and those who are deliberately ignoring them—have kept this issue off the

[376] Mission statement of the Tom Lantos Human Rights Commission in the United States House of Representatives, available at http://tlhrc.house.gov/about.asp.

[377] Available for viewing at http://www.gpo.gov/fdsys/pkg/BILLS-112hr440eh/pdf/BILLS-112hr440eh.pdf

human rights agenda and distracted us with their own, politically motivated ones. They want to fool us into believing that there is no persecution of Hindus in Bangladesh so it can continue under the radar; to keep us from putting the issue of anti-Hindu ethnic cleansing front and center so people have to deal with it; hence, the generalities about minorities (not Hindus per se) and extremists (not the "good people" running Bangladesh). Thanks to Congressman Dold, that is over. The genie is out of the bottle; the toothpaste is out of the tube; the persecution of Hindus in Bangladesh is part of the United States Congressional Record.

It is also significant that as Dold made his speech, Congressman Frank Wolf, who sponsored the bill and is the long time TLHRC co-chair, sat beside him and nodded approvingly. Dold's speech almost immediately increased interest and help in our fight to save the Hindus of Bangladesh. According to Dold's staff, the YouTube video of his minute and a half speech gets more hits than any other. Because of the Internet's worldwide reach, Dold's words were able to give hope to perhaps millions of Bangladeshi Hindus languishing in camps in India or living fearfully inside Bangladesh.[378]

As of this writing, Dold and his staff (with my assistance) are about to sign off on a letter to US Secretary of State Hillary Clinton that addresses the plight of the Bangladeshi Hindus and asks "that the Secretary of State evaluate how the United States can use its trade and aid largesse to influence the Bangladeshi government to put a stop to these human rights abuses against its Hindu citizens."

Once Congressman Dold gives his final approval to the letter, we will circulate it to a select group in Congress to demonstrate significant concern that is growing in Washington over these atrocities. We will make it impossible for people to

---

[378] "Oppression of Hindus in Bangladesh raised at US Capitol," *NewsGram*, July 29, 2011. Also available at http://www.interfaithstrength.com/Dold.htm, where the video of Dold's speech is also accessible.

pretend that they do not exist or that if we wait for the current Bangladeshi government to live up to its pledges they simply will go away. (A general circulation is more involved and would take a great deal more time). *It is the first time a US Congressional letter addresses the plight of Hindus in Bangladesh specifically* instead of burying it with general terms. It thus identifies the anti-Hindu essence of so many atrocities. This was absolutely necessary to raise the level of inquiry and concern about this quiet case of ethnic cleansing to a new level where it had never before been addressed.[379]

While all of us hope that Secretary Clinton will act on our request and take a serious look at how the United States can help stop these atrocities, we expect the letter to open up several other avenues by which the United States can help end this great human rights travesty. First and foremost, we expect to use this documented Congressional concern as the basis for holding hearings before the TLHRC. The hearings will again provide heretofore absent light and focus so people can no longer allege (as governments, perpetrators, NGOs, and others have) that this is not any more serious than the isolated actions of "extremists" and other non-governmental rogue actors. "Congressman Dold and I also spoke about initiatives to confront the Bangladeshi government over their complicity and what the US could do if things do not change. Finally, we expect to take it beyond that to Congressional Committees with jurisdiction over matters like trade.[380]

There are several ways in which a large cross-section of Americans will help insure the success of these efforts. Once the letter is circulated, it will be important for constituents of

---

[379] It is highly significant that we are preparing this as Congressman Dold and the rest of our elected officials are involved in and focused on an all-consuming debate about the US debt and deficit.

[380] For instance, Congressman Dold is a member of the US House Committee on Financial Services and specifically its Subcommittee on International Monetary Policy and Trade. I also have received encouragement for action in the United States Senate from Senator Kirk and Senator Tom Coburn from Oklahoma.

the Congressional Representatives to telephone their elected officials and let them know how important this issue is and that they urge his or her signature on the letter. When we move to requesting hearings, we again will want a broad cross-section of American voters to call their elected officials and voice their strong support for such hearings. Others will be instrumental in obtaining media coverage in both the United States and India (which we hope will spur action there, as well). Can you imagine what Indian politicians will be faced with if it is confirmed that Hindus are being oppressed in a country bordering India, and it is some Americans who are defending them? What Indian politician would not be forced to stand up on this issue or face defeat and disgrace?

This is an effort to mobilize individuals and groups to become part of a broad consensus of Americans in Congress and among the general population. The United States, like India, is a democratic Republic whose leaders ultimately do listen to the voters, especially on issues like ethnic cleansing. Our effort is premised on a belief that our cause is supported by basic American values: defending the defenseless, standing up against oppressors, and standing for human rights. It supersedes things like politics and religion, which should not be issues, even if some people try to make them such. Congressman Dold's speech and letter are enormous steps in that mobilization, but they are only first steps and part of the story of how we will end this quiet case of ethnic cleansing.

There is much more we can do. In the meantime, I maintain a regular check on legislation to see if any would affect issues of commerce with Bangladesh. Trade provides us with perhaps our greatest source of leverage for dismantling the system of ethnic cleansing, and we do not want to lose it by default or through passivity. Here is an example of the danger and the responsibility. Some years back, when I was working to keep Bangladeshi journalist Salah Uddin Shoaib Choudhury from being re-incarcerated or otherwise harassed by the Bangladeshi government and its minions, I found that a bill had been introduced in the US Senate that would give Bangladesh and other nations some tariff relief. The intention behind the bill was a good one: to build markets in the named countries that, Americans generally believe, will strengthen democracy and counter radicalism whether Islamist or leftist. But the issue of potential trade sanctions and benefits had played a key role in our efforts to get the Bangladeshis to adhere to basic standards of press freedom and human rights with regard to Shoaib Choudhury. So I was concerned that we could lose this important tool for human rights. I noticed that one of its co-sponsors was US Senator from California, Dianne Feinstein, and so contacted a colleague in the struggle who lived in her state. She contacted the Senator's staff and explained the situation. The staff person got back to her and said that when told of it, the Senator said she was aware of the case and "had no idea" that bill would have that affect. While Senator Feinstein never formally withdrew her co-sponsorship, the bill also never made it out of subcommittee; and we appreciate her sensitivity to the issue. By the way, we did not out of hand reject the notion behind the bill, even suggested some options, but we made sure to make lawmakers aware of the human rights consequences that would follow from its passage. This incident demonstrates not only the importance of staying current on matters of legislation, but also of working with colleagues across the country and with contacts in Washington. The same methods are at work in developing our case to fight the ethnic cleansing of Hindus in Bangladesh.

This is not a project that one person can accomplish alone. Our representatives in Washington need to know that this is something that concerns their constituents—who must make a noise so loud that the media cannot ignore it and remain credible. Indiana Congressman Mike Pence once noted that any Member of Congress who receives at least ten telephone calls from constituents on any issue will sit up and take notice, call staff meetings about it, and if it involves a piece of legislation will consider that in determining how to vote. That means Hindus and others here need to contact lawmakers and register their outrage at what is being done to innocent people in Bangladesh.[381]

These phone calls can be random but will have a much greater impact if organized in some way. Organization does not suggest anything other than genuine concern by the callers, but it does suggest making that genuine concern more effective; and we have been working on such organization. While we lack an overall single structure for our effort, there already are several elements with call lists ready to be activated in different Congressional districts and states. Moreover, in the 2010 midterm elections, Hindus as a recognized religious group played a significant role in several elections.[382]

Whether organized nationally or locally, these calling efforts will be more successful—both in animating people to call and in how they are received by Senators and Members of Congress—if they are made in conjunction with a piece of legislation or specific effort on Capitol Hill. So, for instance, calls made that urge someone to vote against a bill that would award Bangladesh tariff relief without being contingent on human rights action would tend to be effective.[383] Calls asking

---

[381] To be effective, the contacts need to be made by telephone. Emails tend to get lost or skimmed, and even if looked at often have a marginal impact; they also show much less of a personal commitment. Snail mail takes weeks and weeks because of necessary security measures implemented after several lawmakers received mail with anthrax germs some years back.

[382] Richard Benkin, "Is Hindu-American Community Coming into its Own?" Dr. Benkin," *Hindu Janajagruti Samhiti,* October 29, 2010.

[383] Note, too, that the caller is not simply saying "no," but leaves open the possibility that all of the positives the bill suggest are possible—but only in connection with positive action (not words) that save lives! In that sense, the Senator or Member of Congress can be a real leader for human rights and also for helping to build markets, to take one example.

a representative to request those TLHRC hearings on the Bangladeshi Hindus would be another example of effective action. Effectiveness, remember, requires coordination, so interested parties should contact me through my web site, http://www.interfaithstrength.com.

Bangladesh is heavily invested in advertising itself to Americans and other potential trading partners as a "moderate Muslim country." Laying aside the issue of what, precisely, is a moderate Muslim, we do know that Bangladeshi Muslims traditionally were less intolerant of their non-Muslim neighbors. Over the last few decades, however, they have come more and more under the thumb of radical *jihadis.* Yet, they have not stopped trying to portray themselves as what they perhaps were at one point, and few Americans know that the reality is not what they are saying it is.[384] But if Americans might be less aware than others about events in countries half way around the world, they are smart, and they hold to their values. If they have information about the ethnic cleansing of Bangladeshi Hindus, they will ask how a country can call itself "moderate" and wage *jihad* against its non-Muslim citizens. The façade that the Bangladeshis try to maintain will crumble, but again, not of its own accord; nor will it happen simply because we believe we are right. It will come through the relentless effort of dedicated individuals to shine that disinfecting light bright enough so that it cannot be ignored.

In early 2009, the US Commission on International Religious Freedom issued its report on nations it has deemed problematic in their citizens' freedom to practice their faiths freely. On the heels of the December 2008 election that ended two years of military rule in Bangladesh and brought a party to power that promised to end discrimination against religious minorities; USCIRF upgraded its rating. Previously, Bangladesh had been on USCIRF's "Watch List," the second

---

[384] At various forums and seminars, I am often asked what US policy is on Bangladesh. My response: What policy?

most severe category it has with regard to religious freedom. In recognition of Bangladesh's significant move back to a democratically elected government, USCIRF placed it in the least severe category, "Other Countries Monitored." It was a smart move that recognized apparent progress in the hopes of encouraging more. As we know, however, that progress was a chimera. USCIRF moving Bangladesh back to the Watch List—or even to the most severe "Countries of Particular Concern"—would be a very clear statement that Bangladesh is, in fact, not what it portrays itself to be.

While that would be a powerful blow to the deadly status quo, recognize that USCIRF commissioners and professional staff maintain rigorous standards.[385] They will need to be presented with evidence not only of atrocities but of the government's complicity—directly or indirectly—in them. And the information will somehow have to be verified. This is a long and hard task, and one that we have begun. But the process has only started, and it will take more work gathering and verifying evidence. As the TLHRC also will need some concrete evidence to pursue the subject matter, the two efforts can be undertaken simultaneously perhaps with the result of a one-two blow to the ethnic cleansing of Hindus in Bangladesh.

And while I do not favor boycotts, as they tend to be misguided and ineffective, and often have unintended and nasty consequences, I can tell you that US businesses are not going to buy products from a country that is guilty of ethnic cleansing—*or more to the point that customers know are guilty of ethnic cleansing*. Nor will they be anxious to take on joint ventures with those who stand accused by official US bodies of spreading *jihad* and wantonly killing innocents because of their religion. I do not suggest or endorse a boycott, but free people—consumers and business leaders alike—have choices to make in the way of purchases and business

[385] This information is available at the United Nations' web site, http://www.un.org.

partners. If we give them access to free and unfettered information, we can expect them to use it when they make those choices. *Whether the message comes from government, private enterprise, or both, we want the Bangladeshis to recognize that once they carry out their responsibility to protect all of their own citizens, the opposition will end and they can realize all sorts of benefits for the 150+ million people.*

There is another major weapon we can unsheathe against those who continue participating in or allowing the atrocities that are killing the Hindu community in Bangladesh; although I recommend we hold it in reserve only if others fail to move the Bangladeshis to action. As noted before, Bangladesh depends on receipts from its 10,000 or more citizens employed as UN peacekeepers.

Stationing "peacekeepers" in international hot spots is one of the UN's most prominent efforts. These personnel from various nations are placed in places around the world that are temporarily peaceful as a result of a ceasefire. The premise is that their presence will prevent renewed hostilities or the violation of UN resolutions that were accepted at the time of a cease fire. There have been 62 such missions in the UN's history, including 15 current operations. Two of them—in the Middle East and between India and Pakistan—have been in operation almost since the birth of the UN. The reader can decide whether that money was well spent in reducing tensions or preventing conflict.[386]

What two nations contribute the greatest number of peacekeeping troops to these UN missions? What two nations' economies are bolstered more than any other by payments for these services? The answer is Pakistan and Bangladesh, which averaged 10,712 and 10,634 troops every month in 2010. By

---

[386] United Nations Peacekeeping, Monthly Summary of Contributors of Military and Police Personnel; available at http://www.un.org/en/peacekeeping/contributors/.

contrast, India averaged 8,815 and the United States 86.[387] Every year, United States taxpayers pick up the tab for about 22 percent of the UN's budget—more than any other country by far.[388] They also pay for approximately 35 percent of the entire UN budget for peacekeeping missions.[389] But they doubtless are unaware that their tax dollars are going to support Islamic terror and ethnic cleansing. Given the size of the US contribution to the peacekeepers' budget, we would expect that it could play a role in moving the UN to take action on that score—or at least pull its funding if the UN ignores it. Most Americans are less than infatuated with the UN these days and are likely to react angrily upon this additional revelation of how the UN spends their dollars in ways contrary to their nation and their values.

The Bangladeshi economy is so dependent, in fact, that the threat of losing them was the real cause of Bangladesh's 2007

---

[387] "Assessment of Member States' contributions to the United Nations regular budget for the year 2009," United Nations Secretariat, December 24, 2008. In addition to these "assessed" contributions, countries might also make additional contributions, and the total amount of US taxpayer dollars that went to the UN in 2009 was almost $6.5 billion. Once the UN has it, the donor nation has no control over how it is spent, but the United States in 2009 specifically earmarked money for the UN Relief Works Agency (UNRWA) equal to 35 percent of its entire budget. See "Annual Report on United States Contributions to the United Nations," Executive Office of the President, Office of Management and Budget, June 7, 2010. UNRWA is the only UN agency ever set up for the benefit of one people—and a people not even part of a member state; in this case the Palestinian Arabs. It has been chugging along for over six decades, never once settling a single refugee or providing substantial aid. In recent years UNRWA has been dodging extensive charges of corruption and terrorist ties, specifically with Hamas. A less than objective UN investigation claims—incredibly to pretty much everyone—that UNRWA has no Hamas ties. The thought that any organization could operate in the Hamas police state of Gaza without cooperating with the terror group is laughable. See, for instance, Mitchell G. Bard, "Myth and Fact: UNRWA and Terrorism," *The Jewish Federations of North America,* 2011.

[388] *Op. cit.,* "Annual Report on United States Contributions to the United Nations."

[389] Private communications I received while present before and during the 2007 coup, which I subsequently verified via independent sources.

military coup.[390] Besides the loss of those receipts, the prospect of 10,000 young, unemployed, angry, *and armed* young men being thrown into the country is enough to scare the heck out of anyone. There is no reason why we cannot or *should* not challenge the United Nations for its support of ethnic cleansing; that is, why it continues to reward a country where a portion of its citizenry is being eliminated steadily and deliberately. There is no reason why we cannot mount an effort—with the help of our nations' leaders—to have the UN decertify this ethnic cleanser for participation in peacekeeping missions.

These efforts relate to the United States because it is my country, and I believe in its people and values. There is no reason why similar principles cannot be applied in other countries as well. The European Union, for instance, is Bangladesh's largest trading partner, and some years back, the EU expressed support and passed a resolution in its parliament in support of our human rights effort in Bangladesh to free anti-jihad Muslim Salah Uddin Shoaib Choudhury. In February 2011, my colleague and co-founder of Forcefield Miriam Guttman-Jones , was in West Bengal and Assam with me. She was looking to bring back verified evidence of the atrocities to her county of Australia. Bangladeshi exports to Australia jumped 176 percent between 2007 and 2008;[391] and Bangladesh's exports to India are expected to hit $1 billion in 2011.[392] Besides the economic impact of any actions taken by India, the two countries' common border and the consequent issues give an additional layer of impact to Indian actions. Most Bangladeshi Hindu refugees have fled to India, although the Indian government has not aided or taken them in or

---

[390] "Trading with Australia," *Daily Star (Dhaka),* June 2, 2010.

[391] "Bangladesh Exports to India to Reach $1 bln by 2011," *Bangladesh News,* August 24, 2009.

[392] Personal conversation with BJP leader L K Advani in New Delhi, February 13, 2010.

recognized their refugees status. Some entities like the state government of Assam have attempted to expel them. While India faces numerous challenges, it is a far more formidable entity than Bangladesh. Opposition icon, L K Advani might have given us a path toward an impact on India. After seeing my evidence, he said, that "if the [Indian] government is telling us that there is no problem with the Hindus in Bangladesh and that is not so, the people [of India] need to be told that."[393]

We face formidable obstacles including apathy, ignorance, disinformation, and vested interests. As the acknowledged leaders of the free world for decades, Americans have had their concern channeled in so many areas of the world for so long. I long have lived with my people's attention drawn to matters other than the atrocities in South Asia and how they relate to the threat we face—the same threat that reared its ugly head on September 11, 2001. At the time of this writing, the nation and our leaders in Washington are focused almost exclusively on domestic issues related to our economic crisis, our growing debt, and whether the United States will move toward a European-style social welfare state or retain its role as the champion of free markets and individual initiative. In the November 2010 elections, those issues obscured foreign policy considerations for many voters and candidates.[394] No

---

[393] For instance, a Bloomberg poll conducted one month before the election gave voters a list of issues and asked them which was the "most important" to their vote. Seven percent said the war in Afghanistan, and everything else was domestic. More telling, perhaps, CBS news polled voters at the same time and asked them their top concern without giving them a list, and none answered with any foreign policy issue. Scott Rasmussen is arguably the most accurate pollster in the United States, and his organization's polling showed that one in five Americans put "national security" at the top of their list of priorities just after Obama's election, but that number fell to nine percent by the 2010 contest.

[394] Statement made to Indian press after an address at Lucknow University, February 20, 2008.

doubt, activists in other countries encounter the same phenomenon, especially in this extended period of economic uncertainty. But it is confounding when we find the same lack of concern among Indians. Recall my statement to the press in Lucknow in 2008: "If I were an Indian Hindu, I would be ashamed that an American Jew had to come half way around the world to stand up for the Bangladeshi Hindus.[395] As noted before, many people we seek to gain as allies wonder the same thing: If it isn't that important to Hindus, why should it be important to me?

This does not make our task impossible, but it does mean that people of good will cannot sit and wait for the Bangladeshi Hindus' ethnic or religious brethren to take action—or use the latter's inaction to excuse our own.

Ultimately, our foes are the proponents of radical Islam and violent *jihad.* If we help others see that, we will gain broader, worldwide support for taking action to stop the destruction of Bangladesh's Hindus. As more people recognize it as part of the threat they face, instead of a tragedy in some other part of the world, that support will continue to grow. It also makes sense to seek out other communities whose members are being reduced by radical Islamists and the inaction of others. In the summer of 2011, for instance, the aforementioned Robert Dold asked me to form and lead a "Human Rights Advisory Council" to bring him credible information to help him and the US Congress continue to battle human rights abuses even amidst our focus on domestic issues. The Council will educate the general public about human rights issues and build coalitions among various groups committed to supporting each other's human rights issues; and it has enabled me to find common cause with some of those other communities under duress from radical

---

[395] Lee Smith, *The Strong Horse: Power Politics, and the Clash of Arab Civilizations.* (Doubleday: New York, 2010), p.17.

Islamists; namely, Baha'i and Assyrian Christians. Can Hindus, Sikhs, and Chakmas, for instance, find the same common ground in South Asia?

A different and at least equally important focus is the mass of "average" Muslims; getting them to recognize the inhumanity that is being done in the name of Islam and refusing to be a part of it. This is not about apostasy; one's religion is a purely personal matter and should be nobody's concern. An individual's religious choice is of no consequence; his or her actions, however, are another matter. Let us recall the 14-year-old Hindu girl I met in Uttar Dinajpur. Her attackers were not radical Islamists per se, not members of *Al Qaeda* or *Jamaat.* They were simple neighbors, but because of a prevailing ideology and biased laws—and the fact that no one is telling them that either is wrong—they and others like them are willing to engage in heinous actions for personal gain or some other motives, which they might otherwise find reprehensible.

The lifeblood of the violent *jihadis,* therefore, comes not from petrodollars or arms so much as it comes from the unwillingness of other Muslims to oppose them and the passivity of Islamic governments even when their own citizens are victims of ethnic cleansing. As much as it is one of their great strengths because it turns small numbers of people into great ones, it is also their Achilles Heel. *The Islamists' greatest vulnerability is that they are dependent on the continued inaction by governments and "average" people. The ethnic cleansing of the Bangladeshi Hindus requires continued complicity and passivity by the government and people of Bangladesh if the Islamists' nefarious designs are to succeed.* Force an end to them and you frustrate the designs of Islamists. For many, that sets up a battle for the "hearts and minds" of that greater population. Perhaps it is, but it is not a battle that will be won through appeasement, weakness, and pretensions of "outreach." As the late Osama bin observed, "people naturally prefer the strong horse to the weak one."[396] Among those people we are trying to win over, those outreach efforts will fail as long as we fail to grasp their understandings; to operate in their world and not assume ours is the only reality. If the people we wish to affect see Iran spurn US warnings and march closer to nuclear weapons capability, they will see the forces of democracy and freedom as weak. If they see radical Muslim regimes gaining allies and footholds in Latin America—the United States' back yard with an unprotected border into the US—they will see them, not us, as the likely winners. And if they see the US running scared from its traditional support for Israel, and democratic nations tolerating Islamist destruction of non-Muslim populations; that will confirm their perception that we are indeed the weak horse. It does not matter if history provides a clearer perspective; that for a while, many (including pundits and "authorities") believed of both fascism and communism that they were on an inexorable march that would eclipse the age of democracy. What matters is how people perceive today's actions.[397]

For the people we want on our side, there is another critical but simple reality that I have been hearing consistently from South Asian and Middle Eastern Muslims and non-Muslims alike. If we really believe that we are waging war against

[396] This book is being written almost three-fourths of the way into Barack Obama's first term as President of the United States. Comments made about US foreign policy, the "weak horse," and European-style socialism, all revolve around Obama initiatives that might or might not be reversed by his successors, or even by him should he win a second term. He has backed off his oft-repeated mandate to close the terrorist detention center at Guantanamo Bay, Cuba, as well as his insistence to try terror suspects in US civilian courts; and he has unshackled military action and drone strikes against Islamist leaders. Whether or not Obama will win a second term is as yet unclear, but the November 2010 midterm elections certainly showed a national discontent with his policies among US voters.

[397] Martin Kramer, "Suicide Terrorism in the Middle East: Origins and Response (Prepared Remarks)," *Washington Institute for Near East Policy,* November 8, 2005. In his remarks, Kramer also rejects the notion that Bangladeshi Salafists are any less dangerous than Saudi ones.

injustice and a warped and retrograde sense of right and wrong, then we need to show it. Half-hearted efforts and pretensions of "understanding" our enemy's concerns only weaken our case. On the other hand, they see that *jihadis* seem to have no doubt about the moral superiority of their goals. In an address to the Washington Institute for Near East Policy, Martin Kramer, posits that the rise of "Islamist sensibility" would not have been possible without a "moral logic," and that the only way to defeat them is to undermine it. No territorial concessions or other finite measures will do it.[398] That is, our goal has to be victory, not some hoary notion of peaceful co-existence. After all, who are we to condemn others to atrocity and death?

At times, I know, the task seems daunting, but we can address that trepidation with an old question, if you will excuse the expression from this vegetarian: Do you know how to eat a dinosaur? The answer is: One bite at a time. Let us start today, working together for those small victories that will lead to larger ones. Do not let anyone tell you that you are too "small" or too "alone" to make a difference. It just is not so. Do not let anyone tell you that the only way to get people's attention is with a lot of money or influence. That, too, is a lie, and our past successes are proof of it. No, you do not need all of that.

What we do need is this just cause and the dedication and determination not to let ANYBODY stand in the way of a just end. What we need is dedicated people to undertake relentless, moral effort, and carry it out with no respite even if initially only a few people notice, continuously day after day. Officials at Bangladeshi embassies should get sick of walking among you every day when they come to work; the same for West Bengal government workers. Again, however, they are most effective when part of an organized program that targets

---

[398] *Op. cit.*, Knowles, editor, *Oxford Dictionary of Modern Quotations*, 301. Attributed to Joseph Stalin.

media, elected officials, and specific groups and individuals with a specific the population. Whether we are protesting to Bangladeshis, or petitioning the US or India, they must know that if they ignore us today, they will see us again tomorrow; and if they ignore us tomorrow, they will see us the next day, next week, next month, and next year, and on and on until our cries become too loud for them to ignore.

Joseph Stalin is said to have remarked, "One death is a tragedy, a million deaths a statistic."[399] That 14-year-old rape victim—that child—I met in Uttar Dinajpur was no statistic, and neither are the countless others like her. God help us if we make them one!

[399] Many Indians continue to resent USCIRF, especially after the its last attempt to come to India for a fact-finding mission. Many people were concerned that the mission would help maintain misinformation and a partial story about events in places like Gujarat and Orissa; but I believed then that the refusal to allow USCIRF into India was a mistake, and this situation shows why it was. India is the only country that has refused USCIRF entry, and it remains on its list of "Countries of Particular Concern." Bangladesh, on the other hand, has always cooperated with USCIRF, which as is clear has encouraged that country's efforts at reform. For in fact the only way that USCIRF can alter its perception of religious freedom in India would be if the evidence it had pointed in that direction. A visit in which they had the opportunity to gather it would be to India's benefit. For it could also go a long way in dispelling myths about India and perhaps even change the standard narrative about the events alluded to above. My personal opinion is that such a cooperative venture—on India's terms—is more valuable than an empty (and essentially misguided) gesture about "national sovereignty," but ultimately, the decision is not mine or any other American's but that of the Indian people.

APPENDIX I

GOVERNMENT-TOLERATED ATTACKS ON BANGLADESHI HINDUS

The tables that follow in this Appendix list attacks on Hindus in Bangladesh. They are not presented as an exhaustive list of such attacks but have been limited to: attacks that have taken place while the Awami League government has had responsibility for them; attacks on Hindus, even though there have been numerous attacks on other minorities like the Chakmas of the Chittagong Hill Tracts and the Ahmadiyya, among others; attacks that the government tolerated by its inaction or active cover-up; attacks that we have been able to confirm through independent sources. Still, the lists demand attention. The first contains major 2009 attacks that average almost one per week for the entire year. The second contains a list of seven verified attacks that took place in a mere 26-day period, March 12 through April 6, 2010. While several individuals and groups are responsible for documenting these events, my deepest thanks go to Rabindra Ghosh, a Bangladeshi Advocate (or attorney) who has dedicated his life to investigating, exposing, and opposing these and many more attacks on the Hindus of Bangladesh.

Attacks on Bangladeshi Hindus in 2009*

Date	State Locality	Name	Age/ Sex	Offense	Narrative	Sources	Government
1/1/2009	Barisal, Kalapara, Patuakhali	Subarna Karmakar	14 F	Kidnapping	On her way home from school, several Muslim males (led by one named Jewel, age 22) grabbed Subarna, forced her onto their motor cycle, and fled. Subarna cried loudly for help, but no one came to her aid.	BDMW; Daily Destiny; BHBCUC	Subarna's father complained to the police, who took no action.
1/15/2009	Khulna, Dumuria	Choyon Bairagee	8 M	Kidnapping; assault; breaking and entering; threats.	On January 15, nine kidnappers went to the family home, kicked in the door, and forcefully entered. They grabbed Choyon Bairagee and when his mother Aduri lamented, the kidnappers threatened to kill the child if she reported the matter to anyone. They demanded 20 million taka ransom.	Janakantha; Daily Purbanchal; BDMW; BHBCUC	Moniuzzamn, Officer-in-charge of Dumuria police station, told newsman that there was no case to pursue.
1/24/2009	Khulna, Chandipur	Thakur Das Mondol	M	Severe beating.	Attacked by 5-6 Muslim fundamentalists on his way home and left in a "senseless condition." Taken to Khulna Medical College Hospital. Mr. Mondal is a member of the Hindu Union Council and Chairman of Magur Khali Union Jubo Dal in Khulna.	BHBCUC, CDA	Police have taken no action despite numerous appeals.
1/26/2009	Faridpur, Banesordi	Hindu Temple	***	Religious desecration.	Around 9pm, a group of local, heavily armed Muslim Fundamentalists, led by Mohammed Siraj, former Banesordi chairman, attacked a Hindu funeral site	BHBCUC, CDA; Shri Monoronjon Biswas (filed	Police have taken no action despite numerous appeals.

					and a nearby Kali temple, burning down the temple completely and destroying its Hindu Kali deity. As locals tried to save the temple, the attackers threatened them with arms. Their motive was to grab the Hindu-owned temple area land.	case with police).	
1/28/2009	Dinajpur, Kantaji	Hindu Temple	***	Religious desecration; land grab.	Madrassa built on land of Kantaji Mandir (Hindu, Kali) Temple.	BHBCUC, Daily Shamokal	Police have taken no action despite numerous appeals. BHBCUC presented an appeal directly to Vice Counsel (to the Prime Minister), AFM Zahid Hasan on February 19, 2009. Still no action.
1/30/2009	Chittagong, Hathazari	Hindu Temple; worshi-ppers	M&F	Religious desecration; assault.	A group of 10-15 Islamists attacked the Swaraswait Pandal, destroying the temple and a deity and leaving ten hurt.	BHBCUC	Police have taken no action despite numerous appeals. BHBCUC presented an appeal directly to Vice Counsel (to the Prime Minister), AFM Zahid Hasan on February 19, 2009. Still no action.
1/30/2009	Dhaka, Mondal	Mcnindra Shib Rampur	M Nath	Theft of land.	Md. Hasan Habib, Organizing Secretary of Bhangura Union Awami League of Pabna district, forceibly occupied 4 Bigha and 1 acres of lands belonging to a Hindu, Monindra Nath Mondal As soon as the new	BHBCUC, Daily Naya Diganta.	Mr. Monindra filed a complaint at Bhangura police station, but no action has been taken—even though the Officer-

Date	State Locality	Name	Age/ Sex	Offense	Narrative	Sources	Government
					government came into power, Habib illegally, and with duress and threats, occupied those lands from a poor Hindu.	Bhangura	in-Charge of the police station admitted the offense.
2/2009	Dinajpur		M&F	Rape, thievery, assault	Muslims (as identified by victims) committed the following on this family: beat the father, stole the land, and gang raped the 14 year old daughter. She at first said they "chased" her and on further questioning said they "caught her and did bad things to her.	Direct testimony from victims.	Family received no help from authorities and so fled to India 22 days before our 3/23 interview.
2/13/2009	Dhaka, Shibchar, Madaripur	Hindu Temple.	***	Religious desecration	Muslim fundamentalists attacked the Sidditala Durga temple and destroyed at least ten Hindu deities; and demolished the Kali Temple, Shitala Mandir,and Manasha Mandir. Locals caught one attacker whom the police termed a "mental patient," thus preventing any investigation of it as a religious crime, although the other perpetrators were all part of the Islamist JMB.	BHBCUC, Daily Sangbad	Police have taken no action despite numerous appeals and a direct appeal to Vice Counsel (to the Prime Minister), AFM Zahid Hasan on February 19, 2009 by BHBCUC.
2/15/2009				Home seized; land grab.	Minority home occupied by Awami League operatives.	BHBCUC, Daily Naya Diganta.	Police have taken no action despite numerous appeals. BHBCUC presented an appeal directly to Vice Counsel (to the Prime Minister), AFM Zahid Hasan on February 19, 2009. Still no action.

2/19/2009	Barisal, Ratanpur, Das	Adhir Chandra Sadar	57 M	Murder	Retired Hindu school headmaster shot in the chest by 4-5 attackers. Police blamed it on unidentified "previous enmity."	BHBCUC, Bangladesh Observer	Police have taken no action and declared it not to be a religious crime.
2/26/2009	Barisal, Mohadipur, Kaharul	Tanusree Roy	14 F	Rape, abduction	Per the girl's father, Rajendra Nath Roy, at about 10am, Tanusree was abducted by two Muslims, Babul Hossain Zihad alias Zikrul Islam (24) and Md. Razzak Ali (22). In his FIR filed with Kotwali Police Station, he notes that the kidnappers repeatedly threaten to kill him and his family.	BDMW; BHBCUC	Case Number -04 was filed on the matter on March 2nd under section 7/30 of Nari—O—Shishu Nirjatan Ain. No action has been taken by the police, however, to recover the girl or punish the known perpetrators.
3/8/2009	Sarishkandi; Kamalgong	Dipali Roy; others	26 F	Assault	Prantosh Roy, a Hindu, arranged a marriage of his daughter Dipali Roy (26), but several Muslims (including Papu, son of Tera Mia of Bikram Kalash Village) disrupted the ceremony and shut off the lights. When Jagadish Baydya (intended groom) tried to stop them, 10-12 disruptees became violent and attacked, wounding eight.	Daily Prothom Alo; BDMW; BHBCUC	No action by the police.
3/10/2009	Moulovi-bazar, Dolapar, Sadar	Fulfuli Rani Roy	15 F	Murder	Per the girl's father, she was kidnapped and murdered by Mahabul Islam, son of Rayaz Uddin.	Daily Prothom Alo; BDMW; BHBCUC	Father filed a complaint, but police have taken no action.

Date	State Locality	Name	Age/ Sex	Offense	Narrative	Sources	Government
3/13/2009	Dhaka, Sutrapur, Dhamrai	Milon Moni Das	3 M	Kidnapping; murder	Family reported Milon's kidnapping to the police on March 13, but the police took no action; two days later, a neighbor found the Hindu child dead in some bushes. Local Muslims are suspected, but with the police refusing to act, the perpetrators feel capable of acting with impunity according to locals.	BDMW, GHRD; BHBCUC	A case was registered at Dhamrai Police station on March 15; case No.18 under section 302/201/34 of Bangladesh Penal code. Police took one Muslim into custody, but released him after intervention by the local (party?) chairman. There has been no further action taken.
3/23/2009	Rajshahi, Samaj Bazar, Chatmohar	Multiple; Hindu Temple	***	Land grab; assault; religious desecration	Sharif Uddin Master, a Muslim, of Samaj village at Nimaichara Union, Chatmohar, Pabna tired to seize the land of the Hari Temple. He, his brother Farid, and other Muslims (all armed) rushed the temple; and attacked local Hindus who tried to protect it with their presence. They wounded 30 men and women. Shushil Halder (45), Vela Halder (35), Gobindo Sutradhar (55), Manoshil (45), Ajit Halder (26), Goutom Sutradhar (26), Lata Rani (30), Shuva Rani (45), Bimal Halder (55), Nepal Halder (35), Paritosh Maitra (40), Komal Sutradhar (35), Shyamol Sutradhar (30), Dolo	Daily Ittefaq; BHBCUC	No action by the police.

3/25/2009	Khulna Sarkar	Suvadra	F	Assault; threats	Rani (45), Shipra Rani (20), Alo Rani (33). Hindus are frightened since the occurrence. Ms. Sarakar, an attorney, was beaten and injured in the hall of the Khulna Bar Association by a Muslim colleague, K M Iqbal. She was admitted to Khulna general hospital for treatment. Iqbal tried to beat Sarakar's client, and when she tried to intervene, he beat her, further yelling that he would "kill her if he got the opportunity."	Daily Independent; BDMW; BHBCUC	Victim filed a complaint with the Khulna police, but no action has been taken to date.
3/25/2009	Dhaka, Chandlara, Kendua, Netrokona	Satish and his nephew Kajal	M	Assault	Giashuddin and gang of associates attacke two Hindus. aged 55 and 26, without provocation, injuring them seriously.	Daily Samakal; BHBCUC	Case filed but no action thus far.
3/28/2009	Rajshahi, Sadar, Joypurhat	Bimol Chandra Sarkar	50 M	Property destruction; arson; murder of livestock	Attackers burned down victim's home and barn, killing three cows, injuring three more.	Daily Samakal; BHBCUC	Hindus gathered in from of District Commissioner's office in Brahmanbaria, but police took no action.
3/30/2009	Khulna, Jagannat-pur, Devhata, Satkhira	Suvash Chandra Ghosh	M	Land grab	Muslims forcefully grabbed 132 Bigha of shrimp farming; Faijul Bayajid, Kala, Jihad, and Shafikul were armed and claimed these lands as a domain estate.	Daily Samakal; BHBCUC	Police sided with the attackers, and local Hindus are scared and also intimidated to go to police.
4/2/2009	Chittagong, West	Multiple	***	Torture; assault;	Crime ongoing; date given is date of newspaper report. Muslim Mia,	Daily Samakal;	Case filed but no action thus far.

Date	State Locality	Name	Age/ Sex	Offense	Narrative	Sources	Government
	Payratala, Brahmin-baria			land grab; extortion.	district President of Awami League and others often extort up to 100,000 refusing to pay are assaulte and "torture[d] them in various ways." They also seize land (name of one victim, Nanda Lal Das) and hold people hostage until paid.	BHBCUC	
4/6/2009	Dhaka, Satish Chandlara, Kendua, Netrokona	Chandra, Bishaw Sharma and Prafulla Sharma	M	Torture; assault; land grab	Hindu families by influential, Muslim neighbor Giashuddin who also seized their land.	Daily Samakal; BHBCUC	Case filed but no action thus far.
4/17/2009	Dhaka, Sutrapur; Vusir Goli	Multiple; Hindu Temple	***	Religious desecration; assault; massive land grab.	Hundreds of local Muslims forcibly victed 400 Hindus. Abdul Kayum, ebrother of Awami League General Secretary, Asad Mahabub Bipu, Saleh Ahamed, and local Awami leader Tofael led the demolition of three houses (88, 96 and 97) and the area's oldest Hindu temple, Kalir Ghat Shiva Mondir. The Hindus have owned those and other houses an property for at least 150 years, paying taxes and utilities regularly. The government, however, declare the to be "vested" under the Vested Property Act, and Asad Mahabub Bipu claimed owner-ship filing title suit. The attackers also threatened	Daily Star of Dhaka; New Age of Dhaka; Daily Samakal; BHBCUC	Local police participate in the attack, assisting the land grab and citing the Vested Property Act. Neither did police act to stop the property destruction or religious desecration. The Vested Property Act, maintained and upheld by the current and past Bangladeshi

							the local Hindus. governments, provided justification for the act and has given the police reason for not acting on Hindu complaints. The police claim to have started an investigation, however, although there is no evidence of any activity.
4/20/2009	Mulavi-bazar, Tilagor, Surjogram, Kamalgong Sumita Rani		F	Unspecified assault	Patonusa High School student Nayaiganta; arassed by Muslim males on way home from school and attacked in her home that night.	BHBCUC	Case filed but no action thus far.
4/23/2009	Chittagong, Mojllishpur, Kosba, Brahmin-baria	Minor	F	Rape	Two (minor) Muslims raped the young girl, who was rescued by locals and taken to the Thana Health Complex and later Sadar Hospital for treatment.	Daily Jaijaidin; BHBCUC	A case was been filed at Kosba Police Station, but rapists and companions are threate-ning to kill to the family if the case is not dropped.
4/23/2009	Jessore, Khalilpur, Bagerpara	Bhim Das; Shibu Dutta	M	Robbery	Muslim robbers looted cash and valuables worth 200,000 taka from two Hindu homes.	Daily Independent; BHBCUC	No action by the police.

Date	State Locality	Name	Age/ Sex	Offense	Narrative	Sources	Government
4/29/2009	Dhaka, Sutrapur	Shib Mandir	***	Religious desecration; assault.	Awami League supporters drove out Hindus surrounding the temple and beat them mercilessly.	Nayaiganta; BHBCUC	Witnesses claim police were present, but took no action to stop the attack. When confronted by locals about this, police claimed it was not a temple but only a place with a ffew Hindu deities. Police have refused to act on this case. Note that the temple was in dilapidated shape since a March 30, 2009 attack; and after an attack by Pakistani troops in 1971, local government officials prevented the temple from being refurbished. asked the government to take action against the perpetrators return the temple to the Hindus.

4/30/2009	Dinajpur	Shri Noran-doy Nath Roy	62 M	False prosecution; abduction	On March 16, Mr. Roy filed case against the local school committee charging he was not allowed to vote in the school committee election where his son Ranjit Kumar Roy is a student. of One of the accused is the brother general secretary of local Awami league. On April 30, seven Muslim men forcibly took him to Ranigonj Market an on the way, forced a bag on him and took him to police station. The next day the police took Roy to court, filing a case to recover 20 "Fensidel" he allegedly stole from his attackers.	CDA	False prosecution continues.
5/2009	Barisal, Ujirpur	Dinesh Hazari	M	Attempted murder; seriously wounded	Muslim fundamentalists attacked victim victim with lethal weapons in an effort to grab his land.	Prof. Sukdev Biswas	Pedestrian apprehended two perpetrators; police released them on bail with no follow up.
5/2009	Khulna, Mongala	Swapan Sikari of Datter-math	M	Land grab; intimidation.	Lands ("Fishery") grabbed by local Awami League leader, Md.Idris Ezardar, brother of Md.Khaleq Talukdar, Khulna City mayor. Victims have fled in fear.	Prof. Sukdev Biswas	Government refuses to act or to evict perpetrators from land.
5/2009	Khulna, Mongala	Susanta Kirtyaniya of Datter-math	M	Land grab; intimidation.	Lands ("Fishery") grabbed by local Awami League leader, Md.Idris Ezardar, brother of Md.Khaleq Talukdar, Khulna City mayor. Victims have fled in fear.	Prof. Sukdev Biswas	Government refuses to act or to evict perpetrators from land.

Date Locality	State	Name Sex	Age/	Offense	Narrative	Sources	Government
5/2009	Khulna, Mongala	Gopal Mondal of Datter-math	M	Land grab; intimidation.	Lands ("Fishery") grabbed by local Awami League leader, Md.Idris Ezardar, brother of Md.Khaleq Talukdar, Khulna City mayor. Victims have fled in fear.	Prof. Sukdev Biswas	Government refuses to act or to evict perpetrators from land.
5/2009	Khulna, Mongala	Arun Roy of Basir-khanda	M	Land grab; intimidation.	Lands ("Fishery") grabbed by local Awami League leader, Md.Idris Ezardar, brother of Md.Khaleq Talukdar, Khulna City mayor. Victims have fled in fear.	Prof. Sukdev Biswas	Government refuses to act or to evict perpetrators from land.
5/2009	Khulna, Mongala	Dr.Jogen Babu of Basirkh-anda	M	Land grab; intimidation.	Lands ("Fishery") grabbed by local Awami League leader, Md.Idris Ezardar, brother of Md.Khaleq Talukdar, Khulna City mayor. Victims have fled in fear.	Prof. Sukdev Biswas	Government refuses to act or to evict perpetrators from land.
5/2009	Khulna, Mongala	Sushovan Mistry of Burburiya	M	Land grab; intimidation.	Lands ("Fishery") grabbed by local Awami League leader, Md.Idris Ezardar, brother of Md.Khaleq Talukdar, Khulna City mayor. Victims have fled in fear.	Prof. Sukdev Biswas	Government refuses to act or to evict perpetrators from land.
5/3/2009	Faridpur, Hathata, Modhu-khali	Sree Anil Kumar Ghosal	M	Assault on a priest.	A priest of Shyam Rai Mondir was attacked and almost killed.	Daily Bohrer Kagoj; BHBCUC	No action by the police.
5/4/2009	Chittagong	Shilpak and Krish-na Dhar	M	Torture; assault; kidnapping; extortion,	Two Hindu Gold merchants were kidnapped, tortured, and forced to pay 50 Karat gold before being freed.	Daily Dinkal; BHBCUC	No action by the police.

5/12/2009	Dhaka, Noagon	Rahima Akter	26 F	Public whipping	Hindu woman made a claim of paternity on a married Muslim man, one Abdul Karim. She was taken to the local madrassa where a committee had issued a fatwa for her to be whipped because of the charge. She was taken to Dhaka Medical College, according to one doctor there, "in a very bad situation " The madrassa spokesman insisted the whipping was being carried out "according to Islamic Shariah law."	Daily Samakal; BHBCUC, CDA, UPI Asia	Police took victim to the hospital. The victim's father filed a case against the six people on the fatwa committee, but police arrested only three.
5/24/2009	Barisal, Pir-Noagaon	Multiple	M	Threats, theft, land grab	Multiple, armed attackers rushed several places of Hindu businesses and took over the land; they also plundered valuables from the owners, physically assaulted them, and threatened to kill the victims "if any Hindu claims the land."	Daily Janakantha; BHBCUC	Police refuse to act on filed case; pressured victms to come to agreement with the "forced occupiers." Hindu residents are intimidated as a result.
6/13/2009	Nandail, Ghosai Chandura	Koli Goswami	21 F	Abduction; forced conversion	Touhidul Islam Bhuiya (Sumon) and others broke in the house of Koli Goswami at about 12:45am, gagged her, vandalized the home, and abducted her. The victim tried to escape creating a hue and cry, but the kidnappers scared off potential . help by firing pistols in the air	GHRD, BDMW, unnamed news-papers	Police refused to act or recover the victim for her family, calling it a "love affair." Human rights organizations report secret testimony contrary to law and the manufacture of "marriage documents." Police refuse to take any

Date Locality	State	Name	Age/ Sex	Offense	Narrative	Sources	Government
							additional action, even though they have evidence of vandalized property in their possession (i.e., that it was not a voluntary elopement).
6/24/2009	Sultanpur, Maniganj, Dhaka	Archana Rani Rajbangshi	17 F	Kidnapping, Gang rape, Attempted murder	About 10-11:00pm, this adolescent girl went to fetch water when multiple (and known) Muslim males grabbed her from behind, dragged her into the bushes, stole her ornaments, stripped her, bit her face and thigh, and raped her one after another. They left her unconscious, and assuming she was dead, tied her to a tree and tried to make it look like a suicide. The victim fell, awoke, screamed for help, and was taken to Sir Salimullah Medical College for treatment and where rape and injuries were confirmed.	GHRD	Victim and her brother went to lodge FIR at Harirampur Police station on June 26, but the Officer-in-Charge insulted her and pushed them out of the station. The victim got medical treatment and obtained injury report, but police refused to register the case and destroyed the evidence. Officials including Superitendant of Police have refused to lodge case, intimidated family, and taken bribes. Appeal to Sheikh Hasina has gone unanswered.

6/27/2009		Shymoli Rani Mondal	14 F	Abduction; forced conversion	At about 6:30am, the victim, was kidnapped and raped by seven Muslims, identified by witnesses; married to one of them, and converted to Islam. Rape was confirmed at the Medical Colleage, and the minor girl was recovered.	Daily Karatoa; GHRD	Per law, the marriage of the minor was null and void; her father produced a birth certificate with a 1995 date of birth, but police claim she is 18. Police up to the Superintendant have warned investigators to stay away from the case.
7/2/2009	District-Manik-ganj	Anguri Biswas	23 F	Abduction; forced conversion	was kidnapped and seduced by seven perpetrators from the road towards	GHRD, BDMW	Police refused multiple times to accept an FIR, admitting the act took place but calling it a 'love affair.' GHRD, for acceptance of case, but no action has been taken.
7/5/2009	Jessore	Farul Das	16 F	Gang raped	railway station for wrongful purposes witnessed by 1) Md. Shafikul	OMCT	Complaint filed with police, but despite promises to act, there has been no action to find and arrest perpetrators.

Date Locality	State	Name	Age/ Sex	Offense	Narrative	Sources	Government
7/16/2009	Gopalput, Bogra	***	***	Religious Desecration	Islam, 2) Sree Rajen Saha, 3) Sree Kanta Das of village – Bara Bandar,	Bhorer Kagaj, HAF	No action by the police.
7/22/2009	Paikgachha, Khulna	Rupa Mandal	12 F	Abduction; forced conversion; battery	Victim was first abducted on July 22 by an identified Muslim male and accomplices after family rejected his marriage proposal and held at a nearby company (Jewel Fish Product) owned by a member of parliament and various police and government officials. Police retrieved the girl but refused to lodge a complaint. They released the kidnapprers who kidnapped the victim again on July 27, August 19, and August 22. She remains missing, and the kidnappers have threatened repeatedly to kill the family. They also beat the victim's mother and sister.	AHRC	Mother sought help from the Paikgachha police, and was directed to a Sub Inspector (SI) Delwar Hossain. She said he then kicked her and said: "Do you expect the police to guard your daughter all around the world? Go away and find her yourself." She went straight to the Jewel Fish Product office and found the kidnappers taking her daughter in a boat from the adjacent river port. She shouted for help but no one came. She later forced an FIR, and a court ordered an investigation

							and recovery of the victim. Local and Khulna police and officials have threatened the family and have prevented any action in the case.
7/24/2009	Rangunia, Chittagong	Jatindra Lal	65 M	Murder, Land grab Dey	P.S. Kotwali, Distrtict – Dinajpur. On interrogation the witnesses	Bhorer Kagaj, GHRD	Local police refused to act; family filed case in Chittagong. Police have admitted the violation but are preventing any action.
8/27/2009	Pubail Union, Feni, Chittagong	Multiple	***	Beatings, Attempted murder	At 9pm, 15-16 Muslim males under the leader-ship of Ripon, President of Fazilpur Union Awami League attempted to kill Baramali Das. Other minorities protested, and the hoodlums became more furious, attacked Hindu homes, and beat women and children, seriously injuring	Bhorer Kagaj, BDMW	No action by the police.
11/2/2009	Tajpur, Natore, Rajshahi	Multiple	***	Arson, burning people, murder	ten. Over 100 witnesses testified that more than 100 armed Muslims set fire to Hindu inhabitants, locking them in their houses. All witnesses named accused attacked at night with deadly weapons, ransacked the Hindu village, looted belongings, and set fire to the houses, pouring petrol on them. Raj Behari Ghosh (90) died at the hospital two days later from his burns.	Daily Sangbad, GHRD, BDMW	Police claim that order has been restored, but residents are fearful and no one is currently in custody.

Date Locality	State	Name	Age/ Sex	Offense	Narrative	Sources	Government
11/22/2009	Hatbaria, Jhenaidaha, Khulna	***	***	Religious desecration	Large number of Muslims demolished two hundred year old temples and brought in eight to ten truckloads of dirt to cover the area. Witnessed by entire community.	Daily Sangbad, BDMW	Police claim it is not religious desecration but a land dispute that will be settled; no action taken, except to threaten BDMW advocate who inquired about the case.

(*) All incidents have been verified, involve Hindus, and inaction by authorities. The list is not expected to be comprehensive
GHRD=Global Human Rights Defence
AHRC=Asian Human Rights Commission
CDA=Christian Development Alternative
BDMW=Bangladesh Minority Watch
BHBCUC=Bangladesh Hindu Buddhist Christian Unity Council
HAF=Hindu American Foundation
FIR=First Incident Report, necessary to launch police investigation.
OMCT=World Organisation Against Torture

APPENDIX II

Atttacks on Bangladeshi Hindus - March 12 through April 6, 2010

Date	Division	Locality	Name	Age	G	Offense	Narrative	Sources	Gov't
3/12/10	Khulna	Gach Baria, Lohagora, Narail	Beauty Biswas	5	F	Child rape; attempted murder.	This Class I (youngest class) student, was raped at night by an identified Muslim perpetrator, Badsha Mollah (27). She fell unconscious, bleeding from her vagina, after the assault. She regained consciousness, and her assailant was found by her family trying to strangle the child.	GHRD; BDMW; Daily Purbanchal	Despite the media coverage, involvement of the rights group, and evidence including witnesses and pictures, as well as the perpetrator's previous criminal history, the police have taken no action.
3/14/10	Rajshahi	Bogra Kundu	Rani Deepa	23	F	Abduction; rape; forced conversion to Islam	On her way to the Youth Development Training Center about 9 am, four Muslim men attacked her and kidnapped her, later demanding a ransom from her father. One of them raped the young woman. They forcibly converted the woman but still demand ransom from herfather. They also claim to have married her to one of her assailants.	GHRD	Police have refused to pursue the matter, and the special Women and Children Repression Tribunal refused as well. There are also allegations of briber.

3/16/2010	Dhaka	Serajganj	Sumitra Dutta	14	F	Child abduction; forced conversion	A minor Hindu girl and a student of Class Nine was abducted by Muslims on her way to school and forcefully converted to Islam.	BDMW; HRCBM; Daily Ajkaler Khabar	Police refused to find and save the victim, whose family did that at some peril to them-selves. Police refuse to pursue a case against these known perpetrators.
3/19/2010	Barisal	Patuakhali Rani Das	Anju	16	F	Child abduction; rape	This adolescent Hindu shool girl (Class IX) was taken from her older brother's custody by eight identified Muslims. They abducted her taking her to the Muslim area, Kaina, where all eight gang raped her in turn. She also was assaulted and her belongings looted.	BDMW; Amader Shomoy	Eight perpetrators have been identified by name, but the police arrested only two, bringing no charge. The area police superintendent is aware of the incident, admitting that the violation occurred.
3/21/2010	Chitta-gong	Dhanua, Faridganj, Chandpur	Archana Rani Das, Sanjit Das, eight others.	*	M/F	Religious destruction; home desecration; assault	At about 4pm, 15-20 armed Muslims attacked the Hindu village Dhanua sending two Hindus to the hospital. They destroyed part of the local Temple and several dwellings	BDMW; Daily Samakal	Police arrested only two of five known and 10-15 unidentified assailants; no court action has been set for the two.

Date	Division	Locality	Name	Age	G	Offense	Narrative	Sources	Gov't
3/23/10	Dhaka	Kaliazuri, Netrakona	N/A	N/A	N/A	Religious desecration; land grab	Mohammad Sanowaruzzaman Josef (Awami League official and U.P. Chairman) and his brother Mr. Shamsuzzaman Talukdar Soeb (President of Juba League) forceably occupied lands of the regional Kali Temple and started building on it.	BIHR; BDMW; Daily Jugantor; Daily Star	Mohammad Asaduzzaman, Officer in Charge of the Kaliazuri police station, claimed not to have known about the incident, told the BDMW to file a complaint, and later said the police superintendent said they would take "necessary steps against the perpetrators"; but so far have not.
4/6/10	Chittagong	Sitakunda	Multiple	*	M	Attempted land grabs; theft; assault	Cadres from Awami lawmaker Abul Kashem Master have been attacking Hindu fisherman, demanding their land (sometimes already seizing possession, and if they show any resistance beating and vandalizing them and stealing their catch and equipment. They also specifically order Hindus out of their homes according to a minority leader.	BDMW; Daily Star	Despite media covereage and demonstrations to national leaders of the Awami League, authorities have taken no action.

GHRD=Global Human Rights Defence

BDMW=Bangladesh Minority Watch

HRCBM=Human Rights Congress for Bangladesh Minorities

BIHR—Bangladesh Institute of Human Rights

APPENDIX III

LETTERS PROVIDING EVIDENCE OF THE ETHNIC CLEANSING OF HINDUS IN BANGLADESH, 2012 & 2013

This Appendix contains a letter I sent to Akramul Qader, Ambassador to the United States from Bangladesh, after a meeting I held with him in May 2012, and a letter I sent to Muhiuddin Khan Alamgir, Bangladesh's Home Minister, after a meeting I had with him in February 2013. Both men denied that Hindus had any problems in their country, and the letters were written in response to these Bangladeshi officials' (cynical) requests for evidence of their ethnic cleansing of Hindus. Both men promised to investigate the crimes and see that the perpetrators were prosecuted; neither did anything of the kind. Copies of both letters, including the officials' empty promises, their disingenuous arguments, and evidence of atrocities and Bangladeshi government complicity were also sent to several US lawmakers and other officials. Senator Tom Coburn of Oklahoma immediately referred the letter to the Home Minister to the US Senate Foreign Relations Committee through Senator Bob Corker of Tennessee.

Dr. Richard L. Benkin

521 North Pine Street
Mount Prospect, IL 60056-2056
http://www.InterfaithStrength.com
http://www.interfaithstrength.blogspot.com/
Also available on FACEBOOK

Evening Phone: (847) 506-0881
Mobile Phone: 847-922-6426
Fax Number: (847) 506-1006
Email: drrbenkin@comcast.net

June 12, 2012

H. E. Mr. Akramul Qader
Ambassador of Bangladesh
The Embassy of the People's Republic of Bangladesh
3510 International Drive NW
Washington, DC 20008

Dear Mr. Ambassador,

Thank you for making a special trip to the Embassy for our recent meeting. I hope you return to good health. While our discussion was not always an easy one, it is my sincere hope that it contributes to better things for *all* the citizens of Bangladesh.

The issue at hand is the ethnic cleansing of Hindus in Bangladesh and your categorical denial of it. In your nation's defense, you referred to third hand reports (e.g., from the US Department of State); and I countered with the results of evidence I or my reliable network of associates in South Asia confirmed directly. You asked that I send it to you, and here it is. While the Bangladeshi government is not carrying out organized ethnic cleansing of its Hindu citizens; it enables one by refusing to prosecute those who do and maintaining anti-Hindu laws.

Hindus were almost a third of East Pakistan's population according to its 1951 census. In 1971, when East Pakistan became Bangladesh, the census counted them as almost a fifth. The 2001 census had them as nine percent; and reliable estimates have them between seven and eight percent today. You did not dispute these objective facts when we met; but alleged that they was the result of voluntary emigration: that Bangladesh's Hindus "cannot find suitable matches for their children," you said, "so they go to India where there are more Hindus." Making that account for this sea change in population requires a level of spin heretofore unknown, and there are at least four reasons why that explanation does not hold water: (1) The decline in Bangladesh's Hindu population—the world's third largest—is in stark contrast to *growing*

Dr. Richard L. Benkin

521 North Pine Street
Mount Prospect, IL 60056-2056
http://www.InterfaithStrength.com
http://www.interfaithstrength.blogspot.com/
Also available on FACEBOOK

Evening Phone: (847) 506-0881
Mobile Phone: 847-922-6426
Fax Number: (847) 506-1006
Email: drrbenkin@comcast.net

H. E. Mr. Akramul Qader
June 11, 2012
Page 2

Hindu populations elsewhere where Hindu parents have fewer choices for their children. (2) Professor Sachi Dastidar of the State University of New York (who recently testified before the Tom Lantos Human Rights Commission) concluded that demographic forces plus voluntary emigration cannot achieve that level of population shift. (3) Studies by demographer and veteran of Bangladesh's War of Independence Bimal Primanik found that the Hindu population is actually decreasing in India's West Bengal where the impoverished Hindus flee. (4) I have met personally with refugees in India, and they overwhelmingly find matches for their children among fellow refugees from Bangladeshi persecution. These figures are documented in numerous sources, including my book, *A Quiet Case of Ethnic Cleansing: The Murder of Bangladesh's Hindus.*

In addition, Bangladesh continues to support anti-minority laws. Your Prime Minister admitted that when in April 2009 she told visiting Vice Admiral of the French Navy Gerard Valin that her government would repeal the country's "anti-minority laws," as reported in your leading newspaper, *The Daily Star.* Not only have there been no repeals, but Sheikh Hasina and her government passed on at least two opportunities to effect them without repercussions. Just prior to the 2008 elections, the Bangladesh Supreme Court issued a *Rule Nisi* directing the government to show cause why the Vested Property Act was not contrary to the constitution. Military leaders then in power told me that they would leave that response to the soon-to-be-elected government, which turned out to be the Awami League; and it never gave one. In 2011, the Supreme Court questioned the legitimacy of several constitution amendments, including the Eighth which declares Islam to be the state religion and grants it preferential treatment. As requested by the Court, the government offered substitutes; but not for the Eighth Amendment, leaving the preferences and disabilities in place.

Dr. Richard L. Benkin

521 North Pine Street
Mount Prospect, IL 60056-2056
http://www.InterfaithStrength.com
http://www.interfaithstrength.blogspot.com/
Also available on FACEBOOK

Evening Phone: (847) 506-0881
Mobile Phone: 847-922-6426
Fax Number: (847) 506-1006
Email: drrbenkin@comcast.net

H. E. Mr. Akramul Qader
June 11, 2012
Page 3

Verified Cases of Anti-Hindu Actions

During our meeting, you stated categorically that you knew of no anti-Hindu incidents in your country since those that transpired around the time of the "2006 election" (it was actually 2001). I have direct evidence of a very different picture and am attaching summaries. Unfortunately, minorities face attacks pretty much everywhere. The critical factor is how the government reacts: does it prosecute the perpetrators; or does it send a message that attacks on minorities can proceed with impunity. Successive Bangladeshi governments consistently send the latter message. The incidents I have cited:

- ❑ Occurred under the current, Awami League government
- ❑ Were not prosecuted by the government; in some cases, government agents participated in the attacks or in their cover-up
- ❑ Were verified by two or more independent sources
- ❑ Were specifically anti-Hindu and not random

Let us also be clear that these are incidents that I have been able to confirm with my limited resources; many more have been reported that could meet the above four criteria. Samir Kalra, Director and Senior Fellow for Human Rights of the Hindu American Foundation, noted "nearly 1,200 incidents of violence directed against religious minorities (mostly Hindus) between 2008 and 2011." Its annual reports have consistently cited a clear pattern of anti-Hindu actions going unpunished in Bangladesh. Two of them can be found as appendices in my book, note above:

- ❑ During the Awami League's first year in office, major anti-Hindu incidents occurred at the rate of almost one per week. They included murder, rape, child abduction, forced conversion to Islam, physical attacks, land grabs, religious

Dr. Richard L. Benkin

521 North Pine Street
Mount Prospect, IL 60056-2056
http://www.InterfaithStrength.com
http://www.interfaithstrength.blogspot.com/
Also available on FACEBOOK

Evening Phone: (847) 506-0881
Mobile Phone: 847-922-6426
Fax Number: (847) 506-1006
Email: drrbenkin@comcast.net

H. E. Mr. Akramul Qader
June 11, 2012
Page 4

desecration; and at least one three-day pogrom that occurred immediately behind a Dhaka police station.

- During one 26 day period in 2010, there were seven major anti-Hindu actions; almost one every three days.
- During the first quarter of 2012, there were 15 such incidents, or almost one and a quarter every single week. In at least two cases, local or other officials warned human rights activists to stop investigating the matter.

Since then, I have received allegations of more incidents, including:

- According to *The Daily Purbaanchal* and my own sources, several Muslim males repeatedly raped a child on her way to a Hindu festival on May 25.
- According to a May 20 article in *The Daily Kaler Kantha,* my associates went to Vingravo village in Narayangonj to investigate the recent murder of Samrity Rani, wife and mother, while her husband was away. This involved a home invasion in broad daylight. According to video testimony, Hindus have been threatened not to continue their efforts at prosecution; and the police have taken no action.
- The gang rape of Sanju Rani Dev (28) on May 27 at night in Golapgonj Upazila of Sylhet, as confirmed by Bangladesh Minority Watch
- The abduction of Julie Sinha (23) on May 18 at about 11 am, as she was on her way to class at Sha Jalal University in Sylhet.

There also have been attacks on human rights activist, Advocate Rabindra Ghosh, including attacks on his aged mother; police have refused to protect Mr. Ghosh or prosecute the crimes against him or his family.

Dr. Richard L. Benkin

521 North Pine Street
Mount Prospect, IL 60056-2056
http://www.InterfaithStrength.com
http://www.interfaithstrength.blogspot.com/
Also available on FACEBOOK

Evening Phone: (847) 506-0881
Mobile Phone: 847-922-6426
Fax Number: (847) 506-1006
Email: drrbenkin@comcast.net

H. E. Mr. Akramul Qader
June 11, 2012
Page 5

One final mention is the recent arrest of author Salam Azad on charges of blasphemy, based on a book he recently published in Kolkata. The author maintains that this is part of a pattern of harassment he has experienced at the hands of Bangladeshi officials ever since he began writing protests about the seizure of Hindu land under government auspices. Blasphemy, as you know, carries a possible death sentence and a surety of extended trials. This is not the first Bangladeshi author charged with blasphemy, and it is hardly indicative of a moderate or secular nation.

Sir, I did not collect the evidence presented through a Google search, but through five years of exhaustive work in South Asia, sometimes under unhospitable circumstances. I have looked into the eyes of the victims and confronted victimizers. What is happening to Hindus in your country is real, and I stand by the facts presented here.

Thank you. I look forward to your government's response to these outrages and its rectification of the decades long persecution of Hindus in Bangladesh.

Dr. Richard L. Benkin

Cc: Senator Richard Durbin, Majority Whip
Senator Mark Kirk
Senator Tom Coburn
Congressman Robert Dold
Congressman Eric Cantor, Majority Leader
Congressman Peter Roskam, Chief Deputy Majority Whip
Congresswoman Judy Biggert
Hindu American Foundation
United States Commission on International Religious Freedom

Dr. Richard L. Benkin

521 North Pine Street
Mount Prospect, IL 60056-2056
http://www.InterfaithStrength.com
http://www.interfaithstrength.blogspot.com/
Also available on FACEBOOK

Evening Phone: (847) 506-0881
Mobile Phone: 847-922-6426
Fax Number: (847) 506-1006
Email: drrbenkin@comcast.net

Dr. Muhiuddin Khan Alamgir
Minister of Home Affairs
Government of the People's Republic of Bangladesh
Bangladesh Secretariat
Dhaka

February 22, 2013

Dear Mr. Minister,

I want to thank you for the time you afforded me the other day to discuss the ethnic cleansing of Hindus in Bangladesh. In all candor, however, and as you probably discerned, I found the discussion itself troubling to say the least. Your response was, in essence, that your government has no intention of doing anything other than it is doing now and that the status quo is what we all should expect from Bangladesh's Awami League government. Yet, as I noted during our meeting, your various and sundry responses did not even attempt to address what is happening to Hindus in your country except to say that you are, in effect, 'working on it.' That you have been in office for over four years and your efforts remain marginally helpful at best, should make any discerning individual wonder why you find that acceptable.

Allow me to review briefly the situation you find acceptable. With my own meager resources, I have been able to confirm the following with at least two independent eye witnesses, and many of them were also covered in local media; as of last year, the government has not prosecuted these matters or punished the perpetrators (save in a few cases a few moments of comfortable detention, followed by what amounted to permanent bail).

- ❑ During the Awami League's first year in office, there was about one major anti-Hindu incident a week; incidents including murder, rape (including gang rape), child abduction, religious desecration, forced conversion, land grabbing, and physical attacks.

Dr. Richard L. Benkin

521 North Pine Street
Mount Prospect, IL 60056-2056
http://www.InterfaithStrength.com
http://www.interfaithstrength.blogspot.com/
Also available on FACEBOOK

Evening Phone: (847) 506-0881
Mobile Phone: 847-922-6426
Fax Number: (847) 506-1006
Email: drbenkin@comcast.net

Dr. Muhiuddin Khan Alamgir
Minister of Home Affairs
Government of the People's Republic of Bangladesh
February 22, 2013
Page 2

- ☐ The second year showed no letup in such attacks, and there was one 27-day period that saw over seven major attacks, or almost one every three days. Yet, your administration never thought that significant enough for more action than what you were doing already.
- ☐ Organizations including Bangladesh Minority Watch and Hindu American Foundation both have extensive evidence that the third year, 2011, was no better.
- ☐ As we moved into the Awami League's fourth year in office, I confirmed at least 15 major, specifically anti-Hindu attacks; and as we moved out, there were about 1.25 such attacks per week in the fourth quarter. In between, there was one nine-day period in May that saw a murder in broad daylight, the abduction of a child walking to a Hindu festival, and two gang rapes. Four horrific actions in nine days and the government took it as a normal nine days in Bangladesh.

As if to confirm the problem for Hindus in your country, you told me that I should provide you with specific cases and you would investigate them. Wonderful, but as I noted during our meeting, it is rather odd that you, the Home Minister sitting in Dhaka would be dependent on some man from Chicago for evidence of human rights abuses in Bangladesh. If that is the case, it suggests even more serious problems. Moreover, if the system of law and order is functioning correctly, these crimes would be handled on the local level by local officials and would not require action by the Home Minister of the country.

Further confirmation of the problem came when I raised the issue of ethnic cleansing of Hindus in Bangladesh, and you replied by telling me you "have

Dr. Richard L. Benkin

521 North Pine Street
Mount Prospect, IL 60056-2056
http://www.InterfaithStrength.com
http://www.interfaithstrength.blogspot.com/
Also available on FACEBOOK

Evening Phone: (847) 506-0881
Mobile Phone: 847-922-6426
Fax Number: (847) 506-1006
Email: drrbenkin@comcast.net

Dr. Muhiuddin Khan Alamgir
Minister of Home Affairs
Government of the People's Republic of Bangladesh
February 22, 2013
Page 3

seen the enclaves of the Red Indians in the United States." Another answer you gave to these terrible things was that "union membership has declined in the United States." As I noted when we met, how that can have any relation to the atrocities occurring in your country bespeaks of a true disinclination to recognize their severity. Similarly, your repeated insistence that "33 people were killed in Connecticut" indicates your determination to do nothing that will effectively protect Hindu citizens of Bangladesh.

I will also refer you to the esteemed Bangladeshi Supreme Court lawyer and human rights activist, Advocate Rabindra Ghosh, who was with us in your office. He has extensive evidence of anti-Hindu atrocities, investigated and vetted; and has been fighting this battle for years, including every day that the Awami League has been in office. Just recently, however, I have confirmed even more atrocities, including:

- ❑ Eti Biwas (23 years old) from Khulna district was abducted on 21 December 2012 after her family resisted the seizure of their land by local officials and miscreants (a very common action against the Hindus of your country). The distraught family met with me after the government has taken no action, despite their pleas, to help recover the young woman who remains missing.

Dr. Richard L. Benkin

521 North Pine Street
Mount Prospect, IL 60056-2056
http://www.InterfaithStrength.com
http://www.interfaithstrength.blogspot.com/
Also available on FACEBOOK

Evening Phone: (847) 506-0881
Mobile Phone: 847-922-6426
Fax Number: (847) 506-1006
Email: drrbenkin@comcast.net

Dr. Muhiuddin Khan Alamgir
Minister of Home Affairs
Government of the People's Republic of Bangladesh
February 22, 2013
Page 4

- In far north Dinajpur, an impoverished village of Hindus was attacked by over 100 marauding Muslims who went from hovel to hovel, destroying homes, personal effects, crops, and livestock. While the poor villages have rebuilt the best they can, the invaders continue to threaten to "finish the job" if the villagers do not leave. The only thing preventing that right now is four local Muslim policemen who come to the village while the local police and administration itself refuses to act.
- In the same area, a young mother told us how the local village official came to her home and raped her while her husband was working in the field. She lives in a hovel; he in a mansion. This is a common practice by this and other officials, and there has never been a prosecution of any of these rapes.

While I have some more evidence in these cases, Advocate Rabindra Ghosh has evidence of the two Dinajpur cases and many others.

You might also be interested to know that many MPs in your party (including the MP for the third part of Dinajpur) are actively involved in the seizure of Hindu land. It is well known to so many Bangladeshis that I am surprised that you seem unaware of it. Again, Advocate Rabindra Ghosh has additional evidence.

Dr. Richard L. Benkin

521 North Pine Street
Mount Prospect, IL 60056-2056
http://www.InterfaithStrength.com
http://www.interfaithstrength.blogspot.com/
Also available on FACEBOOK

Evening Phone: (847) 506-0881
Mobile Phone: 847-922-6426
Fax Number: (847) 506-1006
Email: drrbenkin@comcast.net

Dr. Muhiuddin Khan Alamgir
Minister of Home Affairs
Government of the People's Republic of Bangladesh
February 22, 2013
Page 5

You should also know that numerous Bangladesh human rights activists investigating these matters (including Mr. Ghosh), have been arrested and beaten by your own police and other members of your government.

I am also attaching some information from my book, A Quite Case of Ethnic Cleansing: the Murder of Bangladesh's Hindus, which will come out with a second edition later this year. In June of last year, I provided that same information to Bangladeshi Ambassador to the United States Akramul Qader. Like you, he believes that current government actions are sufficient and that it needs take no further action.

You insisted that you need take no action save on individual cases; but you belied that when I asked what would happen if you found it difficult to sell your garments competitively on the international market. You said that fixing the problem would be expensive and this would take money from you. So, as you admit there is a problem that is amenable to solutions. Good, that is a start. Let us work together and give effective protection to the minority citizens of your county. The choice and consequences of that choice are yours.

Please know that, as I said when we met, I have a great deal of affection for the people of Bangladesh (unlike many in your government, that includes ALL the people); and I would like to see these atrocities end amicably—but end they must and they will. I shall not rest until they do.

Dr. Richard L. Benkin
United States Citizen

Dr. Richard L. Benkin

521 North Pine Street
Mount Prospect, IL 60056-2056
http://www.InterfaithStrength.com
http://www.interfaithstrength.blogspot.com/
Also available on FACEBOOK

Evening Phone: (847) 506-0881
Mobile Phone: 847-922-6426
Fax Number: (847) 506-1006
Email: drrbenkin@comcast.net

Dr. Muhiuddin Khan Alamgir
Minister of Home Affairs
Government of the People's Republic of Bangladesh
February 22, 2013
Page 6

Cc: Senator Richard Durbin, Majority Whip
Senator Mark Kirk
Senator Tom Coburn
Congressman Eric Cantor, Majority Leader
Congressman Peter Roskam, Chief Deputy Majority Whip
Congressman Ed Royce
Congresswoman Tulsi Gabbard
Hindu American Foundation
United States Commission on International Religious Freedom

Index

I

J

K

S